Also by Judith Blahnik

With Daniel Leader
BREAD ALONE

With Ruth and Skitch Henderson
RUTH & SKITCH HENDERSON'S SEASONS IN THE COUNTRY
RUTH & SKITCH HENDERSON'S CHRISTMAS IN THE COUNTRY

Also by Phillip Stephen Schulz

COOKING WITH FIRE AND SMOKE
AS AMERICAN AS APPLE PIE
AMERICA THE BEAUTIFUL COOKBOOK
CELEBRATING AMERICA

MUD HENS AND Mavericks

The New Illustrated Travel Guide to Minor League Baseball,
Including Team Histories and Anecdotes, Legendary Ballplayers,
Records and Stats, Stadium Quirks and Characteristics, Home Team Contests and
Traditions, Indispensable Ballpark Information, and
Colorful Itineraries for Baseball Vacations

Judith Blahnik AND Phillip Stephen Schulz

VIKING STUDIO BOOKS

VIKING STUDIO BOOKS
Published by the Penguin Group
Penguin Books USA Inc., 375 Hudson Street, New York, New York 10014, U.S.A.
Penguin Books Ltd, 27 Wrights Lane, London W8 5TZ, England
Penguin Books Australia Ltd, Ringwood, Victoria, Australia
Penguin Books Canada Ltd, 10 Alcorn Avenue, Toronto, Canada M4V 3B2
Penguin Books (N.Z.) Ltd, 182–190 Wairau Road, Auckland 10, New Zealand

Penguin Books Ltd, Registered Offices:
Harmondsworth, Middlesex, England

First published in 1995 by Viking Penguin,
a division of Penguin Books USA Inc.

1 3 5 7 9 10 8 6 4 2

AUTHORS' NOTE
Major league affiliates and minor league franchises have a tendency to
change every year. There was a lot of movement after the 1994 season,
when many club contracts expired. We have followed developments
closely and have kept this book as up to date as possible. Ticket prices
are based on 1994 information and may change without notice.

ISBN 0 14 02.4016 0
CIP data available

Printed in the United States of America
Set in Garamond

Designed by Joseph Rutt
Maps by Claudia Carlson

Contents

Acknowledgments

The authors thank Sharon Creal and George Moskowitz for their assistance and infinite patience, and also Ron Schultz, whose research was invaluable. Thanks to Michael Fragnito and Barbara Williams at Viking Studio Books, for seeing this book through, to Carolyn Hart Bryant, who edited it, and also to Joseph Rutt, who designed it.

We are grateful to Larry Wiederecht and Missan Ellmaker at the National Association of Professional Baseball Leagues, to Michelle Ridgely at Major League Properties, and especially to all team general managers, assistant general managers, and media relations directors, who have been so generous with their knowledge and time. A big thanks also to all the amateur and professional photographers who provided us with photographs. And a special thanks to all the fans who so willingly talked to us about their hometown minor league ballclubs. This book could not have been written without their help. Nor would we have survived without *Baseball America*, a biweekly newspaper that contains a goodly amount of minor league coverage and all the statistics that anyone could possibly want. *Baseball America* is *the* paper of minor league ballplayers.

When we began this book, we were just a couple of fans who wanted to know more about minor league baseball. We discovered that, unlike the major leagues, the minor leagues haven't been adequately documented, especially the years before 1902. We relied on several publications for historical facts and statistics. First and foremost is *The Encyclopedia of Minor League Baseball*, edited by Lloyd Johnson and Miles Wolff (Baseball America, Inc., Durham, NC, 1993). Two publications by The Sporting News Publishing Company in St. Louis came in handy, both 1994 editions: *The Sporting News Official Baseball Register* and *The Sporting News Baseball Guide*. We also made extensive use of *The Ballplayers*, edited by Mike Shatzkin (Arbor House, William Morrow, NY, 1990) and the humongous ninth edition of *The Baseball Encyclopedia*, Rick Wolff, Editorial Director (Macmillan Publishing, NY, 1993). Miscellaneous information was gleaned from *Stolen Season* by David Lamb (Random House, NY, 1991); *Fascinating Baseball Facts* by David Nemec and Pete Palmer (Publications, International, Ltd., Lincolnwood, IL, 1994); and *Fungoes, Floaters and Fork Balls: A Colorful Baseball Dictionary* by Patrick Ercolano (Prentice-Hall, Inc., Englewood Cliffs, NJ, 1987).

Introduction

Major league baseball may be suffering from loss of television revenues—and from having to cope with all those multimillion-dollar salaries, strike or no strike—but minor league baseball is doing just swell, thank you. Last year alone, some thirty million fans showed up at minor league parks to cheer on their hometown teams. In fact, minor league baseball is becoming so popular that a club that was hard to give away only fifteen years ago easily sells for seven figures today.

On any given night from April to September, hundreds of minor league teams play to capacity crowds in small, user-friendly stadiums throughout the U.S. Teams such as the Buffalo Bisons, the Toledo Mud Hens, the Birmingham Barons, the Durham Bulls, the Brevard County Manatees, the Quad City River Bandits, the Portland Sea Dogs, and the Rancho Cucamonga Quakes provide rousing baseball action in ballparks where you are so close to the field that not only do you hear the crack of the bat, you feel it reverberate through your bones.

It's this pleasure of an old-fashioned summer night's game, at old-fashioned prices (usually $3 or $4—the majors average $10.50) that draws as many fans to the drama and lights of the ballpark as theatergoers to Broadway. And drama there is, as the hometown crowds cheer on the young men who play their hearts out in hopes of landing a major role. Not in a Broadway show, but in "the Show," as the players refer to the major leagues.

The player–fan relationship in the minors is unparalleled in the majors. Fans nurture and support their players enthusiastically, showing up night after night, getting to know individual players on a first-name basis, charting their progress, hoping that the good players will move up, carrying a bit of their hometown with them. For their loyalty, fans are virtually guaranteed a night of good baseball—hard hitting, daredevil baserunning, diving catches, and double plays (and sometimes double rundowns, much to our chagrin).

There's a homey yet exuberant atmosphere of celebration in most minor league stands—a touch of Americana, straight out of the late 1940s. And while the billboards that surround the outfield offer the inevitable Miller Lite and Silver Bullet, we also find Gem Jewelry Shop, Bob's Stores, Tops Propane, Joe Bob's Furniture Heaven, Revel's Tractor, and Rosol's Meat Products, all giving us a real sense of where we are.

Fans come from all walks of life. They include office workers (from senior vice-presidents to janitors), church groups, Boy Scout troops, Little Leaguers, entire families (including baby), and old folks, too. Some parks allow fans to bring picnic suppers, which they spread over the bleachers before game time. The majority, however, have their own picnic facilities (with quite reasonably priced menus) that groups may rent out before the game.

The contests and promotions between innings grab everyone's attention as fans vie for a free fill-up of propane, gift certificates for the hardware store, and free pizzas. Or, if really lucky, a trip, a car, even a house on occasion. You never know what to expect. At one game in upstate New York that we were at on a very muggy afternoon, the local Wendy's, when the temperature reached 80 degrees, passed out free ice cream for everyone in the park. At another game in the Midwest, a steady stream of customers queued up for $10 haircuts on the third-base side courtesy of the "Lovely Gina," and for $5, heavenly therapeutic massages from Sister Rosalind (yes, she's really a nun) on the first-base side. Worth every penny, too.

Promotion is the name of this game, and, though it varies from team to team, anything goes—anything, that is, that will draw fans out to the ballpark. In the 1988 film *Bull Durham*, the promoters turned loose a pack of kids on the diamond as a helicopter hovered overhead dropping a thousand one-dollar bills. In real life, at a Southern League park on Mother's Day, they bury a $5,000 diamond somewhere in the infield dirt and let a pack of moms go at it armed only with tablespoons. Down Florida way, Jericho the Miracle Dog, an eleven-year-old golden retriever, may have recently retired from his duties as "ball dog," but his son Toucan ("the Diamond Dog") is filling dad's shoes (paws?) quite nicely. Out in Pennsylvania, one team has a "Kiss the Pig" contest that results in a local celebrity (a radio or TV personality, maybe even the mayor or a powerful CEO) having to kiss a 200-pound pig for charity. On the snout! Another Pennsylvania club has its fans in stitches when opposing teams participate in a milking contest. Some of the young players have never even been within two miles of a cow and need a little fan razzing to get into the swing of things.

Mascots seem to be all the rage in minor league ballparks. Just about every team has one—and there are some doozies. The Reading Phillies "Screwball"—a cross-eyed ball with legs—is one of the silliest. The Carolina Mudcats' "Muddy," a so-ugly-you-love-him catfish in a uniform, is probably the funniest. And the hairy green ball of a Grump, the creature belonging to the Scranton/Wilkes-Barre Red Barons, has to be one of the weirdest. Fans love them, one and all. The mascots, in turn, are more than just clown entertainers during the game—they are often called upon to make public appearances for charitable causes in their communities, lead parades, and visit schools and hospitals.

The most famous mascots of all, the Phillie Phanatic and The Famous Chicken, have flown their major league coops (Philadelphia and San Diego, respectively), or so it seems, as they are always on hand for guest shots at one minor league park or another. Other prominent "acts" on the minor league circuit are people acts: Max Patkin, The Blues Brothers, Captain Dynamite and Lady Dynamite. Max, who is always covered with dirt and dressed in an oversized pinstriped uniform, is so manic and funny that he has earned the nickname the Clown Prince of Baseball. The Blues Brothers, Jake and Elwood, are just a couple of guys who use their acrobatic skills in their Aykroyd-Belushi–inspired routine, while lip-synching to rhythm and blues and rock 'n' roll. Captain Dynamite and Lady Dynamite climb into (styrofoam) boxes and quite literally blow themselves up. And we probably should mention that ELVIS IS BACK!! He's been seen around the country at a number of minor league ballparks on Elvis Night. All of these performers are extremely popular and can easily fill up a grandstand.

The stadiums themselves are part of the fun, too. Some are cozy wooden structures that make you feel as if you've walked right into a Norman Rockwell painting. Others are shiny aluminum-

and-steel sort-of-spacy-looking structures that shimmer and shake, and sound like the end of the world is nigh when the fans stomp in unison in support of their team. Some of the newest ones have been designed as reminders of the past, having all the traditional brick-and-iron feel of a Wrigley Field, but all the spacious amenities of a modern park. And minor league parks are everywhere—from downtown Buffalo to the wooded countryside of North Carolina. One is on a city island; another sits in wide-open California high desert. Wherever they are, the grass is green, the lights are bright, and the peanuts, Cracker Jacks, hot dogs, and beer are as real as they are in Metropolis, but you can bet they are lots cheaper and, some say, much, much tastier.

Mud Hens and Mavericks is a guide to the hometown pleasures of professional minor league baseball. It's not about winning or losing or salaries or statistics. It's about teams and ballparks and players and fans. Look up any one of the Triple-A, Double-A, and Class A regular-season minor league teams, and you'll get an up-to-date picture of each club, a description of the home game experience, how to get there, and what not to miss while you're there.

We've profiled all the regular-season minor league teams—116 of them. We do not include the spirited and colorful rookie leagues, the short season leagues, and the new independent leagues that seem to be popping up all over. They could fill another book! They are, however, briefly noted at the back of this one.

Also at the back of the book you'll find suggested itineraries for some great minor league baseball jaunts and vacations. We've included information that will make organizing a trip just a little easier, whether you plan to stray not too far from home or pack up the RV and hit the road.

THE MAJOR LEAGUE AFFILIATES— IN SHORT

ATL—Atlanta Braves
BAL—Baltimore Orioles
BOS—Boston Red Sox
CAL—California Angels
CUB—Chicago Cubs
CWS—Chicago White Sox
CIN—Cincinnati Reds
CLE—Cleveland Indians
COL—Colorado Rockies
DET—Detroit Tigers
FLO—Florida Marlins
HOU—Houston Astros
KCR—Kansas City Royals
LAD—Los Angeles Dodgers
MIL—Milwaukee Brewers
MIN—Minnesota Twins
MON—Montreal Expos
NYM—New York Mets
NYY—New York Yankees
OAK—Oakland A's
PHI—Philadelphia Phillies
PIT—Pittsburgh Pirates
STL—St. Louis Cardinals
SDP—San Diego Padres
SFG—San Francisco Giants
SEA—Seattle Mariners
TEX—Texas Rangers
TOR—Toronto Blue Jays

IND—Independent
COOP—Cooperative (a minor league team supported by more than one major league team)

How It Works

Although there have been loosely organized independent leagues since 1877, the Northwestern League, created on October 27, 1882, was the first minor league to sign an agreement with the major league National League and American Association (a major league from 1882 to 1891). The agreement was called the "Tripartite Agreement," and what it did was bind the clubs to honor the contracts of players, to recognize territorial rights, and to seek arbitration in settling disputes. It also established minimum salaries, setting a much higher pay scale for the two major leagues. As baseball expanded, both on the major and minor league fronts, new territorial wars (and major league raids on minor league players) prompted the minor leagues to band together for self-protection. On September 5, 1901, at a meeting of leagues at the Leland Hotel in Chicago, the National Association of Professional Baseball Leagues (the NAPBL) was formed.

Baseball has changed dramatically since 1901. For one thing, there were no farm clubs then. Major league teams drafted players directly from the minor league teams who owned them and, even in 1905, were allowed to draft only one player from a club per year (by 1911, the number had increased to eight). All that ended in 1919, when the National Association withdrew from all major league agreements. Two years later the two sides reached a new agreement that changed the face of baseball forever. For the first time, a major league club was allowed to own a minor league team outright. The St. Louis Cardinals was the first major league team to go out and buy controlling interest of teams in different class levels for the sole purpose of gaining total control of a young prospect's training, thus inventing the modern-day farm system.

The NAPBL today governs 19 leagues, which have a combined membership of 216 teams. It is run by a board of trustees consisting of one owner from each league, each league having its own elected president and playoff structure. Aside from being a support system for the minor leagues, often acting as a buffer between the minors and the majors, the NAPBL runs the annual winter meeting and keeps updated records on all players. Over 1,000 new players a year sign up for the minors. That's in addition to the 4,000 players already active *and* the countless other inactive or retired players. The

---

WHO INVENTED THE SEVENTH-INNING STRETCH?

The actual origin is disputable, but the best-known and most well-loved explanation is that when President William Howard Taft was in attendance on opening day in 1910 at Washington's League Park (the Senators beat the Athletics 3-0), he stood up to stretch in the middle of the 7th inning. Well, the fans thought he was leaving—after all, he was a busy man—and everybody stood up out of respect. They continued standing until the President sat back down. We've all been standing and stretching ever since.

NAPBL also oversees the training of young umpires who hope one day to make it to the Show, too.

Major league teams essentially farm out players to minor league teams; hence the nickname "farm clubs." With few exceptions, minor league teams (those belonging to the NAPBL) are affiliated with major league teams. Just like the majors, most farm clubs play five or six months of baseball within their leagues every summer.

The 19 minor leagues are divided into five classes: Triple-A, Double-A, Class A, Class A-Short Season (season starts in June instead of April), and Rookie. Triple-A, established in 1946, is currently the highest classification. Under the original 1901 structure, Class A was the highest, then Class B, C, and D. (Double-A was added in 1908.) In the class restructuring of 1963, all B, C, and D leagues were moved into the Class A category. The Rookie League, primarily for first-year players, was also established in 1963.

Nowadays, a player usually starts (sometimes fresh out of high school) at Rookie level and is promoted up through Class A, Double-A, and Triple-A as the major league farm manager sees fit. Triple-A teams rank just a step below the majors and usually hold a major league team's backup players—who are always at the ready (and chomping at the bit) should one of the regular starters become injured or, God forbid, fall into a slump. Some general managers jokingly call it the "spare parts" league. These players generally earn the highest salaries in the minors, and they travel by air.

Double-A players, on the other hand, travel by bus, sometimes over very long distances. There are fans who will tell you that Double-A ball is the most fun to watch. The players at this level have a lot to prove; it's crucial to their careers that they move up. The Double-A Southern League, in particular, has a reputation for being fiercely competitive. An exceptional player can jump straight to the big leagues from Double-A, but he's got to have a lot of heart and the guts to "hack it," as they say. Some players who have managed the feat in recent memory are Mark Langston, who went from Chattanooga to Seattle in 1984; Terry Steinbach, who jumped straight from Huntsville to Oakland during the 1986 season; and Bobby Thigpen, who went up to Chicago from Birmingham, also in 1986.

A major league team might have as many as eight affiliated minor league clubs, though six is average. The Chicago White Sox, for instance, has a Triple-A affiliate, the Nashville Sounds; a Double-A affiliate, the Birmingham Barons; three Class A affiliates, the Prince William Cannons, the South Bend Silver Hawks, and the Hickory (NC) Crawdads; and a Rookie League team in Sarasota, called the White Sox. The minor league team is just a franchise owned by an individual, or sometimes a town. Its major league big brother, also known as "the Big Club," owns the players and equipment and chips in for some road expenses. The minor league franchise, in turn, provides the field, transportation to games, and the remaining road expenses.

Farm team owners have no say as to who is on their rosters or for how long. The Big Club drafts the players, pays their salaries, and, for the most part, moves them around without much regard for the consequences to their sibling farm clubs. Case in point: the undoing of the 1983 Denver Bears.

The Bears, the Triple-A affiliate of the Chicago White Sox at the time, had had a great year and

THAT KNOTHOLE GANG OF MINE

Abner Powell was a minor league manager in the late nineteenth century who introduced the kid-friendly concept to baseball. It seems there were kids who watched every game at New Orleans's Sportsman's Park through the holes in the pine fence. Powell lobbied until the kids got free admission into two games every week. Nowadays the Knothole Gang program offers free and/or discounted tickets to kids at most minor and major league parks.

were headed into the league playoffs against the Louisville Redbirds. Just before the series began, however, the "Chisox" bigwigs decided that it was time to promote some players to Chicago. When the smoke cleared, not only were eleven players gone, but the manager as well. The new, quickly-put-together Bears were swept, needless to say. Such is life in the minor leagues. But then, where else might you see a young Reggie Jackson, Carlton Fisk, or even Willie Mays up close, in action, and full of potential?

Life in the minors is no bed of roses. Players come to town on one day's notice from spring training with a couple of suitcases in hand. The hometown booster club is critical to a player's well-being. Boosters will take players into their homes if need be, and if a player is in financial trouble, they'll try to help out. One car dealer we know loans the guys cars to use—as long as they

pay the insurance premiums. An elderly woman we talked to told us that she once had to discipline a young player who was living with her family because he would have a big social calendar on game day and drank too much. One day she hid his car keys so he couldn't get to the park. "When you're pitching," she said, "you can't fool around." But that's the exception to the rule. Most kids are grateful to be taken in by the locals, even if it means getting unsolicited advice. And boosters do love to give advice, be they the owners of the local hardware store or farmers from out over the hill. They know a lot about the game, and the players do well to listen. When "their boys" move on to the Show, they're so proud they could bust. And one thing is for certain: those "boys" will always remember those farmers in Iowa, that car dealer in Virginia, and the shopkeepers in New Mexico who took them in at a critical time in their development.

This life is especially hard on married players; the nomadic nature of the game, along with the long hours a player puts in, can be very stressful on young couples. When the players get to town, they often don't have enough stuff to furnish an apartment, even a small one, and are dependent upon generous fans to lend them whatever they need. Which is usually a lot, since the pay is not the reason these athletes play minor league ball.

The average player at the Class A level makes as little as $850 a month; about $1,200 a month in Double-A; and up to $2,000 a month in Triple-A. Plus, they only get paid for the six months they work. It's all a big risk, but they take it for the love of the game. They take it for that shot at making it to the Show—even though the averages are against them. From a team's twenty-three-player roster, only five are expected to make it to the majors—some for just one day, one game. But, as any player will tell you, risk and unpredictability are what make the game (on or off the field) worth playing.

Unpredictability, as a matter of fact, has always been in the nature of minor league ball. In order to survive in the baseball marketplace, teams have

AN APPETITE FOR THE GAME

Words from the American kitchen have added color and humor to baseball parlance for over a hundred years. *Pepper*, for example, is the fielding exercise in which a player tosses balls one after another to a batter who hits grounders or flys at the infielders.

A show-off player is a *hot dog*, while a *meal ticket* is the player who always performs well. If either gets caught in a rundown between two basemen, he's in a *pickle*.

The *fork*ball is a pitch that curves down. The batter tries to hit it with the *meat* (fat part) of the bat. (If he's got a bat made from bad wood, it's a *banana stick*.)

A grounder that takes a high and easy bounce is a *gravy* hop, and a good throw from third to first will have *mustard* on it. A bobbled ball, however, is a *hot potato*.

If the pitcher hurls *cheese*, it's a fastball with zing (over ninety mph). A *pretzel* is a curve with twists. His *bread-and-butter* pitch is the best one he's got. If it's too high and too close to the batter's chest, the pitch is in the man's *kitchen*. The argument that breaks out on the field is called a *rhubarb*.

An easy pop-up is a *can of corn*, and a catch made with the ball showing at the top of the glove is called an *ice cream cone*.

A pitch that's easy to hit is a *cookie*, and a home run is a *tater*. The *ham and egg reliever* comes into a game that has been pretty much decided (he's reliable but indistinct).

A quick appearance in the majors is *a cup of coffee*, and when the player goes back down, it's to the *hamburger* (minor) league.

CY YOUNG

True, the great pitcher, Denton True Young, whose major league career began in 1890 and lasted twenty years, spent little time in the minor leagues, but he did get his famous nickname there. As the story goes, he was trying out for the Canton, Ohio, minor league team when the catcher who was warming him up was so amazed at Young's speed that he nicknamed him Cyclone. Pretty soon, thanks to the sportswriters of the day, it was hello Cy, so long Denton True.

had to move to different towns or change their affiliates. There has been a great deal of shuffling of teams around the various leagues, especially over the last few years, particularly in Class A ball. Much of the frantic movement has been due to the Professional Baseball Agreement of 1990. With the old agreement about to expire that year, the major leagues, irked by the wild success of some of the minor league franchises, demanded that the minors (1) give up all shares of the Big Club's TV revenues, (2) pay a share of their ticket revenues to the majors, and (3) bring minor league ballparks up to major league standards by 1994—later reprieved to 1995. It is the third requirement, known as Article 11-13 of Attachment 6 (of the Professional Baseball Agreement of 1990) that has created the havoc. A great many ballparks were so "quaint" that they didn't have on-site locker rooms, and since most ballparks are community-owned, the burden of ballpark improvements fell directly on local leaderships' shoulders. For some that has meant a $25,000 investment; for others a $250,000 investment; and for those in the worst conditions, cities were looking at an investment of millions of dollars. Unfortunately, no matter how hard owners and fans worked to protect teams from being forced to find greener pastures, some small towns have had to say forget it, leaving baseball fans high and dry. Others have somehow raised the funds to make improvements, and still others have built brand-new stadiums just to keep their hometown teams home. When the dust settles after 1995, the mad scramble to satisfy the Professional Baseball Agreement should produce some long-sought-after stability.

Triple-A Teams

American Association

Buffalo Bisons (Indians)

Indianapolis Indians (Reds)

Iowa Cubs (Cubs)

Louisville Redbirds (Cardinals)

Nashville Sounds (White Sox)

New Orleans Zephyrs (Brewers)

Oklahoma City 89ers (Rangers)

Omaha Royals (Royals)

International League

Eastern Division

Ottawa Lynx (Expos)

Pawtucket (RI) Red Sox (Red Sox)

Rochester Red Wings (Orioles)

Scranton/Wilkes-Barre Red Barons (Phillies)

Syracuse Chiefs (Blue Jays)

Western Division

Charlotte (NC) Knights (Marlins)

Columbus Clippers (Yankees)

Norfolk Tides (Mets)

Richmond Braves (Braves)

Toledo Mud Hens (Tigers)

Pacific Coast League

Northern Division

Calgary Cannons (Pirates)

Edmonton Trappers (Athletics)

Salt Lake Buzz (Twins)

Tacoma Rainiers (Mariners)

Vancouver Canadians (Angels)

Southern Division

Albuquerque Dukes (Dodgers)

Colorado Springs Sky Sox (Rockies)

Las Vegas Stars (Padres)

Phoenix Firebirds (Giants)

Tucson Toros (Astros)

Double-A Teams

Eastern League

Northern Division
Binghamton (NY) Mets (Mets)
Hardware City (CT) Rock Cats (Twins)
New Haven (CT) Ravens (Rockies)
Norwich (CT) Navigators (Yankees)
Portland (ME) Seadogs (Marlins)

Southern Division
Bowie (MD) Baysox (Orioles)
Canton-Akron Indians (Indians)
Harrisburg Senators (Expos)
Reading Phillies (Phillies)
Trenton Thunder (Red Sox)

Southern League

Eastern Division
Carolina Mudcats (Pirates)
Greenville (SC) Braves (Braves)
Jacksonville (FL) Suns (Tigers)
Orlando Cubs (Cubs)
X-XPRESS (Mariners)

Western Division
Birmingham Barons (White Sox)
Chattanooga Lookouts (Reds)
Huntsville (AL) Stars (Athletics)
Knoxville Smokies (Blue Jays)
Memphis Chicks (Padres)

Texas League

Eastern Division
Arkansas Travelers (Cardinals)
Jackson (MS) Generals (Astros)
Shreveport Captains (Giants)
Tulsa Drillers (Rangers)

Western Division
El Paso Diablos (Brewers)
Midland (TX) Angels (Angels)
San Antonio Missions (Dodgers)
Wichita Wranglers (Royals)

Class A Teams
California League

Northern Division

Bakersfield Blaze (COOP)

Modesto A's (Athletics)

San Jose Giants (Giants)

Stockton Ports (Brewers)

Visalia Oaks (COOP)

Southern Division

High Desert Mavericks (Orioles)

Lake Elsinore Storm (Angels)

Rancho Cucamonga Quakes (Padres)

Riverside Pilots (Mariners)

San Bernardino Spirit (Dodgers)

Carolina League

Northern Division

Frederick (MD) Keys (Orioles)

Lynchburg (VA) Hillcats (Pirates)

Prince William (VA) Cannons (White Sox)

Wilmington (DE) Blue Rocks (Royals)

Southern Division

Durham (NC) Bulls (Braves)

Kinston (NC) Indians (Indians)

Salem (VA) Avalanche (Rockies)

Winston-Salem Warthogs (Reds)

Florida State League

Eastern Division

Brevard County Manatees (Marlins)

Daytona Cubs (Cubs)

Kissimmee Cobras (Astros)

St. Lucie Mets (Mets)

Vero Beach Dodgers (Dodgers)

West Palm Beach Expos (Expos)

Western Division

Charlotte Rangers (Rangers)

Clearwater Phillies (Phillies)

Dunedin Blue Jays (Blue Jays)

Fort Myers Miracle (Twins)

Lakeland Tigers (Tigers)

St. Petersburg Cardinals (Cardinals)

Sarasota Red Sox (Red Sox)

Tampa Yankees (Yankees)

Midwest League

Eastern Division

Battle Creek Golden Kazoos (Cardinals)

Fort Wayne Wizards (Twins)

South Bend Silver Hawks (White Sox)

West Michigan Whitecaps (Athletics)

Central Division

Beloit (WI) Snappers (Brewers)

Kane County (IL) Cougars (Marlins)

Rockford (IL) Cubbies (Cubs)

Wisconsin Timber Rattlers (Mariners)

Western Division

Burlington (IA) Bees (Giants)

Cedar Rapids Kernels (Angels)

Clinton (IA) LumberKings (Padres)

Peoria Chiefs (Red Sox)

Quad City (IA) River Bandits (Astros)

Sultans of Springfield (Royals)

South Atlantic League

Northern Division	**Southern Division**
Asheville (NC) Tourists (Rockies)	Albany (GA) Polecats (Expos)
Charleston (WV) Alley Cats (Reds)	Augusta Greenjackets (Pirates)
Fayetteville (NC) Generals (Tigers)	Capital City (SC) Bombers (Mets)
Greensboro (NC) Bats (Yankees)	Charleston (SC) RiverDogs (Rangers)
Hagerstown (MD) Suns (Blue Jays)	Columbus (GA) Redstixx (Indians)
Hickory (NC) Crawdads (White Sox)	Macon Braves (Braves)
Piedmont (NC) Phillies (Phillies)	Savannah Cardinals (Cardinals)

Triple-A Teams

Omaha

Des Moines

Buffalo

Indianapolis

Louisville

Nashville

Oklahoma City

New Orleans

N
W E
S

American Association
TRIPLE-A

American Association

Class A 1902–1907; Double-A 1908–1945;

Triple-A 1946–1962, 1969–

The American Association was founded in 1901 by Thomas J. Hickey, who served as league president for twenty-one years. His initial effort was unusual, to say the least. Hickey actually wrote to the postmasters in eight cities asking their opinion on the prospects of their individual cities joining a new professional baseball league. Those cities were Columbus, Indianapolis, Kansas City, Louisville, Milwaukee, Minneapolis, St. Paul, and Toledo. All eight replied in the affirmative, which should not have been all that surprising since every city on that list, with the exception of the Twin Cities, had once belonged to the American Association when it had major league status (1882–91).

The Association's original lineup remained for fifty years. After several franchises moved or joined other leagues, the American Association suspended play from 1962 to 1969, when it was reactivated. Now Indianapolis and Louisville are the only two charter cities left in the league.

The American Association is made up of eight teams, which are scheduled to play 144 games during the regular season. Since the Association's teams are not grouped into divisions, the play-off format is structured so that the first place team plays the fourth place team and the second place team plays the third place team in a best-of-five series. The winners of that round then play the best-of-five series for the league championship.

Buffalo Bisons

(Cleveland Indians)

Pilot Field
275 Washington Street
Buffalo, NY 14203

When Bob Rich Jr. bought the Buffalo Bisons in 1983, the 100-year-old team was a member of the Double-A Eastern League. At the time, this Cleveland Indians' farm club was drawing only 1,000 or so spectators per game, limping through each season in worn-down, paint-peeling War Memorial Stadium. Then the baseball gods smiled down on Rich and the Bisons. Out of the blue, the team got a call from a film production staff seeking a location for *The Natural,* the baseball movie starring Robert Redford. Just the spark the Bisons needed. By 1984, attendance had shot up to over 220,000! And then Rich surprised everyone. He sold the Indians' franchise to a group in Waterbury, Connecticut, who moved it there, then went out and bought the Triple-A Wichita franchise and moved that team to Buffalo, effectively making the city into one of the minor leagues' premier baseball markets. Buffalo now draws by far the most spectators in minor league baseball, about a million a year. There's an old joke in Buffalo: "Q: How come, even on the hottest days, it's always comfortable at Pilot Field? A: Because the Bisons have so many fans in the stadium."

On April 14, 1988, the Bisons, newly affiliated with the Pittsburgh Pirates, opened the brand-new 19,500-seat Pilot Field (Pilot Air Freight paid $1.02 million for naming rights). The cast and crew of *Good Morning America* broadcast live from the stadium, and that day was the beginning of a new era for Buffalo. From that point on, the Herd, as they are affectionately called, has usually either challenged for or won the American Association playoffs. Among the present-day Pittsburgh

stars who once earned the cheers of Buffalo fans are Jay Bell, Moises Alou, Orlando Merced, Carlos Garcia, and Al Martin, who in 1992 became the only left-handed hitter with a twenty-homer season since Pilot Field opened. Future stars from Buffalo will most likely wear a Cleveland uniform. As of 1995 the Bisons are an affiliate of the Indians.

You can't find a more classic-looking ballpark facade than that of Pilot Field. There are several large stone and glass arch entrances decked with flying flags. And it's right downtown, where they built ballparks in the old days. Inside, the grandstand wraps snugly around the diamond, tucking the very last seats down the line close to the foul poles. From everywhere in the stands, you can feel the soothing breeze that blows in off nearby Lake Erie.

Buffalo Bisons fans are exuberant, loyal, and really quite nuts. On *fridaynightbash* night, the big weekly event, they dress up like the Coneheads, Zorro, Elvis, or the Flintstones. On "Famous Franks Night" there are thousands of Sinatras (and more than a few weenies) in the stands. The women are just as fanatical as the men, according to Bison historian Joe Overfield. Gone is the era of the 1930s, when women had to be coaxed into the park on fifty-cent Ladies' Days. Now female fans make up nearly 45 percent of the hollering Buffalo crowd.

Buster T. Bison is the mascot—a buffalo in a Bison uniform, who adds to the atmosphere of the unexpected. He and his buffalo protégé, Chip (as in "chip off the old block"), surprise fans in their seats, sign autographs for the kids, and sail Frisbees into the stands between innings.

Aside from giveaway nights scheduled throughout the summer, there are special events that draw fans in. For the BisonFest on Memorial Day weekend, the back parking lot is turned into a carnival of rides and games, and celebrities show up for a softball game. Turn-Back-the-Clock Night and Wedding Day (get married in the park or renew your vows) are favorites, too. There are ap-

Bisons giveaways like caps, bats, and gloves attract hundreds of young fans.

pearances by the Blues Brothers, The Famous Chicken, and the Phillie Phanatic. Three free concerts are staged on the field each year as postgame entertainment.

Gates open one hour before game time. The autograph booth is located on the first base side of the main level across from Section 114. Bison players are available twenty minutes prior to the start of each game to sign autographs.

GETTING THERE

Buffalo is the hub of the Greater Niagara region and a great place to visit at the height of baseball season. The area has some really nice hotels, lots of motels (especially in Niagara Falls), and numerous campgrounds and state parks.

Pilot Field is located in downtown Buffalo right off I-190, which loops through town. Take the Elm Street exit and turn left onto Swan Street to Washington Street. There is plenty of parking—in lots and parking structures around the stadium—which costs $4.

Club Level (front upper deck) and Special Reserved (main level) seats go for $7.75. Reserved seats (field lines and rear main level) go for $6.25, and general admission tickets (out in right field and back upper deck) cost $3.75. Seniors and kids fourteen and under get in for $3.25.

For schedule of events and ticket information, call (716) 846-2000.

For tourist information, contact the Greater Buffalo Convention and Visitors Bureau, 107 Delaware Avenue, Buffalo, NY 14202, (716) 852-0511 or (800) BUFFALO.

| | | HOMETOWN STATS—BUFFALO | | | |
| | | *The Last Ten Years* | | | |
Affil.	Year	League	Wins	Losses	Attendance
CWS	1985	American Association	66	76	362,762
	1986		71	71	425,113
CLE	1987		66	74	495,760
PIT	1988		72	70	1,147,651
	1989		80	62	1,116,441
	1990		85	62	1,174,358
	1991		81	62	1,188,972
	1992		87	57	1,117,867
	1993		71	73	1,058,620
	1994		55	89	982,493

Indianapolis Indians

(Cincinnati Reds)

Bush Stadium
1501 W. 16th Street
Indianapolis, IN 46202

Indianapolis's very first professional baseball team was the major league Hoosiers, who played in the National League in 1878 and then again for the 1887–89 seasons. In 1884, the Hoosiers played for one year in the original American Association (1882–91), also a major league at that time. When the American Association was revived as a minor league in 1901, Indianapolis became a charter member and since that time has been affiliated with the Cleveland Indians, the Montreal Expos, the Chicago White Sox, and currently the Cincinnati Reds. Since the early 1900s, they have been called the Indians. Locally, their affectionate nickname is "The Tribe." The club is owned by several hundred stockholders.

The Tribe has been very successful, winning four straight championships from 1986 through 1989. Randy Johnson, Luis Rivera, Marquis Grissom, Dennis Martinez, Otis Nixon, and Larry Walker were all part of those championship seasons. Lately the Indians have been up and down in the standings, but the fans who come no matter what got to witness a league record being set in 1990, when relief pitcher Jay Baller finished with thirty-four saves. Attendance averages 4,700 per game, enough to fill up the prime seats at grand old Bush Stadium, a spacious sixty-five-year-old park named for Indianapolis native Owen J. Bush, who was an outstanding shortstop for the Detroit Tigers during the Ty Cobb era. State-of-the-art in its day, the stadium's classic facade is eye-catching from the White River side of the ballpark.

Inside, the large grandstand rakes up gently from just above field level to the last seats under the roof, and sweeps from foul pole to foul pole. It may not be a cozy park, but the expansive foul areas here give fans a panoramic and relaxing view of the game. And for all its grandeur, this is an informal park. Coolers and food from home are allowed, so many fans picnic in the stands before the game. (The cooler must, however, fit under the seat.) 1995 could be the last season for Bush Stadium, however. Since refurbishing the park would cost $8 million, Indianapolis has passed a bond issue to build the Indians a brand-new stadium that might be ready for the 1996 season.

Although the Indians and their fans believe that baseball itself is its best promotion, everybody does have a good time with the standard giveaways and special events. Some of the gifts that fans show up early for on Souvenir Sundays

INDIANAPOLIS INDIANS
BASEBALL ™

are baseball caps, autographed balls, and T-shirts. On Used Car Night, ten cars are given away between innings.

The Indians' mascot Rowdie is a six-foot-tall, red kind-of bear thing who, in the second inning of the game, surprises two lucky fans way up in the "nosebleed" section with tickets for special field box seats. He also dashes through the stands delivering birthday cakes and cavorts with The Famous Chicken, the Blues Brothers, and the Phillie Phanatic when they come to entertain, though the fans here are wacky enough to entertain themselves. When the PA system blares out the Village People's song "YMCA" between innings, everybody gets up and not only sings along, but makes all the right gestures, too.

Gates open one and a half hours before game time. The best place to get autographs is along the third base line up until about twenty minutes before the game starts.

The Famous Chicken pays regular visits to Bush Stadium, much to the delight of Indians fans.

GETTING THERE

Indianapolis, the capital city of the Hoosier state, is nationally recognized as an ideal place to live and visit. There are quite a few good hotels and motels, and a couple of campgrounds, right in town.

Bush Stadium is located on the northwest side of town. Take Meridian Street to 16th Street and go west for about one and a half miles. Parking is free at the stadium and at the soccer stadium lot across 16th Street, but there are not nearly enough spaces to go around. So unless you are an early bird, you will have to find a space in the sur-

rounding neighborhood, which usually isn't too much of a problem, as local entrepreneurs sell parking spaces in vacant lots and driveways.

Box seats on the field cost $7, while reserved seats go for $6. General admission tickets cost $4. Kids and seniors get $1 off.

For schedule of events and ticket information, call (317) 269-3545.

For tourist information, contact the Indianapolis City Center, 201 South Capitol Avenue, Indianapolis, IN 46225, (317) 237-5206 or (800) 369-INDY.

		HOMETOWN STATS—INDIANAPOLIS			
		The Last Ten Years			
Affil.	Year	League	Wins	Losses	Attendance
MON	1985	American Association	61	81	209,041
	1986		80	62	220,285
	1987		74	64	250,250
	1988		89	53	293,721
	1989		87	59	287,595
	1990		61	85	314,264
	1991		75	68	348,089
	1992		83	61	332,941
CIN	1993		66	77	300,397
	1994		86	57	339,208

Iowa Cubs

(Chicago Cubs)

Sec Taylor Stadium
350 SW 1st Street
Des Moines, IA 50309

In Des Moines, Iowa, in 1887 the local team was simply called the Des Moines Baseball Club. (Now there's a thought.) But after the team won its first championship, it became the Des Moines Champs. When they won again, they became the Des Moines Champs II. Over the years, they've been the Colts, Prohibitionists, Midgets, Undertakers, Water Cures, Legislators, Underwriters, Boosters, Demons, Bruins, Sox, Astros, and Oaks. Tucked into their colorful past is the unique distinction of having hosted the first night baseball game played under proper permanent stadium lighting—not under car lights, household bulbs, or lanterns. It was the night of May 2, 1930, and the Demons (as they were called then) took the field against the Wichita Aeros, both of the now-defunct Class A Western League. The game was the first night game that was broadcast nationally, too. The Demons, by the way, won 13 to 6.

This current team has been with the Cubs since 1981 and has been a member of the American Association since 1969. They've produced some notables, like major league second baseman (then) Tony La Russa, who went up three times from Iowa to Oakland and back to Iowa again (in 1969, 1970, and 1971) before going on to his impressive career as manager of the A's. In 1993 the club won the league championship. One of the stars of that Cubs team was a young pitcher named Turk Wendell, who was doubly popular because not only was he a good pitcher, but he had some mighty odd habits to boot. "Turk's Quirks" are what the fans called them. He drew crosses on the mound, brushed his teeth between innings because he chewed licorice, and superstitiously jumped the third base line on his way to or from the dugout. This is the stuff minor league ball is made of.

On September 10, 1991, the old Sec Taylor Stadium, originally built in 1947, met the wreckers' ball. Exactly one month later, excavation began on the same spot and, amazingly enough, the new Sec Taylor Stadium opened for the 1992 season with the first game sold out. The stadium, which seats 10,500, has the warmth and charm of an old-fashioned ballpark, but all the modern amenities, too—including a restaurant out in the left field corner called the Cub Club, which is open to the public before games but to members only during a

An aerial view shows the splendid location of Sec Taylor Stadium.

game. Next to the Club, along the left field foul line, is a picnic area and beyond that is a play area for kids complete with batting cage. The concession concourse offers dining areas (with tables and chairs) for the tired and hungry. The grandstand is "open air" except for a bit of roof that covers the last few rows. Foul balls fly virtually everywhere in this stadium, but it's a little tricky to figure where they are going to drop if they go up on, but not over, this roof. The suspense is fun; rousing cheers await whoever is quick enough to catch the ball. Beyond the outfield walls, the Des Moines and Raccoon rivers meet. It's a pretty sight, and just up the hill is a splendid view of the state capitol.

Iowa fans are attentive to the nuances of the game and like to keep score and statistics. But they also can make noise, and the acoustics here are great for thunderous rallies. One favorite on-field event is the Celebrity Pop-Up. As fans enter the stadium, they are given a card that is either red, white, or blue. As the manager hits pop-ups to celebrities who represent each color, the fans cheer "their" player. Whatever celebrity catches the most wins a prize for everybody who holds his color. And be sure you take Mom on Mother's Day—all the moms get roses.

Gates open an hour and a half before game time. The best place to get autographs is before the game between the bullpen and the dugout on the third base side of the park.

GETTING THERE

Des Moines's 600-acre Living History Farms, with its "living" exhibits dating back to the 1700s, is a must-see. This capital city has good hotels and motels, and campgrounds can be found in many of Iowa's state parks.

To get to Sec Taylor Stadium take I-235 to the 3rd Street exit. Take 3rd Street South to Court; take a left on Court and go to 2nd. Take a right on 2nd, which takes you right to the parking lot. Parking at the stadium costs $2.50 and is always in short supply. But since the stadium is right at the edge of town, most fans find a spot to park on the street and walk to the ballpark.

Club box seats cost $8. Field box seats and reserved seats go for $6.50. General Admission tickets cost $4.50. Outfield corner bleachers go for $3 (bleachers, $2).

For schedule of events and ticket information, call (515) 243-6111.

For tourist information, contact the Division of Tourism, Iowa Department of Economic Development, 200 East Grand Avenue, Des Moines, IA 50309, (800) 345-4692.

Affil.	Year	League	Wins	Losses	Attendance
	HOMETOWN STATS—DES MOINES *The Last Ten Years*				
CUB	1985	American Association	66	75	269,513
	1986		74	68	257,986
	1987		64	74	257,857
	1988		78	64	266,845
	1989		62	82	252,289
	1990		72	74	270,215
	1991		78	66	308,814
	1992		51	92	453,386
	1993		85	59	446,860
	1994		69	74	485,734

Louisville Redbirds

(St. Louis Cardinals)

Cardinal Stadium
Freedom Way and Phillips Lane
Louisville, KY 40213

Baseball in Louisville dates back to 1876, when the Louisville Grays helped found the major league National League. They played in the National League in 1876 and 1877 and then again from 1892 to 1899. In between, from 1882 to 1891, they played in the old major league American Association. In 1901, when the Association was transformed into a minor league, Louisville became a charter member. Except for four years in the mid-1960s, Louisville hosted baseball until 1972. That was the year the then International League Colonels stormed out of town after the Commonwealth of Kentucky authorized the addition of 18,000 seats to Fairgrounds Stadium, turning the ballpark into a veritable football stadium.

When the strike hit the major leagues in 1981, the minor leagues were suddenly thrown into the spotlight (just like in 1994). At that point, Louisville banker Dan Ulmer and his son Gary thought it a darned good idea to bring Triple-A ball back to the Derby City. They lined up $4.5 million for the renovation of Fairgrounds Stadium and convinced A. Ray Smith, the owner of the Springfield (IL) Redbirds, to move his team to Louisville.

On April 17, 1982, the newly renovated and renamed Cardinal Stadium opened, but it wasn't quite ready. The bullpens were minus the mounds, and forty-five minutes before game time water was spurting out of the ground near second base. The sound system wasn't working, either, so young P.A. announcer Steve Bugg stood near home plate introducing players with a bullhorn. Even so, when the Redbirds took the field, the

19,622 fans in the grandstands gave them a standing ovation. A year later, the Redbirds became the first minor league club to draw more than a million fans in one season. And no wonder, with players like Willie McGee, who was quickly promoted to the soon-to-be World Champion St. Louis Cardinals, Rafael Santana, Eric Rasmussen, Jeff Lahti, and Ricky Horton.

Cardinal Stadium is the largest in the minor league system, seating 33,000. Built in 1959 on the grounds of the Kentucky Fair and Exposition Center, it has a large, wide, and spacious concourse with concession stands so brightly lit that the place feels like a carnival. It's also a bit of a museum, as the complete history of baseball in Louisville is displayed in boxes along the concourse. At the third base end is the Stadium Club Sports Bar, one of the biggest and busiest sports bars anywhere. The ballpark has two picnic areas that can accommodate 5,000 people. (That's a heck of a party!) Beyond the outfield walls you can see the skyline of Louisville and the University of Louisville football complex.

The fans are drawn in by both the game and the special events. There are great postgame concerts here featuring the likes of the Beach Boys, Three Dog Night, and Tanya Tucker. Fireworks nights are always popular, as are appearances by The Famous Chicken, the Phillie Phanatic, the Blues Brothers, and Max Patkin. And no one ever misses "Stupid Human Tricks" Night (à la David Letterman). Giveaways are plentiful, too.

Billy Bird is the tremendously popular team mascot who rides a unicycle on top of the dugouts, challenges the umps to line dances, and pulls off a wildly cheered disappearing act during the seventh inning. Using a trampoline to propel himself, Billy Bird flies out of Cardinal Stadium over the center field wall. The fans go nuts! Meanwhile, Billy lands on a mattress behind the fence. On one recent night, however, his buddies in the front office covered the mattress with a mountain of shav-

Louisville mascot Billy Bird waves to fans as he speeds around during mid-inning warm-ups.

ing cream! In retaliation, Billy ran back on the field, covered with the shaving cream, and hugged everybody in sight, including the umpire.

Gates open one and a half hours before game time. The best spot to get autographs is down along the third base line before the game starts.

GETTING THERE

Louisville is a nationally recognized cultural arts community and home to bluegrass, thoroughbred horses, and the Kentucky Derby. There are first-rate hotels and motels. There are a couple of small campgrounds right in town, and more to the south.

Cardinal Stadium is located on the grounds of the Kentucky Fair and Exposition Center, which is at the junctions of I-65 and I-264. There is ample parking available, which costs $1.

Reserved seats (there are no box seats) go for $7, $4 for kids and seniors. General admission tickets cost $3.50, $2 for kids and seniors.

For schedule of events and ticket information, call (502) 367-9121.

For tourist information, contact the Louisville and Jefferson County Convention & Visitors Bureau, 400 South First Street, Louisville, KY 40202, (502) 582-3732 or (800) 626-5646.

Affil.	Year	League	Wins	Losses	Attendance
STL	1985	American Association	74	68	651,090
	1986		64	78	660,200
	1987		78	62	516,329
	1988		63	79	574,852
	1989		71	74	580,270
	1990		74	72	616,687
	1991		51	92	565,716
	1992		73	70	646,951
	1993		68	76	643,833
	1994		74	68	573,174

HOMETOWN STATS—LOUISVILLE
The Last Ten Years

Nashville Sounds

(Chicago White Sox)

Greer Stadium
534 Chestnut Street
Nashville, TN 37203

There has been baseball in Nashville since 1885, and from 1901 to 1963 the local team went by one name only, the Nashville Vols, for "volunteers." Tennessee is, after all, the "Volunteer State." After the 1963 season (when the old South Atlantic League disbanded) the club moved out of Nashville, and baseball was gone for the next fifteen years. Then, in 1978, Larry Schmittou came along. Schmittou (now president and general partner of the Sounds) was head baseball coach at Vanderbilt University and he, along with Nashville businessman Hershel Greer, put a group together that brought professional baseball back to Nashville. The new team was an expansion club of the Double-A Southern League and was named after the great Nashville "sounds" of country music. That's why, on the team logo, a guitar has taken the place of a bat. The team moved up to the Triple-A American Association in 1985.

Since their first season in 1978, the Sounds have been relentless about developing major league talent. Jeff Combe, Steve Balboni, Rob Dibble, and Skeeter Barnes played here, as did Buck Showalter, who played for three years (1981–1983) before moving to coaching in the Yankees farm system. Don Mattingly hit .316 and had a league-leading thirty-five doubles in 1981 for Nashville, too.

After a six-year affiliation with the Cincinnati Reds, the Sounds are now with the Chicago White Sox (since 1993). The timing couldn't have been much better. When word went out that basketball great Michael Jordan had been signed to a minor league contract with Chicago, the Sounds sold more than $200,000 worth of tickets in four and a half days. That Jordan ended up in Double-A Birmingham didn't hurt their sales, either.

Located in a residential and business area three miles south of downtown, Greer Stadium is all open-air—no roof! The grandstand seats 17,000, and the team draws more than 300,000 fans a year. The place is alive with country music before the game and between innings. So if you like country, this is the place to be. The Stadium Club Restaurant, which offers good food and a great view of the game, is usually reserved for pregame dinners, but then opens to everybody (space permitting) once the game starts. The can-you-top-this surprise of this ballpark is the giant 115-foot-high guitar-shaped exploding scoreboard. When Nashville hits a home run, a huge fireworks display explodes right out of the guitar!

Giveaways are great—wristwatches, umbrellas, sunglasses, beach towels, backpacks, baseball gloves, and lunch boxes. Special crowd-pleasers for the summer include appearances by the Blues Brothers and The Famous Chicken and several fireworks shows. One of the most popular on-field contests is the Pizza Hut Pop-Up. If a fan can catch three pop-ups in a row, everybody in the stadium wins a free pizza.

Gates open one hour before game time. Come early to get autographs. You'll find the players next to the dugouts.

GETTING THERE

Nashville, of course, is home to country and western music, the Grand Ole Opry, and Dollywood. There are some first-class hotels here and motels aplenty. Bed-and-breakfasts and a good selection of campgrounds can also be found in the immediate vicinity.

Greer Stadium is located three miles south of downtown Nashville. Take I-65 to the Wedgewood exit (exit 81). Go west one block to 8th Avenue. Turn right on 8th. Go to the next light (Chestnut). Take a right on Chestnut and proceed to the top of the hill. You'll see the guitar-shaped

The Sounds' huge scoreboard clearly pays tribute to Nashville's great tradition of country music stars.

scoreboard from there. Parking, which costs $2, is plentiful.

Box seats, which most of the seats are, cost $7. General admission tickets go for $3. Kids 12 and under get $1 off.

For schedule of events and more information, call (615) 242-4371.

For tourist information, contact the Nashville Convention & Visitors Bureau, 161 4th Avenue North, Nashville, TN 37219, (615) 259-4700.

HOMETOWN STATS—NASHVILLE *The Last Ten Years*					
Affil.	Year	League	Wins	Losses	Attendance
DET	1985	American Association	71	70	364,225
	1986		68	74	364,614
CIN	1987		64	76	378,715
	1988		73	69	317,695
	1989		74	72	441,500
	1990		86	61	556,250
	1991		65	78	454,575
	1992		67	77	489,991
CWS	1993		81	62	438,745
	1994		83	61	300,827

New Orleans Zephyrs

(Milwaukee Brewers)

Privateer Park
University of New Orleans Lakefront
New Orleans, LA 70148

The first New Orleans team, the Pelicans, played in one league or another from 1887 until their final season in 1959, when they flew the coop. A Cardinal franchise tried to roost in the Crescent City in 1977 but was gone in a year. Baseball returned in 1993, after Denver was awarded a major league franchise (the Colorado Rockies), and the city's minor league team, the Denver Zephyrs, was left high and dry and looking for a home. The team quickly moved to New Orleans even though the facilities there left a lot to be desired. But the Zephyrs brought with them a winning spirit: Denver teams had been very successful over the years, providing the majors with such players as Eric Davis, Barry Larkin, Chris Sabo, Gary Sheffield, and Pat Listach, who went from Denver in 1992 to Milwaukee and received the AL Rookie of the Year honors for his efforts.

For the time being the Zephyrs play in Privateer Park, the ballpark on the campus of the University of New Orleans, about five miles north of the French Quarter. Voters have already floated a bond issue to build a new stadium seven miles away in Jefferson Parish, and the Zephyrs hope it will open for the 1996 season. In the meantime, everyone is making do at Privateer. The problem is that the park is next to the concert arena on the university's East Campus, and the players' locker rooms are in the arena. So after the game the players have to walk by all the fans, out of the stadium, and across an open field to reach the locker room. Summer concerts can create even more havoc. When Tina Turner came to town, the promoters took over the visiting team's locker room; the players had no choice but to change at their hotel.

However, there are other unique features (i.e., limitations) that actually create old-fashioned charm here. For instance, the left outfield fence has a large gap in it. How large? Well, fans with families pull up in their vans and pickups to watch the game from there. They bring beach chairs and

1993 American Association All-Star Zephyr outfielder Troy O'Leary shows restraint at bat.

blankets. It's a great place to catch homers, too. The 5,000-seat grandstand is all open-air, with a tiny concourse where on hot summer nights the big-selling items are large fruit-flavored "snowballs" (we call them sno-cones). Beyond the outfield fence you can see a large green levee where the annual Lollapalooza concert is held. And if you sit way up in the stands you can see Lake Pontchartrain, which is about a quarter-mile from the park. The breezes that blow off the lake are like "zephyrs," which means "gentle breeze"—most welcome when game temps average a hot and humid 88 degrees.

Fans are becoming legion. 1994 saw an increase of around 25,000 over 1993, and that figure will probably skyrocket when the new stadium opens. In the meantime, the diehards (the real screamers) congregate in the reserved seats at third base. For the most part, though, the crowd is laidback, there just to be there, win or lose. The music is great; lots of the Neville Brothers, Fats Domino, Creedence Clearwater Revival, and zydeco. Favorite promotions are Turn-Back-the-Clock Night (to the 1970s and disco) and Ladies' Night (women pay half-price). Kids gather outside the stands on the first base side, where an open field attracts foul balls.

Gates open one hour before game time. Autographs are easy to get, as the players head back across the field to the locker rooms after practice.

You can also try the dugout on the third base side. Then, too, up until ten minutes before the game two players man the autograph booth on the concourse.

GETTING THERE

The French Quarter, Dixieland jazz, jambalaya, crawfish pie, filét gumbo, and Grand Isle oysters. Need one say more? New Orleans is full of world-class hotels, motels, and bed-and-breakfasts. The few campgrounds offer bus service to the French Quarter.

Privateer Park is about five miles due north of the French Quarter on the University of New Orleans East Campus. Take I-10 to Franklin Avenue. Proceed north on Franklin to Leon C. Simon, then west to Press Drive. Take a left on Press to the parking area. Parking is free and plentiful, so plentiful, in fact, that nobody uses the lot adjacent to the stand on the first base side (too many foul balls to cause dents and broken windshields).

Reserved seats go for $7, while general admission tickets cost $5. Seniors, kids, and military personnel get in for $2.

For schedule of events and ticket information, call (504) 282-6777.

For tourist information, contact the Greater New Orleans Tourist & Convention Commission, 1520 Sugar Bowl Drive, New Orleans, LA 70112, (504) 566-5031.

HOMETOWN STATS—NEW ORLEANS *The Last Ten Years**					
Affil.	Year	League	Wins	Losses	Attendance
MIL	1993	American Association	80	64	161,846
	1994		78	66	186,806

*Statistics are given only for the years in which the team played in New Orleans.

Oklahoma City 89ers

(Texas Rangers)

All Sports Stadium
89er Drive/State Fairgrounds
Oklahoma City, OK 73147

Oklahoma City has had a team in town since 1904, when the club was a member of the Class D Southwestern League. From that time until the early 1960s, the team spent most of its time in either the Texas or Western leagues. The team, affiliated with the Rangers since 1983, first joined the American Association in 1962. After a five-year stint in the Pacific Coast League from 1963 through the 1968 season, the team rejoined the Association in 1969. They are now the 89ers, named in honor of those pioneers who dashed for land in the great Run of 1889 after Oklahoma was opened up for settlement. The team has had some great ups and dispiriting downs. They were stellar in 1992 and won the league championship. The bottom fell out in 1993, but attendance increased to more than 350,000 for the year. (Go figure!) Over fifty major league players have come through Oklahoma City, including Mark Davis, Jeff Russell, Ryne Sandberg, Ruben Sierra, Julio Franco, Keith Miller, Tom Henke, Steve Buechele, and Bobby Witt. And then there is Steve Balboni, who had a great three seasons with the 89ers after having spent ten years in the majors with the Royals and Yankees. Steve led the 89ers to the 1992 title, walloping thirty home runs.

All Sports Stadium is a roomy ballpark on the northwest side of the State Fairgrounds. At thirty-two years old, however, the park is showing its age. Oklahoma City voters have finally passed a bond issue that will finance a new stadium to open, fans hope, for the 1996 season. Will the Marlboro Man (currently sticking up above the left field fence) be back? Who knows? But one thing is certain, the flagpole that for thirty years had been right in the way *in the field of play* in center field will not be back. Even though, strange as it seems, no one, in all those years, ever ran into it.

The team mascot, Robo Niner, is a puffy, metallic-gray, Michelin man–like guy with a big baseball head. He works his way through the crowd, signing his own baseball cards for the kids, until he reaches the roof of the dugout, where he thrills the crowd with his dancing. In 1993, he fell from the visitor's dugout, suffered a concussion, and was out for two months. The fans cheered when he made his comeback. While Robo is great for morale, so is Helen Kirk, otherwise known as "the Cowbell Lady." Kirk has been a mainstay fan since 1978. She rattles her cowbell at key moments of the game and gets the crowd more excited than any trumpets or scoreboard antics ever could.

The almost nightly giveaways keep the fans coming back for more. There are after-the-game concerts, too, and Free Dog Night (just what it sounds like) once a week. On Cheap Seat Night fans can sit in the right field bleachers for just $1. Another favorite place to sit is the grassy hill along the left field foul line; for the price of a general admission ticket fans can sit on blankets or lawn chairs and take in the game. At the top of the hill is the Terrace Club picnic area, which is reserved for groups of twelve or more.

Gates open one hour and fifteen minutes before game time. Before the game, you can get autographs at the autograph booth on the concourse. After the game, head to the top of the dugout. The players don't just disappear, because they all have to walk down the right field line to get to the clubhouse at the end of the grandstand.

GETTING THERE

Oklahoma City was settled in one fell swoop, thanks to the Great Land Run. A capital city, it is home to many of the nation's energy-related companies. There's a wide variety of hotels and motels in the area, and camping at Lake Arcadia.

To get to the Fairgrounds and the stadium, take I-44 to the 10th Street exit and follow the signs to the Fairgrounds. You can't miss the stadium. There is plenty of free parking surrounding the fairgrounds. Parking in the stadium lot costs $2.

Tickets for box seats (which have backs and arms) cost $6.50. Reserved seats (folding chairs) go for $5.50, and general admission tickets (benches) are $4.50. Seniors and kids get $1 off.

For schedule of events and ticket information, call (405) 946-8989.

For tourist information, contact the Oklahoma City Convention & Visitors Bureau, 123 Park Avenue, Oklahoma City, OK 73102, (800) 225-5652.

According to current stats, two-thirds of the 89ers fans are male. Here are two who have come early to watch a practice.

		HOMETOWN STATS—OKLAHOMA CITY			
		The Last Ten Years			
Affil.	Year	League	Wins	Losses	Attendance
TEX	1985	American Association	79	63	364,247
	1986		63	79	282,752
	1987		69	71	277,722
	1988		67	74	260,363
	1989		59	86	250,850
	1990		58	87	282,773
	1991		52	92	347,427
	1992		74	70	362,394
	1993		54	90	364,673
	1994		61	83	397,922

Omaha Royals

(Kansas City Royals)

Rosenblatt Stadium
1202 Bert Murphy Avenue
Omaha, NE 68107

More than 6,000 fans show up for every Royals home game.

Omaha was a founding member of the Class A Western League in 1902, and for the next thirty-four years the city's Class A baseball fortunes more or less flourished. In 1936 the league disbanded and Omaha took a decade off from baseball. In 1947 the league was revived and there was A-ball again in the city, but that ended when Omaha left the Western League in 1954. Then in 1955 Omaha's mayor, Johnny Rosenblatt, helped bring Triple-A baseball to town, and the Omaha Cardinals played until 1959. The Dodgers came in 1961—and were gone in 1962! Finally, in 1969, the Omaha Royals moved into Rosenblatt Stadium and began what has turned out to be one of the longest affiliations in minor league history; Omaha and Kansas City have been together twenty-six years. That's almost as long as Richmond and the Atlanta Braves, who hold the Triple-A record of twenty-nine years. The team has won ten divisional titles and four league championships and has sent up a veritable Who's Who of baseball to the majors: George Brett, David Cone, Jeff Conine, Clint Hurdle, Bud Black, Frank White, Dennis Leonard, and ace Charlie Leibrandt, who was actually just passing through in 1984 (from Cincinnati to Kansas City) when he wowed everybody by throwing three shutouts in a total of nine games with a record of 7–1 and an ERA of 1.24.

Rosenblatt Stadium, named after Mayor Johnny Rosenblatt and nicknamed "the Blatt," was built in 1948 and sits atop a hill right next to the city zoo. The park has been renovated over the years and now seats 22,000. Remarkably, this large stadium still feels cozy, perhaps because of the way the bleachers around the outfield enclose the park. If you want to see anything other than the action on the field (such as the Omaha skyline), you have to sit way up in the stands off first base. What you can't miss from any seat is the huge scoreboard in left field. Keep your eye on it. Periodically it explodes with fireworks—after a home run, at the seventh-inning stretch, after a crucial strikeout, or merely at the operator's whim. Nobody knows when it will happen.

The atmosphere here is old-fashioned and relaxed. There's a circle of picnic tables and umbrellas just inside the main gate, where a dixieland band plays for pregame picnickers. You can bring your own food if you want to, but why bother? There's plenty already here—fajitas, burritos, nachos grandes, bratwurst and grilled chicken sandwiches, hand-tossed pizza, Philly cheese steaks, funnel cakes, and cotton candy.

There's live organ music between innings. Omaha's organist, in fact, is the only musician in a Triple-A park ever to be ejected from a game. Check your 1988 *Guinness Book of World Records*—the organist played the Mickey Mouse Club theme after an umpire's call and got the hoist. Some fans, however, prefer rock 'n' roll with their baseball, so GM Bill Gorman and staff have struck a compromise. The organ plays between innings, but at the middle of each inning, taped music fills the park and fans sing out loud to "Who you gonna call . . . Ghostbusters," or "Do Wah Diddy Diddy-dum-diddy-doo," even the Partridge Family theme song.

Major promotions here, like a visit from The Famous Chicken, usually take place on weekends. There are good giveaways: wristbands, bats, helmets, and replica jerseys. Each weekday night is special, too. Our favorite is 2 Buck Tuesday: two adults and two kids can get in for two bucks total! No kidding!

Casey the Lion made his debut as team mascot at the 1994 season opener. Thousands of fans, especially kids, turned out to see him because the team had been announcing his arrival over radio and TV for weeks: "Come out and see Casey at the Blatt." They did. Casey's been a big hit since.

Gates open one and a half hours before game time. For autographs, you have to get there early. The players are usually available right after batting practice down by the dugouts.

GETTING THERE

Omaha flourishes on the western bank of the Missouri River. Its beef is famous; there's a steak house on every corner. The city has plenty of nice, very reasonably priced hotels and motels, and there are a number of campgrounds, some right on the Missouri.

Rosenblatt Stadium is two and a half miles south of downtown. To get there, take I-80 to the 13th Street South exit and go south one block to the stadium. The stadium is on a hill next to the zoo. Parking is free, but the two parking lots fill quickly. Get there early for the best parking.

Field box seats are $6, while the slightly-higher-up View box seats go for $5. General admission tickets cost $3. Kids and seniors get $1 off.

For schedule of events and ticket information, call (402) 734-2550.

For tourist information, contact the Greater Omaha Convention and Visitors Bureau, 1819 Farnam, Suite 1200, Omaha, NE 68183, (800) 332-1819.

HOMETOWN STATS—OMAHA *The Last Ten Years*					
Affil.	Year	League	Wins	Losses	Attendance
KCR	1985	American Association	73	69	175,329
	1986		72	70	255,290
	1987		64	76	251,995
	1988		81	61	287,096
	1989		74	72	314,683
	1990		86	60	341,129
	1991		73	71	329,797
	1992		67	77	407,249
	1993		70	74	384,972
	1994		68	76	439,277

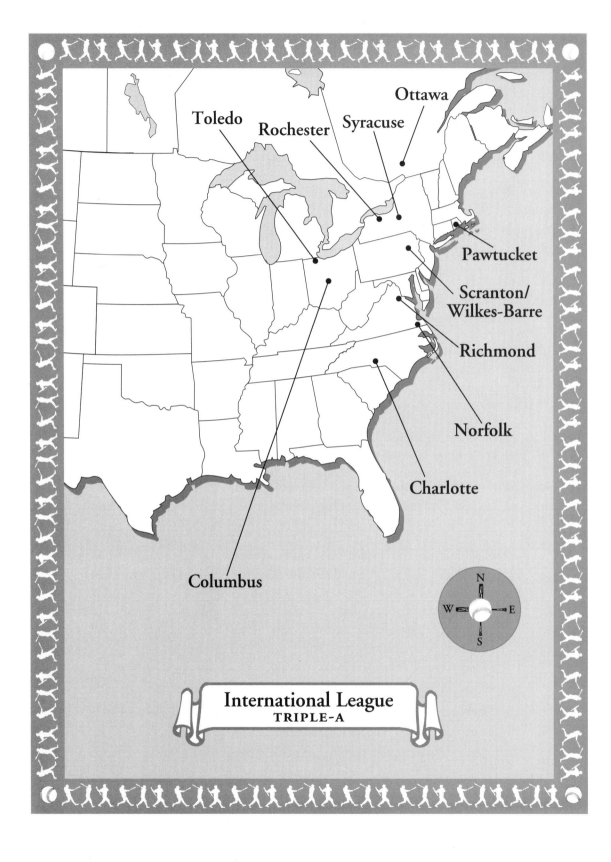

Ottawa
Toledo
Rochester
Syracuse
Pawtucket
Scranton/
Wilkes-Barre
Richmond
Norfolk
Charlotte
Columbus

N
W — E
S

International League
TRIPLE-A

International League

Double-A 1912–1945; Triple-A 1946–

The International League has a slightly complicated past. It was formed in 1887 when three established leagues joined forces—the original Eastern League, the New York State League, and the Ontario League. Present-day league members Richmond, Rochester, and Syracuse were charter members of that union. Then in 1888 the clubs in the north withdrew from the league, claiming that the southern clubs were just too distant; they quickly reorganized as the International Association. Rochester and Syracuse were in; Richmond was dumped, and the old International League instantly folded. In 1891 the circuit was reorganized into the Eastern Association, which became the Eastern League the following year. Finally, after the 1911 season, the league regrouped once again and became the then–Double-A International League.

Since that time, so many teams in so many cities have come and gone that it is nearly impossible (not to mention tedious) to keep them all straight. The latest additions are Charlotte and Ottawa. Both joined in 1993, which ended up being a banner year for the International League; it became the first minor league to attract more than four million fans.

The International League is made up of ten teams, which are scheduled to play 142 games during the regular season. First-place teams in each division play second-place teams in that division in a best-of-five series. Division winners then play a best-of-five series for the league championship.

Charlotte Knights

(Florida Marlins)

Charlotte Knights Stadium
2280 Deerfield Drive
Fort Mill, SC 29716

When the forty-five-year-old wooden stadium at Crockett Park burned down in 1985, most of Charlotte's eighty years of recorded baseball history went with it. The team at that time was the Charlotte O's, the Double-A Southern League affiliate of Baltimore. They hung on for the next few seasons, playing out of trailers on the old site and undergoing a change of ownership, a change of affiliation (from the Orioles to the Cubs), and, in 1988, a change of name to the Knights.

Then along came Doyle Jennings, who donated a large parcel of farmland just across the border in South Carolina. A new state-of-the-art Charlotte Knights stadium finally opened in 1990. And though the park is technically in Fort Mill, just off the interstate, the Knights will always belong to Charlotte, their "Queen City" (the town's nickname). And these Knights are the pride of Charlotte!

In 1993, the city's first year with the expansion Triple-A affiliate of Cleveland, the team won the International League championship. It also managed to keep Cleveland happy by sending up players like Wayne Kirby, Mark Lewis, and Manny Ramirez. Ramirez actually started 1993 with another team, Double-A Canton-Akron, but when he passed through Charlotte he got forty-six hits and twelve home runs in only forty games. Charlotte ended its association with Cleveland after the 1994 season, opting to go with the Florida Marlins in 1995.

The 10,000-seat Charlotte Knights Stadium sits in the middle of bucolic nowhere—plopped on Doyle Jennings's pastureland. The gray and black stone facade with its old iron lampposts and the colorful flags and banners blowing in the wind create a magical effect that has earned the stadium its popular nickname, "the Castle."

Get to the Castle before the seats fill up and behold a rainbow of purple, red, black, green, blue, and yellow. The clothes designer Alexander Julian took charge of the color scheme in the park, and it's stunning. The double-decked grandstand stops at first base and third, and at either end are large grass berms that can hold an overflow crowd of 5,000. On Fireworks Nights the seats and the berms are jam-packed! There are two large picnic areas down right and left fields. Beyond the right field one is the kids' playground. Beyond the playground is an eighteen-hole putt-putt golf course (like miniature golf without the windmills).

Beyond the center and left field fences lie pastures, woods, and, in the distance, Jennings's house. You can see him leave and cross the pasture to come to the game; this ballpark is his dream come true.

Before game time musicians, jugglers, and dancers (especially cloggers and line dancers) entertain out front and on the concourse. Music is piped everywhere, creating a carnival atmosphere. Concession carts roll along the concourse amidst more concession stands and novelty shops.

Between innings, team mascot Homer the Dragon hits whiffle balls into the stands (it's called the "Homer Slam"); whoever catches one wins a prize. At the seventh-inning stretch, three chosen fans come down out of the stands to lead a rendition of "Take Me Out to the Ball Game." Once in a while, a celebrity sneaks in and leads it, and the crowd goes wild!. Popular giveaways include those huge foam #1 fingers, neon caps, and fan packs (pennant, button, bumper sticker).

The park is open until 5:00 P.M. every weekday for visitors and guided tours. It reopens one and a half hours (one hour on Sundays) before game time. Players are available for autographs near the

dugouts before the game or at the booth on the concourse, where one player at each home game spends twenty minutes signing. The players park right outside the front gate, so you can also catch them as they leave the park after the game.

GETTING THERE

Charlotte is really booming and has a lot to offer, including a new arts center and the Carowinds amusement park. There are fine hotels in town as well as other accommodations. Campgrounds are located right at Carowinds (just north of the stadium).

Charlotte Knights Stadium is located south of Charlotte in Fort Mill, South Carolina. From Charlotte, take I-77 south to Goldhill Road (exit

The triple-deck outfield billboard fence reveals tremendous local support for the Knights.

88). Then follow the signs to Deerfield Drive and the stadium. There is plenty of free parking available.

Field box seats, as well as the upper-level club box seats, cost $6.50. Reserved seats are $5.50 and general admission tickets cost $4.50. Kids, seniors, and the military get in for $3.

For schedule of events and ticket information, call (704) 332-3746 in North Carolina, (803) 548-8051 in South Carolina.

For tourist information, contact the Charlotte Convention & Visitors Bureau, 122 East Stonewall Street, Charlotte, NC 28202, (704) 531-2700.

		HOMETOWN STATS—CHARLOTTE			
		The Last Ten Years			
Affil.	Year	League	Wins	Losses	Attendance
BAL	1985	Southern	78	65	104,085
	1986		71	73	106,426
	1987		85	60	129,246
	1988		69	75	102,467
CUB	1989		70	73	157,720
	1990		65	79	271,502
	1991		74	70	313,791
	1992		70	73	338,047
CLE	1993	International	86	55	403,029
	1994		77	65	391,730

Columbus Clippers

(New York Yankees)

Cooper Stadium
1155 W. Mound Street
Columbus, OH 43223

Longtime Clippers manager Stump Merrill meets on the mound with pitcher Rick Hines and Jorge Posada.

Baseball in Columbus began with the Buckeyes, who had two brief stints with the major league American Association, from 1883 to 1884 and from 1889 to 1891. Then when the American Association came back in 1901 as a minor league, the Columbus team, by that time known as the Senators, became a charter member. They changed their name to the Red Birds in 1931, opened their new Red Bird Stadium in 1932, and stayed on until 1955, when they moved to Omaha. The Triple-A Jets then took up residency until 1970. By the end of the Jets' last season the thirty-nine-year-old park was in desperate shape, and fan attendance was dwindling.

Six years later Franklin County officials, led by then–County Commissioner Harold Cooper (who would go on to become the president of the International League), bought the old park, renovated it (installing Astroturf), and secured a new team for the 1977 season. Since the city is named in honor of Christopher Columbus, "Clippers" (think of the Niña, Pinta, and Santa Maria) was a natural choice for the team name. They took the field for the first time on April 22, 1977, in the newly renovated Franklin County Stadium. In 1984 the 15,000-seat ballpark was renamed to honor Harold Cooper.

After a brief affiliation with Pittsburgh, the Clippers became the Triple-A affiliate of the Yankees in 1979. The team has been very successful, drawing half a million fans a year. Some Yankee stars and famous alumni include Doug Drabek, Roberto Kelly, All-Star Don Mattingly, Deion Sanders, and Dave Righetti, who moved on to the Yankees in 1981 and was honored as A.L. Rookie of the Year. Try to get to the park early so you can see the murals of these athletes lining the concourse. You can also check out the many names of Columbus's great ones etched into monuments in the Columbus Baseball Hall of Fame, located in Dysart Memorial Park just behind the stadium's right field fence. Then head to the stadium, where you will be greeted at the gate by team mascot Captain Clipper (a real live person in a 1490s costume with an oversized puppetlike head).

Fans love Cooper Stadium. The steep rake of the grandstand puts everyone extremely close to the action. Hitters love this park, too. The right field fence is twenty feet closer to home than the left field fence, giving this park the same configuration of Yankee Stadium. Steve Balboni, on his way up to an impressive Yankee career, loved it. By hitting ninety-two over the fence from 1981 to 1983, he established and still holds the all-time Clippers home run record. And out-fielders love the low six-foot fence in left field, which makes for exciting plays. Many have been able to leap the fence and rob hitters of home runs.

Promotions run the gamut from the ever-popular "Dime-a-Dog" night (which is just what it sounds like) to wildly successful baseball/concert "doubleheaders" featuring the likes of the Beach Boys, REO Speedwagon, and the Temptations immediately following the game. Every Monday night, kids under sixteen who are members of the Clippers Kids Club get in free. Every Friday, stay for fireworks after the game!

Two of the Clippers' secret weapons are their original theme songs "Ring Your Bell" and "Hometown Heroes." Right after the National Anthem, when the Clippers take the field, "Ring Your Bell" blares over the sound system. The lyrics flash on the scoreboard and the crowd sings—and rings handheld bells! That's right, the fans come equipped with victory bells that don't stop. (You can buy one for $3.50 on the concourse.) The Cllippers get serenaded with either "Ring Your Bell" or "Hometown Heroes" at least two more times during the game (much to the consternation of the visiting team).

Gates open an hour before game time. Head to the dugouts, where the players will sign autographs until half an hour before the game starts. If you miss them there, wait outside the players' locker rooms after the game.

GETTING THERE

Columbus, Ohio's capital city, is known for its art galleries, museums, theater, and historical districts. Downtown and North Columbus have some really nice hotels. There are a variety of motels, as well as camping facilities north of the city in Delaware.

Cooper Stadium is located just southwest of downtown Columbus off I-70. From the east, heading west on I-70, get off at Exit 98B (Mound Street), turn left onto Mound, and proceed to the stadium. From the west, heading east on I-70, you have to get off at Exit 97 (Broad Street), turn left onto Broad, take a right on Glenwood, and then proceed to the stadium. Parking facilities can handle up to 3,500 cars at $2.00 each.

Box seats go for $6, while reserved seats are $4.50. General admission tickets cost $3.50. Kids under twelve and seniors over sixty get in for $1.50.

For schedule of events and ticket information, call (614) 462-5250.

For tourist information, contact the Greater Columbus Convention & Visitors Bureau, 10 West Broad Street, Columbus, OH 43215, (800) 345-4FUN.

HOMETOWN STATS—COLUMBUS					
The Last Ten Years					
Affil.	Year	League	Wins	Losses	Attendance
NYY	1985	International	75	64	568,735
	1986		62	77	548,417
	1987		77	63	570,599
	1988		65	77	536,171
	1989		77	69	504,224
	1990		87	59	584,010
	1991		85	59	570,605
	1992		95	49	583,918
	1993		78	62	580,570
	1994		74	68	535,145

Norfolk Tides

(New York Mets)

Harbor Park
150 Park Avenue
Norfolk, VA 23510

Norfolk and her neighboring towns have been devoted to baseball for nearly a century now. And although the area went without a professional team for six years after the Norfolk Tars and the Portsmouth Merrimacs folded in 1955, eventually a Florida businessman set up a Double-A franchise in Portsmouth. The new Portsmouth Tides would go on to represent the Norfolk area in the Carolina League from 1963 to 1968. Then, in 1969, the New York Mets decided to move their Triple-A International League Jacksonville (FL) club to Tidewater. With the Mets' help, Norfolk built Met Park, where the Met-owned Tidewater Tides played from 1970 to 1992. The Mets sold the club in 1992 to a group of businessmen, which included some proud hometown entrepreneurs. The new owners promptly changed the club's colors, logo, and even its name, to the *Norfolk* Tides, but kept the longstanding affiliation with the Mets. World Series–class players have come up through Norfolk, including Wally Backman, Gary Carter, Ron Darling, Mookie Wilson, Kevin Elster, Sid Fernandez, and Lenny Dykstra. Dykstra played his last minor league game in Norfolk in 1985 before getting the call to New York, as did Kevin Mitchell.

The Norfolk Tides played the 1993 season in the newly constructed Harbor Park on the waterfront in downtown Norfolk. The stadium, located on the western bank of the Elizabeth River, seats 12,000. There are 9,000 seats on the lower level and 3,000 on the upper level, which, as it turns out, is the closest deck that architects have ever built to a baseball field. The team finished their first year here with a just okay 70–71 record. The fans don't seem to care, however, and come no matter what, especially for opening night when there is always a show. Skydivers land on the field, and tugboats and fireboats churn up the river beyond the outfield fence, sounding their horns and shooting off water cannons. Once a flyby of F-14s got everybody up and cheering.

The stadium is fabulous. The wide and airy concourse area that wraps around the grandstand from foul pole to foul pole bustles with a festival atmosphere. There are brightly lit concession stands and game booths. Our favorite is a baseball card photo booth, where you get to be the star player on your own baseball card. The picnic area, where you can reserve tables, is built in three terraces along a grassy berm just over the left field fence. Because the tables sit right at the river's edge, the area is a popular place on those eighty-five-degree nights. For those in the stadium proper there is an open grill concession off the third base line, where you can sit and eat freshly grilled sausages, ribs, chicken, and dogs. And don't miss the concession stands that sell that enormously popular regional favorite, crabcake sandwiches.

"Rip Tide," the team mascot, is a scary little number. A blue and fuzzy creature with a nose that lights up and honks, he (it?) zooms around the field in his own four-wheeler. Word of warning: in the posted "Rules of the Stadium" is a notice that

Tides coaches confer in the dugout.

When not busy stealing popcorn from fans, mascot Rip Tide mugs for the camera.

"Anyone abusing Rip or his costume will be ejected from Harbor Park." (This doesn't apply to the players, who hold, tackle, or otherwise distract him during his nightly race around the bases.) Giveaways are the good ones, like T-shirts, caps, jackets, beach towels, beach bags, and so forth.

Gates open about an hour before game time. Fans can seek autographs by the railings along the field up to fifteen minutes before the game starts.

GETTING THERE

Norfolk is a 300-year-old port city on the Chesapeake Bay. The Greater Norfolk area is sometimes called Hampton Roads, and includes Williamsburg and Jamestown. There are great hotels and motels, and plenty of campsites.

Harbor Park is just off I-264 at Exit 9. Parking is plentiful at $2.00. There are 2,000 spaces at the stadium, but when that lot is full, there are four town parking garages nearby (also $2.00) to handle overflow. If you are staying in beautiful downtown Norfolk, you can easily walk to the stadium.

All seats are reserved. The box seats that wrap around the baselines cost $6.50. The Lower Reserved seats and the Upper Reserved seats on the outfield lines are $5. Students (through high school), seniors, and military personnel get in for $4.

For schedule of events and ticket information, call (804) 622-2222.

For tourist information, contact the Norfolk Convention & Visitors Bureau, 236 East Plume Street, Norfolk, VA 23510, (804) 441-1852 or (800) 368-3097.

HOMETOWN STATS—TIDEWATER/NORFOLK *The Last Ten Years*					
Affil.	Year	League	Wins	Losses	Attendance
NYM	1985	International	75	64	153,100
	1986		74	66	171,589
	1987		81	59	175,104
	1988		71	64	194,089
	1989		77	69	210,258
	1990		79	67	193,055
	1991		77	65	196,988
	1992		56	86	174,362
	1993*		70	71	529,708
	1994		67	75	546,826

*Tides move from Tidewater into Norfolk's Harbor Park.

Ottawa Lynx

(Montreal Expos)

Ottawa Stadium
300 Coventry Road
Ottawa, Ontario, Canada K1K 4P5

It continues to amaze us that baseball truly knows no boundaries. Not to wear out that now-old cliché, "Build it and they will come," but be it the cornfields of Iowa, the tobacco fields of North Carolina, or the outskirts of a major city, the truth is, the fans *do* come. When Ottawa Lynx owner Howard Darwin built "it"—the state-of-the-art, 10,000-seat Ottawa Stadium—"they" came in droves. In their inaugural 1993 season the Ottawa Lynx set an all-time International League attendance record of 663,000 (second only to the American Association's Buffalo Bisons). A total of 44 sold-out games proved that baseball fever was sweeping Canada, due in large part to the huge national popularity of the Lynx's affiliate, the Montreal Expos, and, of course, those incredible World Champion Toronto Blue Jays.

Darwin purchased the Montreal Expos affiliate from Indianapolis in September 1991 and chose the name "Lynx." "I didn't want a really *ferocious* animal," he says, "I wanted one the kids could put on their pajamas." And, perhaps more pointedly, "lynx" has the same spelling in both English and French—one astute, user-friendly solution to the language wars in Canada.

Another amazing thing about the Lynx is that in their first season, they made it to the first round of the playoffs. Even more impressive, of the fifty-seven who wore the Lynx uniform that year, twenty-five actually went on to play for the Montreal Expos. Some of these players include Denis Boucher, Chris Nabholz, Kirk Rueter, Joe Siddall, Rondell White, Archi Cianfrocco, Frank Bolick, and Curtis Pride, who is the first hearing-impaired player in the majors. Pride, who reads lips, has the uncanny ability to judge how hard a ball is hit by the angle it comes off the bat. And what speed he has—he hit twenty-one home runs and stole fifty bases in 1993 before heading up to Montreal late in the year.

Ottawa Stadium has been called a baseball fan's dream. Opened just in the nick of time for the 1993 season, it is a wide-open (no roof) stadium that, except for a few designated out-of-the-way areas, is also smoke-free. The park gets rave reviews for its comfortable seats and good sight lines. Fans tend to arrive early for pregame on-field contests and stay until the last out. The park's most talked about feature is the picnic area off the left field foul line, where fifty tables are usually packed with friends and families. Kids roam about with mitts ready for foul balls, and yes, reservations are a must.

The second most talked about feature has to be Lenny the Lynx, a furry, big-headed lynx-lookalike mascot who pops up unexpectedly—quite often in different costumes. Early in the game he might be found lounging on top of the dugout in beachwear, then perhaps signing autographs in uniform at his own booth on the concourse. He might show up later trying to follow the fantastic Queensview Athletic Club instructors as they lead the crowd in an aerobic seventh-inning stretch workout.

Stay in your seat at the end of the fifth inning. Lynx fans do, just to see the water truck. A tiny cartoonlike truck, driven by a guy who looms out of it, peels into the outfield, speeding bottled water deliveries to the umpires. Then, just as quickly, the truck makes the rounds again to pick up the empties. When you do leave your seat, be sure to try one of those Ottawa standbys: sugar-coated, deep-fried pastries called "beaver-tails." A kissing cousin, perhaps, of the Cajun "pig's ears?"

Gates open one and a half hours before game time. Get autographs down by the dugout and for ten minutes before every game at the autograph booth on the field.

GETTING THERE

Ottawa (and Canada's Capital Region) is a blend of English and French cultures and is filled with world-renowned museums, galleries, boutiques, sidewalk cafes, and charming neighborhoods. There's an exceptional variety of accommodations, including nearby campsites.

Ottawa Stadium, or the Ottawa Multipurpose Recreation Complex, is located in Ottawa off Highway 417. Get off the highway at the Vanier Parkway North exit. Then take a right onto Coventry and head to the stadium entrance. Parking costs $5.50 per car.

Box seats cost $8.45, while reserved seats go for $6.35. General admission tickets cost $4.25.

For schedule of events and ticket information, call (613) 749-9947.

For tourist information, contact the Ottawa Tourism & Convention Authority, 111 Lisgar Street, Ottawa, Ontario K2P 2L7, (613) 237-5150.

Even though the Ottawa runner is tagged by Norfolk's first base defender, the Canadian team went on to better Norfolk in the 1994 overall standings.

HOMETOWN STATS—OTTAWA					
*The Last Ten Years**					
Affil.	Year	League	Wins	Losses	Attendance
MON	1993	International	73	69	663,926
	1994		70	72	596,858

*Statistics are given only for the years in which the team played in Ottawa.

Pawtucket Red Sox

(Boston Red Sox)

McCoy Stadium
One Columbus Avenue
Pawtucket, RI 02861

Since 1977, Pawtucket players have been taking "the bait" from autograph seekers.

Ben Mondor, owner of the Pawtucket (RI) Red Sox, is known as a class act. He took over this bankrupt franchise in 1977 and turned it into one of the finest clubs in the minor leagues. Up until then, Pawtucket's experience with baseball had been sporadic, with teams totalling, at best, fifteen years of playing time since 1908. But that was before Ben Mondor.

Mondor's philosophy is simple—give the fans good baseball and make them feel like part of the family. It's not unusual to catch sight of him and the PawSox management staff greeting people at the gate and mingling in the stands during the game. They care about what the fans want, right down to the local brand of hot dogs they carry. And they listen. Mondor was considering replacing the three dozen billboards that line the outfield fence with new green padding until he consulted the fans, who nixed the idea; the fans didn't want the park to lose its old-fashioned look and feel. Mondor's attitude has won him a very loyal following—that and, of course, the quality of the players who have come through McCoy Stadium on their way to Fenway Park. A few of McCoy's alumni are Jim Rice, Mo Vaughn, Bruce Hurst, Roger Clemens, and Wade Boggs, who had 167 hits in Pawtucket and a league-leading batting average of .335 in 1981.

McCoy Stadium was originally built in 1942, the dream come true of Pawtucket mayor Thomas P. McCoy. By the time Mondor took over, the thirty-five-year-old stadium was falling apart. After Mondor spent nearly $2 million of his own money, the city and state finally passed a $2.5 million renovation project. Now the park is a good-as-new stadium, where the comfortable seats hug the field from the first base bag to third, and fans sit so close to the action they can hear the infielders talk. Colorful murals on the walls along the concourse celebrate all the players who have gone on to "the Show." And the view for those on the first base side provides some of the most spectacular New England sunsets we've seen.

In 1994 seating capacity was expanded to 7,002 from 6,010, since nearly half of the 1993 season's games were sold out. Good news, though: the barbecue area off left field is still intact. For groups of 125 or more, the club provides drinks and all the hot dogs and hamburgers you can eat throughout the game.

Expect the unexpected in Pawtucket baseball. The longest game in professional baseball history took place here in 1981. Against the Rochester Red Wings, the game went *thirty-three* innings

Renovated McCoy Stadium seats 7,002.

and took three days to finish. The first pitch was at 7:35 P.M. on April 18. At 4:18 A.M. the next morning, when the game was still tied at two after thirty-two innings, it was suspended until Rochester could come back to town on June 23. The game started at 6:00 P.M. on the 23rd and was over at 6:20 P.M. Pawtucket won it, 3–2, in the bottom of the thirty-third. The longest game had come to the shortest end.

Gates open two hours before game time. To get autographs, you can wait until the players leave the park, or you can go fishing. That's right, fishing. The stands are built right over the dugouts, so kids place programs, photos, or whatever into plastic bottles or buckets and lower them on ropes to the players for signing. The clever ones cut holes in the sides of soda bottles and lower baseballs inside. The dedicated ones lower their baseball mitts.

GETTING THERE

Only five miles north of Providence, Pawtucket, the birthplace of the American Industrial Revolution, is in the beautiful Blackstone River Valley. Steeped in history, the region has a plentitude of hotels, motels, and campsites.

To reach McCoy Stadium from the north, take I-95 south to Exit 2A (Newport Avenue). Follow Newport Avenue for two miles to Columbus Avenue. Take a right on Columbus and continue on for one mile. The stadium is on the right. From the south take I-95 north to Exit 28 (School Street). Follow School Street two blocks to Pond Street. Take a left on Pond to Columbus (the stadium is right in front of you). Take a right on Columbus; the stadium entrance is on the left.

For adults, box seats run $5.50; seniors and kids pay $4.50. General admission tickets cost $4.00 for adults, $3.00 for kids and seniors.

For schedule of events and ticket information, call (401) 724-7300.

For tourist information, contact the Blackstone Valley Tourism Council, P.O. Box 242, Lincoln, RI 02865, (401) 334-7773.

Affil.	Year	League	Wins	Losses	Attendance
BOS	1985	International	48	91	166,504
	1986		74	65	186,517
	1987		73	67	220,838
	1988		63	79	246,940
	1989		62	84	271,025
	1990		62	84	290,953
	1991		79	64	349,338
	1992		71	72	358,318
	1993		60	82	466,428
	1994		78	64	469,029

HOMETOWN STATS—PAWTUCKET
The Last Ten Years

Richmond Braves

(Atlanta Braves)

The Diamond
3001 N. Boulevard
Richmond, VA 23230

In 1887 Richmond was a charter member of the old International League, which fell apart a year later when the league's northern members withdrew. Richmond then joined the Class C Virginia League in 1906, and since that time has gone without baseball for only a total of *three* seasons—the Depression years 1929 and 1930, and 1965. An incredible record for a minor league city. The club over the years has been called the Virginians, Giants, Crows, Johnny Rebs, Bluebirds, Lawmakers, and Colts. Since 1966, the year they became affiliated with Atlanta, they have been the Braves. Some fine major league players have come through Richmond, among them the pitching brothers Phil and Joe Niekro, who both went on to long major league careers—Joe for twenty-two years, mostly with Houston, and Phil for twenty-three years, mostly with Atlanta. Some other players to move up were Henry's younger brother Tommy Aaron, who went on to play for the Braves, Jim Acker, Steve Bedrosian, David Justice, All-Star Braves aces John Smoltz and Steve Avery, and Atlanta's great outfielder Deion Sanders.

The Diamond, built in an amazing 226 days, opened in 1985. It was actually named by an anonymous fan who wrote a letter suggesting the name to honor the game itself, and to symbolize the stadium as a shining jewel in the community. And it is, indeed, a jewel. There are fifteen luxury super boxes that ring the field just behind the field box seats. The rest of the stadium is raked above. The grandstand wraps from just beyond third to just beyond first base and seats 11,978;

7,000 are located in the upper level. But no matter where you sit, you are close to the field. Even the last seat in the last row feels as close as a front mezzanine seat in any major league park. Two reasons for this are a very small foul area and what seems to be no space between home plate and the backstop.

When you enter the stadium there's a festive feeling on the concourse. A giant ten-by-twenty-foot bust of Chief Connecticut (the official guardian Brave) looms over the first concession stand. You are instantly hit with the aroma of sausages and peppers cooking on a grill, pretzels baking, and cotton candy spinning. There's a small picnic area down off left field, which is a great spot for birthday parties. Or try the Diamond Room restaurant overlooking right field. It opens at 4:30 P.M. for those who want to watch batting practice and get something to eat. There's a complete buffet that is served throughout the game.

The Braves organization doesn't hold to on-field contests, preferring to keep a "serious eye" on the game. Fans don't seem to mind, however, because the club hosts some popular promotions and giveaways. The most well-liked freebies of the summer are seat cushions because all the seats here are metal chairs. Second best are the foam hatchets that everybody waves when they do the "tomahawk chop." On Turn-Back-the-Clock Night the Braves play in their 1960 Richmond Virginians uniforms, and nostalgic fans really turn out in droves. And every night without fail Diamond Duck, the team mascot, gets a clog dance going in the middle of the sixth inning. Fans join him on the top of the dugout.

Gates open one hour before game time. Every Sunday two players sign full-color action photos supplied by the team at the autograph booth on the concourse. The players are only there from 1:10 to 1:30 P.M., and the line starts forming at 12:30 P.M., so get there early. You can also try your luck around the dugouts after batting practice.

Ball girls are a common (and welcome) sight in both the minors and the majors these days.

GETTING THERE

Richmond, Virginia's capital city on the James River, has some of America's finest plantations. The state capitol was designed by Thomas Jefferson. There's a variety of accommodations, from quaint inns to grand hotels. Americamps has campsites just north of town.

The Diamond is located right at the junction of I-64 and I-95 (exit 78) on N. Boulevard, across the street from the Greyhound bus terminal. There is plenty of parking, which costs $2.

Box seats (on the field) cost $6 and are usually available on a day-of-game basis. Reserved seats (first ten rows of the upper deck) go for $5. General admission tickets cost $4, $2 for kids and seniors.

For schedule of events and ticket information, call (804) 359-4444.

For tourist information, contact the Metro Richmond Convention & Visitors Bureau, 550 East Marshall Street, Richmond, VA 23219, (800) 365-7272.

	HOMETOWN STATS—RICHMOND *The Last Ten Years*				
Affil.	**Year**	**League**	**Wins**	**Losses**	**Attendance**
ATL	1985	International	75	65	379,019
	1986		80	60	381,364
	1987		56	83	332,440
	1988		66	75	355,704
	1989		81	65	424,265
	1990		71	74	427,552
	1991		65	79	434,994
	1992		73	71	453,915
	1993		80	62	533,076
	1994		80	61	507,322

Rochester Red Wings

(Baltimore Orioles)

Silver Stadium
500 Norton Street
Rochester, NY 14621

Rochester should be given an award for dependability. The city has hosted professional baseball since 1885, and for all but two of those years Rochester teams have been part of the International League or its predecessor, the old Eastern League. What's even more impressive is that the current team, the Red Wings, has had only two affiliations in the last sixty-five years; they were with the Cardinals from 1929 to 1961 and have been with the Baltimore Orioles ever since. Before 1929 they were, at various times, called the Hop Bitters, Broncos, Beau Brummells, Hustlers, Champs, and Florists (after Rochester's reputation for cultivating acres of commercial flowers). They became the Red Wings in 1929, and the name stuck. Among the Orioles greats who played with the Red Wings are Jim Palmer, Cal Ripken Jr., Bobby Grich, and Don Baylor, the Rockies manager who hit 42 home runs and had 212 RBIs in his two years (1970–71) with Rochester. Stan Musial and Bob Gibson were Red Wings, and Earl Weaver and Frank Robinson were managers. A total of seventeen Hall of Famers played or managed with the Red Wings.

Silver Stadium, one of the oldest minor league parks anywhere, has been home to the Red Wings since May 2, 1929. This place rumbles with history. Even the Babe pitched and hit here in 1933 in an exhibition game. The stadium was dedicated on August 19, 1968, in honor of Morrie Silver, who led the effort to keep baseball in Rochester in the late 1950s and early 1960s. (Over 8,000 people now own stock in the team.) The park is noted for its sixty-five-foot-high scoreboard just to the left of center field and the wildly colorful three-tiered billboards rising forty feet over the left field wall. The roof, which covers a good two-thirds of the grandstands, has bounced many a foul ball into the third base–side parking lot.

The stadium was most recently renovated in 1986, making its seating capacity 12,503. But even though all the facilities were upgraded, the concession area is still cramped. Buffalo wings and barbecued chicken are served next to bistro food, down-home chili, and flavored popcorn. All this and Red Wing Ale, too, which is brewed exclusively for the team by the Rohrbach Brewery. While this is very cozy, it's too cozy for some, which is why Silver Stadium might be replaced soon. Word has it that the Red Wings would like to move downtown to Oak Street and build a new stadium in the shadow of the Kodak tower.

Meanwhile, management's philosophy is this: during the innings, the players keep the fans on the edges of their seats; between innings, management keeps the fans on the edges of their seats. There are, consequently, a lot of on-field contests. One of the most popular involves team mascot Wild Fang, a batlike creature (the winged kind) who races a young opponent around the bases to home plate while he (Wild Fang) pushes a cart full of groceries (from the local sponsor). Guess what! WF never wins. Something always happens. Once a policeman came out on the field and arrested the Fang right in the middle of the race!

There is always something going on at Silver Stadium, which is why over 360,000 fans come out annually. Some of the popular sponsored giveaways include Wild Fang cards, team photos, gym bags, sports bottles, and replica jerseys.

Gates open about one hour before game time. On Sundays there is an autograph booth set up on the concourse. But most days, if you get there early enough, you can grab the players by the dugouts. One nice event they hold here in Kodak country is Camera Day. Once a season, fans get to go out on the field with the players and have their pictures taken.

LEFT: *Red Wings pitcher Kevin McGehee winds up.*

RIGHT: *Bruce Dostal is at bat for Rochester.*

GETTING THERE

Rochester is located on the shore of Lake Ontario. The famous Lilac Festival in May is a fantastic display of blooming flowers, spread over twenty-two acres of Highland Park. There's a good selection of hotels and motels, and a lot of campsites can be found in the area.

Silver Stadium is located in a residential area at 500 Norton Street, two blocks south of Route 104, between Clinton and Seneca Avenues. (Route 104 is accessible from US 390 or US 590.) There is very limited parking at the stadium, but parking on the street is usually not a problem.

Lower box seats go for $7.75, while the upper boxes cost $6.75. Reserved seats are $5.75 and general admission tickets go for $4. Seniors and kids get 75 cents off.

For schedule of events and ticket information, call (716) 467-3000.

For tourist information, contact the Greater Rochester Visitors Association, 126 Andrews Street, Rochester, NY 14604, (716) 546-3070 or (800) 677-7282.

		HOMETOWN STATS—ROCHESTER *The Last Ten Years*			
Affil.	Year	League	Wins	Losses	Attendance
BAL	1985	International	58	81	208,955
	1986		75	63	308,807
	1987		74	65	315,807
	1988		77	64	300,794
	1989		72	73	284,394
	1990		89	56	331,927
	1991		76	68	345,167
	1992		70	74	305,205
	1993		74	67	361,676
	1994		67	74	364,188

Scranton/Wilkes-Barre Red Barons

(Philadelphia Phillies)

Lackawanna County Stadium
235 Montage Mountain Road
Moosic, PA 18507

The Red Barons were not named after the World War I flying ace who has given Snoopy so much grief. The story is much less dramatic. Back in 1905 northeastern Pennsylvania was home to not one but two very popular minor league baseball teams: the Scranton Red Sox and the Wilkes-Barre Barons. These two rivals had shared histories, first with the New York State League and then with the New York-Pennsylvania League and its successor, the new Eastern League. Unfortunately, neither team could hang on and by 1959, both had folded. After a thirty-year drought, the civic leaders of Lackawanna County wanted to bring baseball back to northeastern Pennsylvania. In 1989 they teamed up with local business people and bought the Philadelphia Phillies' Triple-A franchise in Old Orchard Beach, Maine. When it was time to name the new team, the Pennsylvanians wanted to honor their old teams, so they combined the original names, and the Red Barons were born.

The new $25 million Lackawanna County Stadium sits at the foot of Montage Mountain, which lies between Scranton and Wilkes-Barre. The double-decked grandstand wraps from foul pole to foul pole, and the view from any seat is splendid. Beyond the outfield fence is a stunningly beautiful rocky and wooded terrain—a kind of dramatic counterpoint to the park's AstroTurf. All of the 10,800 seats are great, but if you have kids in tow, head for the upper level bleachers along the baselines because that's foul-ball-catching territory.

Lackawanna officials gambled that county residents would support a team. They did, and they do. The Red Barons usually draw over 500,000 fans a

Mascot The Grump relaxes in the dugout with a fan and 1993 Red Baron Bruce Dostal.

Lackawanna County Stadium is home to the Red Barons.

year, packing in over 8,000 each game. It also hasn't hurt that the Philadelphia Phillies, who have been getting better and better each year, made it to the 1993 World Series. A few Red Barons graduates who went on to play on that National League championship team are Dave Hollins, Kevin Stocker, Wes Chamberlain, Steve Stanicek—who set a Red Barons' record in 1990 with seventy-six RBIs—and 1988 U.S. Olympian Mickey Morandini, who also set a team record in 1990 with ten triples.

The official mascot for the Red Barons is the Grump, a green and hairy fella who, according to the coloring book bearing his name, was hatched from a prehistoric egg that was uncovered when the stadium's foundation was being excavated. As he grew up he became an avid fan of the Red Barons.

All giveaways are for kids fourteen and under: neon caps, super sport bottles, bats, sports bags, baseballs, cups, T-shirts, team photos, and more.

The special crowd-pleasing events staged throughout the summer include fireworks displays, a Phillie Phanatic appearance, the $5,000 Dash for Cash, and free baseball clinics.

Gates open about an hour and a half before game time. The best place to get autographs before the game is along the infield fences, or wait until the game is over and catch the players as they leave the clubhouse.

GETTING THERE

Lackawanna County is an old coal mining center in the lush green mountains of northeastern Pennsylvania. It's now most famous for its spectacular fall foliage. There are hotels and motels in Scranton and Wilkes-Barre and numerous campgrounds throughout the region.

Lackawanna County Stadium is located between Scranton and Wilkes-Barre just off I-81 (and south of I-380). Heading north or south, get off at Exit 51, Montage Mountain Road. There is ample parking, which costs $1.

The few lower box seats available (most are taken by season ticket holders) cost $6.50. The upper grandstand seats go for $4.50 and the bleacher seats on either end run $3.50.

For schedule of events and ticket information, call (717) 969-BALL (that's 2255).

For tourist information, contact Pennsylvania's Northeast Territory Visitors Bureau, Airport Aviation Center, 201 Hangar Road, Suite 203, Avoca, PA 18641, (800) 245-7711.

HOMETOWN STATS—SCRANTON/WILKES-BARRE *The Last Ten Years**					
Affil.	Year	League	Wins	Losses	Attendance
PHI	1989	International	64	79	434,106
	1990		68	78	545,844
	1991		65	78	535,725
	1992		84	58	560,464
	1993		62	80	531,620
	1994		62	80	476,053

*Statistics are given only for the years in which the team played in Scranton/Wilkes-Barre.

Syracuse Chiefs

(Toronto Blue Jays)

MacArthur Stadium
Hiawatha Boulevard
Syracuse, NY 13208

Syracuse's first professional baseball team, the Stars, played here for fifty years, from 1878 to 1928. They had two go-rounds with the major leagues, first in 1879 with the National League (1876–   ) and then in 1890 with the American Association (1882–91). The team was a member of the Class B New York-Pennsylvania League in 1929 when, on June 16th, old Star Park literally collapsed and the club was forced to move to Hazelton, Pennsylvania. Baseball would not return to Syracuse until 1934, when Mayor Roland Marvin lured the Triple-A franchise from Jersey City with the promise of a new stadium. In order to get the townspeople involved with the new team the owner, John Corbett, asked them to name it. They suggested seventy names, including the "Syracuse Chiefs." Corbett chose that name because Syracuse is located in the heart of Indian country, and the new stadium was about to be built near the setting of the famous saga "The Legend of Hiawatha."

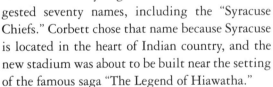

The 8,416-seat Municipal Stadium was built in 1934 as a WPA project. Construction began on March 2, and the Chiefs' first game (in a not-quite-finished park) was an unbelievable forty-eight days later before a crowd of 10,000 fans. At the time, the ballpark had a combined seating of 10,500 (8,400 grandstand seats plus another 2,100 bleacher seats). In 1947, the stadium was renamed in honor of General Douglas MacArthur.

The franchise was sold in 1955 to a group in Miami. A Class A team moved in in 1956 and was gone two years later. Then, in 1961, a new Triple-A team, affiliated with both the Minnesota Twins and the Washington Senators, opened in Mac-Arthur Stadium. The team was floundering in the summer of 1969 when a fire tore through the ballpark. The offices, the concession area, and over 5,000 seats were destroyed. In spite of, or perhaps because of, this tragedy the team turned its season around in one of the great comebacks of all time. Playing in their burned-out stadium, the Chiefs took a deep collective breath and made a run for the playoffs. They finished by winning the league championship, four games to one. Since that time, the team has had some good years, particularly in the 1980s when they won two league championships. The Chiefs have also sent some good players up to play for the World Champion Blue Jays, their affiliate since 1978. Among them are Pat Borders, Rob Butler, Tony Castillo, Juan Guzman, Pat Hentgen, and Tony Fernandez, who played in Syracuse from 1981 to 1984 and led all league shortstops with eighty-seven double plays in 1983.

Syracuse is a big sports town. Thousands of fans support the university's football and basketball teams. Come warm weather, that same enthusiasm is turned toward baseball and the Chiefs. The Chiefs don't hold any on-field contests between innings because they feel it distracts from the level of play. They do, however, have a different giveaway every night and sponsor special appearances by "Elvis," the Blues Brothers, the Dynamite Lady (who blows herself out of a box in center field), and a benefit Soap Opera Star softball game in which real soap opera stars compete against local radio personalities. The team mascot, Scooch, is an orange furry creature that defies description, but don't worry, you can't miss him as he makes several appearances during the game.

Do not leave the stadium without trying the knockwurst and sauerkraut on a roll at Gladys's concession stand or swigging a beer with the very jovial Dently at Dently's Dugout.

Gates open an hour and a half before game time. Players are available for signing autographs before the game down by right field.

In 1994, the Chiefs' pitching and hitting was good enough to get them into the championship playoffs, where Richmond defeated them 3–0 in the best-of-five series.

GETTING THERE

Syracuse, located in the heart of New York State, is home to Syracuse University, with its famous Carrier Dome, the only major domed stadium on a college campus. There's a variety of hotels and motels and plenty of campsites throughout Onondaga County.

MacArthur Stadium is on the north side of town. From westbound Route 81, get off at Exit 22 (Hiawatha Boulevard). From eastbound Route 690, get off at Exit 7 (Court Street.) Follow the signs to the stadium.

Box seats cost $6, while reserved seats go for $5. General admission tickets cost $3.50 (seniors and kids are half-price).

For schedule of events and ticket information, call (315) 474-7833.

For tourist information, contact the Greater Syracuse Chamber of Commerce, 572 South Salina Street, Syracuse, NY 13202, (315) 470-1800.

Affil.	Year	League	Wins	Losses	Attendance
	HOMETOWN STATS—SYRACUSE				
	The Last Ten Years				
TOR	1985	International	79	61	222,813
	1986		72	67	187,758
	1987		68	72	211,315
	1988		70	71	184,910
	1989		83	62	226,244
	1990		62	83	245,045
	1991		73	71	307,993
	1992		60	83	269,067
	1993		59	82	262,760
	1994		71	71	329,594

Toledo Mud Hens

(Detroit Tigers)

Ned Skeldon Stadium
2901 Key Street
Maumee, OH 43537

M*A*S*H cast member Jamie Farr (with Harry Morgan, who played Colonel Potter) is still the #1 Mud Hen fan.

The Toledo Mud Hens are probably one of the most famous minor league teams ever, thanks to actor Jamie Farr, who immortalized them through his character Max Klinger on *M*A*S*H*. And except for a few brief periods totaling no more than fourteen years, the Glass City, as Toledo calls itself, has had baseball for just over 100 years. Toledo's first team, the Blue Stockings, took the field in 1883. In 1884 and again in 1890, they played in the original major league American Association (1882–91). They became the Mud Hens in 1896.

Just what is a Mud Hen? Well, it's not a chicken, though team mascot Muddy the Mud Hen can look a little befowled now and then. A mud hen, also known as a marsh hen or rail, is a bird with short wings and long legs that lives in swamps and marshes. Back in 1896 the team played in Bay View Park, adjacent to the marshlands where these birds thrived. Up until that year, the team had been called by several other colorful names—besides the Blue Stockings there were the Toledos, Maumees, Black Pirates, White Stockings, Swamp Angels, Sowmichers, Iron Men, Glass Sox, and finally, Mud Hens, which stuck.

The Hens have produced some players with great nicknames, too, like Mule Trader, Egyptian, Blazing Sun, Scissors, Sunny Jack, Waffle Iron, and Rin Tin Tin. The historic roster is also a Who's Who of great players: Kirby Puckett, Frank Viola, and Willie Hernandez were Mud Hens; Jim Thorpe, hero of the 1912 Olympics, played for the Hens in 1921; Hack Wilson of Chicago Cubs fame and Pete Gray, the one-armed player, were Hens; and Casey Stengel, who coached the team for six years, was a Hen (he thought nothing of calling his own number for pinch hitter).

In 1956 the team was moved to Wichita, leaving Toledo without baseball until 1965 when, thanks to the efforts of then–county commissioner Ned Skeldon, a nonprofit organization was set up to finance new recreational facilities for the city, including a new ballpark. (Nonprofit status was necessary, as the county could legally finance but not own a baseball team.) Once that was accomplished the organization went out and bought the New York Yankees Triple-A affiliate in Richmond and moved it to Toledo. Since 1967, Toledo has had a number of affiliates. Detroit (there originally from 1967–74) settled in for good in 1987.

Ned Skeldon Stadium in the Lucas County

Recreational Complex seats just slightly over 10,000, yet the atmosphere is cozy and familial. This is one of very few parks where fans actually do picnic in the stands. That is, if there is not a "Ballpark Blowout Bash" going on. The Bash is one big tailgate party that takes place three times each season. Tents are set up in the parking lot two hours before game time, and it's come one, come all, where tons of food and buckets of beer are devoured by the fans.

Team mascot Muddy the Mud Hen is a giant yellow bird in pinstripes who can get 290,000 fans each season to rally, chant, clap, and sing. It's Muddy who leads the chorus on Kazoo Night—one of the Hens' favorite promotions. The first 4,000 fans through the gate get a free kazoo; between innings the PA announcer conducts a kazoo-along.

Gates open two hours before game time, and that is the best time to get autographs as well. The best place to get a signature is near the locker room on the first base side, which is also a great place in the stands to catch foul balls. Diehard fans sit right behind home plate and have been known to razz opposing batters pretty mercilessly. The third base line is also great for fans, particularly for the kids who want to be near the Hens dugout.

GETTING THERE

Toledo, on the Maumee River, is home of the real Tony Packo's Cafe (the cafe's Hungarian hot dogs were fondly remembered by Klinger on *M*A*S*H*), the Ohio Baseball Hall of Fame, and the Toledo Museum of Art. There's a good selection of hotels, motels, and bed-and-breakfasts. And there's camping at the 1,860-acre Maumee Bay State Park.

Ned Skeldon Stadium sits south of Toledo just off the Ohio Turnpike. Take Exit 4 (from east or west) and take the northbound exit to Toledo onto Reynolds Road. Go one block and take a right at Heatherdowns, and then another right at Key. The stadium is on the left. There is plenty of free parking.

Box seats go for $5, reserved seats for $4, and general admission for $3. Seniors and kids fourteen and under get $1 off.

For schedule of events and ticket information, call (419) 893-9483.

For tourist information, contact the Greater Toledo Convention and Visitors Bureau, 401 Jefferson Avenue, Toledo, OH 43604, (419) 321-6404 or (800) 243-4667.

Affil.	Year	League	Wins	Losses	Attendance
MIN	1985	International	71	68	167,787
	1986		62	77	145,909
DET	1987		70	70	194,001
	1988		58	84	193,097
	1989		69	76	172,454
	1990		58	86	159,009
	1991		74	70	217,662
	1992		64	80	242,692
	1993		65	77	274,047
	1994		63	79	293,124

HOMETOWN STATS—TOLEDO
The Last Ten Years

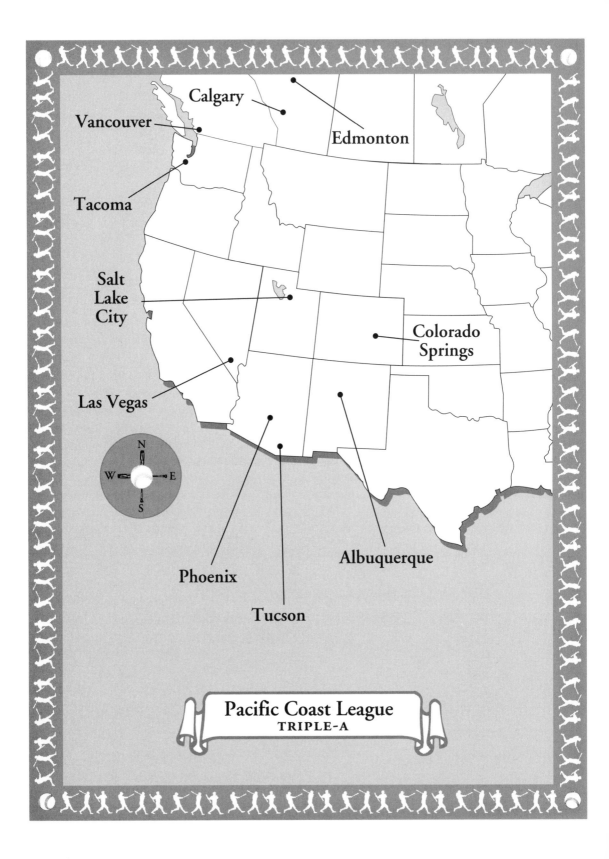

Calgary

Vancouver

Edmonton

Tacoma

Salt
Lake
City

Colorado
Springs

Las Vegas

N
W E
S

Albuquerque

Phoenix

Tucson

Pacific Coast League
TRIPLE-A

Pacific Coast League

Class A 1904–1907; Double-A 1908–1945;

Open 1952–1957; Triple-A 1946–1951, 1958–

The Pacific Coast League was created in 1903 when four teams of the then California League merged with two additional clubs to form a new alliance. (The league, however, did not join the NAPBL until 1904.) The charter members were Los Angeles, Oakland, Sacramento, San Francisco, Seattle, and Portland. Some of these teams were hugely successful. The San Francisco Seals, for instance, drew more fans and paid better salaries than many major league teams. Much of the reason for the league's success was that, believe it or not, into the late 1950s there was only one major league team playing west of the Mississippi (St. Louis doesn't count), and that was Kansas City of the American League. The West was hungry for baseball, and the Pacific Coast League had designs on major league status. To bolster that effort, the NAPBL even gave the league an O (open) classification, ranking it a notch higher than Triple-A. All hopes were dashed, however, when on May 28, 1957, the National League granted permission to the Dodgers and the Giants to move to the West Coast. Today, none of the charter cities are members of the Pacific Coast League.

The Pacific Coast League is made up of ten teams, which are scheduled to play 144 games during the regular season. First-half division winners play second-half division winners in a best-of-five series. If the same team wins both halves, it plays the team with the next best overall record in its division. Division playoff winners then play each other in a best-of-five series for the league championship.

Albuquerque Dukes

(Los Angeles Dodgers)

Albuquerque Sports Stadium
1601 Stadium Boulevard, SE
Albuquerque, NM 87106

Albuquerque's history with professional base-ball dates back to 1915, when it had a team in the Class D Rio Grande Valley Association; that Association folded after just one year. In 1932 another team set up shop with the Arizona-Texas League, which promptly disbanded on July 24th of the same year. The team and league came back in 1937, and Albuquerque has had steady baseball ever since. Its teams have been affiliated with the L.A. Dodgers since 1963, first as its Double-A Texas League franchise and since 1972 as its Triple-A club. For most of that time the team has been called the Dukes. Albuquerque's nickname, you see, is Duke City, for the 10th Duke of Alburquerque, who ruled the area for Spain in the 1700s. (Somewhere along the line the first "r" in Alburquerque got lost.) The

teams have won eight Pacific Coast League championships (including 1994) and produced a host of major league players. Among them: Steve Garvey, Davey Lopes, Doyle Alexander, Sid Bream, Mike Marshall (who hit 34 homers in 1981), Dave Hansen, Mickey Hatcher, and Orel Hershiser. Tommy Lasorda, the Dukes' first Triple-A manager in 1972, led his team to a 92–56 record and beat the Eugene Emeralds three games to one in the league championship.

The Albuquerque Sports Stadium is a 10,510-seat park that turned twenty-five years old in 1994. It's a unique place, with its outfield "drive-in" area, lava rocks, right field grass hill, and often-times tricky winds. It's beautiful, too; tremendous sunsets to the west create dramatic shadows on the eastern mountains. The partially covered grandstand sweeps from the first base bag around home to third base. The grass hill off right field extends from the end of the grandstand down to the right field foul pole and is open during a game only when large crowds (10,000+) are expected. This area can also be reserved for pregame picnics catered by the concession stands, but you will have to move to your seat in the stands before the game starts. You can pic-

A seat along the first base line at Albuquerque Sports Stadium offers a view of incredible desert sunsets.

nic in the stands, too, if you get there early enough. Beyond the outfield fence, there is an incline of lava rock leading up to the "drive-in" area of the park, in which you can sit in or on your car to watch the game. We counted seventy-two cars on the rim, parked side by side and facing down into the ballpark. (There's room for another 50 or so to park in an overflow area). Tailgating and barbecuing thrive out there. Alcoholic beverages are not allowed.

The Dukes have a loyal following. Around 375,000 showed up in 1994. Some of the special events that get everybody into the stadium are the back-to-back fireworks shows around July 4th and several appearances by Hall of Famer Bob Feller and performers Myron Noodleman and Billy Bird (all the way from Louisville).

The Dukes have the usual freebie nights, where they give away magnetic schedules, helmets, cartoon maps, sports bottles, and so forth. They also have a Funny Nose & Glasses Night; the stadium is packed with Groucho Marx lookalikes. Kazoo Night is especially fun. Imagine, if you will, thousands of fans kazooing "Take Me Out to the Ball Game" during the seventh-inning stretch.

The team mascot, Lee the Duke, is just a guy with a beard (no typically costumed mascot, he) who happens to look a lot like the "Duke" on the Dukes' logo. He thrills the kids with magic tricks.

Gates open one hour before game time. The best times to get autographs are from 6:20 to 6:45 P.M. down by the left field bleachers before the game, and outside the clubhouses after the game.

GETTING THERE

Albuquerque, founded in 1706 on the banks of the Rio Grande, lies just to the west of the Sandia Mountains. The city has a variety of hotels and motels to choose from. RV and other campground facilities can be found right in town.

To get to Albuquerque Sports Stadium, take I-25 to Stadium Boulevard. Go east one block to the stadium. There is some parking ($1) at the stadium and plenty of free parking across either Stadium or University boulevards.

Box seats are $4 for all ages, while general admission tickets cost $3 for adults, $2.50 for seniors and students, and $1 for kids. The Drive-In costs $2.50 ($1 for kids).

For schedule of events and ticket information, call (505) 243-1791.

For tourist information, contact the Albuquerque Convention and Visitors Bureau, P.O. Box 26866, Albuquerque, NM 87125, (505) 842-9918 or (800)733-9918.

HOMETOWN STATS—ALBUQUERQUE *The Last Ten Years*					
Affil.	**Year**	**League**	**Wins**	**Losses**	**Attendance**
LAD	1985	Pacific Coast	67	76	252,453
	1986		54	88	235,737
	1987		77	65	300,035
	1988		86	56	314,186
	1989		80	62	318,896
	1990		91	51	324,046
	1991		80	58	340,685
	1992		65	78	362,283
	1993		71	72	390,652
	1994		83	56	376,272

Calgary Cannons

(Pittsburgh Pirates)

Foothills Stadium
2255 Crowchild Trail NW
Calgary, Alberta, Canada T2M 4M4

In 1995, Calgary expects to improve on the team's 1994 71–72 record.

Calgary's baseball teams have had their ups and downs since 1907, when its first team played in the Class D Western Canada League. That team stayed through 1914. In the early 1920s and again in the mid-1950s Calgary clubs played in the Class A Western International League. In the 1970s and 1980s Calgary was home to the Rookie Pioneer League's Calgary Expos. Then in 1984 the Triple-A Salt Lake City Gulls (Seattle's financially shattered PCL team) came up for sale and was immediately snapped up by Russ and Diane Parker, who moved the team to Canada. At the time, the Parkers owned Calgary Copier Ltd., the fourth-largest Canon dealership in the country. When it came time to name the team, the "Cannons" (just add an n) seemed only natural. Since their inaugural season in 1985, the Cannons have become one of minor league baseball's most successful teams, having made it to the playoffs four times. The players who have gone to The Show through Calgary include Edgar Martinez, Bret Boone, Dave Fleming, Tino Martinez, Danny Tartabull—who hit an incredible forty-three home runs here in 1985—and pitcher Mike Campbell, a fifteen-game winner in 1987. And there will be many more now that the Cannons have signed on with the Pittsburgh Pirates.

Foothills Stadium is a 7,500-seat ballpark located amid other sports facilities; Calgary's football stadium can be seen right over the outfield wall. You enter the ballpark through a gate in left field, which gives you a great outfielder's-eye view of the park. The grandstand, which is partially covered, hugs the field from first base to third, and bleachers extend down both sidelines. Tucked underneath the grandstand is the concession concourse. However, more vending is done in the stands here than on the concourse (or so it seems). The vendors or "hawkers" carry big baskets filled with cookies, peanuts, popcorn, M&M's, red licorice, chips, ice cream, pretzels, and beer, and they provide their own brand of entertainment. They have regular customers among the fans and seem to know them by name. You do still have to stand in line on the concourse, however, for a Cannons hot dog, which is served on toast instead of a bun. Try it before you knock it!

The fans here are polite, but not afraid to show enthusiasm. When a Cannon hits a home run the players (and everybody else) stand while he runs the bases, and when he crosses home plate a cannon is fired in his honor. Calgary has some great contests and giveaways. 1994 was their tenth anniversary, and in the course of the celebration year there were a lot of promotions: On Mother's Day they gave away a diamond pendant and later, during their "Diamond Jubilee" celebration, they gave away 10 more to Pop-Up contest winners; they handed out electronic equipment, ten trips to Las Vegas, ten trips to Seattle, ten used cars, and a $10,000 shopping spree, too. Of course, there were the usual everyday giveaways, as well: grab bags for kids, hot dogs and Cokes, mugs, ponchos, and barbecue aprons.

"Wabash the Cannonball," the team mascot, has a cannonball head and a big snout; the kids love him. They love the Cannoneers, too—high school students who double as cheerleaders and ushers. They even help with the tarp if it rains.

Wabash, on the other hand, gets to help with the on-field contests and gets to run the mascot race. One new contest added in 1994 is the Money Grab—contestants try to grab as much fake money blowing around in a glass cage as they can in fifteen seconds. The next day the winner gets to spend that amount of real money at the mall. There is a big fireworks display on Canada Day (June 30) and special visits by the Phillie Phanatic and The Famous Chicken.

Gates open about one hour before game time. You can get autographs down by the dugouts before the game.

GETTING THERE

The Calgary Stampede put this western Canadian town on the map; the 1988 Olympics brought it worldwide attention. Canada Olympic Park and the Olympic Hall of Fame are major attractions. First-class hotels, motels, and campgrounds are plentiful.

Foothills Stadium is located ten minutes west of downtown Calgary. Take Sixth Avenue west to Crowchild Trail. Go south on Crowchild to 23rd Avenue and take a right into parking lot. There is ample free parking.

Lower boxes go for $7.50, while the upper boxes cost $6.50. Reserved and rush seats cost $5.50, $4.50 for kids and seniors.

For schedule of events and ticket information, call (403) 284-1111.

For tourist information, contact the Calgary Convention & Visitors Bureau, 237 8th Avenue SE, Calgary, Alberta, Canada T2G 0K8, (403) 263-8510.

	HOMETOWN STATS—CALGARY				
	The Last Ten Years				
Affil.	Year	League	Wins	Losses	Attendance
SEA	1985	Pacific Coast	71	70	272,322
	1986		66	77	288,197
	1987		84	57	304,897
	1988		68	74	332,590
	1989		70	72	316,616
	1990		66	77	312,416
	1991		72	64	325,965
	1992		60	78	277,307
	1993		68	72	278,140
	1994		71	72	297,981

Colorado Springs
Sky Sox

(Colorado Rockies)

Sky Sox Stadium
4385 Tutt Boulevard
Colorado Springs, CO 80922

The Sky Sox namesake was the Class A Western League affiliate of the Chicago White Sox, which played in Colorado Springs from 1950 to 1958. The name honors the high altitude of the city (6,000 feet) and the tie with the White Sox organization. When the Triple-A Hawaiian Islanders moved to Colorado Springs thirty years later, it seemed logical to revive the name. From 1988 to 1992 the Sky Sox were affiliated with the Cleveland Indians and the team, even though they had a winning record, did not draw the fans; Cleveland seemed so distant. But when the Colorado Rockies took over the franchise in 1993, things changed big-time. The fans could relate to the Rockies, even though the team didn't have a good first season. Much of that problem stemmed from the fact that the Rockies had no Double-A franchise at the time. So the Sky Sox, when depleted of players by the Rockies, had only Class A to call up. There was so much back and forth of players between the Springs and Denver that the route became known as the I-25 Shuttle—or "Sox to Rox," and vice versa.

Sky Sox Stadium has an open-air grandstand—no roof and no upper deck to get in the way of the fabulous view. The ballpark is northeast of the city in a yet underdeveloped area of rolling green hills at the foot of the Rockies. The brilliant blue sky and billowing white clouds seem close enough to hit with a fly ball. The 6,000-seat grandstand stops at first and third. The foul area is minute, and there are only 28 rows in the stands— 14 of which are box seats and 14 of which are aluminum bleachers with backs. Grass berms flank left and right fields and allow seating capacity to expand for fireworks nights and special promotions. Just above the left field berm is a picnic area with its own concession stand and bandstand. If it hasn't been reserved, anyone can sit there.

The most unique feature of the stadium, however, is at the far end of the right field berm. Sky Sox Stadium has started something that, thanks to the 1994 strike, has come to national attention. Yes, it's hot tub mania! The best seats in the house are in the hot tub that sits on a deck over the "smokehouse" (actually the storage house for grounds equipment) and even has AstroTurf to keep the splinters at bay. It's big enough for eight, but only six are allowed in the tub at any given time. For eighty bucks (1994 prices) you get a box supper for eight, champagne, and the game. Only problem is, at last check, there was a waiting list a mile long—in fact, almost the whole season was reserved a year in advance!

Every game starts with fireworks that punctuate the end of the national anthem. There are annual events like the before-game baseball card and memorabilia show; the daylong health fair; Secretaries' Day, when a lucky fan gets to beat the hell out of a typewriter or fax machine with a bat; and the Diamond Dig, a most popular event for the ladies.

The giveaways are top-quality merchandise—no cheap stuff here. If you come on Cap Night, you'll get a good cotton twill (not mesh) cap; the same cap costs $15 downtown. The music is good, too—rock 'n' roll and country.

Even if you're not hungry enough to eat an elephant, you might stop on the concourse and get yourself some "elephant ears," Colorado's version of funnel cakes (large fried pieces of sweet dough sprinkled with powdered sugar). Or try the hot items—chicken fingers and batter-fried jalapeño peppers—at "Fry Babies" (yes, everything is fried).

Gates open one hour before game time. You can get autographs down by the dugouts until about twenty minutes before the game starts.

These Sky Sox fans might be too busy to wonder who's on first! Nonetheless, the 1994 Sox went on to the division playoffs.

GETTING THERE

The location of Colorado Springs near Pikes Peak, along with the Garden of the Gods, the Air Force Academy, NORAD (North American Aerospace Defense Command, buried deep in Cheyenne Mountain), and quaint Manitou Springs, makes it a prime tourist destination. The world-famous Broadmoor Hotel is here, and motels and campgrounds are plentiful.

To get to Sky Sox Stadium, take I-25 to Garden of the Gods Road. Head east and continue on for about four miles (the name will change to Austin Bluffs Road). Bear right onto Barnes Road for another mile until you go over a rise, and there you are. There is ample parking, which costs $2.

Box seats cost $6, while general admission tickets go for $4. Kids and seniors get $1 off.

For schedule of events and ticket information, call (719) 597-1449.

For tourist information, contact the Colorado Springs Convention and Visitors Bureau, 104 South Cascade Avenue, Colorado Springs, CO 80901, (719) 635-1632 or (800) 88-VISIT.

		HOMETOWN STATS—COLORADO SPRINGS *The Last Ten Years**			
Affil.	**Year**	**League**	**Wins**	**Losses**	**Attendance**
CLE	1988	Pacific Coast	62	77	168,248
	1989		78	64	203,955
	1990		76	67	201,642
	1991		72	67	174,731
	1992		84	57	187,645
COL	1993		66	75	189,293
	1994		70	69	211,671

*Statistics are given only for the years in which the team played in Colorado Springs.

Edmonton Trappers

(Oakland A's)

New Trappers Stadium
10233 96th Avenue
Edmonton, Alberta, Canada T5K 0A5

The Edmonton Trappers are owned by local entrepreneur Peter Pocklington, who brought the franchise into the Pacific Coast League in 1981. For the next ten years, as affiliates of the California Angels, the team was steadfast if not exactly stellar. They made it to the playoffs in 1983, 1984, and 1990 before switching their affiliation to the Florida Marlins in 1993.

In their first year with the Marlins, the Trappers challenged for a first-half championship and then struggled through a record twelve-game losing streak. Amazingly enough, the team executed its first-ever triple play in the franchise's thirteen-year history. It happened on August 21, 1993, in the game against the Las Vegas Stars.

Even if 1993 wasn't a banner year, the Trappers still managed to send a dozen outstanding players to the Marlins, among them pitchers Dave "Stormy" Weathers and Matt Turner. Catcher Bob Natal played just seventeen games before getting the call. Another catcher, Mitch Lyden, finished in Edmonton with a .300 batting average, and Geronimo Berroa went up after his batting average of .327 matched his at bats—327. The year 1995 brings a change of affiliation. The Marlins, stating that the distance between teams was just too great, left Edmonton for Charlotte in the International League. The Oakland A's have taken their place.

The brand-new (1995) Trappers stadium sits on the same spot as the original (1953) park. And even though it doesn't bear the name of John Ducey, as did the classic wooden park that it replaces, the man who did so much for baseball in Edmonton is well remembered here with bust and plaque. Ducey, who died in 1983, devoted his life to baseball. He started as a bat boy, then became an umpire, and finally general manager of the famous (in Canada) 1957 Edmonton Eskimos. That team played in the independent Western Canada Baseball League and went up against the Japanese team in the championship game of the Global World Series in Detroit.

In the farewell ceremonies at the old park there were testimonials from all sorts of people—peanut vendors from the 1950s, bat boys all grown up, trainers from the 1960s, umpires, players, and fans—who knew John Ducey. Then, as a final farewell, while a crowd of 4,000-plus watched in silence, a single bagpiper played and slowly led Ducey's family (wife Grace, son Brant, and daughter Duane) around the bases to home plate one last time.

While the original 6,200-seat park may be

For the Trappers' Klondike Days annual celebration, a special singing of the Canadian National Anthem.

missed in Edmonton, the old cramped concession and restroom areas, where many people spent a whole inning waiting in line, are not. Space and comfort is the order of the day at the new 8,000-seat state-of-the-art stadium, where every seat in the grandstand is a chair, and the bleachers down both lines are the comfortable kind with backs. Speaking of comfort, there are thirty enclosed suites on the field level from first base to third. During spring rains they are a cozy haven for fans, but each has its own patio deck, too, for those lovely summer days in Edmonton. No, they're not available day-of-game; these suites are sold out on five-year contracts. Meanwhile, for the rest of us, the grandstand will feel like the perfect place to be looking out over the river valley, which runs along the North Saskatchewan River.

Game time is lively, with at least three on-field contests during each game. Team mascot Homer gets a lot of attention, too, with his mischief. Once he distracted a young man away from his pretty date while everybody watched. Then he took the man's seat, and his girl!

The Trappers claim to have the best hot dog in all of baseball—the so-called "Ducey Dog," which must be heaped with chopped raw or fried onions and a good helping of sauerkraut. And if you love these the way most of the fans do, you will not want to miss the great Hot Dog Giveaway. Four thousand (that's 4,000) dogs are given away absolutely free. Gates open one hour before game time. You can get autographs from the guys near the dugouts up to 20 minutes before the game starts.

GETTING THERE

Edmonton, Alberta's capital, is located on the banks of the North Saskatchewan River, which runs right through the heart of the city. Edmonton is home to West Edmonton Mall, the world's largest shopping and entertainment complex. Accommodations are varied, ranging from moderate to expensive. There are campgrounds in town.

New Trappers Stadium is located downtown at the corner of 96th Avenue and 102nd Street. The parking, on grassy fields adjacent to the park, is adequate and costs $3.

Grandstand seats cost $8.00, and general admission tickets go for $7.25. Seniors and kids get $2 off.

For schedule of events and ticket information, call (403) 429-2934.

For tourist information, contact Edmonton Tourism, 9797 Jasper Avenue, Edmonton, Alberta, Canada T5J 1N9, (403) 496-8400 or (800) 463-4667.

| | | HOMETOWN STATS—EDMONTON | | | |
| | | *The Last Ten Years* | | | |
Affil.	Year	League	Wins	Losses	Attendance
CAL	1985	Pacific Coast	66	76	229,112
	1986		68	73	229,682
	1987		69	74	229,381
	1988		61	80	243,419
	1989		65	76	230,728
	1990		78	63	229,307
	1991		70	66	252,813
	1992		74	69	257,146
FLO	1993		72	69	261,361
	1994		67	75	272,631

Las Vegas Stars

(San Diego Padres)

Cashman Field
850 Las Vegas Boulevard N.
Las Vegas, NV 89101

Present-day major league second baseman Paul Faries played for Las Vegas in 1991 and 1992.

In September 1982, Larry Koentopp announced that he was moving his Triple-A team from Spokane to Las Vegas in time for the 1983 season. When they arrived a citywide "Name the Team" contest was held, and the "Stars" came out the big winner. Almost 11,000 people jammed into the 9,334-seat Cashman Field for their first game. That year they saw a young Kevin McReynolds hit thirty-two homers. Over the next five seasons, fans watched the team distinguish itself by making four playoff appearances and taking two league championships. They also saw Sandy Alomar Jr. lead the league catchers in 1989 with 702 putouts; Alomar was named Minor League Player of the Year by the *Sporting News*.

The team was bought in 1992 by sports entrepreneurs Hank Stickney and his son Ken. The Stars have continued to be very popular with fans in Las Vegas, which is quite an accomplishment given the myriad of other distractions in this city. Even though spring days can easily top one hundred degrees, the Stars have one of the minor leagues' top attendance records.

Cashman Field was completed in 1983 just in time for the Stars' first season opener. It is part of a fifty-acre, $26 million complex that includes a 100,000-square-foot convention center and a 1,954-seat theater—all built on land donated by James "Big Jim" Cashman, a community leader and "Southern Nevada pioneer." Except for about 900 covered seats, the grandstands (and bleachers) are wide open to the elements—which, being in the desert, is usually no problem if you're watching a night game. The natural turf field is backed up by a grassy berm dotted with palm and olive trees. (The trees are illuminated during night games.) On the occasions when the numbers swell—July fireworks shows and big league exhibition games, for instance—fans spread out onto the outfield berms and along the upper deck of the club level. On the horizon looking northeast, the valley is lined with craggy desert mountains that were formed, we were told, by an ancient geologic fault. It's a beautiful setting for a ballpark.

You never know who you are going to see in this park. It is not unusual to spot a major headliner from the Strip enjoying a ball game. There are giveaways every night and promotions galore. Although they have pitch-through-the-hole games in many parks, you can make money in Las Vegas. Big money, up to $500. You could win a house or a car, too! Then there are the wacky antics of the contestants in the water balloon Catch or Splash contest or the spin-around-the-bat Dazed and Confused race. Beach towels, mitts, bats, jerseys, and hats are always popular giveaways. Appearances by The Famous Chicken and four fireworks nights attract big crowds. And be sure to look up—you never know when the "Into the Fire" skydiving team (featured as the "Flying Elvi" in the movie *Honeymoon in Vegas*) will fly in the American flag at the conclusion of the national anthem.

Gates open an hour before the game. There is usually one player at the autograph booth on the concourse before the game, but you can get autographs along the rail above the dugouts before the game, too.

GETTING THERE

Las Vegas, with its casinos, wedding chapels, showrooms, and now the incredibly imaginative theme parks, is becoming one of the world's premier tourist attractions. It's loaded with luxury casino hotels, first-class motels, and RV campsites.

Cashman Field is two blocks north of world-famous "Glitter Gulch" in downtown Las Vegas on Las Vegas Boulevard. Either take Las Vegas Boulevard or take I-95 to the Cashman Field/Las Vegas Boulevard exit. There is ample parking, which costs $2.

Field-level seats cost $6; plaza-level seats go for $5. Reserved seats are $4.50, and general admission tickets cost $4. Kids, seniors, and military personnel get $1 off general admission.

The Stars' fireworks events sell out early.

For schedule of events and ticket information, call (702) 386-7200.

For tourist information, contact the Las Vegas Convention and Visitors Authority, 3150 Paradise Road, Las Vegas, NV 89109, (702) 892-0711.

		HOMETOWN STATS—LAS VEGAS *The Last Ten Years*			
Affil.	**Year**	**League**	**Wins**	**Losses**	**Attendance**
SDP	1985	Pacific Coast	65	79	313,783
	1986		80	62	291,060
	1987		69	73	299,198
	1988		74	66	305,622
	1989		74	69	315,517
	1990		58	86	312,522
	1991		65	75	330,699
	1992		74	70	382,838
	1993		58	85	386,310
	1994		56	87	338,834

Phoenix Firebirds

(San Francisco Giants)

Scottsdale Stadium
7408 East Osborn Road
Scottsdale, AZ 85251

For many a New Yorker, 1958 was not a good year. It was the year that the Brooklyn Dodgers moved to Los Angeles and the New York Giants to San Francisco. And when the Giants moved west, their Triple-A affiliate in Minnesota moved southwest to Phoenix and joined the Pacific Coast League. This was a big deal in Phoenix, where the P-Giants, or P-Gees as they were affectionately called, played at the old Municipal Stadium at Central and Mohave. The move obviously did them good. Led by Dusty Rhodes, Andre Rodgers, and Willie McCovey, the team took over first place on July 30, 1958, and never looked back. They clinched the league title on September 5th.

After just two years, however, the Giants left Phoenix, saying the stadium was too old and so far out of town that the fans weren't coming anymore. They spent the next five years in Tacoma. Meanwhile, Phoenix built a new Municipal Stadium and persuaded the San Francisco Giants to use it for spring training. Horace Stoneham, owner of both the San Francisco Giants and the Tacoma Giants, was so impressed with the new park that he brought his minor league team back to Phoenix in 1966. In 1984, Martin Stone, the largest stockholder of World Paper, chairman of the Adirondack Corporation, and director of Canyon Ranch, Inc. and W. R. Berkeley Corporation, bought the team. He owns it still.

In 1986 the Phoenix Giants, in search of its own identity, changed its name to the Firebirds. Over the years, the Giants/Firebirds have had some mighty impressive players come through Phoenix. Aside from Rhodes, Rodgers, and McCovey, the team has produced Bobby Bonds, Matt Williams, Bob Brenly, George Foster, Gary Matthews, Dave Kingman, Jack Clark, Chili Davis, Dan Gladden, Terry Mulholland, Charlie Hayes, and Dave Dravecky. In 1992 the team moved into its new home, Scottsdale Stadium.

One of the comfy characteristics of Scottsdale Stadium is the grass berm seating around the entire outfield. These general admission spots are available on a first-come basis. Chairs of any sort are not allowed, but cushions, blankets, and towels are. Others opt for the "misting area," a large section of the terrace/reserved box seats. The roof above this area is equipped with dozens of small nozzles that emit a superfine cool mist spray that keeps everybody at least ten degrees cooler than the air temperature. Not wetter, just cooler. Scottsdale Stadium is a nonsmoking facility.

Phineas T. Firebird, the team mascot, entertains and helps with giveaways. Used Car Night, Turn Back the Clock Night, and the annual exhibition game with the San Francisco Giants always attract huge crowds.

Gates open one hour prior to game time. Fans can seek autographs from players next to the bullpens and down the sidelines before the start of the game. On weekends, two players man an autograph booth before the game, too.

GETTING THERE

The Valley of the Sun conjures up breathtaking desert beauty, outdoor recreation, top-rated golf courses, and luxury resorts. There are world-class hotels and resorts in Phoenix and Scottsdale, and motels and campgrounds everywhere.

To get to Scottsdale Stadium, take I-10 to the Broadway Road East exit and continue on to Rural Road. Go left on Rural Road and head north (Rural becomes Scottsdale Road) approximately four and a half miles to Osborn Road. Take a right

There are pregame activities at Scottsdale Stadium that conclude with the parade of colors and the National Anthem.

on Osborn to the ballpark, which is on the left. Parking is free around Scottsdale Stadium. Public parking garages are located north of the stadium and at 2nd Street, west of the Scottsdale Center for the Arts.

Field-level box seats are usually sold out and cost $7. The terrace boxes go for $6, while the reserved boxes go for $5. General admission tickets cost $4. Kids and seniors get $1 off general admission and reserved.

For schedule of events and ticket information, call (602) 275-0500.

For tourist information, contact Phoenix & Valley of the Sun Convention & Visitors Bureau, One Arizona Center, 400 E. Van Buren Street, Phoenix, AZ 85004, (602) 254-6500.

HOMETOWN STATS—PHOENIX
The Last Ten Years

Affil.	Year	League	Wins	Losses	Attendance
SFG	1985	Pacific Coast	80	62	168,820
	1986		81	61	161,583
	1987		77	67	183,798
	1988		67	76	171,030
	1989		67	86	199,157
	1990		63	76	248,660
	1991		68	70	247,791
	1992		66	78	278,798
	1993		64	79	246,414
	1994		70	72	315,859

Salt Lake Buzz

(Minnesota Twins)

Franklin-Quest Field
77 West 1300 South
Salt Lake City, UT 84105

1994 was the first season for the Salt Lake Buzz—in Salt Lake City, that is. Before that, the team had been the Portland Beavers. They moved after owner Joe Buzas, who owns several other minor league teams, couldn't get the city of Portland to upgrade their facilities to meet major league demands. So when Salt Lake City offered them a brand-new stadium, it was bye-bye Portland. Too bad for the Portland fans; a lot of good players came through there, including Lou Piniella and Luis Tiant. In 1991 Brian Harper, Scott Leius, and virtually the Twins' entire current lineup came up through Portland. Still others include Denny Nagel of the Pirates and Paul Sorento of the Indians.

Utah is nicknamed the Beehive State, and back in the early 1960s Salt Lake's Triple-A team was called the Bees. Buzas wanted to name the new team in honor of that old team, but the Burlington Bees (Iowa) of the Class A Midwest League own the copyright to the name. So, in keeping with the Bees and Beehive theme, Buzz seemed like a good choice.

Franklin-Quest Field is named after the time-management company of the same name that donated $1.4 million to help build the new park. The stadium, a brick facility with green iron gates, has an old-fashioned look and a roomy feel about it. It's located at the edge of the business district and the beginning of a residential area, so there's a mix of small businesses, high-rise buildings, and one-family homes nearby. When you enter the stadium you walk up to the concourse area, and as you look out over the outfield wall, you see one of the most spectacular views in all of baseball—the Wasatch Mountains, which remain snowcapped through June, at which point they turn brilliantly fresh and green.

The stadium has 12,000 chair seats (with arms), room for 500 more in the suites, and room for another 2,000 fans in the outfield terrace. The opening night crowd in 1994 was 14,500, though the average attendance has settled in around 9,600. The fans here are notoriously late, so the park rarely fills up until after the game has begun. But then again, 95 percent stay to the very end, even if the Buzz are down by ten runs. The fans know the game, and get excited by its finer points. Be that as it may, we feel that half the excitement is due to the 4,500-foot altitude. This is, needless to say, a hitter's park. So anything can happen.

During the game, you can try your hand (if you are chosen, that is) at the Domino Frisbee Toss (land a Frisbee on a large vinyl domino and win pizza for a year!), and there's the Swing for the Fences (hit a 70-mph ball pitched from the pitching machine out of the park and win a Saturn), or try the Pop-Up contest (catch 4 in a row for $400).

Gates open one hour and fifteen minutes before game time. Many of the young players, even if they came from other teams, aren't used to all the attention and are flattered to sign autographs. They really are stars here. They get stopped in malls, on the street, everywhere. At the stadium, down by the dugouts is your best bet.

GETTING THERE

When in Salt Lake City, Utah's capital and headquarters of the Mormon religion, do visit the historic Temple Square, with its six-spired Temple, Tabernacle, and Assembly Hall. There are plenty of hotels, motels, mountain resorts, and campgrounds in the area.

Franklin-Quest Field is located just south of downtown on the corner of 1300 South and West

Temple. Take I-15 to the 13th South exit and go two blocks to West Temple. There is ample parking, which costs $3.

Baseline box seats are $7, while upper and lower reserved seats go for $6. General reserved seats cost $5; $4 for seniors and students; and $3 for kids.

For schedule of events and ticket information, call (801) 485-3800.

One of the most compelling views from any minor league stadium is found at Franklin-Quest Field.

For tourist information, contact the Salt Lake Convention & Visitors Bureau, 180 South West Temple, Salt Lake City, UT 84101, (801) 521-2822.

Affil.	Year	League	Wins	Losses	Attendance
HOMETOWN STATS—SALT LAKE CITY *The Last Ten Years**†					
IND	1985	Pioneer	46	24	57,683
MIN	1994	Pacific Coast	74	70	713,224

* Statistics are given only for the years in which the team played in Salt Lake City.
† Salt Lake City did not have a baseball team from 1986 to 1994.

Tacoma Rainiers

(Seattle Mariners)

Cheney Stadium
2502 S. Tyler
Tacoma, WA 98405

Tacoma had its first baseball team in 1902 and has belonged to eight different leagues over the years. And though the city was briefly a member of the Pacific Coast League (Class A) in 1904 and 1905, it didn't rejoin the league until 1960, when the Triple-A affiliates of the San Francisco Giants moved their team up from Phoenix. In 1961 the Tacoma Giants won their first league championship. The Giants went back to Phoenix in 1966. For Tacoma, a series of different affiliations followed until the Oakland A's came to town in 1981. And stayed. Until 1995, that is, when the A's moved out to Edmonton and the Seattle Mariners moved in. The Rainiers (formerly the Tigers) are currently owned by George and Sue Foster, who also own Foster Farms poultry. They are baseball fans as well as owners, and are improving the stadium's

facilities while keeping its old charm. And although the best the team has done in the last few years is to finish third in the Northern Division (in 1993), the fans seem to appreciate the effort; over 4,000 show up for each game. Some high-powered players have developed in Tacoma, among them Juan Marichal, Dusty Rhodes, and Gaylord Perry from the 1961 Giants and, more recently, Mark McGwire, Jose Canseco, Tim Belcher, and Jose Rijo.

Cheney Stadium is named in honor of the legendary industrialist, philanthropist, and sportsman Ben Cheney, who played a major role in getting the stadium built and bringing Triple-A ball to Tacoma. The grandstand starts at first and stops at third; the last five rows are covered. The seats rake gently down to the field; a walkway separates the box seats (the first 10 rows) from the reserved and general admission seats. The fans here call the park very user-friendly. The box seats are comfortable plastic theater seats. And many of the seats in the reserved seating section are wooden theater seats from the old Seals' Stadium in San Francisco. The place holds 10,000 and is located in a residential neighborhood. The view over the outfield wall is of the local high school, perched atop a hill the locals call

Tacoma catcher Henry Mercedes makes the play at the plate against Calgary.

"Tightwad Hill." It seems that some fans used to sit up there and watch the game for free. There is a great view of Mount Rainier out over the right field bleachers. And since foul balls regularly fly out of the park on both sides, the local kids line the park outside the stands and wait for balls to come sailing over the top.

The concession area is pretty tight, but the crowd flocks in anyway for the chicken nuggets, which always outsell the hot dogs. (Perhaps in honor of the owners? We don't know.) There are two sports bars—one on either side of the concourse—where you can have a beer and watch the game on a big-screen TV. Both are mobbed on rainy days.

Even though overall attendance suffers with the rainy weather in the great Northwest, the team still drew more than 347,000 fans in 1994. Promotions are plentiful. Mondays are always half-price nights, and you can even purchase tickets in advance. Used Car Night is always a big hit. The club gives away more used cars than any other team that we know of—twelve in one game. The place is packed. Only once did a car look like it came straight from the demolition derby. It didn't start, either, much to everybody's delight. (It had to be pushed from the field.)

Gates open one hour before game time, one and a half hours on big promotion nights. Autographs are easy enough to get before the game down by the dugouts, or after the game as the players leave the clubhouse.

GETTING THERE

Tacoma, nestled between the shores of Puget Sound and majestic Mount Rainier, is located in beautiful Pierce County, which has one of the best park systems in this country. There's a variety of hotels and motels, and several campgrounds right in town.

To get to Cheney Stadium, take I-5 to Exit 132 and go west on Highway 16. Get off at the 19th Avenue East exit. The stadium is on your right. There is ample parking, which costs $2.

Box seats cost $6.50, while reserved seats go for $5.50. General admission tickets cost $3.50. Kids, seniors, and the military get 50 cents off.

For schedule of events and ticket information, call (206) 752-7707.

For tourist information, contact the Tacoma–Pierce County Visitor & Convention Bureau, 906 Broadway, Tacoma, WA 98401, (206) 627-2836 or (800) 272-2662.

| | | HOMETOWN STATS—TACOMA | | | |
| | | *The Last Ten Years* | | | |
Affil.	Year	League	Wins	Losses	Attendance
OAK	1985	Pacific Coast	66	76	208,534
	1986		72	72	247,098
	1987		78	65	293,366
	1988		62	82	280,168
	1989		77	66	313,077
	1990		75	67	309,210
	1991		63	73	293,418
	1992		56	87	329,000
	1993		69	74	316,475
	1994		61	81	347,719

Tucson Toros

(Houston Astros)

Hi Corbett Field
3400 E. Camino Campestre
Tucson, AZ 85716

In 1969, Tucson baseball fans gathered for the first time since 1958, the year when the old Tucson Cowboys (and the Class C Arizona-Mexico League) bid adios to the world. Baseball was finally back when the new Triple-A affiliate of the Chicago White Sox moved to town. The local newspaper sponsored a contest to pick a name for the new team, and "Toros" came out on top, beating out "Tacos" (which is sort of okay, actually) and hundreds of other entries. The team became affiliated with the Oakland A's in 1973, followed by the Texas Rangers in 1977. Then, in 1980, the Houston Astros took hold of the reins and haven't let go.

When the team came up for sale in 1988, it was purchased by Rick Holtzman, a real estate developer who also owns the Quad City River Bandits (Class A Midwest League), the Chattanooga Lookouts (Double-A Southern League), and the Albany Polecats (Class A South Atlantic League). That deal has made all the difference in Tucson baseball. The Toros had always been known as a perennially weak team, but after Holtzman hired veteran GM Mike Feder, the club won two league championships and has continued to draw more than 300,000 fans each of the last four seasons. Some of the players Tucson has sent on to the major leagues are Eric Anthony, Craig Biggio, Ken Caminiti, and Darryl Kile.

Hi Corbett Field is an old-fashioned stadium that was originally built in 1937 as the home field for the Tucson Lizards, who played in the Class D Arizona-Texas League. Named for Hiram Corbett, who was president of the Tucson Baseball Commission for twenty-four years, the stadium is part of Reid Park, a complex that includes the municipal zoo and a golf course. It was given a facelift in 1989 by Holtzman, who likes to restore all the stadiums in which his teams play. (Hi Corbett is also the Colorado Rockies' spring training facility.) The ballpark seats 8,000, and there are always good seats available on a day-of-game basis. At either end of the grandstand is a large picnic area that can be reserved for groups. Game time temperatures might hover around one hundred degrees, and the air can be as dry as an oven, but the view of the park and trees beyond the outfield fence is cooling.

GM Mike Feder and staff see to it that there are lots of giveaways every year at Hi Corbett Field. In 1994, the replica '93 Championship rings that were handed out became instant collector's items. Some of the usual giveaways include T-shirts, caps, bumper stickers, and cowbells! Some of the special events that the Toros sponsor are appearances by the Phillie Phanatic, The Famous Chicken, and the Blues Brothers. And Roll-Back-the-Clock Night is always a big draw, especially when the year is 1932 and the uniform says "Lizards."

Toros players successfully turn a double play.

At the end of the 1993 league championship series against Portland, the Toros celebrate victory.

Tuffy, the Toros mascot, is a young sweet bull with horns folded unthreateningly over his head. Unlike most other mascots, Tuffy will win the Dash-for-Cash on occasion (but he never competes against tiny tots). Should you get hungry, chow down on some nachos; here in the Southwest, the jalapeños are fresh.

Gates open one and a half hours before game time. The best time to get autographs is before the game from the reserved seating area along the third base side.

GETTING THERE

Tucson is a fast-growing city set in a desert valley ringed by five mountain ranges. There's a lot of history to explore here. Tucson has luxury hotels and resorts, spas and guest ranches, a variety of motels, and campgrounds galore.

To get to Hi Corbett Field, take I-10 to the Broadway exit. Go east on Broadway to Randolph Way, and then south on Randolph for about one mile to the stadium. There is plenty of free parking.

Box seats cost $6, while reserved seats go for $5. General admission tickets cost $4. Kids, seniors, and the military get $1 off.

For schedule of events and ticket information, call (602) 325-2621.

For tourist information, contact the Metropolitan Tucson Convention & Visitors Bureau, 130 South Scott Avenue, Tucson, AZ 85701, (602) 624-1817.

HOMETOWN STATS—TUCSON *The Last Ten Years*					
Affil.	Year	League	Wins	Losses	Attendance
HOU	1985	Pacific Coast	65	75	128,540
	1986		71	72	116,117
	1987		75	67	157,744
	1988		68	75	173,889
	1989		56	86	186,270
	1990		71	71	238,629
	1991		79	61	317,347
	1992		70	74	300,134
	1993		83	60	307,791
	1994		81	63	309,623

Vancouver Canadians

(California Angels)

Nat Bailey Stadium
4601 Ontario Street
Vancouver, BC, Canada V5V 3H4

Vancouver's foray into professional baseball dates back to 1904, when the city made its debut with the Oregon State League. That lasted one year. The club joined the Northwest League in 1905 and played for one year, and then again from 1907 to 1917. That franchise was called everything from the Beavers, Bachelors, Maple Leafs, Bluecaps, Canadians, to, if you're ready for this, the Old Maids. (There were a few other choice unprintable names when the team went 34–106 in 1907, finishing 53 games out of first place.)

In 1951, brand-new Capilano Stadium opened, just three years before the Class A Capilanos (named after a brewery) folded. And then in 1956, Vancouver's first Triple-A team, the Vancouver Mounties, took the field. The Mounties didn't have much success either, although in 1959 a young man named Brooks Robinson made quite a sensation. The team left in 1962, came back in 1965, and then left again in 1969. Vancouver then went without baseball until Molson Brewery brought it back in 1978 and, none too subtly, named the team the Canadians after their own brand name.

The Canadians were affiliated with the Oakland A's in 1978; then came the Milwaukee Brewers, the Chicago White Sox, and the California Angels in 1993. Vancouver teams have been in the playoffs six times in the last eight years and won the Pacific Coast League championships in 1985 and 1989. Some of the players the Canadians have sent to the majors are Chris Bosio, Tom Candiotti, Dion James, 1983 Rookie of the Year and All-Star Ron Kittle, and 1992 Gold Glove second baseman Jose Lind.

Nat Bailey Stadium is charming, a tiny bandbox of a park nestled in the lee of Little Mountain. The setting, at the foot of Queen Elizabeth Park, is really quite spectacular. The 6,500-seat stadium, built in 1951, was designed as a smaller version of Sicks Seattle Stadium, considered a showcase of minor league baseball. When baseball left in 1969 the park was more or less abandoned to teenagers who held drag races across the outfield. It didn't take long before more pickets were missing than remained—stolen from the outfield fence. The stadium fell into such disrepair that there was a move to tear it down. But then, with the return of baseball in 1978, the ballpark was renovated back to life. It was dedicated in honor of Nat Bailey, founder and owner of the White Spot restaurant chain and a long-time supporter of baseball in Vancouver. Now the team is usually second or third in the league in attendance. Average per game is about 5,000 fans, which is really good in a stadium this size.

There are picnic areas down both foul lines. The First Base Barbecue is extremely popular for groups of thirty or more; you can watch the whole game right there from your table. Die-hard fans, known as the "Bleacher Bums," sit at the top of the stands behind third base. The music is as old-fashioned as the stands: organ, of course.

The team does not have a mascot, but The Famous Chicken makes an annual pilgrimage to Vancouver, much to the delight of the fans. Other special events include fireworks and McDonald's Restaurants Baseball Clinics.

Gates open one hour before game time. The best time to get autographs is an hour before the game down by the dugouts. Players are usually available until about 20 minutes before the game starts.

GETTING THERE

Vancouver is surrounded by some of the most spectacular scenery on earth. Towering snow-capped mountains rise high above this beautiful

city, which sits on Canada's west coast. There are luxury hotels downtown, with motels and camp-grounds nearby.

To get to Nat Bailey Stadium, take Highway 99 to Oak Street and go right on 41st Avenue and then left on Ontario Street to the Stadium. There is ample free parking.

Box seats go for $7.50. Lower reserved seats cost $6.50, while the upper reserved seats are $5.50. Kids and seniors get in for $3.25.

Fan-friendly, cozy, and comfortable, Nat Bailey Stadium fills almost to capacity for every home game.

For schedule of events and ticket information, call (604) 872-5232.

For tourist information, contact the Vancouver Travel InfoCentre, 200 Burrard Street, Vancouver, BC, Canada V6C 3L6, (604) 683-2000 or (800) 663-6000.

HOMETOWN STATS—VANCOUVER _The Last Ten Years_					
Affil.	**Year**	**League**	**Wins**	**Losses**	**Attendance**
MIL	1985	Pacific Coast	79	64	199,781
	1986		85	53	231,819
	1987		72	72	338,614
CWS	1988		85	57	386,220
	1989		73	69	281,812
	1990		74	67	281,540
	1991		49	86	288,978
	1992		81	61	333,564
CAL	1993		72	68	349,726
	1994		77	65	320,863

Double-A Teams

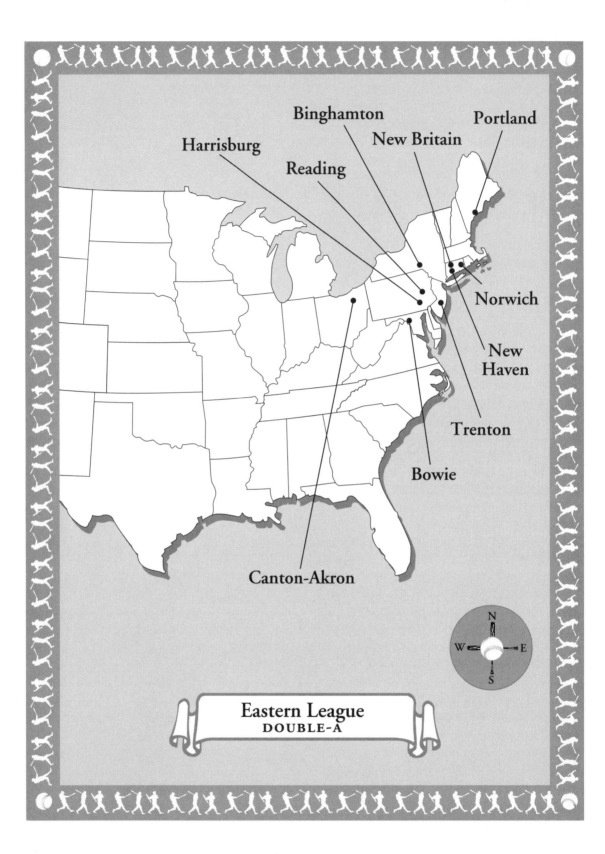

Binghamton

Portland

Harrisburg

New Britain

Reading

Norwich

New
Haven

Trenton

Bowie

Canton-Akron

N

W   E

S

Eastern League
DOUBLE-A

Eastern League

Class A 1938–1962; Double-A 1963–

The Eastern League's history is somewhat confusing, as that name has been used in the past by several different leagues, including the precursor of the International League. Although there was an Eastern League operating from 1916 to 1932, that league has no connection to today's Eastern League. No, today's Eastern League grew out of the original New York-Pennsylvania League (not to be confused with today's New York-Penn League), which was created in 1923 as a Class B league and then became a Class A league in 1933. The league's charter members were Binghamton, Elmira, Scranton, Wilkes-Barre, Williamsport, and York. After Trenton joined the league at the end of 1937 and Hartford joined in 1938, the name was changed to the Eastern League.

The league, which obtained a Double-A ranking in 1963 (with only three of the original cast intact—Binghamton, Elmira, and York), has undergone many changes over the years, including the recent move of the Yankees' franchise from Albany-Colonie (NY) to Norwich (CT). Then, too, the league expanded in 1994 to include the Colorado Rockies and Florida Marlins expansion teams in New Haven (CT) and Portland (ME).

The Eastern League in made up of ten teams, which are scheduled to play 142 games during the regular season. First-place teams in each division play second-place teams in the same division in a best-of-five series. Division playoff winners then play each other in a best-of-five series for the league championship.

Binghamton Mets

(New York Mets)

Binghamton Municipal Field
211 Henry Street
Binghamton, NY 13901

Binghamton's local team, called the Triplets for much of its history, is the only member of the Eastern League that can trace its origins back to the league's predecessor, the old 1923 New York–Pennsylvania League. Binghamton did, however, lose its team after the 1968 season when the Yankees moved its franchise to Manchester (NH). The town went without pro ball until 1992, when the Mets took the field. Their arrival was a joint effort of the town of Binghamton and the New York Mets, who together built the 6,000-seat Binghamton Municipal Field. The Mets had a great first year, beating Canton-Akron three games to two for the league championship. Their star ace, Bobby Jones, who went 12–4, was named 1992 Eastern League Pitcher of the Year; late in 1993 he went on to make his New York debut. Close to 260,000 Binghamton fans showed up for the regular season (another 19,309 showed up for the playoffs).

Binghamton Municipal Field is right downtown on the site of what was once a busy rail yard. Actually, tracks run along outside the left field fence, and every once in a while you can see the tops of railroad cars rolling slowly by. The twenty-four-row grandstand is partially covered, and every seat is comfortable and full-backed. The park features two picnic areas off the left and right field lines, which are usually reserved for pregame chowdowns. Once the gates open, however, anybody can come order food and watch the game from here. For the kids, there's a speed-pitch batting cage, down left.

Mets fans everywhere are vocal (if not crazy), but no more so than in Binghamton. One fan in particular stands out. His name is Jingles, and we were told to watch for him to do a dance in the aisles or on the dugout roof every time the Mets scored. Sure enough, he did. Even if there is no chance for the team to win, he'll still do his routine.

Binghamton is a college (Binghamton University and Broome Community College) town, and the team gets a big turnout from students, faculty, and their families. Tourists find their way to the park, too, and so do diehard fans from New York City. The ballpark itself is part of the draw. Like Fenway Park or Wrigley Field, which are also right downtown, this place is so much a part of everyone's life that the whole town buzzes on game nights. Parking is not ample here. Most fans have their favorite parking spots in the surrounding neighborhood, which, by the way, is friendly and safe, so not to worry.

Although the food is more or less standard ballpark fare there is one delectable standout called a "Spedie" (named, we think, for how fast they sell). Order one and you get skewered, marinated chicken cubes that are grilled and served on a hoagie. Do not, however, put any condiments on the sandwich; only out-of-towners would do such a thing. The Italian dressing marinade provides all the flavor!

The Mets are big on promotions and on-field fun. One of the more unusual on-field contests we've run across is the Conklin Grand Prix. For this one, a kid on foot gets to compete against a Formula 1 race car that suddenly appears, engines roaring, in the right field corner. The kid, starting at home, has to run the bases before the mean machine makes it to the left field corner. We also like the "Lady Fan" of the game, who receives a bouquet of flowers just for being there. Home game giveaways include the usual items plus frisbees and gift certificates.

The park is open for visitors and tourists from 10:00 A.M. to 4:00 P.M. The gates reopen at 5:30

P.M. Players are available for signing autographs between 6:30 and 6:45 P.M. down the right field line near the bullpen.

GETTING THERE

Binghamton, about two hundred miles northwest of New York City, is set in a lovely valley on the banks of the Susquehanna and the Chenango rivers. Accommodations range from motels to charming bed-and-breakfasts and luxury hotels. Campgrounds are available.

To get to downtown Binghamton and Binghamton Municipal Field from I-81, get off at Exit 4S, which puts you on Route 11. Get off at Henry Street and proceed to the stadium. The limited parking lot (for 300 cars) costs $3. Parking is easy enough to find on local streets, however.

Box seats cost $6, and reserved seating goes for $5. General admission tickets cost $4. Seniors and kids get $1 off.

For schedule of events and ticket information, call (607) 723-6387.

For tourist information, contact the Broome County Convention & Visitors Bureau, P.O. Box 995, Binghamton, NY 13902, (607) 772-8860.

Relaxed in the dugout at Binghamton Municipal Field, the 1994 Mets went on to win the 1994 Eastern League Championship, beating Harrisburg 3–1 in the best-of-five series.

HOMETOWN STATS—BINGHAMTON *The Last Ten Years**					
Affil.	Year	League	Wins	Losses	Attendance
NYM	1992	Eastern	79	59	259,284
	1993		68	72	225,467
	1994		82	59	217,600
*Statistics are given only for the years in which the team played in Binghamton.					

Bowie Baysox

(Baltimore Orioles)

Prince George's Stadium
4101 NE Crain Highway
Bowie, MD 20716

Up until a couple of years ago, the Bowie Baysox played in Hagerstown as the Eastern League's Hagerstown Suns, a Baltimore Orioles affiliate since 1981. (The team of the same name that plays there now is a Class A South Atlantic League club.) While there, the club sent a bunch of players up to the Orioles, including Manny Alexander, Damon Buford, John O'Donoghue, Mike Oquist, Jim Poole, Arthur Rhodes, and Paul Carey, who led the Eastern League outfielders with four double plays in 1991.

When the franchise moved in 1993 to Bowie, south of Baltimore and east of D.C., they took the name that won in a name-that-team contest. The winner received lifetime season tickets. The "Bay" in "Baysox" refers to the nearby Chesapeake Bay, and "Sox" is, well, just a good old baseball name. Because Prince George's Stadium wasn't ready until 1994, the team played its 1993 season in Baltimore's vacant Memorial Stadium. No one was sure how that would go over, since Baltimore is just crazy about its Orioles, but the Baysox did amazingly well, drawing over 250,000 fans and placing third in attendance in the Eastern League. For his efforts, GM J. Keith Lupton received the league's Executive of the Year Award that year. (It was his third, having received the Carolina League's honors twice when he was with the Frederick Keys.)

The Baysox were slated to open the 1994 season in the new state-of-the-art Prince George's Stadium. Unfortunately, the harsh winter of

In their first game at the new Prince George's Stadium on June 16, 1994, Bowie Pitcher Rick Forney opened against Binghamton's Ricky Otero. Bowie won 14–6.

1993–94 held up construction work, and the team had to play the first part of the season on the road. But once in, the wait was worth it. The 10,000-seat stadium is very modern, low-slung and sleek-looking. The field is built down into a bowl, so that when you enter through the main gate you are on the concourse looking out over the field. The open-air grandstand extends to just beyond the bases. Some of the stadium's state-of-the-art features are skyboxes, a restaurant, a full range of concession areas, a big playground, and a picnic area. The view is very pretty, nothing but verdant woods over the outfield fence.

The concessions are really worth talking about: popcorn shrimp, crab cakes, barbecued pork, Pit beef, funnel cakes . . . good stuff. There are also theme food days: Meatball Mondays (meatball sub with cheese), Taco Tuesdays (chimichanga/burrito platter), Wings Wednesdays (chicken wings), Tasty Thursdays (gyros), and Fish Fry Fridays (fish & chips). There's also a great selection of draft beers for the thirsty. And, for kids fourteen and under only, there's a $1 hot dog stand.

The Baysox calendar for special events might include the usual appearances by the Blues Brothers, Max Patkin, and the Dynamite Lady, but also the Silver Bullets women's pro baseball team and Morganna the Kissing Bandit. Very impressive. Our favorite is probably Disney Trip Giveaway Night, when one fan wins a getaway to the Magic Kingdom. On other promotion nights free golf visors, cups, checkbook covers, and Kan Koolers are given away along with the usual items.

Gates open one hour before game time. You can get autographs before the game down next to the dugouts.

Another run helps to build Bowie's impressive 84–58 1994 season.

GETTING THERE

Bowie, with its wonderful 200+-year-old trees, is located in historic Prince George's County. Old Bowie is famous for its antique shops. There are beautiful small hotels and inns, lovely bed-and-breakfasts, and numerous motels throughout Bowie. Some campsites are available nearby.

Prince George's Stadium is located in the southeast quadrant of the US 50 and US 301 interchange and is visible from both highways. There is plenty of free parking.

Box seats are $7; there is no reserved seating. General admission tickets cost $5, $3 for kids, seniors, and military. (Kids in Little League uniforms get in free.)

For schedule of events and ticket information, call (301) 805-6000.

For tourist information, contact the Prince George's County Conference & Visitors Bureau, 9475 Lottsford Road, Landover, MD 20785, (301) 925-8300.

HOMETOWN STATS—BOWIE *The Last Ten Years**					
Affil.	Year	League	Wins	Losses	Attendance
BAL	1994	Eastern	84	58	293,665†

*Statistics are given only for the years in which the team played in Bowie.

†Figure reflects 27 "at home" games played elsewhere due to delayed stadium opening.

Canton-Akron Indians

(Cleveland Indians)

Thurman Munson Memorial Stadium
2501 Allen Avenue, SE
Canton, OH 44707

Although Canton and Akron both had professional baseball teams dating from 1905 (Canton in the Class B Central League and Akron in the Class C Ohio-Pennsylvania League), neither had baseball after the 1942 season. Almost fifty baseball-less years passed before the Indians came to town. They arrived in 1989 just in time to open the brand new Thurman Munson Memorial Stadium, which was named for the late great New York Yankees catcher, who grew up in Canton. The team was moved here from Burlington, Vermont, by its owner and president, Mike Agganis. The move seemed appropriate because the Canton-Akron area is Cleveland Indians' territory. The fans are loyal, and why not? The C-A Indians have been contenders ever since they came to town, qualifying for the playoffs every year and winning the Eastern League Regular Season Championship in 1992. Some of the players who have moved up are Albert Belle, Jim Thome, Manny Ramirez, Julian Tavarez, and Albie Lopez. Charles Nagy pitched here in 1989 and 1990 before going straight up to Cleveland.

Thurman Munson Memorial Stadium is a 5,700-seat park. No one would call it charming, but it's comfortable enough in a rugged sort of way. With bits of steel here and tons of aluminum there, it's been called everything from the "World's Largest Erector Set" to "a big tin can." And is it noisy when the fans start pounding and stomping! The stadium literally "thunders." The view? Well, I-77 lies beyond left field, the Coen Tire Company is dead center, and the parking lot is beyond right. Every year the team has to pay for broken windshields and dents.

The Manwich Family Section is an alcohol-free, smoke-free area in the general admission seats, section L-5. The picnic area off right field is fun if you can get 25 people together. There's no charge to reserve the area, but you have to order from the stadium menu, which offers the basic hamburgers, hot dogs, grilled steak sandwiches, and chicken. It stays open during the ball game, so you can stay put and watch from the picnic tables.

The season always includes several giveaway promotions and a few special nights as well. For instance, on Dew, Dog & Chip Night you get a Mountain Dew, a hot dog, and a bag of chips for 75 cents. Not bad, huh? There is the Used Car Giveaway—five are given away between innings. (The cars do run.) Once a month, the Stark County Humane Society sets up shop and brings some critters available for adoption. And, our favorite, Canton-Akron's version of Dash for Cash: fake money is dropped from a hot-air balloon tethered fifty feet above the infield and previously selected fans get to chase down and grab as much as they can in a minute. Winners take home the equivalent in real cash.

Don't leave for the night without trying the specialty from the Bases Loaded Grill, located on the concourse—even if it means ducking foul balls (which do, on occasion, come flying in). But then, a kielbasa "with the works" on a hero roll is worth living dangerously for.

Gates open one hour before game time. Players are usually available for autographs before the game down the left field line from 6:00 to 6:45 P.M. for night games and from noon to 1:00 P.M. before day games.

GETTING THERE

Canton, of course, is home to the Professional Football Hall of Fame. Akron is home to the National Inventors Hall of Fame. There's a selection of hotels and motels in the region, as well as campgrounds and an RV maintenance center (in Canton).

To get to Thurman Munson Memorial Stadium,

In spite of successful plays like this one, 1994 was Canton-Akron's first season to end with more losses than wins.

take I-77 to Exit 103 (Cleveland Avenue), make a left on Mills Avenue, then go left on Allen Avenue. Parking is a steal at $1 (if you don't park too close to the right field fence and get clobbered).

Reserved seats cost $5; general admission tickets go for $4. Seniors and kids get $1 off general admission.

For schedule of events and ticket information, call (216) 456-5100.

For tourist information, contact the Canton-Stark County Convention & Visitors Bureau, 229 Wells Avenue, NW, Canton, OH 44703, (800) 533-4302.

		HOMETOWN STATS—CANTON-AKRON *The Last Ten Years**			
Affil.	**Year**	**League**	**Wins**	**Losses**	**Attendance**
CLE	1989	Eastern	70	69	203,986
	1990		76	64	204,193
	1991		76	65	218,397
	1992		80	58	194,662
	1993		75	63	273,639
	1994		69	73	255,002

*Statistics are given only for the years in which the team played in Canton-Akron.

Hardware City Rock Cats

(Minnesota Twins)

Beehive Field
Willowbrook Park Complex
New Britain, CT 06051

Joe Buzas, owner of New Britain's baseball team, loves baseball. Aside from owning several minor league teams, he is himself an ex-ballplayer. He played briefly in the majors with the 1945 Yankees, but he was better known in the minors, having played both Triple-A and Double-A ball. When Buzas bought the franchise way back in 1957 the team was based in Allentown, Pennsylvania. (The journey to New Britain took them through York and then Reading, PA; Pittsfield, MA; Pawtucket, RI; and Bristol, CT.) The team had been affiliated with Boston since 1983, but parted company after the 1994 season when Boston insisted Buzas move the team to Springfield, Massachusetts. When he declined, the Red Sox left in a huff, and the Minnesota Twins took over. Major league players who have made their way through New Britain include Roger Clemens, Ken Ryan, Aaron Sele, Jody Reed, and Jeff Bagwell.

The stadium at Beehive Field is snugly old-fashioned. It seats 4,700—small by any standards, though management claims that they can accommodate 6,000. The covered part of the old wooden grandstand barely wraps around home plate; most of the seats are general admission bench-type bleacher seats. Box seats with backs and arms, however, are usually available on a day-of-game basis. Die-hard fans sit off first base and heckle the ump and the opposing first base coach. The ballpark sits low to the ground, so foul balls have a tendency to go flying up and over the back of the stands. Kids line the entire park outside hoping to catch the next ball, even though they can't see where they're coming from. There's always lots of pointing and shouting on the concourse and in the parking lot. Every once in a while a ball will sail up and over everybody and land in the parking lot, breaking a windshield on its way down. A net was erected to catch the balls before they get that far, but it doesn't always work.

The mascot, a disheveled looking (man-sized)

In New Britain, fans come out early to relax before game time.

bee dubbed Buddy Bee, simply showed up one day. And since his girlfriend at the time was into voodoo, nobody said much. Except once—when a Red Sox pitcher (who shall be nameless) gave Buddy Bee a hard time. The girlfriend put a hex on the pitcher, and he went into a slump. He begged her to remove the hex, and when she did he pitched a one-hitter. True story!

Joe Buzas holds that minor league baseball is its own best promotion. After all, he points out, at four bucks (or less) a ticket a family can see a good ball game, have a hot dog, and still get off cheaper than going to the movies. There may not be a lot of on-field contests, but there is Bat Night, Cap Night, Ball Night, and so forth. Sponsors also give free certificates to fans with the lucky numbers in their programs. The Gem Jewelry Store gives away a gold chain to the fan who comes closest to guessing the actual attendance. One regular on-field contest is the Pizza Hut Ball Toss. If a kid (chosen from the fans) can sink a ball through a hole from ten feet, everybody in the stadium wins free bread sticks; from twenty feet a slice of pizza; from thirty feet, the whole pizza pie! Then, too, Hall of Famers stop by occasionally and are delighted to sign autographs. So is comic Max Patkin, whose manic routines have earned him the title "The Clown Prince of Baseball."

Gates open about one hour before game time.

Get there early if you have kids in tow. After the Sox go through their warm-up exercises in left field, they'll stop on their way to the dugout to sign autographs along the third base line. (You can catch the visiting team over on the first base line.)

GETTING THERE

New Britain, nicknamed "Hardware City" in honor of the local Stanley Tools factory, is in the heart of Central Connecticut, where charming colonial towns and villages dot the hilly countryside. There are plenty of motels, bed-and-breakfasts, and campsites throughout the region.

Beehive Field is located in Willowbrook Park in New Britain. Take I-84 to Highway 72 East (exit 35) to Ellis Street; go left on Ellis and then left on South Main Street for one mile. From I-91 take Route 9 North (exit 22) to Willowbrook Park (exit 24). There is ample free parking.

Box seats, right behind home plate and at the bases, go for $5. Reserved seats, farther behind home plate, cost $4.50, and general admission tickets go for $4. Seniors get in for $2, kids under twelve $1.50.

For schedule of events and ticket information, call (203) 224-8383.

For tourist information, contact the Central Connecticut Tourism District, One Central Park Plaza, New Britain, CT 06051, (203) 225-3901.

	HOMETOWN STATS—NEW BRITAIN				
	The Last Ten Years				
Affil.	Year	League	Wins	Losses	Attendance
BOS	1985	Eastern	75	64	90,802
	1986		64	73	81,617
	1987		61	79	83,338
	1988		47	90	77,965
	1989		60	76	100,943
	1990		72	67	123,017
	1991		47	93	146,632
	1992		58	82	125,393
	1993		52	88	140,915
	1994		59	81	129,696

Harrisburg Senators

(Montreal Expos)

RiverSide Stadium
City Island
Harrisburg, PA 17101

Baseball in Harrisburg dates back to 1907, when the local team played in the Class D Tri-State League. After the 1952 season, the then Harrisburg Senators and the Class B Interstate League they played in at the time called it quits, but not before the team created some controversy. That was the year the club signed Eleanor Engle, a twenty-four-year-old stenographer, to play shortstop, saying, "She can hit a lot better than some of the fellows." For four days in June Engle suited up for the Senators, but she never played. What an uproar—even the team manager didn't want "a girl" playing on the team. Eventually NAPBL president George Trautman voided her signing. Some thought the whole thing was a publicity stunt, but a reporter, after watching her practice, wrote that Eleanor " . . . scooped up hard grounders and threw to first base like a pro."

In 1987, the sport came back to a brand-new ballpark. The new Eastern League franchise was named in honor of the previous tenants, thus linking the new era to the past. The Senators have been phenomenally successful; over the past six years they have sent up more than fifty-five players to the major leagues, among them Moises Alou, Steve Carter, Carlos Garcia, Orlando Merced, and Randy Tomlin.

RiverSide Stadium sits on the exact spot where baseball had been played earlier in the century —on City Island in the middle of the Susquehanna River, which runs through Harrisburg. The 6,300-seat stadium is part of a sixty-two-acre waterfront park and sports complex. The facilities include volleyball courts, softball fields, water golf, nature trails, jogging paths, cycling paths, two marinas, the *Pride of the Susquehanna* paddlewheel riverboat, and a food court called Riverside Village. Many people come for the whole day.

The ballpark is a steel and aluminum noisemaker that is nearly packed for every game. When everybody screams and pounds the sound can be deafening. But, as one fan told us, "the crazier you are, the better you feel when you leave the park." Sounds right to us. Senators fans in fact created the great crowd scenes for the movie *Major League II*, which starred Charlie Sheen and Tom Berenger. RiverSide Stadium was used in the spring training footage.

Special events include fireworks shows, the Mother's Day Diamond Dig, and a big draw, the Annual Milking Contest. Senators compete with the visiting team in an out-and-out milkout. There are two cows on the field— one for each team. Whichever team gets the most milk in the least amount of time is the winner. The fans love it because they know that many of the players have never even seen a cow, let alone milked one!

There are a lot of giveaways throughout the summer—all kinds of freebie baseball paraphernalia, plus occasional mugs, lunch bags, and pizza-oven mitts. Best of all, however, some lucky fans win free trips to Montreal to see the Expos play.

On Friday nights there's live jazz on the concourse, complete with a chicken dinner for $5. Or, if you prefer, you can get great barbecued chicken or steak sandwiches and ribs at the concession stands along the first base side of the concourse. Or, better yet, before the game stop at the food concessions just outside the park. Try some roast beef cooked on a spit over an open pit or some mighty fine crab cake sandwiches.

Gates open about one and a half hours before game time. You can get autographs up to thirty minutes before the game along the first base line.

Expo top prospect pitcher Uqueth Urbina helped Harrisburg get to the 1994 league championship playoffs with a 9–3 record.

GETTING THERE

Harrisburg is the capital of Pennsylvania. Spend some time downtown, or take the twenty-minute drive to Hershey and watch your favorite candy bars being made. Both places have good motels and top-rated hotels. Campgrounds can be found between the two.

To reach RiverSide Stadium from I-83, get off the interstate at Exit 23 (Second Street) and continue to the Market Street Bridge and City Island. Many people park off-island to avoid any hassle and walk the ten minutes to the Stadium. Parking at an on-island lot costs $1. Replica trolley buses also run a shuttle service between City Island and the downtown area, where you will find shops, restaurants, hotels, and museums.

Box seats go for $7 while Reserved Grandstand seats (behind home plate) go for $6. General admission tickets cost $5. Kids under twelve and seniors get $2 off general admission.

For schedule of events and ticket information, call (717) 231-4444.

For tourist information, contact the Capital Region Chamber of Commerce, 114 Walnut Street, Harrisburg, PA 17108, (717) 232-4121.

HOMETOWN STATS—HARRISBURG
The Last Ten Years*

Affil.	Year	League	Wins	Losses	Attendance
PIT	1987	Eastern	77	63	212,141
	1988		65	73	216,940
	1989		71	65	200,196
	1990		69	69	223,033
MON	1991		87	53	233,423
	1992		78	59	209,159
	1993		94	44	250,476
	1994		88	51	234,774

*Statistics are given only for the years in which the team played in Harrisburg.

New Haven Ravens

(Colorado Rockies)

Yale Field
252 Derby Avenue
West Haven, CT 06516

One of the two expansion Double-A teams (Portland being the other) that played their first games in 1994, the New Haven Ravens took this New England town by storm. On opening day in April, 1994, 6,500 fans jammed into 6,200-seat historic Yale Field stadium, and minor league baseball was back to stay. (The West Haven A's left in 1982.) The Ravens owner, Yale alumnus W. Edward Massey, lives in Connecticut and is thrilled to have his first team play at Yale Field.

The landmark stadium, built in 1927, is a perfect model-in-miniature of old Yankee Stadium, complete with a grandstand roof supported by wrought-iron poles, which, by the way, can—like in olden days—create some sight line problems. This park resonates with history. President William Taft was the president of Yale at the time of the stadium's opening. An avid baseball fan, he asked that a special seat be installed allowing for his remarkable girth. The extra-wide Taft seat remained behind home plate for nearly sixty-five years and was only removed during the recent renovation. In the Yale archives, too, there's a photo of Babe Ruth standing at home plate, presenting a copy of his autobiography to the then-captain of the Yale baseball team, none other than George Bush. There are other interesting photographs, too, like the one of the young Yale pitcher Ron Darling on the mound.

Yale Field has been restored with careful attention to keeping the best of the past. The old covered grandstand wraps around from first to third base. New bleachers continue down the left field line, and a new, terraced picnic pavilion down right can handle up to 300 people. The old land-mark hand-operated scoreboard is still in use at every game, but so is the new state-of-the-art dot-matrix message board right next to it. The old scoreboard, by the way, stands 30 feet high—405 feet straight out in center field. Legend has it that Ted Williams is the only batter ever to hit one over the top.

The setting is very New England. From the top rows of the stadium you can see trees, the old homes of New Haven, and part of another national landmark, the Yale Bowl. (In the spring, you might also hear the starting pistol at the Yale track, which is right next door.) Sunsets here can be very pretty—the setting sun shines golden rays through the old columns and portals of this stadium, casting dramatic shadows and dappled light across the outfield and scoreboard.

Special events like the annual Mother's Day Diamond Dig are a big hit. So are between-inning contests like the Dizzy Bat Race, Dash for Cash, and the Mascot Chase. Premium giveaways include T-shirts, caps, and big Louisville Sluggers bats—no minis or Little League bats here.

The team mascot, Rally Raven, literally hatched from a giant egg that sat nesting for weeks in a mall, piquing everybody's curiosity. He just came flitting out one day, and he hasn't stopped flitting since.

Gates open one hour before game time. The best place to get autographs is down by the dugouts before the game.

GETTING THERE

New Haven, a town of spires and steeples, Gothic towers and glass towers, and home to Yale University and the Long Wharf Theater, is a booming New England community. Accomodations are mostly modern hotels downtown and motels on the outskirts. Camping is limited.

Yale Field is located about one-quarter of a mile west of Route 10 at 252 Derby Avenue. From I-95, take Route 10 north to Derby, then turn left on Derby.

The hard-to-come-by luxury box seats go for

$12.50, while the regular box seats are $7. Reserved seats cost $5, and general admission tickets cost $3 for adults, $2 for kids and seniors.

For schedule of events and ticket information, call: (203) 782-1666 or (800) RAVENS 1.

For tourist information, contact the Greater New Haven Convention & Visitors Bureau, One Long Wharf Drive, New Haven, CT 06511, (203) 777-8550 or (800) 332-STAY.

In their first year, the impressive Ravens hit and pitched their way to the 1994 division playoffs.

HOMETOWN STATS—NEW HAVEN
*The Last Ten Years**

Affil.	Year	League	Wins	Losses	Attendance
COL	1994	Eastern	77	63	276,316

*Statistics are given only for the year in which the team played in New Haven.

Norwich Navigators

(New York Yankees)

Navigator Stadium
Norwich Industrial Park
Norwich, CT 06360

From 1985 through 1994 this team played in Heritage Park in Colonie, a suburb of Albany, New York. As far as tradition is concerned, they couldn't have been in a better place. New York State has been the home of dozens of fields of dreams since the 1850s. Albany itself was the site of the first-ever road game back in 1860, when the Brooklyn Excelsiors traveled up the Hudson to beat the Albany Champions 24–6. The problem that inevitably sent the Albany-Colonie Yankees from New York to Connecticut was Heritage Park. Only ten years old, it was already in need of major renovations. When nobody came up with the funds needed to fix the place, the club began to look around for a more secure home.

They wanted to move to Suffolk County on Long Island (NY), but the New York Mets nixed that. So the team decided to stay put in Colonie, but after once again failing to extract promises to fix up the stadium, their search continued. Danbury and Stamford (CT) and Atlantic City (NJ) came courting, but so did Norwich. The Norwich mayor, several Connecticut state legislators, and the State Department of Economic Development came armed with a plan the Yankees couldn't refuse. The plan called for the construction of a brand-new stadium in an attractive industrial park about forty miles southeast of Hartford. Good crowds were assured because around 470,000 people live within twenty-five miles of the new park's location. Then, too, the whole Nor-

wich area was starved for baseball—there had not been a team in town since way back in 1910. Even the franchise president, Hank Smith, who was born in the Bronx and wanted to keep the team in his home state, knew this was a deal not to pass up.

In 1995, the Yankees' Eastern League Double-A Navigators, named for the traditional seafarers who made their way to Norwich via the Quinebaug River, makes its debut here, and Norwich can count on a hard-hitting tradition coming with it. The club has been on a winning track ever since 1988, advancing to the playoffs every year until 1993 and bringing home three Eastern League titles in four years (1988–1991). Some star alumni from this team include Pat Kelly, Deion Sanders, Bernie Williams, Doug Drabek, N.L. All-Star Bob Tewksbury, and Jimmy Leyritz, who, in spite of his 1989 Eastern League record for being hit by pitches (9), has gone on to a healthy career in the majors.

While the old Heritage Park seated 5,000, the Navigators' brand-new park seats 6,000 and offers state-of-the-art luxury boxes and a large picnic area down the baseline. The facade is red brick—a welcome contrast to the modern flavor of the industrial park where the new stadium is located.

The old team mascot, a seven-foot baseball named Grounder (a favorite of ours), has, unfortunately, not made the move from Albany to Norwich. Several successful promotional events though, like the Mother's Day Diamond Dig and appearances by The Famous Chicken, et al., will most likely be as popular here as in New York. There are postgame fireworks on Memorial Day and July 4th and, of course, the usual giveaways—mugs, helmets, caps, bats, baseballs, and gloves.

Gates open one hour before game time. The best place to get autographs is near the dugouts. The Yankees are on the first base side.

GETTING THERE

Norwich is a lovely old New England town that was built in 1659 on land purchased from the Mohegan Indians. It is called the Rose City for its renowned two-acre Rose Garden featuring 2,500 rose bushes. There are some lovely inns and bed-and-breakfasts. Camping, too.

Navigator Stadium is located in Norwich Industrial Park in the northern part of town. Take I-95 to I-395 North (exit 76) and proceed to West Town Street (exit 82). Turn left onto West Town and proceed to the second light. Turn right into Industrial Park and follow the signs to Stoit Avenue and the stadium. Parking costs $2.

Box seats cost $7.50, while reserved seats go for $5. General admission tickets cost $3.50.

For schedule of events and ticket information, call (203) 887-1647.

For tourist information, contact the Norwich Tourism Commission, Eastern Connecticut Chamber of Commerce, 35 Main Street, Norwich, CT 06360, (203) 886-2381.

The Famous (and incorrigible) Chicken delights Norwich fans as much as he does fans throughout the minor leagues.

Portland Sea Dogs

(Florida Marlins)

Hadlock Field
271 Park Avenue
Portland, ME 04102

An incredible fan turnout in 1994 made the disappointing 60–81 season easier to bear for the Portland players.

1994! Brand-new team! Brand-new stadium! 12,000 people living within walking distance, and they were all showing up! They had to turn fans away at Hadlock Field. In April! In Maine! And so it went in Portland, where the Florida Marlins debuted the Sea Dogs, their first-ever Double-A franchise. In fact, no sooner had the 6,000-seat Hadlock Field opened than there was talk of expanding. It was all a dream come true for owner Dan Burke, retired CEO of Capital Cities/ABC.

Baseball, both amateur and professional, has been played on (or around) the site of Hadlock Field since the late 1800s by the likes of Pilots, Duffys, Highs, and Gulls. The last professional team, however, moved out in 1949, and interest in pro ball didn't resurface until Joe Buzas wanted to move his Double-A Bristol Red Sox to town in 1982. It didn't work out for Buzas, who took his team to New Britain instead, but when Double-A bids were requested for the new Rockies and Marlins franchises, Portland was ready.

Hadlock Field is in a residential area just south of downtown, tucked behind the Portland Exposition Building, one of the oldest arenas in the country. It's a friendly place with a traditional red brick facade and waving flags. The grandstand is shaped a bit like a hook, sweeping from first base around home and down beyond third. There are some box seats down the right field line, and a picnic area in the right field corner. It's a casual, open-air, nonsmoking stadium (smoking is permitted, however, behind the left field stands). The outfield wall is double-decked with billboards and graced with a state-of-the-art

modern scoreboard with a traditional look. Even better, when a Sea Dog hits a homer, a lighthouse rises up out of the center field fence, sounding a deep repetitive whistle, while a bright light spins around on top. Fans go nuts.

The fans have a great time here. They come early and stay until the very last out. They're a noisy bunch, too, stomping on the steel-and-aluminum grandstand to rally the team or howling forth with the "sea dog bark." The PA announcer gets into the act as well, inciting fans with sound effects: crashing glass when a ball flies toward the parking lot, screaming and wailing at the umpire's unpopular calls. Fireworks nights are big draws, as are the discount nights, aimed mostly at kids. But then, every night seems to be a big draw, so if you are planning to be in the area and want to come watch the

The Sea Dogs' scoreboard with a landmark look to it complements the neighboring architectural landscape of buildings dating back to 1915.

Sea Dogs, call ahead and reserve your tickets.

Giveaways are good ones: baseballs, bats, and gloves. The team mascot, Slugger the Sea Dog, looks just like the team logo, a seal with a dog's face, and pops up wherever he wants to. And keep an eye out, too, for the Trash Monster, who stomps through the stands keeping things tidy. Nobody's afraid of him, though; in fact, kids collect trash and give it to him.

When you're hungry, try a Sea Dog Biscuit (fried fish on a bun). The clam chowder is good, too.

Gates open one and a half hours before game time. The players will sign autographs down by the dugouts before the game.

GETTING THERE

Portland is right on Maine's rocky coast. Old Port, the restored historic downtown area, is alive with restaurants, shops, movies, and street musi-cians. There's a variety of hotels, motels, and campgrounds right in town and along the coast.

Hadlock Field is located on Park Avenue near downtown Portland. Parking near the park is lim-ited. However, there are designated parking areas in the city where you can catch a shuttle bus (for $1) to the park. The buses run frequently, starting one hour before the game. There are a few private parking garages nearby. (For more information on parking, call the number below.)

Box seats cost $6, while reserved seats go for $5 (kids and seniors get $1 off both). General admis-sion tickets cost $4 (kids and seniors get $2 off).

For schedule of events and ticket information, call (207) 879-9500.

For tourist information, contact the Conven-tion & Visitors Bureau of Greater Portland, 305 Commercial Street, Portland, ME 04101, (207) 772-5800.

HOMETOWN STATS—PORTLAND The Last Ten Years*					
Affil.	Year	League	Wins	Losses	Attendance
FLO	1994	Eastern	60	81	375,197

*Statistics are given only for the year in which the team played in Portland.

Reading Phillies

(Philadelphia Phillies)

Municipal Memorial Stadium
Route 61/Centre Avenue
Reading, PA 19610

Professional baseball here dates back to 1893, when the Reading team—simply called Reading—played in the Pennsylvania State League. Over the years, through memberships in a variety of leagues, they have been called the Reading Actives, Aces, Anthracites (anthracite is a hard coal), Brooks, Chicks, Coal Barons, Coal Heavers, Dutchmen, Indians, Keystones, Marines, Pretzels (our favorite), and Red Roses. They have been the Phillies' Eastern League affiliate since 1967.

Reading has had many future major league stars come through its portals, including Greg Luzinski, Bob Boone, Ryne Sandberg, Andre Thornton, Mark Davis, Dallas Green—who went on to manage the 1980 World Champion Phil-

Reading outfielders Pat Brady (left) and Sam Taylor pose in 1993. Brady went on to the Triple-A Red Barons in 1994.

lies—and Mike Schmidt, the eleven-time Gold Glove third baseman who spent seventeen years with the Phillies.

Municipal Memorial Stadium is located in a mixed business and residential area. Sitting in the recently renovated stands, you see hazy blue mountains in the distance providing a backdrop to the row houses and pine trees just over the center field fence. (Behind the park, out of view, are steel plants.) The latest renovations, undertaken during the 1992–93 off-season, extended the front of the stadium with a new ticket window and entry gates. The park now looks like a classic old stadium (a little like Camden Yards). New offices were added, as well as an expanded left field section on the other side of the reservation-only picnic area, a roof over the entire grandstand, and all-new seats (all with backs). The stadium now seats 8,000, and an average of 4,900 fans show up for each game.

The Phillies' mascot, Screwball, is a cross-eyed baseball on legs who greets fans at the gate and entertains all through the game. Also on the loose in the stands is that masked man, the Rubbish Ranger. Among other characters that make appearances on occasion are the Phillie Phanatic and Captain and Lady Dynamite, who once every season climb into a box in short center field, blow themselves up, and walk away from the debris.

This is one team that goes in big for promotions. Out of seventy home games, there are promotions at sixty-one. There are five fireworks shows throughout the season and giveaways at practically every home game. A fan can really stock up on baseball cards, gloves, tumblers, canteens, equipment bags, sports wallets, and more—just for showing up!

The Food Grove behind the right field bleachers is open to everybody. You can get a variety of foods there, but the grilled sausages and chicken are favorites. Also, don't pass up those homemade pretzels and funnel cakes (deep-fried sweet cakes) that are as big as the paper plates they are served on. The Grove has cast-iron tables and chairs

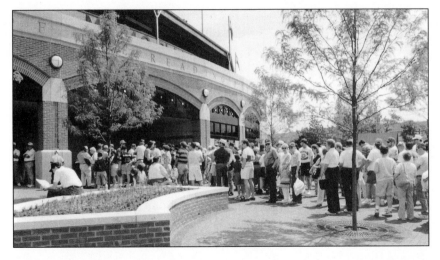

Reading fans, here outside Municipal Memorial Stadium, were second only to Portland in league attendance in 1994.

tucked under shade trees for a brief respite from the madd'ing crowd.

Gates open one hour before the game. The best place to get autographs is near the fences by the dugouts. The players have to walk through the grandstand to get to the dugouts, so there is ample opportunity to get their signatures.

GETTING THERE

Reading is at the foot of the Blue Mountains and calls itself the "outlet capital of the world." There are at least four huge outlet complexes there. The region has a good selection of motels and plenty of campsites with RV parking.

To get to Municipal Memorial Stadium, take Route 222 to Route 61. Go south on Route 61 for one and a half blocks. The stadium is on the right. There is ample parking in the stadium parking lot or in the lot across from the stadium on Front Street. Parking is free.

Box seats go for $6, reserved seats for $5. General admission tickets cost $3. Seniors and kids get $1 off.

For schedule of events and ticket information, call (610) 375-8469.

For tourist information, contact the Reading-Berks Visitors Information Association, 801 Hill Road, Wyomissing, PA 19610, (800) 443-6610.

HOMETOWN STATS—READING *The Last Ten Years*					
Affil.	Year	League	Wins	Losses	Attendance
PHI	1985	Eastern	58	79	76,819
	1986		77	59	83,506
	1987		76	63	100,895
	1988		67	69	144,107
	1989		68	71	178,734
	1990		55	82	204,240
	1991		72	68	250,610
	1992		61	77	287,078
	1993		62	78	313,083
	1994		58	82	338,249

Trenton Thunder

(Boston Red Sox)

Mercer County Waterfront Park
210 Riverview Executive Plaza
Trenton, NJ 08611

Thanks to the severe winter of 1994, Mercer County Waterfront Stadium wasn't quite ready for the opening of the new Trenton Thunder's season. Groundskeepers, in fact, were still laying sod on April 22 with the season in full swing. But despite the delay and the extra early-season games played on the road, baseball was back in Trenton after an absence of forty-four years.

The franchise was previously in London (Ontario), where the team was called the Tigers after its parent club. The Tigers had been in London for five years, but because of poor attendance and an ever-deteriorating stadium, the team's New York owners decided at first to move the team, but then decided to sell it instead to a group of New Jersey businessmen. Among the players from this franchise who have moved on to the Show are Travis Fryman, Milt Cuyler, Danny Bautista—who jumped straight to Detroit in 1993—Sean Bergman, John Doherty—who also went right to Detroit in '92—Greg Gohr, Buddy Groom, and Kurt Knudsen. The Thunder changed affiliates in 1995, going with the Boston Red Sox instead of Detroit.

Before the Thunder came to town, the last baseball teams in Trenton were the Senators and Giants, who played from 1936 to 1950. Willie Mays spent part of that last season here, brushing up his skills before heading over to the New York Giants the following year, where he earned himself the 1951 Rookie of the Year honors.

Mercer County Waterfront Stadium sits on the banks of the Delaware River not far from a very trendy part of downtown Trenton known as Chambersberg. You can actually walk to the ballpark from any number of restaurants and nightspots. Almost three million people live within a thirty-five-mile radius of Trenton, making the area the largest Eastern League market. The stadium is a throwback to an earlier era, with its warm brick facade and graceful arches. It's a small facility, seating 6,300, and it gets pretty cozy, since average attendance (in 1994) is around 6,250. There's a traditional wide-open concourse with two big concession areas. Try the pork roll, which you can only get in Jersey. Or so they tell us.

The grandstand extends just beyond the first and third bases and rakes up gently to sixteen luxury skyboxes and the stadium restaurant right behind home plate. There is a terraced picnic area off right field and another (for pregame parties) outside the stadium. Eighty-four billboards make up the outfield wall. That's a lot. They are stacked three high in left field and then taper down to one in right. The huge thirty-foot-high state-of-the-art scoreboard is in right as well. Homers over the far right field wall go into the drink. The parking lot is beyond center and left, but you can't really see it.

The Thunder host a lot of special events. During the 1994 season the women whose lives were spotlighted in the movie *A League of Their Own* showed up for autographs and first pitches. Turn-Back-the-Clock Night drew a sold-out crowd—hot dogs were seventy-five cents, popcorn was fifty cents—and the Thunder wore the uniforms of the 1947 Trenton Giants in a game against Bowie. Premium giveaways go on all season long.

Gates open one and a half hours before game time. You can get autographs before the game down by the dugouts, after the game outside the clubhouse.

GETTING THERE

Trenton, the capital of New Jersey, has plenty of historic sites and museums to visit. There are first-class hotels just a few miles north of the ballpark and numerous motels nearby. Camping is available at Washington Crossing State Park on the Delaware River.

Mercer County Waterfront Park is located off Route 29 South, adjacent to the Delaware River. There is plenty of parking, which costs $2.

"Club" seats (first 10 rows) go for $7, while "Pavilion" seats (right behind Club) are $6.50.

Trainer Lon Pinhey talks to Thunder players in the dugout at Mercer County Waterfront Park.

"Loge" seats are $6 and "Terrace" seats (benches with backs) cost $5.

For schedule of events and ticket information, call (609) 394-8326.

For tourist information, contact the Trenton Convention & Visitors Bureau, CN206, Trenton, NJ 08625, (609) 777-1771.

HOMETOWN STATS—TRENTON *The Last Ten Years**					
Affil.	**Year**	**League**	**Wins**	**Losses**	**Attendance**
DET	1994	Eastern	55	85	318,252†

*Statistics are given only for the year in which the team played in Trenton.

†Figure reflects 17 "at home" games played elsewhere due to delayed opening.

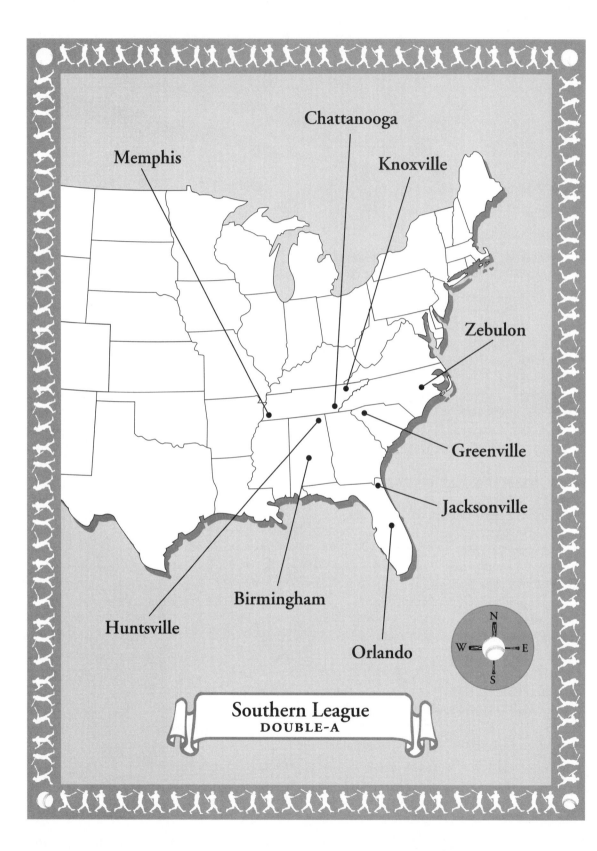

Chattanooga

Memphis

Knoxville

Zebulon

Greenville

Jacksonville

Birmingham

Huntsville

Orlando

N
W   E
S

Southern League
DOUBLE-A

Southern League

Double-A 1964–

Today's Southern League is the successor of the old Double-A South Atlantic League, which closed shop in 1963. (The current Class A South Atlantic League is the successor of the Western Carolina League.) The league's original carryover members from the SAL were Lynchburg (VA), Asheville (NC), Charlotte (NC), Chattanooga (TN), Knoxville (TN), and Macon (GA). Columbus (GA) joined after leaving the SAL after the 1959 season and Birmingham (AL) came on board from the defunct (1961) Southern Association. Only three of those original members—Chattanooga, Knoxville, and Birmingham—are still members.

The Southern League is very proud of its reputation. It was the first Double-A league to institute the three-umpire system. And it is the one Double-A league that sends its best players straight to the majors on a regular basis. Southern League players are known to play hard and fast—the trip to the top can be a short one.

The Southern League is made up of ten teams, which are scheduled to play 144 games during the regular season. First-half division winners then play second-half division winners in a best-of-five series. If the same team wins both halves, it plays the team with the next best overall record in its division. Division playoff winners then play each other in a best-of-five series for the league championship.

Birmingham Barons

(Chicago White Sox)

Hoover Metropolitan Stadium
100 Ben Chapman Drive
Birmingham, AL 35244

Birmingham, a founding member of the Southern League in 1964, had organized baseball as far back as 1885, the year the Birmingham Barons Baseball Club started up. When Birmingham came into the Southern Association in 1901 the team played at the Slag Pile (just off First Avenue). In 1910 they moved into Rickwood Field, just west of town in those days. Between 1910 and 1975 a lot happened at Rickwood Field, in Birmingham and throughout the South. Early on, the Barons shared the stadium with the Black Barons of the Negro American League. Then came the Civil Rights movement and with it, demands for equality on the field and in the stands. Baseball in Birmingham went through a difficult period of adjustment. It is fitting that some of the players most remembered in Birmingham include Willie Mays, Hank Aaron, and Reggie Jackson. More recent alumni include Jack McDowell, Robin Ventura, Frank Thomas, and Craig Grebeck.

After a long affiliation with the Athletics, Birmingham lost baseball when the A's franchise moved north in 1975, to Chattanooga. When Southern League baseball returned in 1981 with the Detroit Tigers, Birmingham had grown up around Rickwood Field, and the old park was in serious need of repair. Even with all the drawbacks at Rickwood the fans turned out, and the Birmingham Barons rewarded them in 1983 by winning the city's ninth league championship. In 1986, the Barons severed ties with the Tigers and signed on with the Chicago White Sox. Then, as a fitting farewell to their last season at Rickwood, the club won a tenth championship in 1987. In 1988 the Barons moved into the barely finished Hoover Metropolitan Stadium and promptly won another title in 1989. In 1993, more than 250,000 fans watched the Barons make their way to yet another title. And in 1994, that attendance nearly doubled as fans consistently turned out to see Michael Jordan in his baseball debut.

The new park is fabulous. It's surrounded by

A Dizzy Bat Race contestant takes ten spins around the bat. (For a full description of the contest, see The Glossary of Fun & Games, page 289.)

rolling land and woods in this so-far-undeveloped section of Birmingham. With room for 10,000 inside, the stadium also features a grassy knoll where fans can lay back and take in the game. You can even rent an air-conditioned suite or reserve a patio or banquet room for a private party. Management was afraid that fans might not follow the team from Rickwood to Hoover, but they did—an average of 4,000 show up per game. One fan, we are told, hikes eight miles along the Interstate to the game; it takes him four hours!

The yearly special events include fireworks displays and appearances by major league mascots. Giveaway nights are frequent, and on-field contests are big here. The most popular event in hot weather is the Water Balloon Pitch. If you are the one to hit and break the most balloons, not only do you end up soaked, you win a prize for every fan sitting in the section of the stands that you represent. Our favorite contest, however, is the Kenny Rogers Roaster Foul (or is it fowl?) Ball Contest. If at any time during a selected inning a foul ball comes flying into your section, you and everybody else there gets a coupon for free chicken or cherry cobbler or pie at the local celebrity's franchise. The food at the concessions on the concourse is state-of-the-art good ballpark fare. And for beer connoisseurs, Hoover Metropolitan Stadium offers the largest selection of foreign beers we've seen.

Gates open an hour and a half before game time. The best spot for getting players' autographs is along the fence near the dugouts before the game. On Fridays and Saturdays, team mascot Babe Ruff mans his own autograph table on the concourse.

GETTING THERE

Birmingham is a city of green hills and valleys that stretch for miles. You'll find plenty of good hotels and motels. Limited camping is available at the Family Fun Center and Sports Amusement Park.

Hoover Metropolitan Stadium is located south of Birmingham two miles off I-459. From the north or the south, get off the interstate at Exit 10 (Highway 150) and follow the signs to Ben Chapman Drive and the stadium. There is plenty of parking available, which costs $2.

Box seats and reserved bench seats cost $5.50. General admission is $3.50. Seniors, kids under fourteen, and military personnel get $1 off.

For schedule of events and for ticket information, call (205) 988-3200.

For tourist information, contact the Greater Birmingham Convention and Visitors Bureau, 2200 Ninth Avenue North, Birmingham, AL 35203, (205) 252-9825.

HOMETOWN STATS—BIRMINGHAM *The Last Ten Years*					
Affil.	Year	League	Wins	Losses	Attendance
DET	1985	Southern	57	86	140,671
CWS	1986		70	73	175,932
	1987		68	75	147,279
	1988		62	82	269,831
	1989		88	55	270,793
	1990		77	67	256,227
	1991		77	66	313,412
	1992		68	74	263,323
	1993		78	64	277,096
	1994		65	74	467,867

Carolina Mudcats

(Pittsburgh Pirates)

Five County Stadium
3501 N.C. Highway 39
Zebulon, NC 27597

When Steve Bryant bought the struggling (69–74) Columbus (GA) Astros in 1988, he sponsored a change-the-name contest to stimulate some interest in the team. "Mudcats" (the breed of catfish whose extra-long whiskers make it one of the ugliest fish to cruise southern river bottoms) came up the undisputed winner. When the logo was revealed, everyone was in turns shocked and delighted. "It's so ugly it's outstanding," one manager proclaimed. During their first year, the merchandising of the Mudcats was phenomenal. Long-gone fans poured back into the park. The team finished only two games better in the overall standings (71–71), but the supply of T-shirts, caps, and anything else that bore the Mudcats' logo just couldn't keep up with the demand.

Then in 1991 Steve Bryant did something totally unthinkable—he moved his team to Zebulon, North Carolina. Not only do the two Carolinas have a combined total of sixteen minor league baseball teams, but Zebulon is just thirty-six miles from Durham, the home of the successful minor league Durham Bulls. Actually, Bryant wanted to move his team to his hometown of Raleigh, only twenty miles from Durham. However, Miles Wolff, then owner of the Bulls, succeeded in getting the league to change the old ten-mile territorial rights distance to thirty-five. So goodbye Raleigh, hello "Field of Dreams."

In the movie *Field of Dreams* Kevin Costner's character built a ballpark in a corn field in Dyersville, Iowa. In North Carolina, Steve Bryant built his smack in the middle of Avon Privette's tobacco field in Zebulon—population 3,000+! "Build it and they will come." They did, too. The site serves a million baseball fans within a distance of thirty miles. "Opening night," according to GM Joe Kremer, "looked just like the movie. There was a long line of headlights stretching from the ballpark down the road." The 6,000-seat park opened with 7,333 in attendance (and 3,000 more were turned away). And the team actually flew in Don Lansing, the real-life owner of Costner's ballpark, who came packing a pail of Iowa dirt to sprinkle over the new mound at what is now called Five County Stadium. Pittsburgh pitcher Tim Wakefield, who went 15–8 here in 1991, is probably the most famous Mudcat to come out of Zebulon, but others who have moved on to the Show include pitchers Rich Robertson and Steve Cooke.

The trek to Five County Stadium can be dramatic. For twenty miles outside Raleigh there is nothing but rolling wooded countryside. Suddenly you see the sign for Zebulon, and as dusk settles you look up and see the stadium's bright lights hovering over the trees like a "close encounter" beckoning. The entrance to the stadium is a rustic one-ticket-booth affair flanked by a chain-link fence. A NO FISHIN' sign greets you as you enter, which is actually a funny idea, since you need a "fishing license" (i.e., ticket) to get in!

There are promotions and contests aplenty; count on giveaways at almost every home game. A popular between-inning contest is the Pizza Scream, in which a Lady Mudcat (usher) delivers a large pizza to whoever screams the loudest. Concessions offer a great catfish sandwich and crispy "Bait Shop" fries in a cup.

Gates open about one and a half hours before game time. For autographs, head for the area behind the dugout. The players are great; they'll sign whatever you throw their way.

GETTING THERE

Raleigh, North Carolina's capital city, is over two hundred years old. The "City of Oaks" has a goodly amount of hotels and motels. Camping is available at several of the county and state parks in the area.

Five County Stadium is located twenty miles east of Raleigh. Get on Highway 264 and head east to Zebulon. In Zebulon continue to Highway 39 and the stadium. There is plenty of free parking available.

Box seats go for $6, reserved seats for $5, and general admission tickets cost $4. Seniors, kids under fourteen, military personnel, and students with ID get $1 off.

For schedule of events and ticket information, call (919) 269-2287.

For tourist information, contact the Greater Raleigh Convention and Visitors Bureau, P.O. Box 1879, Raleigh, NC 27602, (919) 834-5900.

Five County Stadium, home of the Carolina Mudcats, is usually filled beyond capacity on home game dates.

HOMETOWN STATS—ZEBULON					
The Last Ten Years*					
Affil.	Year	League	Wins	Losses	Attendance
PIT	1991	Southern	67	75	218,054
	1992		52	92	263,141
	1993		74	67	328,207
	1994		74	66	319,279

*Statistics are given only for the years in which the team played in Zebulon.

Chattanooga Lookouts

(Cincinnati Reds)

Historic Engel Stadium
1130 E. Third Street
Chattanooga, TN 37403

The first female to sign a professional baseball contract was seventeen-year-old Jackie Mitchell, who signed with the Chattanooga Lookouts during the 1930s. Some say that she was a good pitcher who learned the art from major leaguer Dazzy Vance, the National League's premier pitcher in the 1920s. But like Eleanor Engel, who would follow at Harrisburg in the 1950s, her time in the spotlight was brief. Major League Baseball Commissioner Judge Kenesaw Mountain Landis voided the contract, stating flat out that baseball was just too physically taxing for women.

Current Lookouts owner Richard Holtzman is an ardent baseball fan and a very busy man. The Chicago-based real estate magnate and banker bought the franchise, his fourth minor league team, in 1987. The other teams he owns are the Class A Albany (GA) Polecats, the Class A Quad City River Bandits, and the Triple-A Tucson Toros. Holtzman has a reputation for restoring ballparks. Working in conjunction with local governments, he has renovated each of the stadiums in which his teams play. Historic Engel Stadium in Chattanooga received a $2.2 million facelift before the 1990 season that restored it to the way it looked in the 1920s—complete with brick walls, awnings, wrought iron, and antique lamps on the concourse. The field was totally rebuilt; the traditional bleachers were restored, the box seats were expanded, and a picnic area was opened down the left field foul line for special occasions (advance booking is required).

Holtzman is a man who believes in promotion for promotion's sake—and why not? It's in keeping with the Lookouts' reputation. The very park they play in is named in honor of Joe Engel, one of the all-time great minor league P. T. Barnum–like promoters. Engel built the stadium in 1930 and was famous for his extravagant promotions. He even gave away a $10,000 house once. There were those, of course, who thought the man had taken leave of his senses. Who had ever heard of such a thing? But it worked. Fans filled the park, and through the years players like Danny Tartabull, Mark Langston, Billy Swift, and Reggie Sanders headed to the major leagues.

Not quite as extravagant, but surely as satisfying, is the Lookouts' Annual Used Car (one per inning) Giveaway. The stadium seats about 8,000, but more than 10,000 show up for this event. At the Diamond Dig in June, any woman eighteen or older can take to the infield, tablespoon in hand, to dig for the diamond ring that's buried there. The announcer calls the action while hundreds of diggers work frantically.

Since the park is a registered historic landmark, it is open during the day. Anyone can wander in, sit in the stands, and dream. Be sure to visit the Hall of Fame gift shop located at the end of the concourse on the third base side. It is part museum—boasting lots of Lookouts memorabilia, including that of Lookouts' Hall of Fame players Harmon Killebrew, Rogers Hornsby, Satchel Paige, who played for the Chattanooga Black Lookouts in the 1950s, and Ferguson Jenkins—and part souvenir shop. The park closes in the evening and then reopens about one hour before game time. The best place to get autographs is at the autograph booths on the concourse before the game starts.

GETTING THERE

Chattanooga, a must-see in any tourist guide, sits on the banks of the Tennessee River in the shadow of Lookout Mountain with its legendary Lovers' Leap. There's an abundance of good hotels and motels and excellent campgrounds nearby.

To get to Engel Stadium, take I-24 to I-27 north to the 4th Street exit. Take a right onto 4th and stay on 4th for about one and a half miles when 4th turns into 3rd. The stadium is on the right. There is plenty of parking available, which costs $2.

Box seats cost $5; general admission tickets go for $3.50. Kids under twelve and seniors get in for $2.

For schedule of events and ticket information, call (615) 267-2208.

For tourist information, contact the Chattanooga Area Convention and Visitors Bureau, 1001 Market Street, Chattanooga, TN 37402, (615) 756-8687.

Several generations of fans have supported Chattanooga teams. Some family ties go all the way back to 1885, when the team was first named after nearby Lookout Mountain.

HOMETOWN STATS—CHATTANOOGA
The Last Ten Years

Affil.	Year	League	Wins	Losses	Attendance
SEA	1985	Southern	66	77	112,700
	1986		64	78	118,684
	1987		68	75	110,893
CIN	1988		81	62	136,921
	1989		58	81	156,677
	1990		66	78	135,825
	1991		72	72	186,285
	1992		90	53	269,688
	1993		72	69	270,671
	1994		67	73	292,920

Greenville Braves

(Atlanta Braves)

Greenville Municipal Stadium
One Braves Avenue
Greenville, SC 29607

Greenville, South Carolina, got its first professional baseball team in 1907. Unfortunately, as history would show, Greenville wasn't always appreciative of the sport and many a team failed, including that original team, the Mountaineers. After the Mountaineers went down for the count, the Spinners took up residence. Although the original Spinners would also fail, the team put Greenville on the map. A young local player named Joe Jackson caught everybody's attention on his way to becoming a superstar with the White Sox, only to be caught up in the 1919 Black Sox scandal that would end his career. "Shoeless" Joe Jackson is buried in Greenville.

The 1960s and 1970s saw the Braves, Mets, Red Sox, and Rangers in Greenville playing in the Class A Western Carolina League. Then disaster struck, and the old Meadowbrook ballpark burned to the ground in 1972. Ten years later, a group of prominent businessmen and Greenville civic leaders got together and approached the Atlanta Braves about moving their franchise to Greenville. Atlanta's Double-A team was in Savannah, Georgia, at that time, but after a lot of persuasion and after being eliminated from the playoffs in 1983, they packed their bags and headed to Greenville and a brand-new stadium. Greenville Municipal Stadium was completed in just six months, on April 9, 1984. In the opener on April 10 the Braves beat the Chattanooga Lookouts 4–2.

The grandstand at the stadium is open-air. The field sits below ground level, so when you enter from the concourse the field is laid out before you like an amphitheatre. Beyond the outfield fence are the woods and fields that surround the stadium. Even standing in line at the concession stands, waiting for those ever-popular nachos, you face the field. You can watch the game and also watch for foul balls, which can come zinging by as you wait your turn for boiled peanuts and a pitcher (yes, pitcher) of beer.

The stadium seats about 7,000, including the overflow onto the grassy knolls off the foul lines. The average draw, however, is about 3,800. The crowd is very family-oriented but enthusiastic; these fans can do the wave and the "tomahawk chop" with the best of them. They really care about their players and follow their development and progress. And they've had a lot to follow. Some players who ended up on the World Series–contending 1991 and 1992 Atlanta teams are Tom Glavine, Steve Avery, Ron Gant, and Jeff Blauser. Graduates of the 1992 G-Braves that captured the Southern League Championship with 100 wins are Javier Lopez—the Southern League MVP in 1992 and Melvin Nieves, Mike Kelly, and Tony Tarasco.

The G-Braves, as they call themselves, don't have a mascot, but do schedule appearances by Max Patkin, "The Famous Clown Prince of Baseball," The Famous Chicken, and Billy Bird & Company. And there are promotional giveaways galore. Almost half the home games have free giveaways. Big favorites are the travel mugs, tomahawks (for the chop, no doubt), tote bags, and even boxer shorts! And speaking of shorts, one of the most popular on-field contests is the Big Splash. Some lucky fan, preferably wearing shorts, gets to go digging for silver dollars, quarters, nickels, and dimes in a wading pool filled to the brim with water. The catch is that you have to take the money out and put it right in your pocket. More than a few have almost lost their pants.

Gates open about an hour before game time. The autograph booth on the concourse level is open for half an hour before each game. Autograph hounds may prefer to wait until after the game and catch the guys as they leave the clubhouse, outside the park down the right field line.

GETTING THERE

Historic Greenville is less than an hour from the breathtaking mountains, state parks, and whitewater rivers of the Blue Ridge Mountains' Upcountry. There are numerous hotels, many motels, and plenty of campsites in the region.

Greenville Municipal Stadium is located on Mauldin Road. From I-85 North, take Exit 46 (Mauldin Road), turn right onto Mauldin, and go two and a half miles. The stadium is on the right. From I-85 South, take Exit 46, turn left onto Mauldin Road, and proceed as above. There is plenty of parking available, which costs $2.

"Prime boxes" (those right down on the field along the baselines) go for $6.50. Regular box seats, immediately behind the prime boxes, cost $5.75. Reserved seats in the bleachers behind home plate will run you $5.25. General admission for the remaining bleachers goes for $4.50. Kids under fourteen get general admission for $3.

For schedule of events and ticket information, call (803) 299-3456.

For tourist information, contact the Greenville Convention & Visitors Bureau, P.O. Box 10527, Greenville, SC 29603, (803) 233-0461.

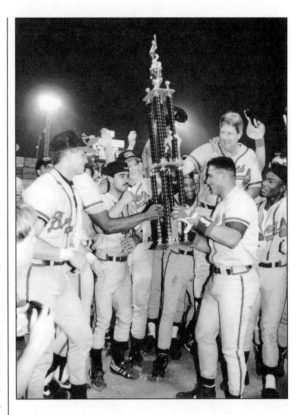

1992 Southern League champions, the Greenville players celebrate their title after beating Chattanooga.

| | | HOMETOWN STATS—GREENVILLE | | | |
| | | *The Last Ten Years* | | | |
Affil.	Year	League	Wins	Losses	Attendance
ATL	1985	Southern	70	74	214,471
	1986		73	71	203,647
	1987		70	74	206,468
	1988		87	57	209,791
	1989		70	69	208,117
	1990		57	87	204,929
	1991		88	56	222,038
	1992		100	43	247,798
	1993		75	67	232,369
	1994		73	63	244,171

Huntsville Stars

(Oakland Athletics)

Joe W. Davis Stadium
3125 Leeman Ferry Road
Huntsville, AL 35801

Huntsville, home of the U.S. Space & Rocket Center, is often called the "space capital of America." So what better name for its baseball team than the "Stars" (the celestial kind, of course)? Steady baseball in Huntsville is a fairly recent phenomenon—more recent, in fact, than even the space shuttle. Although two teams had played here briefly in the past (1911–1912 and 1930), baseball never took off until Larry Schmittou (who also owns several other teams) brought his club here in 1985. Affiliated with the Oakland A's since day one, Huntsville has produced some major league notables in the last ten years: Tim Belcher, Scott Brosius, Jose Canseco, Steve Chitren, Terry Steinbach—who set a Southern League record with 132 RBIs—Mark McGwire, and Wally Whitehurst are some former Stars who moved up.

Joe W. Davis Stadium, named in honor of the Huntsville mayor, was built in 1985 on the site of an old airport about four miles south of town. It's a multisport facility that is full of fans all year long because the Stars share the place with a college football team, six different high school football teams, *and* a soccer team. With seating for 10,000, it's a roomy park. The grandstand sweeps from just beyond first base around home and all the way to the left field foul pole. General admission bleachers extend down the right field line. The outfield wall, in classic minor league tradition, is double-decked with billboards. And the view from the stands? Mountain peaks fill the horizon by day, city lights at night.

The Stars have developed an enthusiastic following; more than 4,000 spectators show up for most home dates. These fans think nothing of driving forty-five miles to see a game. Lots of tourists pop in, too, while they're in town to visit the Space & Rocket Center. The management staff makes sure that everybody has a good time. The club puts on annual fireworks displays that are so popular that they keep adding more and more shows to the schedule. There are lots of half-price nights, including one of our favorites, Free Hot Dog Night. But while the dogs are good on any night, be sure to try the barbecue sandwiches and the chicken filet sandwiches, too.

Of all the classic between-innings contests, The Dizzy Bat Race rates highest in popularity with the fans here. So does the (through the hole) Ball Toss. One of the more celebrated contests, though, is the Space

A Ball Toss contestant tries to get at least one through the hole between innings. (For a full description of the contest, see The Glossary of Fun & Games, page 289.)

Race. Actually, it's just your typical kid-versus-mascot-run-the-bases contest, where the kid always seems to win, but in this case the kid races a spaceman. The funny thing is, the Stars claim they don't have a mascot! So who is the guy in the NASA-type space suit who runs the Space Race every night? Well, the story is that he just sort of appeared one day and that was that! He's been losing the base race every night since. Premium giveaways are plenty and include all the favorite fan freebies.

The park is open all day and closes one and a half hours before game time. Gates reopen one hour before the game starts. The best place to get autographs is just behind third base in the left field stands. Players are available from the time the gates open up to thirty minutes before game time.

GETTING THERE

Huntsville, the birthplace of Alabama, came through the Civil War unscathed, its vast number of historical buildings—many of which are open to the public—intact. Hotels and motels are numerous, and the Space & Rocket Center has its own on-site RV campground.

Joe W. Davis Stadium is located about four miles south of downtown Huntsville. Take I-65 to I-565 east. Then go south on South Memorial Parkway to Drake Avenue and the stadium. There is plenty of parking, which costs $2.50.

Veteran clown Max Patkin entertains Huntsville fans, who saw their team take the 1994 league championship.

Box seats go for $6. General admission tickets cost $4.

For schedule of events and ticket information, call: (205) 882-2562.

For tourist information, contact: Huntsville/Madison County Convention & Visitors Bureau, 7700 Monroe Street, Huntsville, AL 35801, (205) 535-2000.

	HOMETOWN STATS—HUNTSVILLE				
	The Last Ten Years				
Affil.	Year	League	Wins	Losses	Attendance
OAK	1985	Southern	78	66	300,810
	1986		78	63	263,198
	1987		74	70	256,090
	1988		59	85	185,811
	1989		82	61	217,948
	1990		79	65	228,821
	1991		61	83	224,208
	1992		81	63	252,010
	1993		71	70	282,731
	1994		81	57	297,801

Jacksonville Suns

(Detroit Tigers)

Sam W. Wolfson Park
1201 East Duval Street
Jacksonville, FL 32202

Jacksonville has baseball in its blood. The very first team was formed in 1874 and named the Robert E. Lee Base Ball Club of Jacksonville. Although that first ball club was strictly amateur (or so management insisted), the team was so good, and the guys played so hard, that the players were often accused of being paid professionals. The accusers, of course, were the teams that they inevitably beat the pants off!

Professional ball came to Jacksonville in 1904 when the Jacksonville Jays joined the old South Atlantic League. They were succeeded by the Scouts, then the Tarpons, the Tars, the Braves, the Jets, the Suns, the Expos, and finally the Suns again. When the Jays played way back in the early 1900s, the stadium was across the St. John's River, and since there were no bridges at that time, fans came by ferryboats. The park was situated right on the riverbank, so that high-flying balls often flew kerplunk right into the river.

Due to Jacksonville's location on the Atlantic Ocean, the city often played host to major league teams down in Florida for preseason practice. You could say, in fact, that spring training was invented in Jacksonville when the Washington Statesmen came to town in 1888 for what they called "preseason practices." Other teams that Jacksonville hosted were the Philadelphia Athletics, the Brooklyn Dodgers, the Cincinnati Reds, and the Boston Nationals.

In 1953 Jacksonville was affiliated with the Braves, in the days when the Braves were still the Milwaukee Braves and the tomahawk chop wasn't

even a twinkling in Ted Turner's eye. And in that year a nineteen-year-old Hank Aaron made history. Wearing number 5, Aaron, along with two other Braves players, broke the color barrier in the South Atlantic League. Aaron had a remarkable year and the rest, as they say, is history. Peter Bragan Sr. has owned the team since 1984. He is the president of the club and his wife, Mary Frances, is affectionately known as Mrs. President. They, along with son Peter Jr., who is VP/GM, are indeed the first family of Jacksonville baseball.

The present stadium was opened on June 3, 1955, and renamed in 1964 in memory of philanthropist and sportsman Samuel W. Wolfson, the president of the 1955 Braves. This 8,200-seat park has been home field to a number of minor league pitchers who went on to World Series–class status. Jacksonville ace alumni include Tommy John, Nolan Ryan, Randy Johnson, Bret Saberhagen, and Tom Seaver. The team doesn't have a mascot, but they do have Bragan's Blue Monster, an affectionate name for the twenty-five-foot blue billboard smack dab in center field. It just happens to line up with the pitcher's mound and home plate, and hitters will tell you that the billboard makes it a lot easier to see the ball. There is a picnic area down the right field line, near the playground and the Speed Pitch the kids adore. This area is a great place to catch foul balls, too.

The Suns, affiliated with the Detroit Tigers as of 1995, draw fans with a number of premium giveaways and special attractions, including several fireworks shows, guest appearances by big league mascots, and baseball clinics for kids ages thirteen to seventeen. Prior to every Sunday game all kids ages four to fourteen are invited to come out onto the field and run the bases. Prizes are awarded based on speed and style. The kids love it, and moms and dads bring their cameras.

Gates open about an hour and a half before game time. The best place to get autographs is outside the clubhouse after the game.

GETTING THERE

Jacksonville, not far from St. Augustine, straddles the mighty St. John's River just before it flows into the Atlantic Ocean. The area is packed with motels, bed-and-breakfasts, hotels, fancy resorts, and even beachfront campgrounds.

To get to Wolfson Park, take I-95 to the 20th Street East exit and continue on 20th Street to the exit ramp for the Gator Bowl Complex. Follow the signs to Wolfson Park. There is plenty of parking available, which costs $3.

Lower box seats go for $6, while upper-level box seats cost $5. General admission is $4. Kids under fourteen, seniors, and military personnel get $1 off. (Under 3 and over 80 are always free.)

For schedule of events and ticket information, call (904) 358-2846.

For tourist information, contact the Jacksonville and the Beaches Convention & Visitors Bureau, 3 Independent Drive, Jacksonville, FL 32202, (904) 798-9148.

Suns catcher Jim Campanis and his wife, Lisa, exchanged vows on the pitcher's mound in 1991.

Affil.	Year	League	Wins	Losses	Attendance
MON	1985	Southern	73	70	82,907
	1986		75	68	164,772
	1987		85	59	190,456
	1988		69	73	175,396
	1989		68	76	220,803
	1990		84	60	244,494
SEA	1991		74	69	231,139
	1992		68	75	226,273
	1993		59	81	250,002
	1994		60	77	240,580

HOMETOWN STATS—JACKSONVILLE
The Last Ten Years

Knoxville Smokies

(Toronto Blue Jays)

Bill Meyer Stadium
633 Jessamine Street
Knoxville, TN 37917

Knoxville has had a professional baseball team since about 1909. In the 1920s, as a member of the Appalachian League, they were called the Knoxville Pioneers. Then in the 1930s and 1940s they were the Smokies and played in the Class A Southern Association. Although perennial basement dwellers, the Smokies did have one good year in 1939 (finishing fifth instead of last), producing a team full of future major league players, including first baseman Babe Young, second baseman Dutch Meyer, third baseman Tom Hafey, his brother, outfielder Bud Hafey, and pitcher Gordon Maltzberge. Then, smack in the middle of the 1944 season, the team left, virtually sneaking out of town overnight for booming Mobile.

From that time on, baseball struggled in Knoxville. And even though a new stadium was ready in 1955 and a new group of owners, which included local businessman Neal Ridley, brought in another team a year later, the sport didn't take off. After the 1967 season the Smokies were history once again. Then in 1972 Neal Ridley bought the Chicago White Sox Southern League affiliate in Asheville and moved it to Knoxville. Much to everyone's dismay, the White Sox renamed the team—the Knoxville Sox. The "Knox-Sox" did well, though, and they developed a following. The players included such future big leaguers as 1983 Cy Young Award winner LaMarr Hoyt and Gold Glove first baseman Mike Squires.

In 1980, Ridley hooked up with baseball's then-newest franchise, the Toronto Blue Jays. There were those who questioned his sanity. It wasn't every day a club chose to leave an established team like the White Sox for an unknown expansion team. And from Canada yet? But Ridley knew what he was doing, and his gamble paid off big-time: the "new" Knoxville Blue Jays were in the playoff picture in 1982, 1984, 1985, 1986, and 1991. Some of the players that came out of this era are Cecil Fielder, Fred McGriff, Jesse Barfield, Pat Borders, and Juan Guzman.

After Ridley died in 1985 the Toronto Blue Jays bought the franchise from his family. The first thing the Blue Jays did was overhaul the Stadium and then, to everyone's amazement, they renamed the team the "Smokies" to capture Knoxville's hometown pride—Knoxville is known as "the gateway to the great Smoky Mountains."

The ballpark, originally built in 1953, is named in honor of Knoxville native and 1948 National League Manager of the Year Bill Meyer, who managed the Pittsburgh Pirates from 1948 to 1952. Unfortunately, it is in a part of town that has seen better days. Although the ballpark is neighbored by softball fields and a few picturesque Victorian homes, the area is, for the most part, industrial. A huge warehouse towers over left field, its many glass windows primary targets for anyone swinging a bat.

But the stadium itself is a classic, a clean and comfortable place that seats 6,400. Every seat is a chair seat, too; there's not a bleacher in sight. There is also a picnic area off left field where groups can watch the game while eating barbecue and chicken dinners. While you are at the concession stands keep in mind the three "p's:" Polish Dogs, Pretzels, and a fortified beverage called Power Aid.

One of the most popular promotional events, other than the annual appearance by the Phillie Phanatic, is Turn Back the Clock Night, when players from both home and visiting teams wear vintage 1950s uniforms. It costs two bits to get into the park that night. Just flip your quarter into the large bucket as you enter through the turnstiles. Premium giveaways are scheduled throughout the season.

The team mascot is a large, huggable owl

named Owlfredo, who is hopelessly inept at running the bases against younger fans. He's much better at nesting between two huge billboards in the outfield.

The gates open about one hour before game time, and the kids head straight to the chain-link fence down the right field line, where the players will sign just about anything shoved their way. Most kids stay there during the game as well—it's a favorite place to catch foul balls.

GETTING THERE

Knoxville, in the heart of the scenic East Tennessee Valley, is the northern gateway to the Great Smoky Mountains. The city has an abundance of first-rate hotels and motels. There are plenty of campgrounds in the region as well.

Bill Meyer Stadium is just northeast of downtown Knoxville. Take I-40 to James White Parkway and get off the Parkway at the first exit, Summit Hill Drive. Take a right onto Summit Hill. At the first stop light, take a right onto Central. Go about fifty feet and make another right onto Willow Avenue. The road dead-ends at the stadium. There is plenty of free parking.

Box seats, in the first four rows of the stands, cost $5.50. General admission is $4.50. Kids and seniors get $1 off.

For schedule of events and ticket information,

Despite their losing 1994 season, Knoxville placed second in the league in club batting average.

call (615) 637-9494.

For tourist information, contact the Knoxville Tourist Bureau, 810 Clinch Avenue, Knoxville, TN 37901, (615) 523-7263.

HOMETOWN STATS—KNOXVILLE *The Last Ten Years*					
Affil.	Year	League	Wins	Losses	Attendance
TOR	1985	Southern	79	64	108,952
	1986		74	70	109,731
	1987		68	76	124,231
	1988		75	69	87,434
	1989		67	76	69,776
	1990		67	77	82,676
	1991		67	77	123,361
	1992		56	88	90,387
	1993		71	71	140,868
	1994		64	76	145,092

Memphis Chicks

(San Diego Padres)

Tim McCarver Stadium
800 Home Run Lane
Memphis, TN 38104

What do Ron Howard, Maury Povich, Bob Costas, and Tim McCarver have in common? They all own a piece of the Memphis Chicks, that's what. And because principal owner and president David Hersh managed to get these nationally known names to invest in his team in 1991, prominent local businessmen soon followed suit. Hersh also fought long and hard for a plan to spend a total of $3.1 million on renovations to a nearly-thirty-year-old ballpark. All these efforts have paid off, as the Chicks pull in nearly 4,000 fans a game.

Memphis, a longtime member of the Southern Association, dropped professional baseball in 1960 after the fabled Russwood Park was destroyed by fire. A new stadium, Fairgrounds Field, was built in 1963 and was subsequently expanded in 1968 to 4,500 seats when a band of concerned citizens, led by Tim McCarver, succeeded in bringing the New York Mets' Texas League expansion team to Memphis. Professional baseball was back, and in keeping with the local scene the team was called the Blues! The Blues lasted through 1976 (then part of the International League). The stadium was renamed in McCarver's honor in 1978 when the Memphis Chicks, then affiliated with the Montreal Expos, joined the Southern League. In 1980 seating capacity was increased to 10,000 with the addition of the outfield bleachers. Later renovations have added a new infield carpet of AstroTurf, a new stadium club, and, perhaps more importantly, new restrooms, better seats and concession stands, and a new picnic pavilion in the left field corner, where for as little as $6.50 you can have "all-you-can-eat." The Chicks had been affiliated with the Kansas City Royals since 1984, but in 1995 signed up with the San Diego Padres.

McCarver is a truly cozy ballpark, so cozy that general admission ticket holders have to climb up through the box seats to settle in. There is very little foul ball area here. It's also unusual in that while the infield is AstroTurf, the outfield is grass. The stadium has a reputation for being a batter's park —lots of home runs and zinging foul balls. Hitters like Bo Jackson, who played here in 1986, have a great time. Jackson drew 7,000 fans when he made his debut; then, after fifty-three games, he was promoted straight up to Kansas City. Other top-notch players who have played in Memphis are Sean Berry, Brent Mayne, Greg Hibbard, Jeff Conine, Jim Eisenreich, and David Cone, who had his worst year ever here in 1984 with eight wins, twelve losses, and twenty-seven wild pitches.

"If you give us a chance, we will entertain you," says Hersh. And they do, too, with fireworks, Soap Opera Stars Softball, Mother's Day Diamond Giveaway, Max Patkin, The Famous Chicken, and about six after-game concerts presenting the likes of Joe Diffie, Ricky Skaggs, and Patti Loveless. There are ample giveaways and a fairly recent addition, mascot Chief Chickasaw. The Chief, with his ceremonial turtle-shell rattle and traditional leaning pole, represents the strength and tradition of the Chickasaw Nation, in whose honor the team is named. They say that the mascot has the approval of the Chickasaw Nation, but one wonders how the tribal leaders must have felt when the Chief was once thrown out of the game for mooning the ump!

Gates open one hour before game time. There

Mascot Chief Chickasaw reacts to the umpire's call.

Beyond the left field fence at Tim McCarver Stadium are the lights of downtown Memphis.

is always one player manning the autograph booth on the third base side of the concourse, but you might have better luck near the left field bleachers and neighboring picnic area. The guys are available up until about twenty minutes before the game starts.

GETTING THERE

Memphis *is* Graceland and Beale Street, with "rock-and-roll in its heart and the blues in its soul." There's a variety of lodging, including the famous Peabody Hotel with its famous Peabody ducks. There are two state parks in the area that operate campsites.

Tim McCarver Stadium is located on the State Fairgrounds complex next to the Liberty Bowl. Take I-240 south to Poplar Avenue West. Then take a left on Highland, a right on Central, and a left on Early Maxwell to the stadium, which is on the left. Parking, which costs $2, is on the right.

The limited number of box seats go for $6. All the rest are general admission tickets, which cost $5. Seniors, kids, students, and the military get $1 off.

For schedule of events and ticket information, call (901) 272-1687.

For tourist information, contact the Memphis Convention & Visitors Bureau, 47 Union Avenue, Memphis, TN 38103, (901) 543-5333.

		HOMETOWN STATS—MEMPHIS			
		The Last Ten Years			
Affil.	Year	League	Wins	Losses	Attendance
KCR	1985	Southern	65	79	200,682
	1986		69	75	252,036
	1987		72	71	215,749
	1988		79	64	205,568
	1989		59	84	175,334
	1990		73	71	193,758
	1991		61	83	185,409
	1992		71	73	212,768
	1993		63	77	230,181
	1994		75	62	258,311

Orlando Cubs

(Chicago Cubs)

Tinker Field
287 Tampa Avenue South
Orlando, FL 32805

Professional baseball in Orlando dates back to the early 1900s. Like other Florida cities, Orlando has been a spring training home for many of the major league teams. Its minor league franchises have been affiliated with several different major league clubs over the years, but have played almost exclusively in the Florida State League—through 1972, that is. In 1973, much to the delight of local baseball fans, the Minnesota Twins moved their Southern League affiliate to Orlando from Charlotte. And the fans weren't disappointed. Tim Laudner, on the 1981 Orlando team that took the Southern League championship, had forty-two home runs and went on to play on the Twins' 1987 World Series championship team. Orlando players who were part of that team (which beat St. Louis 4 games to 3) and the 1991 championship team (which beat Atlanta 4 games to 3) include Randy Bush, Gene Larkin, and Greg Gagne.

The association with the Twins lasted through the 1992 season, by which time they were the Orlando SunRays. The team was sold after the 1992 season to the *Chicago Tribune,* the corporate parent of the Chicago Cubs. And since every minor league team in the Cubs' farm system is called the Cubs (OK, Rockford has the "Cubbies"), the SunRays became the Cubs, too. So, "On the Road to Wrigley" is the new Orlando battle cry. A long road at that, judging by the last two years' standing (bad).

Tinker Field is one of the oldest ballparks in the country. It was originally constructed in 1914 and then totally rebuilt in 1963. The ballpark is named, ironically, for Hall of Famer Joe Tinker, the legendary shortstop who played with the Chicago Cubs from 1902 through 1912 and then again in 1916. Tinker settled here after managing the Orlando Gulls of the Florida State League in the early 1920s. The stadium was renamed in his honor in 1921.

Kids show up early at Tinker Field on Bat Day, one of the Cubs' most popular promotions.

Tinker Field is located in a residential area adjacent to another landmark stadium—the Citrus Bowl, which sits beyond the right field fence. Off in the distance over the left field fence is Lake Lorna Doone. When Tinker Field was renovated the older scoreboard was kept in an effort to maintain the park's nostalgic charm. There is a picnic area behind the third base bleachers that can be rented out by parties of twenty or more. (The catered picnics have names like Base Hit, Double, and Triple.) There is also a playground with swings, slides, and monkey bars.

One of the more interesting traditions at Tinker Field is the regional concession offerings. Every night features specialties that are native to the visiting team's home base. For instance, if the Memphis Chicks are in town, you'll find barbecue on the menu. If it's the Carolina Mudcats, expect fried catfish. You won't want to miss special appearances by the Blues Brothers and Billy Bird and Company. As usual, locally sponsored giveaways include bats, wallets, mugs, helmets, and so forth.

The team mascot, Spike, is a bear cub. He's constantly on the prowl before and during the game. The kids can't hug him enough.

Gates open one hour before game time. Get there early, after infield practice, if you want to get the players' autographs. You can catch them near the first base dugout.

GETTING THERE

Orlando, home of The Magic Kingdom, EPCOT Center, Disney-MGM Studios, Universal Studios, Sea World, *and* the Orlando Cubs—need we say more? A list of accommodations, including at least ten campsites, could fill a phone book.

To get to Tinker Field, take I-4 to Exit 37 (Gore Street); then go west to Tampa Avenue. Take a right on Tampa to the stadium. There is plenty of parking available, which costs $2.

Box seats cost $6; reserved grandstand, $4; general admission, $3. Kids, seniors, and military personnel save $1.

For schedule of events and ticket information, call (407) 872-7593.

For tourist information, contact the Orlando/Orange County Convention & Visitors Bureau, 7208 Sand Lake Road, Orlando, FL 32819, (407) 363-5871.

		HOMETOWN STATS—ORLANDO			
		The Last Ten Years			
Affil.	Year	League	Wins	Losses	Attendance
MIN	1985	Southern	72	71	62,122
	1986		70	73	75,728
	1987		61	82	69,656
	1988		66	75	68,904
	1989		79	65	93,034
	1990		85	59	147,070
	1991		77	67	110,131
	1992		60	82	154,965
CUB	1993		71	70	217,716
	1994		59	78	195,270

X-Xpress

(Seattle Mariners)

c/o The Southern League of Professional
Baseball Clubs Inc.
1 Depot Street, Suite 300
Marietta, Georgia 30060
(404) 428-4849

This franchise has been the nomadic orphan of the Southern League since it was forced out of its home in Charlotte (NC) after the 1992 season. It's been seeking a permanent home ever since (even as we write this).

Up until 1992, there had been a Southern League team in Charlotte dating back to 1964 (with a four-year break from 1972 to 1976). The Knights, as this club was then called, were affiliated with the Cubs. They were booted out of town when the International League expanded from eight teams to ten and the city of Charlotte brought in a new Triple-A franchise to play in the new Knights Stadium. This displaced Double-A team even lost its name to the new Triple-A affiliate of the Indians. Then, to add insult to injury, the club's plans to relocate to New Orleans were dashed at the last minute when yet another Triple-A franchise, the Zephyrs, moved there from Denver.

Enter Larry Schmittou, owner of the Triple-A Nashville Sounds, who took in the homeless team on a one-year (which stretched to two-year) conditional agreement in 1993. He ran the team and shared the 17,000-seat Hershell Greer Stadium with the by-then new affiliate of the Minnesota Twins, the Nashville Xpress (we think the team really thought they were just zooming through on their way to their real home).

This move brought double the amount of baseball to Nashville; there was a game almost every night at Greer, plus promotions, plus everything else—except fans. The Xpress drew only about 2,600 a game in 1993, while the lion's share of fans—about 6,400 a game—and hoopla went to the Sounds. The stats got worse in 1994, except when the Double-A Birmingham Barons (with Michael Jordan) came to town. Attendance dropped to about 2,100 a game. And too much baseball in town was also affecting the Sounds' attendance—down to 4,500 a game in 1994.

The minimal support and the Xpress's mediocre overall performance, however, did not keep the stepchild team from contributing to the Twins roster. Minnesota's 1994 outfielder Rich Becker had led the 1993 Xpress with ninety-three runs. Catcher Mike Durant went up in 1994, too, as did Marty Cordova.

By early 1994, the new sole owner of the Xpress, Dennis Bastein, was still scrambling to find a permanent home for the team. Lexington (KY) looked good for a while. There were news releases and artists' renderings of the proposed new stadium, but Lexington was not ready to commit by the time the Xpress had to leave Nashville. And leave they had to—the welcome mat had most definitely been yanked.

Enter the Caribbean. And why not? About eight miles outside of San Juan, Puerto Rico, in the heart of tourist-friendly Bayamon, stands the big, beautiful 14,000-seat Juan Ramon Loubiel Stadium, just waiting to be utilized. And Bastein pointed out that having a Southern League team playing in Puerto Rico made sense. A lot of major league players come from Puerto Rico, and winter ball there is phenomenally successful. The Memphis Chicks' owner, David Hersh, a major supporter of Puerto Rican baseball, agreed to manage the franchise in Bayamon on a two-year trial basis. The league approved.

There was only one thing stopping the move—the team's new affiliate, the Seattle Mariners. The Twins had abandoned the Xpress in a reshuffle of affiliates after the 1994 season. When the smoke cleared, the Xpress and the Mariners were the only ones left in the pool. After weeks of heavy-duty negotiations with Hersh, the Mariners finally just flatly refused to continue discussions about going to Puerto Rico. So long, Bayamon.

On January 19, 1995, the Southern league President finally announced that beginning with

Fireworks displays always attract large crowds to minor league ballparks.

the 1997 season, the league conditionally approved the permanent relocation of Dennis Bastein's team to Springfield, Missouri. But we're not holding our breath; the move is pending construction of a brand-new ballpark and season ticket minimums.

For the 1995 and 1996 seasons the team seems destined for a two-year stint in North Carolina somewhere, most likely in Wilmington, where it would be operated by Steve Bryant, who owns the Carolina Mudcats. For the latest on the club's new name and whereabouts, contact the Southern League office.

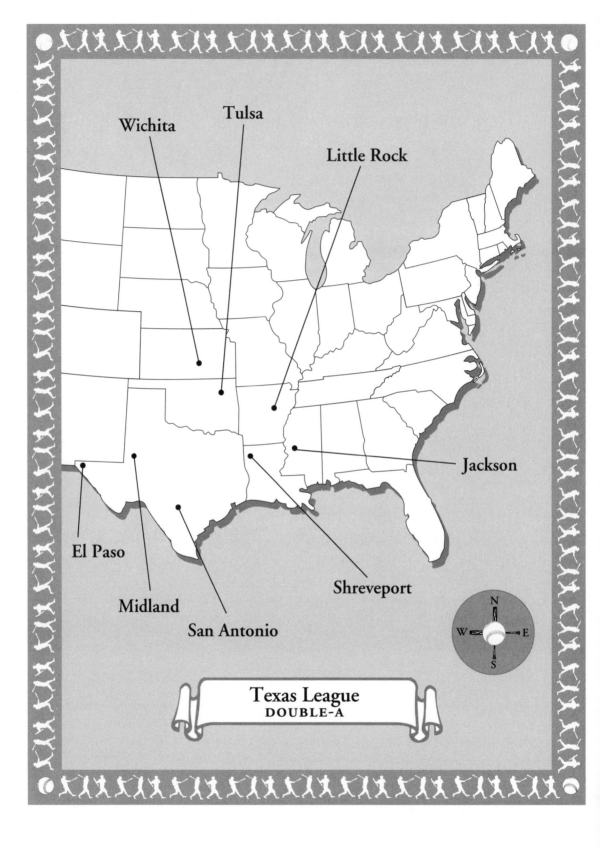

Wichita

Tulsa

Little Rock

Jackson

El Paso

Midland

San Antonio

Shreveport

N
W — E
S

Texas League
DOUBLE-A

Texas League

Class D 1902–1906; Class C 1907–1910

Class A 1921–1942; Double-A 1946–

Professional baseball made its way into Texas in 1888 when the Texas League was organized by Austin, Dallas, Fort Worth, Galveston, Houston, and San Antonio. Though the Texas League over the years has included twenty-five Texas cities and thirteen out-of-state ones, the league today consists of three Texas clubs and five out-of-state ones.

Going to Texas League games in the late 1800s could be exciting. In Fort Worth (and elsewhere), cowboys actually wore their six-guns to the ballpark. As legend has it, a drover once whipped out his revolver and angrily shot at an untimely pop-up as it was flying in the air. No one on the field dared to move. From then on, pop-ups that dropped safely for base hits were called "Texas Leaguers."

The Texas League had money woes at the end of the nineteenth century and so did not play in 1891, 1893, 1894, 1900, and 1901. It reorganized in 1902, joining the NAPBL that same year. A year later, however, the league split into two entities, the Texas League and the South Texas League; they were rejoined in 1907.

The Texas League is made up of eight teams, which are scheduled to play 136 games during the regular season. First-half division winners then play second-half division winners in a best-of-five series. If the same team wins both halves, it gets a bye for the first round. Division playoff winners then play the best-of-seven series for the league championship.

Arkansas Travelers

(St. Louis Cardinals)

Ray Winder Field
War Memorial Park
Little Rock, AR 72205

Minor league baseball has been a big part of Little Rock's colorful history since 1901, when the city was a member of the old Southern Association. And except for the years 1911 to 1914, Little Rock teams were with the Association right through 1958. When Little Rock lost its team in 1959, everybody panicked. Civic leaders and local businessmen quickly joined forces, bought the New Orleans team, and moved it to Little Rock for the 1960 season, where it played as the Arkansas Travelers. And they still do. The Travelers joined the Texas League in 1966 and have been affiliated with the St. Louis Cardinals since then.

GM Bill Valentine has his own colorful history. Before he took over the Travelers in the 1970s, he was a major league umpire. His umpiring career ended in 1968 when he was unceremoniously ejected from baseball after he tried to organize the umpires into a union. These Travelers have flourished under his leadership. Some of the players who have hit and run through Little Rock are Dallas Green, Rick Wise, Grant Jackson, Andy Van Slyke, Garry Templeton—who averaged over .400 in the one month he was there—Tommy Herr, and Terry Kennedy.

Travelers' Stadium, built in 1932, was named, as the team was, after the old rural traveling salesmen who sold goods from wagons in the backwoods. The stadium was renamed in 1966 to honor Ray Winder, a former ticket seller who managed the team for forty years.

The stadium has been renovated on a regular basis, and so it's a clean and comfortable park today. It's located in War Memorial Park, which is a beautiful green complex that includes the city zoo, a fitness training park, and another stadium. Winder seats 6,083, just big enough for the average game attendance of 4,600 fans. Game night here is a social event; it is *the* time to get together with family, neighbors, and co-workers. Even when the Travelers are in last place, the fans show up—loud and loyal. One particular female fan, known by everyone as the woman with "the voice smooth as sandpaper," regularly takes her seat behind home plate and doesn't let up on the opposing players or the umpires. Visiting teams just hate to come to town.

There are promotions almost every night. One of our favorites is Klunker Car Night. And these are real klunkers! There is a cacophony of boos as the car is driven onto the field; then the boos turn to cheers when some lucky (or unlucky) soul wins it. On Tuesdays and Thursdays you get free bingo cards at the gate; the PA announcer calls out numbers between innings. Prizes include free pizzas and a trip to St. Louis. On Saturdays, you might get in on a Dixieland band or a guest appearance by The Famous Chicken. If you catch the doubleheader on Saturday, don't wander too far between games—the Egg Toss between players and their wives is a hoot.

The ballpark organist, Alfreda Wilson, has been playing for Travelers fans since 1972. During the game, as hitters step up to the plate, she gives them "their" tune—a player named Bill gets "He's Just My Bill," one from San Francisco gets "San Francisco Here I Come," John gets "Big Bad John," and so on.

Gates open one hour before game time. The best time to get autographs is up to thirty minutes before game time near the box seats or about thirty minutes after the game by the clubhouse.

Travelers fans turn out for their team, win or lose.

GETTING THERE

Little Rock is a lush, hilly, people-oriented city that is known for its stately government buildings. It has some first-rate hotels, and the nearest campsite is only ten minutes away in the 1,500-acre Burns Park in North Little Rock.

Ray Winder Field is just south of downtown Little Rock. From I-630, take the Fair Park Blvd. exit and follow the signs. You'll come to the top of a hill and see the stadium below. There is plenty of free parking.

Box seats in the covered grandstand go for $6, while general admission, the top twenty rows, and the bleacher seats off right field go for $4. Kids and seniors get in for $2.

For schedule of events and ticket information, call (501) 664-1555.

For tourist information, contact the Little Rock Convention & Visitors Bureau, 1 State Health Plaza, Little Rock, AR 72201, (501) 376-4781.

Affil.	Year	League	Wins	Losses	Attendance
	HOMETOWN STATS—LITTLE ROCK *The Last Ten Years*				
STL	1985	Texas	64	70	207,985
	1986		67	67	222,613
	1987		72	63	256,365
	1988		67	69	251,892
	1989		79	56	296,428
	1990		56	80	256,074
	1991		49	87	265,268
	1992		59	73	265,984
	1993		66	69	285,757
	1994		68	67	275,524

El Paso Diablos

(Milwaukee Brewers)

Cohen Stadium
9700 Gateway North Boulevard
El Paso, TX 79924

With friends who take your check for $1,000 and then leave you hanging with $72,000 in debts, who needs enemies? So Jim Paul was asking in 1974, when he bought the struggling El Paso Sun Kings. This was back when the team played in Dudley Field, where the dry air, gusting winds, and, more pertinently, an outfield fence that measured only 330 feet away made the park a pitcher's nightmare. Scores like 25–13 were not uncommon. A man not to be discouraged, however, Jim Paul renamed the team the Diablos and turned the franchise around. In two years, attendance went from 60,000 to more than 200,000. In the last twenty years, the team has done very well. They have reached the playoffs thirteen times, and more than 300,000 fans come out annually. Some major league stars who have worn Diablo colors are Carney Lansford, the *Sporting News* 1988 Minor League Player of the Year Gary Sheffield, and All-Star big leaguer Greg Vaughn, who led the Texas League with 28 home runs and 105 RBIs in 1988.

Jim Paul knows the way to the fans' hearts: give 'em wild and give 'em crazy is his philosophy. Dubbed the P. T. Barnum of minor league baseball, Paul originated the white handkerchief, "Bye-Bye Baby" tradition—when he handed out white tissues at the gate. After the opposing pitcher was yanked, the announcer played a tape of the guitar intro to Janis Joplin's "Bye-Bye Baby," and the fans stood up waving their tissues and singing, "So long, too bad you had to go, boom, bye bye, baby, bye bye." Pretty soon, opposing teams started countering. When a Diablo pitcher was yanked, the visiting players would come running out on the field waving white towels. The fans went nuts. Still do. It's absolute bedlam.

The fans and players aren't the only ones pulling pranks. Once an announcer got thrown out of the park by an irate umpire who didn't think it funny when, after a dubious call, the announcer played a snippet from Linda Ronstadt's song "When Will I Be Loved?" that went, "I've been cheated, been mistreated." After ignoring the ump and playing it a second time, he got tossed.

The Diablos play in an almost-new (1990) 9,700-seat stadium named after Andy and Sid Cohen, two old-time major league players from El Paso. Andy played briefly for the New York Giants in 1926, 1928, and 1929. Sid pitched briefly for

Record crowds jammed Cohen Stadium in 1994 to watch the Diablos play their way to the league championships, where they swept the Fayetteville Generals 4–0 in a best-of-seven series.

Washington and was the last AL pitcher to strike out Babe Ruth in 1934, his last year in a Yankee uniform. (The Babe did play a symbolic extra year for the Boston Braves in 1935.) The winds of April and May are still wicked, but you couldn't ask for a more beautiful location. The ballpark sits at the juncture of the sage-and-wild-grass-covered desert and the foothills of the Franklin Mountains, which form the southernmost tip of the Rockies. The park is actually in the shadow of the great mountains, which helps enormously to cool down the field on those blistering July and August days. Considered one of the best-designed ballparks in the minor leagues, Cohen Stadium has a roomy concourse above field level, so that while waiting in line for one of the "best-ever" chili cheese dogs the fans don't miss anything. There's a game arcade for kids and the Hard Ball Cafe down the third base line, which serves an all-you-can-eat buffet.

There are the usual giveaways—helmets, bats, and caps—but the Diablos also give away televisions, in-ground swimming pools, and cash. In addition to mascot Casey Chicken, who does a fantastic moonwalk on top of the dugout, the team has four other mascots: Home-Run Honey Bear, Rally Raccoon, Cool Cat, and First Base Bernard. All together, they create a kind of mascot mania. There are six fireworks spectaculars each season. Sundays are always crowded because that's 25 Cent Hot Dog Night.

Gates open one hour before game time. The best place to get autographs is at the autograph booth near the main gate every night before game time. Lots of kids also like to lean over the dugouts after the game.

GETTING THERE

El Paso, with its spectacular mountain vistas and desert sunsets, is steeped in the border heritage of the American Southwest. Don't miss the Ysleta Mission; it's the oldest in Texas. Accommodations are mostly motel rooms. There are at least six campsites in the immediate area.

Cohen Stadium is located in northeast El Paso. Take I-10 to US 54 (North-South Freeway) north to Gateway North Boulevard (Diana exit). The Stadium is right there. There is ample parking, which costs $1.50.

Box seats at field level cost $5.50, while general admission bench-style seats with backs go for $4.00.

For schedule of events and ticket information, call (915) 755-2000.

For tourist information, contact the El Paso Civic, Convention & Tourism Department, One Civic Center Plaza, El Paso, TX 79901, (915) 534-0696 or (800) 351-6024.

HOMETOWN STATS—EL PASO
The Last Ten Years

Affil.	Year	League	Wins	Losses	Attendance
MIL	1985	Texas	86	50	245,744
	1986		85	50	210,261
	1987		75	59	180,633
	1988		74	60	207,236
	1989		63	73	228,261
	1990		77	58	201,068
	1991		81	55	273,438
	1992		73	63	262,727
	1993		75	59	306,948
	1994		88	48	327,542

Jackson Generals

(Houston Astros)

Smith-Wills Stadium
1200 Lakeland Drive
Jackson, MS 39216

Jackson's very first team was a member of the Class D Delta League, which lasted only one year—1904. From 1905 to 1953, Jackson teams played in the Cotton States League, the Mississippi State League, the Dixie League, the East Dixie League, and the Southeastern League. Then, after a twenty-two-year absence from baseball, the city lured the New York Mets–owned Double-A Texas League Victoria Toros to town in 1975. In 1982, New York sold the Jackson Mets to businessman Con Maloney of Cowboy Maloney's Electric City (Mississippi's largest appliance and video dealership). Since then, the club has made the playoffs eight times, winning the league championship three times.

More than 130 Jackson players have gone on to the majors over the years. Among them are several of the 1986 World Champion Mets: Lee Mazzilli, Jesse Orosco, Darryl Strawberry, Rick Aguilera, Roger McDowell, Lenny Dykstra, and Wally Backman. Also Mookie Wilson, who married Rosa Gilbert here at home plate on June 22, 1978; following baseball tradition, they marched back to the dugout beneath an archway of bats held by teammates.

After the 1990 season, the Mets pulled out after Jackson's city council failed to commit to needed stadium improvements. Maloney quickly formed a new alliance with the Houston Astros and held a contest to name the new team. The "Jackson Generals" came out the big winner. A good choice, too, since the city is named after Andrew Jackson, the general (and seventh President of the United States).

Five-thousand-seat Smith-Wills Stadium is located in the midst of several parks, right next door to the Dizzy Dean Museum. The stadium opened in 1975, just in time for the Mets to take the field, and was renovated in 1992 to the tune of $2.5 million. It's a simple ballpark with a covered grandstand that stops just halfway to the bases on either side of home plate. This blue reserved section has theater-type seats. Bleachers extend from first and third down the foul lines. Concession stands on the concourse directly behind home plate serve up an abundance of standard fare. Or you can head over to the Hardball Grill behind the first base bleachers and get a fresh grilled hamburger, a grilled chicken sandwich, or a Big Smokey grilled sausage sandwich, which, according to one fan we know, is 110 percent fat and "the best damn sausage in the South."

In 1993, the team established a new club single-season attendance record on their way to the league championship, drawing 148,228 fans. They would top that in 1994. The fans here may be casual and relaxed, but they are also uninhibited and very vocal. The Human Siren, as one fan is called, distracts visiting players with his uncannily accurate imitation of an ambulance or police car siren. Then there are the third base bleacher bums whose duties, or so it seems, are to mercilessly razz the umpire and opposing team. And they do! And then there's the team mascot, Rally-Gator, the green gator who dishes out trouble and mischief.

Over the course of a season, the Gens (their nickname in Jackson) hold more than sixty-eight special home game promotions. The most well attended are the six postgame fireworks shows, the Diamond Dig Night, and the explosive appearance by Dynamite Lady. Giveaways include some of the best—baseball cards, baseballs, pennants, sunglasses, and floppy hats.

Fans are allowed in the park to watch batting practice, and if you're lucky the players will sign autographs. Everybody must clear the grounds, however, before the gates reopen one hour before game time. If you miss out before the game, you can always find the players afterward outside the clubhouse.

GETTING THERE

Jackson's historic downtown and its Agricultural Museum (a reconstruction of a 1920 Southern town) are the city's big draws. There are some nice hotels here, along with many motels and nearby campgrounds.

Smith-Wills Stadium is situated on the north side of town. To get there, take I-55 to the Lakeland Drive exit. Go east for one-eighth of a mile. There is plenty of free parking.

All reserved seats go for $5. General admission tickets cost $4. Kids, seniors, and the military get $1 off.

For schedule of events and ticket information, call (601) 981-4664.

For tourist information, contact the Metro Jackson Convention & Visitors Bureau, 921 North Presidents Street, Jackson, MS 39202, (601) 960-1891 or (800) 354-7695.

The Generals celebrate their 1993 league championship victory after dousing the El Paso Diablos 3–0 in a best-of-five series.

		HOMETOWN STATS—JACKSON *The Last Ten Years*			
Affil.	Year	League	Wins	Losses	Attendance
NYM	1985	Texas	73	63	132,021
	1986		72	63	118,894
	1987		70	66	131,248
	1988		61	75	134,967
	1989		61	74	87,153
	1990		73	62	124,142
HOU	1991		70	66	114,660
	1992		61	74	140,040
	1993		73	61	148,230
	1994		74	61	148,647

Midland Angels

(California Angels)

Max H. Christensen Stadium
4300 N. Lamesa Road
Midland, TX 79705

Midland had baseball on a steady basis from 1928, the city's first year with the Class D West Texas League, through 1959, the city's last year with the Class D Sophomore League. Lack of interest was the reason baseball left town. A mere 17,000 showed up in 1959. Then when the Texas League realigned its teams in 1972 the Chicago Cubs came to Midland, where they spent the next twelve years. In 1985, Midland became an affiliate of the California Angels.

The Midland franchise in western Texas draws from the smallest-population market in all of Double-A ball, but the club still manages to bring in an average of 3,000 fans each game. Major league pitcher Lee Smith wore the Midland uniform for two years in 1978 and 1979. Other big league luminaries include Devon White, Bryan Harvey, Shawon Dunston, Dante Bichette, and Tim Salmon.

Christensen Stadium (named after the man who brought baseball back to Midland after its thirteen-year absence) is a comfortable no-frills place that sits in a park area on the northeast side of town. Just inside the blue fence and simple facade is a wide concourse that wraps around the grandstand from first base to third. There is a grassy landscaped area off the right field foul line, where families can relax and kids roam about waiting to catch foul balls. Beyond the right field fence is a view of a golf course; oil rigs dot the view over left.

The atmosphere on game night is great; Midland fans turn out in a big way to support the players. Even if the Angels are trailing 10–1 in the bottom of the ninth, the crowd goes wild if one of their own gets a hit. The team mascot, Juice the Moose, a kind of Bullwinkle in sneakers and a jersey, is actually very agile. He can rouse the fans to chants or loud sing-alongs when the opposing pitcher is yanked and "Hit the Road, Jack" or "Happy Trails" blares over the loudspeakers.

GM Monty Hoppel and his staff book The Famous Chicken, the Phillie Phanatic, and Billy Bird for annual appearances. There are five fireworks shows and a laser light show during the season that pack the 5,000-seat park. Giveaways are plentiful—caps, umbrellas, bats, and once a year a TV is given away between each inning. There's always something going on. Sail a Frisbee through a small square window and win $2,000. Be chosen "Fan of the Night" and make a long-distance call on a cellular phone to anywhere in the U.S. from your seat (Hi Mom, guess where I am?). Early in the game, "The Best Seat in the House" is awarded to a lucky fan, who then sits out the game in a deluxe recliner; the big blue chair replaces six ordinary seats right below the press box. You might also be chosen to be a "Bleacher Creature"—you and three of your pals will get to sit on a raised deck area just beyond the dugout, complete with table, umbrella, and VIP waitress service. But here's our favorite, and it's not a contest. Haircuts! For $7.95, Supercuts from downtown Midland will cut your hair while you watch the game from the booth just off the press box. $1 goes to charity.

The favorite fan food here is the Frito Pie, which is a bowl of corn chips topped with lots of chili and melted cheese. Another big seller, "spicy spuds," are spicy thick-cut potato chips deep-fried while you wait. And if you come on one of those hot Texas nights, don't pass up the "ice cream in a helmet" (ice cream served in a small plastic replica helmet).

The park is open all day, but everybody has to clear out one hour and fifteen minutes before game time. The gates reopen after fifteen minutes—one

Although Midland players consistently make baseball exciting for fans, they have yet to capture a league title.

hour before the game. On Wednesday nights, there are four players who sign autographs on the concourse before the game.

GETTING THERE

Midland is a modern city whose two other main attractions (besides baseball) are the Museum of the Southwest and the Confederate Air Force Museum. (Both great for kids.) Accommodations are mostly motels, with a few campsites nearby.

Max H. Christensen Stadium is on the northeast side of downtown Midland. Take Rankin Highway (Big Spring Street) to Loop 250, then exit right at Lamesa Road to the stadium. There is plenty of free parking.

Box seats are $6, while reserved seats cost $5. General admission tickets go for $4. Kids and seniors get in for $2.

For schedule of events and ticket information, call (915) 683-4251.

For tourist information, contact the Midland Chamber of Commerce, 109 North Main Street, Midland, TX 79701, (915) 683-3381 or (800) 624-6435.

Affil.	Year	League	Wins	Losses	Attendance
	HOMETOWN STATS—MIDLAND				
	The Last Ten Years				
CAL	1985	Texas	59	77	127,836
	1986		62	71	129,674
	1987		75	61	137,910
	1988		61	74	133,105
	1989		70	66	135,518
	1990		56	80	168,742
	1991		67	68	180,616
	1992		61	72	195,629
	1993		67	67	196,464
	1994		61	75	190,022

San Antonio Missions

(Los Angeles Dodgers)

San Antonio Municipal Baseball Stadium
5757 Highway 90 W.
San Antonio, TX 78227

This San Antonio francise was a charter member of the Texas League in 1888. When the split came in 1903, San Antonio found itself in the South Texas League—but only until the leagues rejoined in 1907. And with the exception of a few years here and there, the city has been a Texas League member ever since. San Antonio teams have had many major league affiliations over the years—most recently the Cubs, Brewers, Indians, Rangers, and, since 1977, the Dodgers. They've been called the Missions since 1988.

The owner of the Missions is entrepreneur David G. Elmore, who, aside from his business dealings in insurance, real estate, and hotels, also owns the Triple-A Colorado Springs Sky Sox, the Class A San Bernardino Spirit, the Class A (short season) Eugene Emeralds, and the Rookie Idaho Falls Braves. Even though the Missions haven't been all that hot lately, the stadium is always at least 80 percent full, a record in the league. San Antonio fans have seen some great Texas League players come through on their way up. Pitcher Dennis Eckersley had his best year in his minor league career here in 1974 with fourteen wins and three losses, future Dodgers Steve Sax and Sid Fernandez were All-Stars here in 1981 and 1983, and Fernando Valenzuela pitched twenty-two games here in 1980 before skipping right up to L.A.

Located eight minutes from downtown, the San Antonio Municipal Stadium is brand-new. It seats 6,200 and has state-of-the-art skyboxes and a dot-matrix scoreboard. Lest you forget where you are, the entrance to the stadium has two one-hundred-foot-high mission bell towers. When you enter the stadium, you're standing high on the concourse level with a view down onto the field and stadium. There is usually a cool breeze that blows in from the Gulf and right into the batters' faces, making this a great pitcher's park. One relaxing feature about this place is the grass berm that hugs the left field wall. Beautifully landscaped, the grassy area is a favorite place for families to watch the game and play catch.

Special appearances by The Famous (and irreverent) Chicken pack San Antonio's Municipal Stadium. To the best of our knowledge, the bird has never been ejected from a game.

There are a lot of promotional nights here when fans are sent home with free baseball paraphernalia, but you can also score a cereal bowl or backpack. There are several postgame concerts, fireworks displays, and appearances by the Blues Brothers and The Famous Chicken. The Missions' version of Turn-Back-the-Clock Night has the teams in 1939 uniforms; admission is 50 cents for adults, 25 cents for kids.

This is San Antonio, so we would suggest that you chow down on the beef or chicken fajitas. The meat is marinated for twenty-four hours before it is grilled and heaped into a tortilla with all the spicy condiments. We think it's better than a dog any day. Well, maybe, unless the dog is one of the "double dogs" served here—one big bun that has two slits for two dogs. Or try the "catcher's mitt," a pita stuffed with beef or sausage and peppers, or a "puffy taco" (deep-fried).

Speaking of puffy tacos, that's what the Missions' team mascot is—a huge puffy taco called Henry with a tomato head and jalapeño feet. During the middle of the sixth inning, Henry races a kid around the bases. If the kid can tackle him and then beat him to home plate (as always seems to happen), he gets a T-shirt that says I TACKLED THE TACO.

The whole park is open during the day, and local businesses rent out luxury suites for catered lunches. The park closes at 4:00 P.M. on game days and reopens at 6:00 P.M. Autographs are easy to get at the autograph booth on the concourse before the game, or down by the dugouts after the game.

GETTING THERE

San Antonio, home of the Alamo and the world-famous River Walk, has added Sea World and Fiesta Texas amusement park to its list of must-dos. There are elegant hotels right on the River Walk, with motels and campgrounds nearby.

To get to San Antonio Municipal Stadium from downtown, take I-35 south to I-90 west. Get off at the Callaghan exit. The stadium is right there. There is ample parking, which costs $2.

Executive boxes cost $7. Box seats go for $6, reserved seats are $5, and general admission tickets cost $4. Kids and seniors get in for $2.

For schedule of events and ticket information, call (210) 657-PARK.

For tourist information, contact the San Antonio Convention & Visitors Bureau, P.O. Box 2277, San Antonio, TX 78298, (210) 270-8700 or (800) 447-3372.

HOMETOWN STATS—SAN ANTONIO *The Last Ten Years*					
Affil.	Year	League	Wins	Losses	Attendance
LAD	1985	Texas	59	75	106,183
	1986		64	71	122,261
	1987		50	86	122,277
	1988		73	60	130,899
	1989		49	87	158,402
	1990		78	56	180,931
	1991		61	75	185,336
	1992		62	74	177,365
	1993		58	75	189,251
	1994		62	74	411,959

Shreveport Captains

(San Francisco Giants)

Fair Grounds Field
2901 Pershing Boulevard
Shreveport, LA 71109

Shreveport fans have rooted for local professional baseball since 1895, when teams had names like "Gassers" and players like Bill Kemmer had batting averages like .405. Except for the Dixie years (1933, Dixie League; 1934, East Dixie League; 1935, West Dixie League), Shreveport baseball teams have played in either the Southern Association or the Texas League. The city was without baseball when the Southern Association (which they happened to belong to at the time) disbanded in 1961, but baseball came back in 1968 with the Atlanta Braves when the Texas League expanded from six teams to eight. When the California Angels took over the Shreveport Braves in 1971, they renamed the team the Captains in honor of the riverboat captains who once so ably served this port town on the Red River. The team has been affiliated with the San Francisco Giants since 1979.

The Captains have been owned by Taylor Moore since 1977. Moore gets involved not only with his players but with the fans as well. He manages to keep the prices down and has found time to hold focus groups with the fans to keep up with their wants and needs. One of their requests was the recent establishment of a no-smoking *and* alcohol-free section for families, which they got along the first base line.

The Captains have done well over the years, competing in virtually every playoff since the mid-1980s and winning the league championship in 1991. Some of the major league players who have honed their skills in Shreveport are pitchers Russ Swan and Terry Mulholland, catchers Steve Decker and Jim McNamara, and the multitalented out-fielder (and designated hitter) Mackey Sasser.

Fair Grounds Field was built in 1986 and seats about 6,200. It is part of the Louisiana State Fairgrounds, a complex that includes a football stadium. The stunning light blue facade is one hundred feet tall! Inside, the grandstand seating is compact, but a big foul area—fifty feet from the dugout to the baseline—gives the place a spacious feel. Even so, lots of foul balls go up and over the roof and into the parking lots. (Great place for kids to hang out, mitts ready.) One of the stadium's luxury features is the big, glass-enclosed Sky Box that holds up to eighty fans. It sits right behind home plate and, best of all, is air-conditioned! When the air is unbearably humid and the temperature hovers around ninety degrees at game time—which is 7:35 P.M. on weekdays—these seats are prime real estate. Beyond the outfield fence is I-20, but beyond the highway sits the Shreveport skyline.

Shreveport fans are a varied bunch. Some are extremely knowledgeable and come out because they follow the players, the league, and the game. Others come just to mingle in the beer garden down by the bullpen and to enjoy the contests and the promotions. They're in the oil business, cattle business, and light manufacturing, and lately they're in the gambling business from the riverboat casinos that tie up in Shreveport. Gambling has also increased tourism in Shreveport, so tourists are now filing through the gates as well.

Mega-events every season are the four fireworks displays and the Friday night concerts after the game in the beer garden. There are the usual giveaways every weekend, too!

Gates open one hour before game time. You can get autographs up on the concourse before the game, or after the game as the players leave the clubhouse.

GETTING THERE

Shreveport and sister city Bossier City across the Red River are modern cities noted for their Southern hospitality—and riverboat gambling. There are several nice hotels, some good motels,

The Captains led the league in fielding and pitching in 1994.

and about ten campgrounds right in the immediate area.

To get to Fair Grounds Field, take I-20 to the Louisiana State Fairgrounds at the Heame Avenue (US 171) exit. The parking lot is gigantic—and free.

If the air-conditioned Sky Box seats (right behind home plate) aren't totally booked, they sell for $10. Field box seats go for $6, and general ad-mission tickets cost $4. Kids, seniors, and military personnel get in for $3.

For schedule of events and ticket information, call (318) 636-5555.

For tourist information, contact the Shreve-port-Bossier Convention & Tourist Bureau, P.O. Box 1761, Shreveport, LA 71166, (318) 226-8884.

		HOMETOWN STATS—SHREVEPORT			
		The Last Ten Years			
Affil.	**Year**	**League**	**Wins**	**Losses**	**Attendance**
SFG	1985	Texas	72	64	56,025
	1986		80	56	183,560
	1987		78	57	233,524
	1988		74	62	234,587
	1989		75	61	210,669
	1990		65	68	204,872
	1991		86	50	206,540
	1992		77	59	207,925
	1993		66	69	203,479
	1994		73	63	199,465

Tulsa Drillers

(Texas Rangers)

Drillers Stadium
4802 East 15th Street
Tulsa, OK 74112

Tulsa just may hold the record for membership in leagues that disband after one year. The city's first time out was in 1905 with the Missouri Valley League, which promptly folded. In 1906, it was the South Central League; in 1907, the Oklahoma-Arkansas-Kansas League; in 1908, the Oklahoma-Kansas League; and then in 1912, the Oklahoma State League (which actually came back later in 1922). Tulsa ball clubs have been with the Texas League three times—the latest go-round began in 1977.

Tulsa's home team seems to have always been called either the Oilers or the Drillers. And oil is still big business in Tulsa, so don't expect a name change in the near future. Tulsa teams have produced some wonderful seasons and some great players. Eight Hall of Famers have come out of Tulsa, among them Dizzy Dean, Jake Beckley, Frank Robinson, and four-time Cy Young Award pitcher Steve Carlton. More recently, a very im-pressive bunch have made their way through town: Sammy Sosa, two-time All-Star pitcher Dave Righetti, Ranger outfielder Juan Gonzalez, Ron Darling—who at age twenty-one pitched in his first minor league game here—eleven-time Gold Glove first baseman Keith Hernandez, and pitcher Tom Henke are a few.

From 1959 to 1976, Tulsa was affiliated with the St. Louis Cardinals. The club signed with the Rangers in 1977. Through all those years home field was Oiler Park at the fairgrounds. Brand-new Drillers Stadium opened in 1981, but because the team shared it with the local football and soccer teams, artificial turf was installed to cut down on wear and tear. When the stadium was renovated in 1991, making it strictly a baseball park, owner Went Hubbard, who bought the team in 1986, wasted no time switching to natural grass. By the 1993 season, there was a real grass field and a new score-board, twice as big as the old one, in the outfield.

Like old Oiler Park, Drillers Stadium is located at the county fairgrounds. Fans like the park because even with its 10,744-seat capacity it has fan-friendly charm; the grandstand seating cups right around home plate. The ballpark is adjacent to the fairgrounds' race track. Often during a game you can hear the race being called and the horses thundering by. Lots of kids stand near the track and wait to catch the foul balls that fly out of the stands and head that way. Out over left field is a large super-market parking lot. When a good

Drillers teams may have struggled in 1993 and 1994, but Tulsa fans have broken their own attendance records both years.

This brightly lit stadium marquee is a colorful old-fashioned welcome.

wind blows out from home to left field, home run balls can go rolling right up to shoppers pushing grocery carts to their cars.

In April and May, the Drillers conduct baseball clinics for kids before the games and then invite them to stay—for free. There's some kind of promotion at virtually every home game, with lots of giveaways. A big one in 1993 was the night that pieces of the AstroTurf from the old field were given away. Special events might include appearances by the Teenage Mutant Ninja Turtles or the very special Dog and Frisbee Show.

Gates open about one and a half hours before game time. If you get there early you might catch the end of batting practice. It's also the best time to get autographs as the players slowly make their way off the field. They generally hang around until twenty to thirty minutes prior to starting time.

GETTING THERE

Northeastern Oklahoma, with Tulsa its focal point, is renowned for its rich Cherokee history and scenic rivers and lakes. Tulsa has some fine hotels, and there's a wealth of motels and campsites throughout the region.

Drillers Stadium is located on the County Fairgrounds three miles north of I-44 and one and a half miles south of I-244 at 15th Street and Yale Avenue. There is plenty of free parking.

Box seats cost $6.50. Reserved seats go for $5. General admission tickets are $3.50. Sundays through Thursdays, kids and seniors get $1 off.

For schedule of events and ticket information, call (918) 744-5901.

For tourist information, contact the Tulsa Convention & Visitors Bureau, 616 South Boston, Tulsa, OK 74119, (800) 558-3311.

		HOMETOWN STATS—TULSA			
		The Last Ten Years			
Affil.	Year	League	Wins	Losses	Attendance
TEX	1985	Texas	60	76	154,514
	1986		49	85	162,529
	1987		52	84	170,932
	1988		71	65	188,375
	1989		73	63	218,755
	1990		68	68	226,461
	1991		58	78	260,864
	1992		77	59	290,393
	1993		65	69	325,135
	1994		63	73	344,764

Wichita Wranglers

(Kansas City Royals)

Lawrence-Dumont Stadium
300 S. Sycamore
Wichita, KS 67213

Since the early 1900s, Wichita fans have turned out for teams like the Izzies, Aeros, Pirates, and Braves. The town's first team was a member of the Class C Western Association from 1905 to 1908. Local clubs then went on to play in either the Class A Western League or the Triple-A American Association until 1987, when the Wichita Pilots (with the San Diego Padres) came into the Texas League. The team took on the Wrangler nickname in 1989 and changed affiliates in 1995, signing on with the Kansas City Royals.

Baseball is in Wichita's blood, and some great players like the exciting shortstop/second baseman Roberto Alomar; All-Star pitcher Andy Benes; Cy Young Award winner Bruce Sutter; 1978 Gold Glove Award winner Chris Chambliss; and Eric Davis, who in 1984 recorded the highest batting average of his career in Wichita—.314—have all made baseball in Wichita exciting.

It is also in Wichita that a man named Raymond "Hap" Dumont founded the National Baseball Congress (NBC) in 1931. The NBC is an umbrella organization for adult amateur baseball. When old Island Park burned down in 1934, Dumont convinced the town to build a new stadium on the banks of the Arkansas (pronounced AR-KANSAS) River. Lawrence Stadium opened with 3,500 seats and has been the site of the NBC World Series in August and home to the local minor league team ever since. The stadium was renamed Lawrence-Dumont after Dumont's death in 1971.

When the Rich family came along and bought the Wranglers in 1989, the city of Wichita sank $5 million into renovations. These are the same Riches who own the Buffalo Bisons, so they know a thing or two about successful baseball clubs. The expanded 6,800-seat stadium is now a blend of tradition and state-of-the-art modern convenience. Some of the old lights remain, but there is a new roof over the grandstand, and though there is grass in the outfield, the infield is now, because of all the baseball in town, artificial turf.

They say there's not a bad seat in the park, but some are definitely better than others. The club seats, for instance, right behind the dugouts, include waitress service. Just past the first base bag is the Hard Ball Cafe, a three-level terraced dining area with tables and umbrellas. Just beyond is the OK Corral, a safe play area for kids, and the Hitching Post, a long back fence where parents can watch both the game and their kids.

You might get a break at the gate on Two-For-Tuesdays: 2 tickets, 2 hot dogs, and $2 worth of gas from the sponsor, Total Gasoline, for $10. Thursday is Dollar Day: hot dogs, soda, and beer cost only $1. The big events take place on the weekends, when the freebies include caps and helmets. Saturday night might feature fireworks displays, Turn-Back-the-Clock Night, or used car giveaways. The Famous Chicken or Phillie Phanatic might appear. Sundays are always Family Nights; kids get to run the bases after the game. And do they! As many as 300 have stormed the bags.

Wilber T. Wrangler, a big horse of a mascot, appears in a bright red cape over the outfield fence. The PA announcer spots him and shouts, "Look! It's Super Wilber!" For some reason, everybody goes nuts.

Gates open one hour before game time. The best place to get autographs is on the concourse behind home plate from 6:30 to 6:45 P.M., or by the dugouts after the game.

GETTING THERE

Wichita, home of Sheplers, "The World's Largest Western Store," is also home to the Old Cowtown Museum, a seventeen-acre open-air exhibit of Wichita life from 1865 to 1880. Wichita

Just beyond first base, fans can eat and drink at tables without missing any Wrangler action.

has some superb hotels and motels. Camping at nearby Lake Afton.

Lawrence-Dumont Stadium is located downtown. Take I-135 to Kellogg Avenue right downtown to Market Street. Take a right on Market to Lewis. Go left on Lewis over the river and into the park. There is plenty of free parking.

Club seats (with waitress service) cost $7. Box seats go for $6 and reserved for $5. General admission tickets cost $3.50. Seniors and kids under twelve get $1 off.

For schedule of events and ticket information, call (316) 267-3372.

For tourist information, contact the Wichita Convention & Visitors Bureau, 100 South Main Street, Wichita, KS 67202, (316) 265-2800.

HOMETOWN STATS—WICHITA *The Last Ten Years**					
Affil.	**Year**	**League**	**Wins**	**Losses**	**Attendance**
SDP	1987	Texas	69	65	150,952
	1988		60	76	70,525
	1989		73	63	176,424
	1990		67	68	218,109
	1991		71	64	200,217
	1992		70	66	210,990
	1993		67	68	236,378
	1994		54	82	210,482

*Statistics are given only for the years in which the team played in Wichita.

Class A Teams

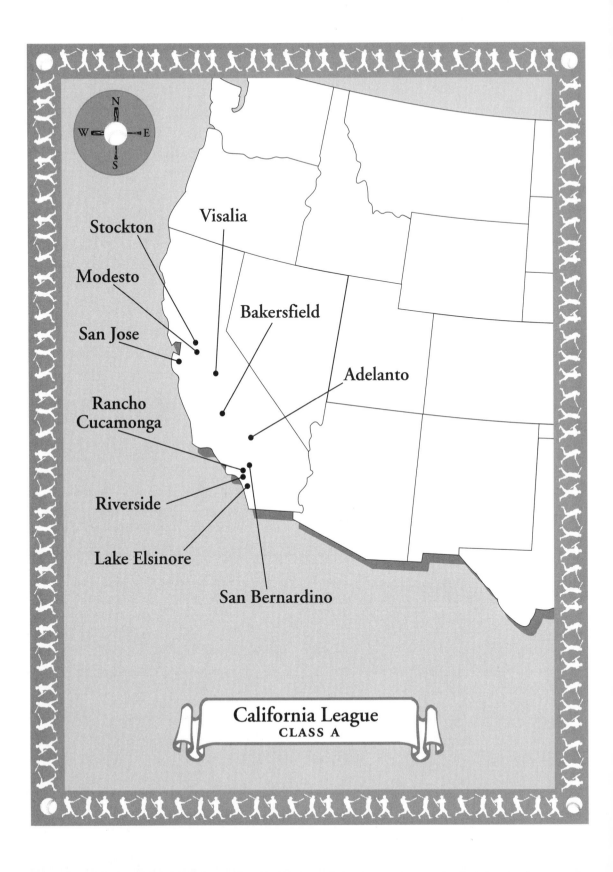

Stockton

Visalia

Modesto

Bakersfield

San Jose

Adelanto

Rancho
Cucamonga

Riverside

Lake Elsinore

San Bernardino

California League
CLASS A

California League

Class C 1941–1942, 1946–1962; Class A 1963–

The "old" California League was founded in 1891. It was sometimes referred to as the "Highway 99 League" because so many of its member cities stretched along this roadway, which ran through the heart of the California agricultural community from Stockton to Bakersfield. The league was doomed when four of its teams left in 1903 to found the Pacific Coast League. Others would eventually play in the California State League (1910, 1913–15, 1929).

The California League as we know it today was founded in 1941, ironically, by members of the Pacific Coast League, who had near-major league status at this time and were looking to form a Class C league in order to bring young, talented players to their own backyards. At the first California League meeting, franchises were awarded to Stockton, Riverside, San Bernardino, Bakersfield, Anaheim, Fresno, Santa Barbara, and Merced. San Bernardino and Riverside never finished the season. Play would be suspended the following year as more and more young men went to war. After the war, the league was reorganized into a Class A league and resumed play in 1946. Of the eight original cities Merced, Anaheim, and Santa Barbara are no longer represented.

The California League is made up of ten teams, which are scheduled to play 140 games during the regular season. First-half division winners play second-half division winners in a best-of-five series. If the same team wins both halves, it plays the team with the next best overall record in its division. Division playoff winners then play each other in a best-of-five series for the league championship.

Bakersfield Blaze

(COOP)

Sam Lynn Ballpark
4009 Chester Avenue
Bakersfield, CA 93301

In 1910 Bakersfield joined the Class D San Joaquin Valley League. That lasted one year. Another team tried in 1929 with the Class D California State League—that ended in a one-year stint, too. Finally, in 1941 the Bakersfield Badgers joined the California League as affiliates of the New York Giants, and they have been active off and on since then. The team became affiliated with Cleveland in 1946 and was renamed the Indians. 1954 marked the club's debut with the Dodgers—the Brooklyn Dodgers, that is. That affiliation dissolved after the 1956 season, resumed in 1960 with the Los Angeles Dodgers, and dissolved again in 1976. In 1984, the team hooked up yet again with Los Angeles, a relationship that lasted until 1995, when the Dodgers moved to San Bernardino.

The B-Dodgers, as they were called here until they renamed themselves the Blaze after the Dodgers left, are a story of struggle. They've played some up-and-down baseball for a few seasons, coming in second and third in the standings. In 1989 and 1990 they played in the league championships, winning in 1989. By 1992, they slipped to seventh in the overall standings with a 68 and 68 record. In 1993 they ended up with 42 wins and 94 losses, almost matching their all-time worst finish of 40 and 102 in 1986.

In spite of recent hard times (after all, that's baseball), Bakersfield has chalked up hundreds of golden moments, if not golden seasons, in its history. The club has produced more than 140 major league players, and some of them have truly been greats! Hall of Famer and Cy Young Award winner Don Drysdale and Cy Young Award winners Mike Marshall and Rick Sutcliffe were young ballplayers in Bakersfield. Other notables whom local fans have watched move up include six-time All-Star Ron Cey, World Series pitcher Juan Guzman, Dodger All-Star catcher Mike Piazza—who hit twenty-nine homers as a B-Dodger in 1991—and first baseman Eric Karros, who in 1989 led the Califor-

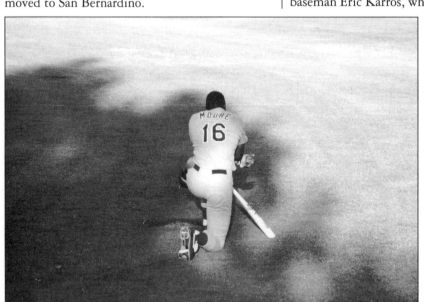

1993 Bakersfield outfielder Mike Moore waits his turn.

nia League with an incredible 1,232 putouts.

Sam Lynn Ballpark is a small place located just one mile north of downtown. Built in 1941, it sits amid a spread of Little League fields and tall cypress trees. The mighty Kern River flows about 100 feet beyond the outfield fence. The compact grandstand begins and ends at first and third bases and seats an average of 2,500 fans every night.

Between-inning lucky giveaways are big here. There's one night when an all-expenses-paid vacation is awarded *each inning*! On another night fans can win a color TV—one per inning. There are at least thirty giveaways per season, though not all as grand as the above. The bats, gloves, helmet banks, baseballs, and baseball cards are always of interest to the kids. Seat cushions, caps, gym bags, and mugs please the adults.

On-field contests are popular here, too. The Taco-Eating Competition is one that we haven't seen anywhere before. Three or four fans are picked to come down from the stands and chow down on platters full of tacos near home plate. Whoever can eat eight first is the winner. In another fun contest some lucky fan is handed a cellular phone right there in his or her seat and given the chance to call "anywhere, USA."

Gates open thirty minutes before game time. You can get autographs down by the dugouts before the game, or outside the clubhouse after the game.

GETTING THERE

Oil-rich Bakersfield, in the southern San Joaquin Valley, is also agriculturally rich; cotton, grapes, almonds, carrots, pistachios, and citrus are its most important crops. There are also many excellent Basque restaurants here. Hotels, motels, and resorts are plentiful. Camping is nearby.

To get to Sam Lynn Ballpark, take Highway 99 to the California Avenue exit. Go east three miles to Chester Avenue. Take a left onto Chester and go two miles to the stadium. The parking lot on the first base side is free.

Box seats are $5, and reserved seats (bench seats with backs) cost $3.

For schedule of events and ticket information, call (805) 322-1363.

For tourist information, contact the Greater Bakersfield Convention & Visitors Bureau, 1033 Truxtun Avenue, Bakersfield, CA 93301, (805) 325-5051 or (800) 325-6001.

| | | HOMETOWN STATS—BAKERSFIELD | | | |
| | | *The Last Ten Years* | | | |
Affil.	Year	League	Wins	Losses	Attendance
LAD	1985	California	65	80	74,054
	1986		40	102	78,635
	1987		78	65	109,120
	1988		71	71	92,360
	1989		82	60	123,572
	1990		80	62	142,280
	1991		85	51	147,655
	1992		68	68	156,233
	1993		42	94	149,095
	1994		69	67	141,505

High Desert Mavericks

Baltimore Orioles

Maverick Stadium
12000 Stadium Way
Adelanto, CA 92301

The Mavericks are as much a phenomenon as anything that manages to thrive in the desert. They were not doing all that well when they were the Red Wave playing in the lush environs of Riverside. In 1989 they were nineteen games back at the end of the season, and in 1990 they were twenty-six and a half games back in the overall standings. They drew only about 82,000 fans to boot. But after moving up here to the middle of arid nowhere in 1991 they took the league championship, beating Stockton three games to two and drawing over 204,000 fans. Go figure. The principle owners are the four Brett brothers. Yes, it is brother George who recently retired from Kansas City. It is brother Bobby, president of the team, who named it after his favorite TV Western character.

The Mavericks went on to take another league championship in 1993 as affiliates of the Florida Marlins. Major leaguer Tim Clark was a Maverick star that year and the league MVP. The parent team then moved the Class A championship franchise to the Florida State League in 1994. The Mavericks stayed in business, however, signing on as an affiliate of major league baseball for the 1994 season. Nineteen ninety-five marks their first year with the Orioles.

You can't miss Maverick Stadium when you turn off Highway 395. A bright turquoise roof makes it look like a jewel set against a backdrop of sagebrush and Joshua trees. The impressive San Bernardino Mountains tower on the horizon. This is a comfortable, modern stadium that puts fans close to the ac-

tion; the first row of seats is only about ten feet from the on-deck circle. Overlooking the Mavs' bullpen off the left field line is the Hard Ball Cafe, a popular vantage point for groups of twenty-five or more. There's a grass berm down the right field line, which is a favorite place for families to stretch out. Kids roam at will, and lots of foul balls find their way there. Since the town is at an elevation of 4,000 feet, game-time temp is usually a cool 75 to 80 degrees after a hot day of 100-degree-plus weather. The blue-black night sky is gorgeous, filled with seemingly millions of stars.

Mavericks fans are great, a mix of retired people and young workers, salt-of-the-earth types who love their team. Many of them commute "down the hill" to Los Angeles or Orange County every day and live here where they say the air is cleaner, housing is more affordable, and life seems "slower, safer, and saner." At the game, however, they are like fans anywhere, and they do go a little crazy.

As people come through the gate they get a white "K" card that measures 8½ by 11″. Every time a Maverick pitcher strikes out a batter, there are thundering cheers as everybody raises their card high. It's better than the wave! PA announcer Dan Hubbard adds spark to the maverick atmosphere with music bites and sound effects. As an opposing batter steps up to the plate you might, for instance, hear Bart Simpson saying "Aw man . . . I don't want to be here." The fans laugh, the batter gets a bit rattled—all is well. And here's a tradition that was new to us: At the end of the seventh inning, two concession guys dressed as chocolate chip cookies get up and dance a little number they call the "cookie crumble." Then they go into the stands with real cookies—and sell out every time.

The team mascot, Cow Bull Wooly Bully, has run off with everyone's heart, even though he constantly loses the fifth-inning race around the bases to a little kid. He tends to get waylaid—either he bumps into a player or someone distracts him with a basket of candy. One night the kid felt so sorry

Twice the league champs (1991 and 1993), the Mavericks hope for a comeback at Maverick Stadium in 1995.

for Wooly that he let him—actually made him—win by pushing him across the plate. The crowd was on its feet.

Giveaways take place on Friday and Saturday nights. There are about twenty-two per season, and they're a little different from most: you are likely to get a free cowboy hat or BBQ apron in addition to the usual ballpark freebies like gloves, T-shirts, bats, and so forth.

Gates open one and a half hours before game time. You can get autographs before the game at the "autograph pit" on the field, so get there early.

GETTING THERE

Adelanto, thirty-five miles north of San Bernardino, was founded in 1915 by inventor E. H. Richardson. This high desert town, known for its clear skies and cool nights, is close to snow skiing, water skiing, fishing, golf, tennis, and boating. Accommodations are limited to a few motels.

To get to Maverick Stadium, take I-15 to Highway 395 and then take 395 to Adelanto Road. You can't miss it. There is plenty of free parking.

The box seats in rows 1 through 8 are presold. Reserved seats cost $5, and general admission tickets are $3.50, $3 for kids and seniors.

For schedule of events and ticket information, call (619) 264-MAVS.

For tourist information, contact the Adelanto Chamber of Commerce, 17451 Raccoon Avenue, Adelanto, CA 92301, (619) 246-5711.

	HOMETOWN STATS—HIGH DESERT				
	The Last Ten Years*				
Affil.	Year	League	Wins	Losses	Attendance
SDP	1991	California	73	63	204,438
	1992		71	65	218,482
FLO	1993		85	52	191,697
MLB†	1994		45	91	171,783

*Statistics are given only for the years in which the team played in Adelanto.

†Major League Baseball.

Lake Elsinore Storm

(California Angels)

Lake Elsinore Diamond
500 Diamond Drive
Lake Elsinore, CA 92530

Baseball may be brand new (1994) to Lake Elsinore, but the Storm (formerly the Angels) isn't new at all. Owner Ken Stickney, son of the Rancho Cucamonga Quakes owner, Henry Stickney, moved the club here from Palm Springs, where it had been since 1986. As a long-time affiliate of the Angels, the team made some great contributions to major rosters. Big league pitchers Mike Butcher and Kirk McCaskill played in Palm Springs, as did Junior Felix and Ty Van Burkleo, who led the league with 22 homers and 108 RBIs

in 1986. But the prospect of a brand-new stadium and a larger fan market finally convinced Stickney to move the team to higher ground.

It wasn't easy. The Storm struggled at the start of 1994, scraping an all-time bottom when they were down 5 and 28. The team worked its way up to a still unimpressive 18 and 39. But no matter! The Storm finished in the middle of the pack but second in the league in unconditional love (attendance). Win or lose, the fans, nearly 5,000 a game, pour in. Even the local Blind Pig Brewery created "Class-A Ale" in honor of the team, and that beer is *the* one to drink at the park.

Lake Elsinore Diamond is a sight to behold. It looks like a turn-of-the-century landmark—brick facade, arched entries, green steel exposed girders and supports. If you glance back over your shoulder as you enter the view is the beautiful lake itself and the wild Ortega Mountains that separate you from the Pacific Ocean. It's exciting to walk around the

With Lake Elsinore at their backs, Storm fans file into The Diamond.

concourse before the game. A speed pitch, where you can measure your pitch against radar, Hockey Slap Shot and Basketball Free Throw games, plus brightly lit concessions and portable carts, turn the place into a festival. Rock 'n' roll, country tunes, and oldies are piped throughout, and the aromas of spicy smoke and grilled chicken permeate the air.

The grandstand starts at first base, cups around home, then hugs the field all the way down the third base line. Down the right field line is a grass berm, where for $3 a ticket you can spread your blanket, stretch out, and wait for the foul flies to sail over. At the very end of the left field line is the Diamond Club restaurant, which is open all day long, all year long. With terraced decks that overlook the field, this is a great place for taking in the park with or without a game going on. The whole place seats just over 8,000, and for a modern park it's an asymmetrical wonder. The outfield is as quirky as any old park that was built to fit an urban neighborhood: Imagine! Extreme right is 310 feet, right center is 338, and dead center is 395. Then, left center is 417, left of left 372, and extreme left 330. The angles make for some wild and unpredictable fielding and baserunning.

Lake Elsinore fans have literally taken the Storm by storm, swamping the stadium's souvenir shop to buy up anything with the team logo on it. So popular are the souvenirs that on one Cap Night when GM Kevin Haughian and staff had 2,000 replica caps to give away, 7,100 fans showed up. Other giveaways that draw crowds are bats, baseballs, and helmets. Fans also turn out for The Famous Chicken, who makes a yearly appearance. And of course fireworks extravaganzas pack the park.

Don't leave the stands during the seventh-inning stretch because the team mascot, a formidable eleven-foot-tall blue sea serpent named Hamlet, and five tiny kids dressed up like the Village People take over the field and dance to the song "YMCA." The mascot race is for real here: a fan races Hamlet for a $1,500 big-screen color TV. Even if the fan loses he still wins a Walkman. We like this win-win notion.

Gates open one and a half hours before game time. Most folks get autographs right down by the dugout next to the fence before the game.

GETTING THERE

Lake Elsinore is a pretty community, known at one time for its spas and mineral springs and now for lake recreation. It's east of the ocean town of San Juan Capistrano (where the swallows return every March 19th). Accommodations vary from moderately priced motels to deluxe resorts. There is lakeside camping.

To get to the Lake Elsinore Diamond take I-15 south from the L.A. area or north from the San Diego area. Exit at the Diamond Drive exit. Go about four blocks, and you'll see the stadium on your right. Parking is plentiful and costs $2.

Five-dollar box seats are available day of game. Reserved seats go for $4. General admission tickets (for the grass berm) cost $3, $2.50 for kids.

For schedule of events and ticket information, call (909) 245-4487.

For tourist information, contact the Lake Elsinore Valley Chamber of Commerce, 132 West Graham, Lake Elsinore, CA 92530, (909) 674-2577.

HOMETOWN STATS—LAKE ELSINORE *The Last Ten Years**					
Affil.	**Year**	**League**	**Wins**	**Losses**	**Attendance**
CAL	1994	California	65	71	357,123
Statistics are given only for the year in which the team played in Lake Elsinore.					

Modesto A's

(Oakland A's)

John Thurman Park
501 Neece Drive
Modesto, CA 95353

This is the team that in 1993 challenged the High Desert Mavericks for the California League championhip and lost. The series was exciting. The teams were tied through the sixth inning of the fifth and final game, but the Mavericks broke the tie in the seventh and went on to take the game by four runs. The A's are highly competitive (they took the 1982 and 1984 championships), and they carry on some heated rivalries. For example, they lost to the Stockton Ports in the 1985 and 1992 divisional playoffs, but then beat them in 1993 for the opportunity to take on the Mavericks.

Modesto baseball goes back further than this recent history, however. The hometown team in 1914 was the Colts, a member of the California State League. Since 1946, when Modesto joined the California League, fans have turned out for a succession of teams with names like the Modesto Cardinals, Reds, Yankees, and Rangers. This team has been the A's since 1975, and a veritable Who's Who of Baseball has played here in the last twenty years. Ten-time All-Star Rickey Henderson played here in 1977, and in 1985 Mark McGwire hit 24 home runs and 106 RBIs. Ironically, Tony La Russa and Reggie Jackson came through Modesto long before it was an A's affiliate. More recently, Brent Gates, Mike Bordick, Ernie Young, Fausto Cruz, and Eric Helfand have gone up.

John Thurman Stadium is a forty-year-old, 2,500-seat ballpark, a well-preserved vestige of the early California League. This kind of town park has almost disappeared from the American landscape. You drive down a tree-lined road to get here. There's a golf course on one side, a river on the other. The stadium is set back off the road and is surrounded by an eighteen-foot ivy-covered fence. Flowerbeds are all around. Bright lights and the sound of a live band playing on the concourse inside lure you past the old ticket booth (a cinderblock kiosk with wood-shutter windows that pull open with ropes) and through the turnstiles that are manned by the same two guys who, we are told, have been here for twenty years. (Their pay is $12 a game, so we're sure they're not in it for the money.) The concession concourse is small, bright, and as inviting as a street fair. Concessions and souvenir stands are right there, and nearby is the player photo booth, where for $2 you can have your picture taken with a player. Autographed, too (a portion of the proceeds goes to charity). There's a restored 1930s milk truck with a candy-striped awning that now serves as a beer wagon.

Right above the entrance to the grandstand is a huge Modesto A's logo and the words "WORLD CHAMPIONS BEGIN HERE." The grandstand is snug, with a few rows of seats that begin and end at the base bags. The closest is twenty feet from home plate. The farthest, well, it feels just about as close.

Modesto fans are actually quite polite. You seldom hear a boo for the ump or anybody else. They're pretty spoiled, too. Since Modesto is so close to Oakland (about an hour away as the crow flies), it's not uncommon for major league stars to rehabilitate here after an injury. In that case the park is packed. But the average turnout is a little over 1,600.

GM Tom Marting and staff guarantee fans a good time. Between innings there's live organ music, and kids run the bases for prizes. There's the Dizzy Bat Race, too. In Baseball Toss if a fan gets three balls through a hole in the target, he or she wins a getaway weekend to Oakland to see the big A's play. During Baseball Trivia the fan who answers the question correctly wins a squeeze bottle that looks just like a cellular phone *and* the chance to win a real one if he or she can answer a somewhat harder question. We like this trivia contest, by the way—all the questions are about the minor leagues. There are fireworks at least once a month, Hall of Famer Bob Feller does an occasional guest appearance, and so does a new performance group called The Dangerous Dinosaurs. There are lots of giveaway nights when good freebies go to the first 500 to arrive.

Gates open one hour before game time. The best place to get autographs is along the third base line before the game.

GETTING THERE

Modesto is 2½ hours west of Yosemite in the San Joaquin Valley—the historic Mother Lode gold country lies between. There are several moderately priced motels, a few bed-and-breakfasts, and a good selection of campgrounds.

To get to John Thurman Stadium from Highway 99, take the Tuolumne/B Street exit. Go one block west to Neece Drive. Turn left and go a quarter-mile to park. There's plenty of free parking.

Reserved seats are $5. General admission tickets cost $3.50; kids get $1 off.

For schedule of events and ticket information, call (209) 529-7368.

An aerial view reveals the rural setting but not the extensive renovations that have enhanced John Thurman Park for the 1995 season.

For tourist information, contact the Modesto Convention & Visitors Bureau, 1114 J Street, Modesto, CA 95353, (209) 577-5757.

HOMETOWN STATS—MODESTO					
The Last Ten Years					
Affil.	**Year**	**League**	**Wins**	**Losses**	**Attendance**
OAK	1985	California	76	68	73,661
	1986		69	73	72,757
	1987		79	63	78,357
	1988		54	88	71,500
	1989		56	86	87,256
	1990		59	82	62,089
	1991		68	68	77,287
	1992		79	57	104,671
	1993		72	64	100,016
	1994		96	40	109,314

Rancho Cucamonga Quakes

(San Diego Padres)

The Epicenter
8408 Rochester Avenue
Rancho Cucamonga, CA 91730

It takes a lot of guts to name a California baseball team the "Quakes," and then design its logo with the letters splitting apart as if along a fault line. And it takes a formidable sense of humor to name that team's stadium the "Epicenter." Wait, it gets better. The team mascot, "Rallysaurus," is called . . . TREMOR!!

Henry Stickney, the majority owner of the Quakes, also owns the Las Vegas Stars of the Pacific Coast League. There are several minority owners as well, including the actor Mark Harmon. In 1986, they bought the Class A Ventura Gulls, then moved the team to San Bernardino, where they played as the Spirit from 1988 until 1992.

When the team moved to Rancho Cucamonga in 1993 and switched their affiliation from the Seattle Mariners to the San Diego Padres, the fan response was greater than anyone expected; better than 330,000 showed up for that inaugural season. The Epicenter is only fifty miles from Dodger Stadium, and Stickney is quick to point out that many of the Quakes fans are ex–Dodger fans who are fed up with the traffic, crowds, high prices, and hassles of a typical L.A. game these days. The fans came from all over southern California, and by June of the first year they were filing in at an average of 4,500 each game. By June 1994, 5,700 fans were turning out for each game, all but packing the 6,100-seat stadium.

The Epicenter is part of a sports complex in a parklike setting of three softball fields, one Little League field, and two soccer fields. The ballpark has a traditional California welcoming feel to it with its three-story facade, arched entrances, palm trees, Spanish tiles, and colorful flags flapping in the wind. The spacious grandstand hugs the diamond from just beyond first base to just beyond third. The skyboxes sold out almost as soon as the stadium opened, but you can sit in the cafes at either end of the grandstand. For a $5 Cafe ticket you can watch the game and get fresh-grilled sausages and peppers, chicken burritos, nachos, even hot dogs and hamburgers. Beyond the cafes down by the bullpens is the Terrace seating (some stadium seats, some benches with backs). And beyond the outfield fence is a fantastic view of the farmland and vineyards that surround the park. Mount Cucamonga, seven miles away, and the magnificent San Bernardino Mountains rise in the distance.

Tremor, the extraordinary six-foot-seven-inch mascot Rallysaurus, is all teeth and snout in a uniform bearing the Richter-scale number 4.8. Other characters in the park are Mr. and Ms. Trash, who walk around in tuxedos picking up, well, trash. The Famous

RANCHO CUCAMONGA

Quakes™

PROFESSIONAL BASEBALL CLUB

The Quakes' John Thompson, a California League All-Star in 1994, makes the play at first.

A rare moment: Tremor stops for a photo.

Chicken makes an appearance during the season, too.

There are lots of premium giveaway nights—pennants, caps, minibats, and our favorite, kazoos. Not only does the club host several impressive postgame fireworks shows during the summer, but fireworks light up the sky after every Quakes home run and victory. One of our favorite promotions is what the Quakes call Sports Heroes Night: one Wednesday each month fans get to meet and talk with some of the greats, like Hall of Famer Orioles third baseman Brooks Robinson, or Cy Young Award–winning pitcher Rollie Fingers, or the great Dodger All-Star Tommy Davis. There's lots of time for autographs and pictures, too.

Gates open one hour before game time. You can get autographs before the game down by the dugouts, or after the game outside the clubhouses.

GETTING THERE

Ontario, just south of mainly residential Rancho Cucamonga, is a big convention city in the Inland Empire with over 3,100 hotel and motel rooms in various price ranges. There's a good assortment of campgrounds in the area. The San Gabriel Mountains lie just to the east.

The Epicenter is part of the Rancho Cucamonga Sports Complex. Take I-10 to I-15 North to Foothill Boulevard. Exit left to Rochester Avenue and then left to Stadium Way. There is parking throughout the complex, as well as additional parking east of the stadium, which costs $2.

Super box seats, which include waitress service, cost $6, and regular box seats are $5. View seats are $4 and the bench seats and Terrace seats are $3.

For schedule of events and ticket information, call (909) 481-5252.

For tourist information, contact the Greater Ontario Visitors and Convention Center, 421 North Euclid Avenue, Ontario, CA 91762, (714) 984-2450.

	HOMETOWN STATS—RANCHO CUCAMONGA *The last Ten Years**				
Affil.	**Year**	**League**	**Wins**	**Losses**	**Attendance**
SDP	1993	California	64	72	331,005
	1994		77	59	386,633

Riverside Pilots

(Seattle Mariners)

Riverside Sports Center
1000 Blaine Street
Riverside, CA 92507

In 1992 this team was still the Silver Sox, playing ball in Reno, Nevada, where the California League had had a team since 1955. The Sox suffered a couple of bad seasons there as independent affiliates of Major League Baseball. They finished $54^{1}/_{2}$ games back in 1988 and 33 back in 1991. After the 1992 season they signed with the Seattle Mariners, moved to Riverside, and changed their name to the Pilots. Riverside fans were thrilled. After forty years of hometown baseball, they had gone two summers without the game. Their last team, the Red Wave, moved out in 1991 to become the High Desert Mavericks, and these folks were starved for baseball.

Opening day 1993 was a big deal. The actor Robert Wagner and the comic Billy Crystal, who owned pieces of the team, were here, and Crystal threw the first pitch. The Pilots went on to do pretty well that first season, too (much better than they had done the year before in Reno, where they finished with a 65–71 record). Here they finished in second place in the first half of the season and tied for first in the second half.

Riverside Sports Center is a 3,500-seat stadium located on the tranquil and tree-filled University of Riverside campus. The old-fashioned grandstand tucks up close to the field, and foul balls regularly fly out of the park and into the lot outside, where a dozen or more kids wait for the chance to catch one. The concession concourse is small but manages to put out some of the best-tasting grilled burgers and dogs. The fans are consistent if not profuse, showing up at an average of 1,300 per game (we think the smaller numbers might have something to do with a no-beer-here city ordinance).

The giveaways every Friday and Saturday night are big draws. New bats, balls, gloves, helmets, baseball cards, and so forth go home with the first 500 who come through the gate. Members of the Co-Pilots, the team's kids club, can come to a free baseball clinic during the season and get into all Sunday games free. Little Leaguers in uniform always get in free, too. On Mothers Day 497 zirconia "diamonds" and three real diamonds are given away at random to moms as they come through the gates. At every game the Pilots' mascot, Homer Hound Dog, appears anywhere and everywhere. One on-field contest that we like is the Hot and Cold Ticket Search. Airline tickets for some getaway vacation lay out on the infield in plain sight of everybody except the contestant, who has been blindfolded and led out onto the field. He/she begins searching for the prize with only the help of the fans in the stands, who yell YOU'RE HOT, YOU'RE COLD. The blindfolded one has ninety seconds to find the dream vacation.

Gates open one hour before game time. Autograph seekers have great access to the players, who will sign autographs next to the fence down the third base line before the game.

GETTING THERE

Riverside is a beautiful city that has wisely preserved its turn-of-the-century buildings. The first navel oranges from Brazil were planted here—the rest is history. There are luxury hotels (including the famous Mission Inn), economical motels, and camping.

Riverside Sports Center is located on the campus of the University of Riverside. From Highway 60, take the Blaine Street exit and head north. The left field wall is right on Blaine Street. Parking is free.

Reserved seats are $5. General admission tickets cost $3, $2 for kids, seniors, and the military.

Homer Hound Dog, Riverside's mascot, tests the umpire's vision.

For schedule of events and ticket information, call (909) 276-3352.

For tourist information, contact the Riverside Visitors & Convention Bureau, 3443 Orange Street, Riverside, CA 92501, (909) 787-7950.

Affil.	Year	League	Wins	Losses	Attendance
SDP	1988	California	85	57	60,509
	1989		64	78	80,154
	1990		64	78	82,420
SEA	1993		76	61	68,821
	1994		87	49	85,358

HOMETOWN STATS—RIVERSIDE
The Last Ten Years*†

*Statistics are given only for the years in which the team played in Riverside.

†Riverside did not have a team from 1991 to 1993.

San Bernardino Spirit

(Los Angeles Dodgers)

John A. Fiscalini Field
1007 E. Highland Avenue
San Bernardino, CA 92404

In 1913, San Bernardino's new Class D Southern California League baseball team, the Kittens, didn't make it through their first season—it folded by mid-July. Another one, the Padres, tried in 1929 as members of the California State League, but quit in June when the league disbanded. Then in 1941 fans got the team that would stay, or so they thought: the Stars, part of the Pacific Coast League's Hollywood Stars farm system. But they didn't finish the season, either. The Anaheim Valencias played here from 1948 to 1950, then they left too. San Bernardinans finally got a team bent for success in 1987 when the Ventura Gulls moved into town, renamed themselves the Spirit, and stayed! For six years, anyway. 1988 was an exciting year; fans saw Ken Griffey Jr. play fifty-eight games before he moved up. And in 1989 and 1990, the fans broke their own team attendance records.

In 1993 the Spirit moved to Rancho Cucamonga, and the Salinas Spurs moved in. The Spurs had been a struggling coop team since 1987, averaging less than 60,000 annual attendance. They were eager to move into a new market, take the Spirit name, and carry on the momentum. However, the team's owners, David Elmore and Donna Tuttle, who also own the Colorado Springs Sky Sox and the San Antonio Missions, among other teams, didn't foresee the reaction of the fans to the loss of their first real team; the locals were downright depressed. Even though the new Spirit had the up-and-coming eighteen-year-old pitcher from Japan, Makato (Mac) Suzuki, who was throwing 96-mph aces, and even though they were playing well, almost winning their first half-season in 1993, the fan turnout limped in at 88,000. By midseason of '94, however, fans were bouncing back and attendance was up 35 percent over 1993. And there's more good news! The Spirit will play in a brand-new downtown stadium by the end of 1995. Stay tuned.

In the meantime, John A. Fiscalini Field, an old 3,200-seat place, built in the 1940s as part of Perris Hill Park, will remain home field. The classic open grandstand starts and stops just beyond the base bags. There's a patio cafe down off first and a sports bar off third. Over the outfield wall is a nostalgic California landscape. Huge pine trees stand in a thick grove from the left field foul pole to left center, and bushy oleander trees hug the rim of the fence all the way to right center. In late spring the sweet fragrance of thousands of pink and white oleander blossoms wafts into the park, along with the smells of the new-mown grass and pine—it's no wonder that the young man went west! Beyond the right field

The picnic area at Fiscalini Field offers a relaxed view of the game.

fence is a tree-covered hill that envelopes half the stadium and is a favorite campsite for home run scouts, who get a free game pass for every returned ball. With dead center only 387 feet, there are lots of homers here (166 in 1993), and a kid could retrieve enough for a general admission season ticket. The concession area is snug. Sometimes there are lines, but the roasted (over coals) corn is worth the wait; peel off the husk yourself and slather it with butter (or not). Yes!

Spirit fans are a good mix of those who really know baseball and folks just out for a good time. During the game, however, everyone is paying attention, focused on the field. Between innings they get to go a little nuts. There are Bat Races, Beat the Bug Races, and Horse Races over the outfield fence. The team mascot, the Spirit Bug, an extraordinary dancer in a Spirit uniform with a large foam baseball head sprouting antenna, does his moves on top of the dugout. Sometimes he's Elvis Bug, or Phantom of the Opera Bug, or Bat Bug, or Zorro Bug. Monday is Splash for Cash Night—contestants get to go kiddie-pool "diving" for hundreds of dollars' worth of coins. On Tuesday, get in for $1 with the sponsor's coupon. Wednesday is fifty-cent beer and soda night, and Friday and Saturday—giveaways! To the first 500 go the balls, bats, squeeze bottles, T-shirts, caps, and more.

Gates open one hour before game time. Players will sign autographs down by the dugouts before the game.

GETTING THERE

San Bernardino is Riverside's "sister city" and home to the National Orange Show. More than 280 acres of parks, lakes, and recreation areas lie within the city limits. There are hotels, motels, and inns, and resorts and several campgrounds are close by.

To get to John A. Fiscalini Field, take I-10 to 215 North to 30 East to the Waterman exit. Go right on Waterman to Highland Avenue. Take a left on Highland, and you'll see the board marquee for the field. There's limited parking, which is free. On-street parking is easily accessible.

Super box seats behind home cost $5. Regular box seats behind the dugouts are $4. Reserved go for $3.50. General admission is $3, $2 for kids and seniors.

For schedule of events and ticket information, call (909) 881-1836.

For tourist information, contact the San Bernardino Convention & Visitors Bureau, 201 N. E Street, San Bernardino, CA 92401, (909) 889-3980 or (800) TO-RTE-66.

Affil.	Year	League	Wins	Losses	Attendance
IND	1987	California	70	72	158,896
SEA	1988		74	68	154,653
	1989		83	59	184,791
	1990		77	65	190,890
	1991		54	82	187,895
	1992		52	84	106,469
IND	1993		62	74	88,468
	1994		48	88	101,710

HOMETOWN STATS—SAN BERNARDINO
The Last Ten Years*

*Statistics are given only for the years in which the team played in San Bernardino.

San Jose Giants

(San Francisco Giants)

Municipal Stadium
588 East Alma Avenue
San Jose, CA 95112

Royce Clayton, a San Jose Giant in 1990, runs home.

San Jose fans got hooked on baseball when their team, the Dukes, played a great season that finished with an impressive ninety wins and fifty-seven losses. That was back in 1891. Nearly fifty years later, in 1942, San Jose joined the California League only to have play suspended due to World War II. The city came back into the league in 1947, and San Jose has been home to a string of teams ever since: the Owls, Red Sox, JoSox, Pirates, Expos, Missions, and the team with perhaps the longest-running nickname, the Bees (1962–76 and 1983–87). In 1988, when the club signed on with San Francisco, they not only became the San Jose Giants, but became relentless winners, making the division playoffs four years in a row.

Well over 100 San Jose players have made it to the major leagues. Former Bees and Missions include George Brett, Jamie Quirk, Steve Howe, Ruppert Jones, and Dave Henderson. Players from the SJ-Giants roster include Royce Clayton, Steve Hosey, and talented pitchers like Rod Beck—who went 11–2 here in 1989—and Kevin Rogers, who finished with a 14–5 record when he played here in 1990.

It's not just players that have gone up, either. San Jose saw annual attendance jump from 69,000 in 1987, when the team was unaffiliated, to 108,000 in 1988. Since 1992, the SJ-Giants have drawn over 130,000 fans a year. Fans come from all over the area, including San Francisco, Oakland, Salinas, and Monterey. Much has to do with the innovative efforts of the SJ-Giants owners, but the team has also benefited from close proximity to the City by the Bay, with its Giants fever.

Locally, fans refer to the 5,500-seat San Jose Municipal Stadium, or Muni, as "the gateway to San Francisco." It is located in a pretty residential area near the San Jose State athletic fields and Kelley Park, which houses a kids' petting zoo, a formal Japanese garden, and the community ice rink. The grandstand is small, only twenty-four rows or so, and it stops at first base and third. The Santa Cruz Mountains sprawl on the horizon over the right field fence. Down the third base line is Turkey Mike's Barbecue, named after the great New York Giants hitter, (Turkey) Mike Donlin, whose six hits sparked the Giants to victory in the 1905 World Series matchup against the Athletics. About forty picnic tables accommodate groups of twenty-five or more, and you can get fresh grilled chicken, ribs, burgers, sausages, turkey burgers, fish steaks, swordfish kabobs, and more.

There are not many giveaway promotions

here, but fans have lots of fun anyway. Catch a foul ball and win a free pizza. At the bottom of the sixth inning there's Pitch for Cash (ye old baseball-through-the-hole trick). During the seventh-inning stretch there is Smash for Cash, something we haven't seen in too many parks. A big truck pulls up into right field, and three players, who have been matched up with three fans, get two chances to hit a ball and bust a headlight. If the player succeeds, the fan wins big money.

The SJ-Giants don't have a mascot, but they still have a traditional mascot race. The challenge of running the bases against a kid from the stands falls to assistant GM Buzz Hardy, and so the event is called Buzz the Bases. Just as in other mascot races, Buzz starts walking from second while a kid starts running from home. Players and umps do everything they can to distract and detain Buzz, who needless to say rarely wins. San Jose, by the way, has a fan who claims to have invented the wave. Krazy George is his affectionate nickname, and he is a fixture here. Besides getting a wave going, he can singlehandedly get the crowd chanting "GO GIANTS GO!"

Gates open one and a half hours before game time. For autographs, there is usually a table set up for twenty minutes before the game. You can also get them down by the dugouts before and after the game.

GETTING THERE

San Jose, capital of the Silicon Valley, has a language all its own, so the convention bureau has put out a glossary to help us ("end users") "interface with the natives." There are first-class hotels, myriad motels, and RV campgrounds right in town.

To get to Municipal Stadium, take I-280 to S. 10th Street; go west on 10th to Alma Avenue; south on Alma to the stadium. Or take U.S. 101 to Tully Road; go north on Tully to Senter Street, and east on Senter to the stadium. There is plenty of parking, which costs $2.

Box seats cost $6. General admission tickets are $5 for adults, $2 for kids and seniors.

For schedule of events and ticket information, call (408) 297-1435.

For tourist information, contact the San Jose Convention & Visitors Bureau, 333 West San Carlos Street, San Jose, CA 95110, (408) 295-9600.

	HOMETOWN STATS—SAN JOSE *The Last Ten Years*				
Affil.	Year	League	Wins	Losses	Attendance
IND	1985	California	55	88	53,423
	1986		65	77	87,235
	1987		33	109	69,120
SFG	1988		91	52	108,386
	1989		81	61	108,458
	1990		74	68	108,478
	1991		92	44	123,905
	1992		78	56	135,891
	1993		79	57	133,138
	1994		74	62	131,091

Stockton Ports

(Milwaukee Brewers)

Billy Hebert Field
Sutter and Alpine Streets
Stockton, CA 95204

Stockton was a charter member of both the "old" California League of 1891 and the "new" California League of 1941. The city, located in northern California in the San Joaquin Delta, is the largest inland port west of the Mississippi. And so the nickname.

Since the Ports signed on with the Milwaukee Brewers back in 1979, the team has played in an unbelievable thirteen divisional playoffs and has won the league championship four times. Some terrifically talented players came through Stockton in the 1980s. Pitcher Mike Warren won nineteen games here in 1982, and Bill Wegman finished with sixteen wins in 1983. Brewers first baseman John Jaha hit twenty-five home runs for the Ports in 1989. And there are others—catcher Dave Nilsson, outfielder Troy O'Leary, second baseman Bill Spiers.

The team's logo, the Mighty Casey at the Bat, has a good story to go with it. Stockton lays claim to being *the* Mudville referred to in Ernest Lawrence Thayer's poem "Casey at the Bat." Even though Thayer always claimed that the poem was not based on fact, there was a team in Stockton in the late 1800s that played on a field on Banner Island, nicknamed Mudville because of its sloshy conditions; the team itself was nicknamed the Mudville Nine. There were players with the names Flynn, Blake, and Cooney, the same as in Thayer's poem. Thayer himself lived in nearby San Francisco and worked for the *Examiner*, which published his poem on the editorial page. The similarities are too many for locals not to believe that the mighty Casey is theirs.

Billy Hebert Field is named after a well-known California League baseball hero who lived in Stockton and unfortunately was the city's first casualty in World War II. Located inside Oak Park, the cozy 3,500-seat stadium is surrounded by softball fields. The view from the stands is pretty—green and lush—and a breeze blows in off the delta, which keeps the temperature quite comfortable. Grandstand seating stops at first and third bases, and bleachers extend down both baselines. The small concourse extends from behind home plate to third base. (Be sure to try a Casey Dog; it's a foot long.) Down the left field foul line is the Casey BBQ, a three-tiered open-air deck with picnic tables that can handle up to 200 people. For twelve bucks you can get a chicken dinner and the game. Foul balls fly everywhere, including into the parking lot.

One of the quirks of this park is the location of the clubhouse—out beyond the center field wall. One of the billboards actually hides the gate in the outfield wall. It's calming to watch the players as they take the long walk across the field after a game and disappear into the fence. Not so calming for a visiting pitcher who gets yanked, however. He has to walk around the warning track under everybody's watchful gaze. As the gate swings open for his departure the PA announcer blasts a slow-creaking door sound, and when the gate closes behind the pitcher there's the inevitable SLAM. The crowd cheers! There is no mercy in Mudville!

About 1,700 extroverted fans show up each game night. Most of them are here from the start, too—everybody up and singing the National Anthem, then cheering the first pitch. At every home game, two Fans of the Game are chosen at random at the gate and escorted to special wooden seats (originally from Wrigley Field). Then in the middle of the first inning Casey the Mascot, a guy with a big head and belly who looks like a 1900s ballplayer, delivers flowers, seat cushions (vintage wooden seats can be a bit uncomfortable), caps, and a BBQ boxed supper. There's also the Pizza

Yell (like the Pizza Scream—the fan with the loudest mouth wins the pizza). Dizzy Bat Race, and Casey Race at every game. And twenty-one giveaway nights per season, too.

Gates open one hour before game time. You can get autographs before the game down by the dugouts.

GETTING THERE

Stockton, the heart of San Joaquin County and its largest city, is surrounded by 1,000 miles of winding California Delta waterways. It is one of the most fertile regions anywhere. Although the city has a few hotels, accommodations are mostly motels. There's camping twelve miles to the north in Lodi.

To get to Hebert Field, from I-5 north take the March Lane exit. Go right for three miles to El Dorado. Take another right to Alpine. Turn left on Sutter and go three blocks to the stadium. From Highway 99, take the Hoover Lane exit and go west two miles to West Lane. Take a left and go three miles to Alpine. Go right on Alpine for three-quarters of a mile to the stadium. There is plenty of free parking.

Reserved seats are $6, and general admission tickets cost $5, $2.50 for kids and seniors.

For schedule of events and ticket information, call (209) 944-5943.

For tourist information, contact the Stock-

Mascot Casey joins the conference on the mound.

ton/San Joaquin Convention & Visitors Bureau, 46 West Fremont Street, Stockton, CA 95202, (209) 943-1987.

		HOMETOWN STATS—STOCKTON *The Last Ten Years*			
Affil.	Year	League	Wins	Losses	Attendance
MIL	1985	California	82	63	69,334
	1986		83	59	56,129
	1987		94	48	61,794
	1988		94	49	58,586
	1989		89	53	72,734
	1990		82	59	85,436
	1991		71	65	90,126
	1992		81	53	112,348
	1993		79	57	108,629
	1994		54	82	114,013

Visalia Oaks

(COOP)

Recreation Park
440 N. Giddings Avenue
Visalia, CA 93291

Since 1946, Visalia fans have turned out for California League teams like the Cubs, Hollywood Stars, Reds, A's, White Sox, Mets, Minnesota's legendary farm club, the Visalia Oaks, and most recently the Central Valley Rockies. From 1977 through 1992 local fans saw the Oaks go to two division playoffs and into seven battles for the league championship (winning in 1978; losing from 1980 to 1983, 1986, and 1992). Future Twins star Kirby Puckett was League Player of the Year in 1983, and a young Kent Hrbek was MVP when he played here in 1981.

In 1993, after fifteen years with Minnesota, Visalia signed on as the Class A team for Colorado. The then-new name, Central Valley Rockies, honored Visalia's location smack in the middle of the great San Joaquin Valley, the agricultural belt of California. Unfortunately, the team didn't do all that well their first year. Although they had a good solid second half, the first half was downright miserable. CV fans did, however, get to see their pitcher, Marcus Moore, make it to the big leagues. When the Rockies pulled out after the 1994 season, the franchise went back to using the Visalia Oaks name.

Recreation Park is straight out of a Norman Rockwell painting, sitting as it does in the center of a lush public park just two blocks northwest of downtown Visalia. There is no facade per se; only a chain-link fence surrounds it. The park was built for 2,000 back in 1946, and it still seats 2,000. This is a wonderful place to watch baseball; every seat feels as if it's right on the field.

The stands fill up early. Sometimes three generations of the same family show up together. These fans get close to the young players, keep statistics, and follow their careers; they love baseball, pure and simple. Management makes sure they have a good time, too. Some promotional nights are like festivals. On Tijuana Taxi Night, for instance the real (so to speak) Tijuana taxi cruises the infield, and the whole place,

After the 1992 season, Visalia's third baseman, Scott Stahoviak, went on to Double-A and then to Minnesota for his first stint in the majors in 1993.

including the concessions, turns Mexican for the evening. Even on regular nights there is an air of celebration here. Despite the fact that Visalia is primarily an agricultural community that is struggling economically, about 1,300 spectators show up for each game. On a hot and dry summer's night (95 degrees average), baseball is often the best entertainment in town that also offers an opportunity to socialize with friends and neighbors.

The club sponsors baseball clinics for kids—and from Sunday to Thursday Little Leaguers get in for free. The kids usually head for the bleachers down the field lines, as those are the best seats for catching foul balls. We noticed that the parking lots outside the park also attract a bunch of well-gloved future minor league ballplayers.

Giveaways are the usual baseball fan goodies. If you come on Free Baseball Night you'll even get one with an autograph. There are a couple of unusual game-time traditions here, too. One is Beachball Volleyball between innings. If the crowd can keep the ball in the air, *and* keep it in the stands, *and* away from the ushers, everybody in the crowd gets any size soda, including large, for $1. The Strikeout Beer Batter of the Game is great too (unless you are the chosen batter, of course). It works like this: A visiting player is designated the Strikeout Batter for the Night. Every time a hometeam pitcher strikes him out, everybody in the stands gets a beer or soda for half-price. The place goes absolutely bananas trying to distract the poor guy at the plate!

Gates open one hour before the game. Come early if you want to get autographs down by the dugout.

GETTING THERE

Visalia, "gateway to Sequoia National Park," is the oldest city between Stockton and Los Angeles. Rich in the lore of the West, from its days as frontier fort through the stagecoach and cattle baron era, Visalia is now an agricultural center. Accommodations consist mostly of motels.

To get to Recreation Park, take Highway 198 into Vasalia and go north on Giddings Avenue for about a mile. The stadium is on the right. There is ample free parking.

Box seats are $5, and general admission seats (which start just 5 rows back and are also great seats) cost $3.

For schedule of events and ticket information, call (209) 625-0480.

For tourist information, contact the Visalia Convention & Visitors Bureau, 720 W. Mineral King, Visalia, CA 93291, (209) 734-5876 or (800) 524-0303.

HOMETOWN STATS—VISALIA					
The Last Ten Years					
Affil.	Year	League	Wins	Losses	Attendance
MIN	1985	California	66	78	74,407
	1986		75	67	72,962
	1987		68	74	60,818
	1988		80	62	47,593
	1989		76	66	83,946
	1990		90	51	78,212
	1991		58	78	67,386
	1992		75	61	86,209
COL	1993		61	75	77,547
	1994		65	71	92,756

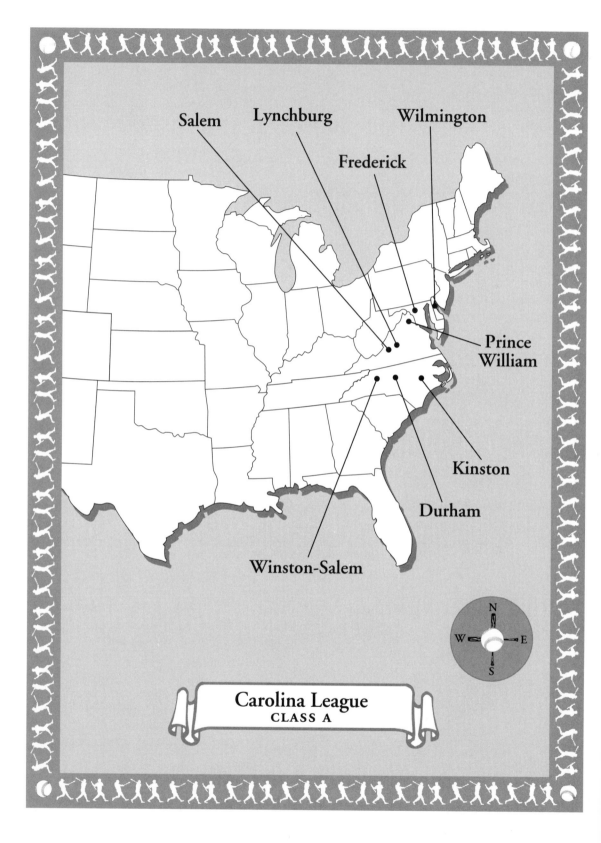

Salem Lynchburg Wilmington

Frederick

Prince
William

Kinston

Durham

Winston-Salem

Carolina League
CLASS A

Carolina League

Class C 1945–1948; Class B 1949–1962; Class A 1963–

The Carolina League was born in 1944 thanks to a man named Herb Brett, a former minor league pitcher who turned to managing in 1934 after a sore arm ended his playing career. He had managed in the Bi-State League, the Piedmont League, and the old Southern Association before he bought the inactive Danville (VA) team and attempted to start a new league. At a meeting in Burlington, North Carolina, on October 15, 1944, six teams decided to join forces: Danville, Leaksville (NC), Martinsville (VA), and Burlington came from the inactive Bi-State League, Raleigh and Greensboro (NC) from the Piedmont League. Two weeks later, at a meeting in Durham, Winston-Salem and Durham joined, bringing the total to eight. Brett declined the presidency of the new Carolina League so that he could stay with his team when the league "officially" opened in 1945, but he remained very influential in the league throughout his career.

The Carolina League has changed dramatically over the years. Teams have come and teams have gone, though it's interesting that the last two cities to join the league are the only charter members still part of it (Durham and Winston-Salem).

The Carolina League is made up of eight teams, which are scheduled to play 140 games during the regular season. First-half division winners play second-half division winners in a best-of-three series. If the same team wins both halves, it gets a bye for the first round. Division playoff winners then play each other in a best-of-five series for the league championship.

Durham Bulls

(Atlanta Braves)

New Durham Bulls Park
200 Willard Street
Durham, NC 27702

It's a Bulls tradition that Little Leaguers join the Bulls players for the National Anthem.

The Durham Bulls gained wide notoriety with the hit movie *Bull Durham,* starring Susan Sarandon and Kevin Costner. Here in Durham, however, they've been notoriously well-loved since 1902, when they were founded. Named after the Duke family's Bull Durham Tobacco Company, "Durham Bulls" quickly came to mean hard-hitting, fun-loving baseball.

No one would have thought of changing the name. But in 1971, when all minor league teams were struggling to make ends meet, the Bulls' owners picked the name "Raleigh Durham Triangles" to draw desperately needed fans from a broader area. Big failure! The home field lay fallow from 1971 until 1980, when new owners unveiled the now-famous Durham Bulls logo and brought the team back. The team had 84 wins and 56 losses that year, winning their division but losing in the finals to the 100–40 Peninsula Pilots. Starved fans packed the old Durham Athletic Park, making the Bulls one of the most successful teams in Carolina League history.

In 1990, when the new principal owner, Jim Goodman, talked about leaving the ailing 5,000-seat park and moving to a new stadium in Raleigh, the Bulls fans stampeded! Theirs was the Durham team that had produced major league stars like David Justice, Brett Butler, and Ron Gant, who hit a league-leading twenty-six homers in 1986. Back in 1936 the great ace Johnny Vander Meer went 19–6 for the Bulls with 295 strikeouts. Veteran power hitters Joe Morgan and Rusty Staub came out of Durham, too. Goodman and the business community had to find a way to build a new park and keep the Bulls in town. Nothing short of that would do!

Next chapter. The Bulls open their 1995 season in a brand-new stadium in downtown Durham while the beloved old park becomes a landmark attraction. The new 7,200-seat stadium has a graceful brick facade and traditional wrought-iron gates. It sits high on a hill with a view of the city. The grassy berm behind the left field wall in the old stadium—where fans would sit on blankets and lawn chairs and kids would scramble to catch home runs—has been recreated here in right field. There are several picnic areas, great seating with intimate sight lines all over the park, and an outfield like the old one, with old-fashioned squared-off corners that give a ball "bouncing room" and an unpredictable rebound off the wall. The famous mechanical bull-board (whose proximity to the warm-up pen, we're told, gave the bullpen its name) has also made the trip to the new park.

The Bulls fans, who fill the stadium to near capacity before the first pitch, are diverse as heck. Students and faculty from the University of North Carolina, Duke, and North Carolina State pack in with politicians from Raleigh, young professionals from Chapel Hill, business owners from Durham, blue-collar workers, CEOs, tobacco farmers, young families, older folks, and church groups. At the sound of the National Anthem, they all stand and sing out in such full voice that they sound like a choir. It's a Bulls' tradition that gives even the umpires goose bumps. Then the fans carry out another tradition—annoying the opposing pitcher. As he throws his warm-up pitches across the plate, thousands of voices let out a long drawn out "whooop" that slides up the scale. When the catcher throws the ball back, there's an "whoo" down the scale.

Between-inning contests like Board Toss—if you get three balls through a cutout of a TV you win a real one—and giveaways like coolers, balls, helmets, and bats are fun. But these fans make their own fun, too. They stay in their seats at the end of the fifth inning just to applaud the five guys on the grounds crew as they hand-drag the infield to the

accompaniment of the *William Tell* Overture.

When you're hungry, try Dillards' "A Buck a Bone" ribs for the best Carolinian barbecue you'll ever eat!

The new park is open all day, but closes at 5:00 P.M. It reopens at 6:00 P.M. on nights when a home game is scheduled.

GETTING THERE

Durham, a city of Civil War landmarks and grand Southern plantations, is also the home of Duke University and Research Triangle Park, making Durham an important center of medicine and technology. Durham has world-class hotels, a variety of motels, and lakeside campgrounds nearby.

The new Durham Bulls Park is located in downtown Durham in the midst of old tobacco warehouses. Take I-40 or I-85 to Highway 147 and exit at Magnum Street (Exit 12). Go straight through the intersection (do not turn onto Mangum). The stadium is right in front of you. Parking costs $2.

Box and reserve seats go for $6. General admission tickets cost $4.

For schedule of events and ticket information, call (919) 688-8211.

For tourist information, contact the Durham Convention & Visitors Bureau, 101 East Morgan Street, Durham, NC 27701, (919) 687-0288 or (800) 446-8604.

	HOMETOWN STATS—DURHAM				
	The Last Ten Years				
Affil.	Year	League	Wins	Losses	Attendance
ATL	1985	Carolina	66	74	182,720
	1986		72	68	197,125
	1987		65	75	217,012
	1988		82	58	271,650
	1989		84	54	272,202
	1990		71	68	300,499
	1991		79	58	301,240
	1992		70	70	280,994
	1993		69	69	305,692
	1994		66	70	259,758

Frederick Keys

(Baltimore Orioles)

Harry Grove Stadium
6201 New Design Road
Frederick, MD 21701

Francis Scott Key practiced law in Frederick and is buried here. So when this Orioles affiliate moved to town from Hagerstown in 1989, it seemed only patriotic to choose the composer of "The Star-Spangled Banner" as a namesake. Whether it's the ghost of Francis Scott Key watching over them or just plain hard work, the Keys have played some terrific baseball since coming to Frederick. They took the league championship in 1990 and won the second half of their division in 1993. A few players who helped create all the excitement were David Segui, Jack Voigt, Ricky Gutierrez, and pitcher Ben McDonald, who went straight up to Baltimore after a brief appearance here in 1989.

The fans come from all over Montgomery and Frederick counties in numbers that exceed 340,000 a year. That's an average of 5,300 fans each night in a stadium that seats 5,500. You will see an impressive wave here, believe it or not, and when fans rally by jangling their car keys, the sound is wildly rousing.

Harry Grove Stadium sits on the edge of town amid lush rolling farmland. It opened in 1990 with the help of a cash gift from Mr. and Mrs. M. J. Grove, who requested that the park be named after Mr. Grove's father. From the outside, the park blends with the traditional look of historic Frederick. Inside, a modern, user-friendly concourse wraps around the top of the grandstand, allowing for a good view of the field. By the way, we like the "kids only" concession stand up there. So do the kids! The Keys Cafe, offering catered suppers for as few as two people (reservations required), is in a prime location behind home plate. But no matter where your seat is in this park, it's a great one. Even the presumed worst seat in the house, which is just past first base near the bullpen up in the last section of the reserved seating, is GM Larry Martin's favorite. It's a great spot to catch foul balls, too. There are grass berms down the right and left field lines, and beyond the outfield fence the view of the Appalachian Mountains is gorgeous.

The team mascot, Keyote, is a big fat furry seven-foot fella who delivers birthday cakes to fans, hands out prizes, and generally pops up everywhere. The Trash Bandit prowls the stands stealing garbage. If you don't turn your cups and wrappers over, beware his water pistol. He'll use it.

Promotions are popular here, more so than giveaways. There are five huge fireworks shows each season that are so phenomenal that traffic stops on the nearby interstate. And no opening ceremony could be more exciting than the one here in 1993. A gigantic Stars and Stripes was unfurled on the field as none other than Francis Scott Key himself arrived in an open carriage while tracer rockets fired their "red glare" into the night. The place went wild.

Theme weekends draw fantastic crowds. If it's Country Weekend, you'll be line-dancing and trying to win a cowboy hat. For Beach Party Weekend tons of sand were dumped at the main entrance, where Keyote the mascot set up his beach chair alongside a Caribbean steel band. At a sixties weekend Elvis impersonators run around while the sounds of the King himself boom over the PA system between innings. On Magic Weekend magicians perform on the dugout roof, and stilt walkers are let loose, too. There is one giveaway night when the handout prize steals the show—Kazoo Night. You can look forward to 5,000 (plus) fans all playing songs together between innings!

Gates open one hour before game time. Getting autographs is easy, either before or after the game, since the players have to move through the fans down near the field to go back and forth to the clubhouse.

Harry Grove Stadium, just outside of town, is surrounded by farmland.

GETTING THERE

The Frederick area is packed with historic eighteenth- and nineteenth-century sites and museums, all set amidst verdant farmland and lush state and national parks. There are wonderful bed-and-breakfast inns, quaint hotels, and numerous motels and campgrounds.

Harry Grove Stadium is at the intersection of I-70 and Route 355 (Market Street exit). There is ample free parking.

Box seats cost $7, while reserved seats go for $6. General admission tickets are $5, $3 for kids and seniors.

For schedule of events and ticket information, contact (301) 662-0013.

For tourist information, contact the Tourism Council of Frederick County, Inc., 19 East Church Street, Frederick, MD 21701, (301) 663-8687 or (800) 999-3613.

		HOMETOWN STATS—FREDERICK *The Last Ten Years**			
Affil.	**Year**	**League**	**Wins**	**Losses**	**Attendance**
BAL	1989	Carolina	73	65	165,870
	1990		74	62	277,802
	1991		58	82	318,354
	1992		69	71	329,592
	1993		78	62	351,146
	1994		76	61	344,563

*Statistics are given only for the years in which the team played in Frederick.

Kinston Indians

(Cleveland Indians)

Grainger Stadium
400 East Grainger Avenue
Kinston, NC 28502

Professional ball has been played in Kinston off and on since 1908. And since 1956, Kinston clubs have been playing fairly regularly in the Carolina League. They've been called the Expos, Pirates, Yankees, Braves, and Eagles. From 1980 to 1985 they were the Blue Jays, independent in 1986, and since 1987, when they hooked up with Cleveland, they've been the Indians. Over the last few years, these Indians have played some edge-of-your-seat, nail-biting baseball. In 1993, when they challenged Winston-Salem in the playoffs and lost; the outcome of each game came down to the last at bat.

There's a roster full of major league stars who once wore the Kinston uniform. Manny Ramirez, Paul Shuey, Albie Lopez, Jim Thome, Mark Lewis, Albert Belle, and Charles Nagy are a few of them.

Grainger Stadium was built back in the 1940s and is one of those charming jewels of the minor leagues. Located in an old residential neighborhood, it has a warm red brick facade with arched entryways and iron gates. The walkway leading up to the entrance is bedecked with planters, antique lamppoles, and colorful flying flags. Once inside the main gate and in your seat, you'll feel how very intimate this park is. Home plate is no more than thirty feet away from the fans, and the foul area is as narrow as we've seen anywhere. The grandstand wraps around from first to third base. Foul balls bounce off the roof over the seats behind home or sail out of the park and into the street or somebody's yard. The kid who catches one can turn it in for a seventy-five-cent reward. Most kids keep them, of course.

Down the right field line is a tented picnic area with tables and a play area for kids. Nearby is the Beer Garden, usually packed with the dating crowd. Throughout the park are the smells of grilled hot dogs, burgers, and (may we recommend the) Cajun fried chicken. The place holds 4,200, but on big nights, like when the archrival Durham Bulls come to town, the crowd swells to 5,500, filling every inch of the picnic area and

Kinston players relax before beginning pregame warm-ups.

Beer Garden. We thought that pretty impressive for a town with a population of 27,000. As it turns out, the whole region is so baseball-crazy that fans will drive the distance from Goldsboro, Jacksonville, and New Bern, all within about 40 miles of Kinston.

On any night there's likely to be a mixed crowd: airmen from the Cherry Point Station in nearby Havelock might be sitting next to cotton farmers, college kids, politicians, shop workers, young families, and older folks. Although they are fiercely loyal, these fans love baseball first and foremost, and they'll applaud a great play even if it's by the opposing team. Once, in 1989, the whole crowd stood up for then-Salem pitcher Randy Tomlin, who had just hurled a no-hitter against Kinston.

The team mascot, Percy Pelican, flies in and out and has been caught picking up little kids to help them get the ball through the hole in the Bojangles sign during the Strike-O contest. One of the most popular on-field contests is Andy's Uniform Race, sponsored by Andy the cheese steak man from downtown Kinston. A pile of baseball uniform clothing is thrown down on the infield, and a fan tries to get it all on in one minute flat. The PA announcer calls the action play-by-play—or, shirt by sock! One night a man who weighed about 300 pounds and stood 6 feet tall somehow managed to squeeze into everything in time.

Gates open one hour before game time. Come early, and you can get autographs near the fence down the left field line. Or stay after the game and wait outside the clubhouse. The players are quite generous with their time. (One night Pete Rose Jr. spent an hour signing after a game.)

GETTING THERE

Located in the center of eastern North Carolina, Kinston is a thriving community that is unique in that both the Revolutionary War and the Civil War are represented here with historic sites and museums. There is a variety of accommodations: motels, inns, bed-and-breakfasts, and campgrounds.

Grainger Stadium is located at 400 East Grainger Avenue, half a mile off U.S. Highway 11 and Route 70 Business. Parking is free.

Box seats cost $5, while reserved seats go for $4. General admission tickets cost $3. Kids, seniors, students, and the military get $1 off.

For schedule of events and ticket information, call (919) 527-9111.

For tourist information, contact the Kinston Convention and Visitors Bureau, 301 North Queen Street, Kinston, NC 28502, (919) 527-1131.

HOMETOWN STATS—KINSTON *The Last Ten Years*					
Affil.	Year	League	Wins	Losses	Attendance
TOR	1985	Carolina	64	73	74,722
IND	1986		60	76	48,845
CLE	1987		75	65	68,199
	1988		88	52	80,623
	1989		76	60	88,154
	1990		88	47	106,219
	1991		89	49	100,857
	1992		65	71	105,090
	1993		71	67	134,506
	1994		60	78	122,557

Lynchburg Hillcats

(Pittsburgh Pirates)

City Stadium
Fort Avenue and Wythe Road
Lynchburg, VA 24501

Lynchburg's history with professional baseball dates back to 1886, when the club was called the Lynchburg Base Ball Association. The team had nineteen wins and six losses that year and took first place in the old State League. One hundred and nine years later the team became the Hillcats; in between, they played as the Hill Climbers, Tobacconists, Shoemakers, Grays, Senators, Cardinals, White Sox, Twins, Rangers, Mets, and Red Sox.

As Mets they won back-to-back championships in 1983 and 1984. As Red Sox they made the playoffs four times, beginning in 1988. Some of the more famous players who have come up through Lynchburg are Gregg Jefferies, Darryl Strawberry, and Lenny Dykstra, who set a league record here in 1983 with 105 stolen bases. That same year Dwight Gooden compiled a 19–4 record and also set a league record with 300 strikeouts. Rumor has it that when Strawberry played here in 1981, he hit homer after homer into the cemetery just beyond the right field wall. Hmm.

Lynchburg is often called the Hill City—hence the team name—and it is that. Built in 1939 as a WPA project on the site of the old Fair Grounds, City Stadium sits up on Cotton Hill. After careful renovations over the years, the ballpark remains a comfortable old place with classic looks and charm. The 4,000-seat grandstand wraps around home from bag to bag, no further. The view over the outfield wall—of the Blue Ridge mountains—is one of the most spectacular in all the minor leagues: When the dogwoods blossom in early spring it's enough to take your breath away. Summer sunsets, reflected in the haze off the mountains, are stunning. To snag foul balls sit at either end of the grandstand, or do as the kids do and stand just outside the right field fence.

The game atmosphere is relaxed and friendly. Lynchburg fans are a tight-knit, baseball-savvy bunch who come out not only for the love of the game but also for the chance to see each other. Some are actually second- and third-generation fans. There are a few giveaway nights—bats, caps, balls—but not many. The club is famous for its July 4th after-game extravaganza, when $5,000 worth of fireworks light up the sky over a park that's packed to standing-room-only capacity. But for the most part, these fans don't need much to have a lot of fun. They didn't even have a mascot until the Green Monster, named in honor of the big Green Monster wall in Fenway Park, made his debut in 1994. In 1995 a new affiliation and a new mascot will get a chance to win the hearts of the fans.

The park is open all day and closes about one and a half hours before the game starts. The gates reopen one hour before game time. The best time to get autographs is before the game down by the short fence that runs along the left field line from the end of the grandstand to the clubhouse.

GETTING THERE

Lynchburg, the City of Seven Hills on the James River, has a lot to offer: the Blue Ridge Mountains, Appomattox, Jefferson's "Poplar Forest" retreat, and more. There are beautiful bed-and-breakfasts, inns, and hotels, and a variety of motels and campgrounds.

To get to City Stadium from the north, take U.S. 29 south to the City Stadium exit. From the south, take U.S. 29 north to the Lynchburg College exit. There is plenty of free parking.

Box seats in the first two rows between the first

base dugout and the third base dugout are $4.75. The remaining general admission tickets cost $3.75. Kids, seniors, and students get $1 off.

For schedule of events and ticket information, call (804) 528-1144.

For tourist information, contact the Greater Lynchburg Chamber of Commerce Visitors Information Center, 216 Twelfth Street, Lynchburg, VA 24504, (804) 847-1811 or (800) 732-5821.

The notorious Phillie Phanatic makes a guest appearance at Lynchburg.

HOMETOWN STATS—LYNCHBURG *The Last Ten Years*					
Affil.	**Year**	**League**	**Wins**	**Losses**	**Attendance**
NYM	1985	Carolina	95	45	95,657
	1986		75	65	87,930
	1987		63	76	88,370
BOS	1988		68	72	81,197
	1989		70	66	74,375
	1990		58	80	92,607
	1991		67	72	88,897
	1992		77	58	92,720
	1993		65	74	100,113
	1994		52	87	100,724

Prince William Cannons

(Chicago White Sox)

Prince William County Stadium
7 County Complex Ct.
Woodbridge, VA 22193

The Cannons' Mike Figga signs autographs.

This franchise started playing as the independent Dukes in 1978 in Alexandria, Virginia. The team became the Mariners in 1979, the Dukes again in 1980, and then the Pirates in 1981, when they signed on with Pittsburgh. In April 1984 the team moved to Woodbridge (just southwest of Washington, D.C.), became the Prince William Pirates, and opened the brand-new County Stadium. They drew hardly over 100,000 fans that year. The team has built a solid and very loyal following since then and now draws more than 200,000 fans each season.

In 1987, when the team joined the Yankees farm system, the club took Cannons as their new name. Whatever the name and whatever the affiliation (White Sox as of 1994), the club has managed to reward fans with pretty good baseball over the years. They won the Carolina League championship in 1982 and 1989, made it to the playoffs again in 1991, and have sent up some impressive players to the majors—Pat Kelly, Kevin Maas, and Sterling Hitchcock have gone on to the Yankees. Barry Bonds had his best year in the minors here in 1985, with thirteen home runs, while young Bobby Bonilla had his worst, with just three.

Prince William County Stadium is an open, friendly place located within a quadrate of baseball diamonds, all of which are plopped right in the middle of a forest. It's not fancy from the outside, but once inside the 5,200-seat ballpark, the grass field and fabulous view of the thick pine and spruce forest more than make up for the no-frills exterior. The Cannon's Cafe, just inside the main gate, is a casual place to eat, meet, and greet before the game. The big picnic area under a huge blue and white tent in the right field corner is set up for large groups. The concourse is a festive food-lovers' kind of place with open grills on both the third base and the first base sides. Don't pass up the barbeque ribs and curly fries.

Cannons' fans are extremely supportive of their team. When they rally, the stomping in this aluminum-and-steel structure can be deafening. Fridays and Saturdays are giveaway nights; everything from seat cushions and caps to beach towels and sunglasses goes home with the first fans to show up. There are several fireworks shows during the season and appearances by big league talent such as The Famous Chicken, the Blues Brothers, and the Phillie Phanatic.

On-field contests are big here between innings. The Cannons tell us that they were the first team in the Carolina League to introduce the wildly popular Dizzy Bat Race. There's the Diamond Dig on Mother's Day, and at other games the management brings out the Big Money Tunnel, which is actually a phone booth flooded with real money. The contestant inside gets to keep all that he or she can grab in thirty seconds. In the $10,000 Grand Slam Inning contest, if a batter hits a grand slam he and a lucky fan split the big money. Even if he just gets a hit, it's worth $100; a run batted in gets $200; two RBIs, $300, three RBIs, $400. Sometimes there's an Ice Cream Sundae Race, when the staff makes a *150-foot-long* sundae that stretches from home plate down the third base line. An equally long line of kids waiting in the outfield then races to devour the stuff. Yes, you bet it gets messy.

Gates open one hour before game time. After practice players will sign autographs down by the dugout before the game. After the game, wait outside the clubhouse. Every Sunday afternoon before the game one player is out front signing autographs, too.

GETTING THERE

Prince William County is brimming with American history. There are Civil War battlegrounds and charming Piedmont villages to visit, as well as all the sights in nearby Washington, D.C. and Baltimore. Accommodations are varied: inns, bed-and-breakfasts, motels, and four campgrounds that offer both camping and RV parking.

To get to County Stadium from the north, take I-95 south to Exit 160 and take a left at the second light onto Davis Ford Road for six miles to the stadium. From the south, take I-95 to Exit 156 and take a right on Hillendale Road, then left on Davis Ford Road to the stadium. Parking is plentiful and costs $2.

Field box seats go for $7.50, while regular box seats cost $6.50. Reserved seats are $5.50 and general admission tickets cost $4.50. Kids and seniors get $1 off.

For schedule of events and ticket information, call (703) 590-2311 or the twenty-four-hour hotline, (703) 730-2640.

For tourist information, contact the Prince William County Conference and Visitors Bureau, 4349 Ridgewood Center Drive, Prince William, VA 22192, (703) 792-6680 or (800) 334-9876.

HOMETOWN STATS—PRINCE WILLIAM
The Last Ten Years

Affil.	Year	League	Wins	Losses	Attendance
PIT	1985	Carolina	65	74	127,356
	1986		67	72	117,000
NYY	1987		66	74	105,749
	1988		55	84	114,403
	1989		72	66	74,810
	1990		64	75	210,262
	1991		71	68	207,103
	1992		69	71	208,416
	1993		67	73	209,273
CWS	1994		71	65	210,401

Salem Avalanche

(Colorado Rockies)

Salem Municipal Field
620 Florida Street
Salem, VA 24153

Back in 1894, the Roanoke Magicians were the first professional baseball team in the Roanoke Valley. Those Magicians were eventually succeeded by the Tigers, the Highlanders, the Salem/Roanoke Friends, the Salem Friends, the Roanoke Red Sox, the Salem Rebels, Salem Pirates, Salem Redbirds, Salem Buccaneers, and, as of 1995, the Salem Avalanche (the new affiliate-inspired name selected in a recent name-the-team contest). The club is owned by Kelvin Bowles, a professional scout by trade. Around Salem, though, he is known primarily as "the man who saved baseball in the Roanoke Valley," because he purchased the team in 1985 and helped keep it in Salem. The club, which starts with the Colorado Rockies in 1995, has had a knack for finishing near the bottom of the standings—one reason being the previous affiliate Pittsburgh's uncanny ability to come in early each season and pluck the best players off the roster. Still, the team has drawn record crowds for eleven consecutive seasons. Close to 2,500 fans a night have watched the likes of ace Randy Tomlin, Orlando Merced, and Carlos Garcia play and move on to the majors.

The new (1995) Salem Municipal Field is a welcome replacement for the old park, which had served baseball here since 1927. The old place was built to fit into a tight little corner of a residential neighborhood and had lots of quirks, like a cinderblock outfield wall and light poles on the field.

Although those characteristics aren't repeated in the new 6,000-seat stadium, some of the charm of the old place is. There are only sixteen rows of seats, for instance, which means that every fan is close to the grass. This place sits high on a hill next to the high school stadium and the civic center arena, so home runs sail up and out of the park and do not bomb the front porches of the neighboring homes as they did at the old park. The grandstand is roomy and makes a wide curve from first base to third. And the view is still the same as always, the Blue Ridge Mountains in the distance.

These fans aren't afraid to make noise. Many are students from Roanoke or Hollins College. Lucky for them that every half-inning you can win a free pizza, chicken dinner, and so forth.

There are six roomy concession areas on the airy concourse, where the club still manages to sell thousands of addictive spicy deep-fried waffle-cut potatoes and juicy Carolina-style barbeque pork sandwiches. There is also a very busy grill that cooks up hamburgers, hot dogs, and chicken.

Count on the Dizzy Bat Race between innings. Some nights there are shopping sprees sponsored by a local market. A lucky fan gets to push a shopping cart around the infield and collect as many grocery items as possible in the allotted time. One woman managed to fill two carts! The Blues Brothers show up during the season to entertain. And there are special first-pitch appearances by such baseball legends as Gaylord Perry and Catfish Hunter.

The giveaways over the course of a season include magnet schedules, baseballs, posters, bumper stickers, umbrellas, baseball cards, and t-shirts.

Gates open one hour before game time. You can get autographs before the game between the dugout and the clubhouses, and after the game outside the clubhouses.

GETTING THERE

Salem (and the entire Roanoke Valley) is rich in Appalachian heritage. There are Civil War battle-fields, plantations, museums, the Natural Bridge, the Blue Ridge Parkway, the great Appalachian Trail, and the Dixie Caverns to explore. Accommodations are varied, from modest motels to charming inns and beautifully maintained campgrounds.

Salem Municipal Field is located near downtown Salem at 620 Florida Street. There is very little parking, so everyone has to find a spot on the streets, which isn't that difficult if you get there early enough.

Box seats go for $5 and reserved seats cost $4. General admission tickets are $3. Seniors and kids get $1 off (except for some special events). The bleacher seats are concrete—bring a cushion. Some fans bring their own lawn chairs.

For schedule of events and ticket information, contact (703) 389-3333.

For tourist information, contact the Roanoke Valley Convention & Visitors Bureau, 114 Market Street, Roanoke, VA 24011, (703) 342-6025.

The Blues Brothers entertain at many of the minor league ballparks.

HOMETOWN STATS—SALEM *The Last Ten Years*					
Affil.	Year	League	Wins	Losses	Attendance
TEX	1985	Carolina	72	65	71,788
	1986		45	93	87,047
PIT	1987		80	59	111,661
	1988		73	66	119,966
	1989		63	75	121,581
	1990		55	84	126,121
	1991		63	77	131,582
	1992		64	76	134,598
	1993		61	79	145,657
	1994		64	75	153,575

Wilmington Blue Rocks

(Kansas City Royals)

Daniel S. Frawley Stadium
801 South Madison Street
Wilmington, DE 19807

Back in 1940, the original Wilmington Blue Rocks (a Phillies affiliate) were named for the beautiful granite rocks in the waters of Wilmington's Brandywine River. Future Hall of Famer Robin Roberts pitched his way straight to Philadelphia with a record of 9–1; he got the call in June 1948.

The team folded in 1952, and there was no baseball in Wilmington for the next forty-one years. The drought ended when the 1992 Carolina League champions, the Peninsula Pilots from Hampton, Virginia, moved in for the 1993 season. Owners Frank Boulton, a seasoned professional baseball operator, and Bud Harrelson, of 1969 Mets fame, changed the name of the Pilots to honor the original Wilmington team.

The stadium's name is another story. Technically, it is Judy Johnson Field at Daniel S. Frawley Stadium. 1933 and 1936 Negro League All-Star Judy Johnson was a native of Wilmington and the only Delawarean who played in the Negro League ever to be inducted into the Baseball Hall of Fame. Daniel S. Frawley, the late former mayor of Wilmington, provided major muscle in getting the new team and stadium for Wilmington. Groundbreaking ceremonies were held on October 9, 1992, and the home opener took place on April 16, 1993, an incredible six months later. This is a beautiful, 5,700-seat, state-of-the-art, comfortable ballpark. The field stretches out below the concourse, which wraps around the grandstand starting at first base and continuing past third down the left field line. Down the right field line are the general admission bleacher seats. There are sixteen luxury skyboxes, a restaurant, two picnic areas, and, beyond the right field wall, a splendid view of Wilmington's skyline. It doesn't get much hotter than eighty degrees here, but it can be very humid at game time.

The Blue Rocks fans come from every walk of life—many are the young professionals who are moving into Wilmington at a rapid rate. The 1993 season drew 330,000 fans, who nearly packed the park each night. The team even made it to the playoffs that year, going 45–24 during the first half-season and 30–40 during the second. They won their first playoff game and then fell apart, but the fans didn't mind. They had a great first year, as did three of the Royals organization's top prospects, Michael Tucker, Darren Burton, and Brian Bevil, names for all of us to watch.

The fans are enthusiastic from the minute they walk through the gate. They stand and clap wildly as the pitcher delivers the first pitch of the game, and they don't sit down until he gets his first strike. There are contests and giveaways during each game, several fireworks displays during the season, and scheduled appearances by big league mascots like the Phillie Phanatic and The Famous Chicken.

The concession stands offer the standard fare, though two regional favorites—Philly cheese steaks and pretzels with lots of condiments—are especially good here.

Gates open one hour before game time. There is an autograph booth on the concourse that is manned on Wednesdays and Sundays. Kids can also get autographs down by the dugouts and along the railing that stretches between the dugout and clubhouse.

GETTING THERE

Wilmington, home of tax-free shopping (and all the world's banks), sits halfway between New York and Washington, D.C. in the beautiful

Built in only six months, Daniel S. Frawley Stadium is a state-of-the-art facility.

Brandywine Valley. Some of America's finest hotels (like the du Pont) and inns can be found here—excellent camping, too.

To get to Frawley Stadium from the south, take I-95 north to Maryland Avenue (exit 6). Then take a right on South Madison and proceed to the park. From the north, take I-95 south to Martin Luther King Avenue (exit 6). Then take a right on South Madison and head to the park. There is plenty of free parking.

Box seats go for $6, and reserved seats cost $5. General admission tickets are $4. Kids, seniors, and the military get in for $2.

For schedule of events and ticket information, call (302) 888-BLUE.

For tourist information, contact the Greater Wilmington Convention & Visitors Bureau, 1300 Market Street, Wilmington, DE 19801, (302) 652-4088.

HOMETOWN STATS—WILMINGTON					
*The Last Ten Years**					
Affil.	Year	League	Wins	Losses	Attendance
KCR	1993	Carolina	74	65	332,132
	1994		94	44	335,024

*Statistics are given only for the years in which the team played in Wilmington.

Winston-Salem Warthogs

(Cincinnati Reds)

Ernie Shore Field
401 West 30th Street
Winston-Salem, NC 27105

Winston-Salem, a founding member of the Carolina League in 1945, has captured ten league championships in its history, the most recent one in 1993. Winston-Salem's first professional baseball team played in the Class D Virginia-North Carolina League, which lasted for one year. Before joining the Carolina League, Winston-Salem teams spent the 1920s, 1930s, and early 1940s in the Piedmont League. Nearly fifty years of Carolina League baseball has produced major league veterans like 1954 All-Star Ray Jablonski and 1967 and 1969 All-Star Rico Petrocelli. In 1981 pitcher Mike Brown threw forty-two shutout innings, a league record, and more recently Pedro Castellano had a league-leading eighty-eight RBIs in 1991; Andy Hartung had ninety-four in 1992.

Ernie Shore Field is named after a famous Winston-Salem native whose brief major league pitching career (7 years) was quite remarkable. Shore had a lifetime 65–42 record with a 2.45 ERA. He pitched on two World Championship teams, the 1915 and 1916 Boston Red Sox. His roommate for five seasons was none other than the great Babe Ruth. Shore came back home to Winston-Salem and served as county sheriff for almost thirty-five years. When the Twin City needed a new stadium, they asked Shore to come out of retirement, find a site, and raise the money. He did. The brand-new ballpark opened in 1956.

The red brick facade with four arched portals gives the place a nostalgic look. The field is laid out below the concourse area, so when you are standing in line for Buffalo chicken wings (the hot item here—no pun intended), you still have a great view. The grandstand starts near first base and stops at third. Bleachers hug both foul lines, and grass hills for overflow crowds extend to the outfield fence. The stadium has just undergone a renovation that increased the seating capacity to 6,200 and enhanced the charm of the old park.

With an average attendance of 2,500, lots of good seats are available on a day-of-game basis. One of the best seats in the house is in the picnic area at the top of the stands on the third base side. It's for parties of twenty-five or more and requires reservations, but what a way to see the game.

It's hot here—and humid. Average summer game-time temps are in the nineties. Not bad, though, if it happens to be Thirsty Thursday, when all drinks are half-price. Contests include the infamous Dizzy Bat Race and Rolling for Bowling (down the field lines). Every fourth night some fan wins the Dirtiest Car of the Night honor. The prize? A free car wash.

There are first-pitch guest appearances by NASCAR drivers like Richard Petty and Harry Gant. (Baseball fans here are also avid fans of the Charlotte Motor Speedway.) Billy Bird and Captain Dynamite appear, as do the Charlotte Hornets' cheerleaders, the Honey Bees.

There are thirty giveaway nights during the season, with the most popular freebies being replica uniform shirts, caps, baseballs, and bats.

Gates open one hour before game time. You can get autographs before the game down by the dugouts or after the game outside the clubhouse.

GETTING THERE

When in Winston-Salem you will want to visit Reynolds House (R. J. Reynolds's former country estate) for its fine collection of American art and Old Salem, which was settled by Moravians in 1766. There are charming inns, hotels and motels, and campgrounds nearby.

A skydiver delivers the ball for the first pitch on opening day at Ernie Shore Field.

To get to Ernie Shore Field, take Business I-40 to the Cherry Street exit and go north on Cherry through downtown to Deacon Boulevard. Take a right on Deacon and continue to the stadium. There is plenty of free parking.

Box seats cost $6, while reserved seats go for $5. General admission tickets cost $4.

For schedule of events and ticket information, call (910) 759-2233.

For tourist information, contact the Winston-Salem Convention and Visitors Bureau, P.O. Box 1408, Winston-Salem, NC 27102, (910) 725-2361 or (800) 331-7018.

		HOMETOWN STATS—WINSTON-SALEM			
		The Last Ten Years			
Affil.	**Year**	**League**	**Wins**	**Losses**	**Attendance**
CUB	1985	Carolina	58	81	98,434
	1986		82	56	136,841
	1987		72	68	133,263
	1988		73	67	79,999
	1989		64	71	89,360
	1990		86	54	102,558
	1991		83	57	111,333
	1992		66	73	159,316
CIN	1993		72	68	164,509
	1994		67	70	160,994

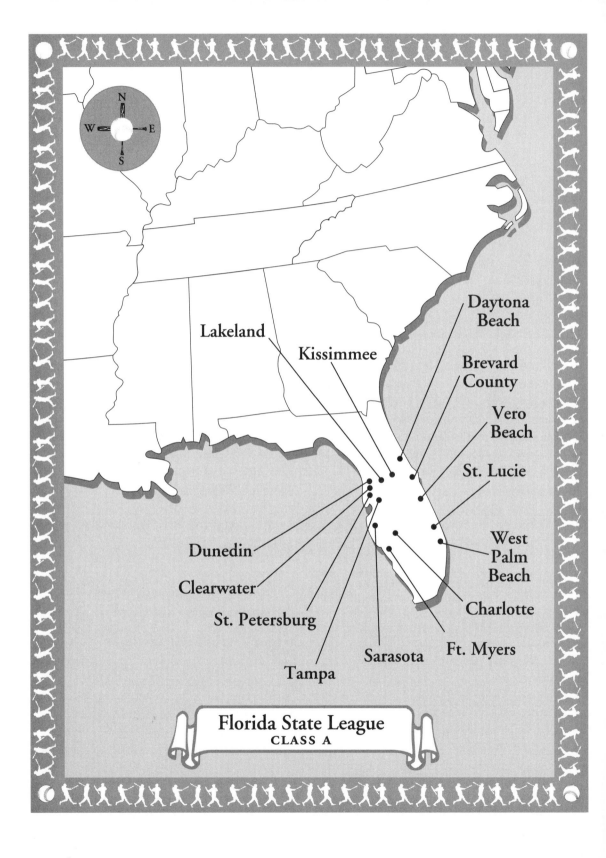

Lakeland

Kissimmee

Daytona Beach

Brevard County

Vero Beach

St. Lucie

West Palm Beach

Charlotte

Ft. Myers

Sarasota

Tampa

St. Petersburg

Clearwater

Dunedin

Florida State League
CLASS A

Florida State League

Class D 1919–1920, 1925–1928, 1936–1941, 1946–1962

Class C 1921–1924; Class A 1963–

Except for two brief interruptions (1929–1935 and 1942–1945), the Florida State League has been in business since 1919, when six cities joined forces: Sanford, Orlando, Lakeland, Bartow, Bradenton, and Tampa. Bartow, Bradenton, and Sanford lasted two years. Orlando jumped ship in 1973 to join the Double-A Southern League. St. Petersburg, which joined along with Daytona Beach in 1920, has the most overall years of membership—forty-eight all told.

The situation in Florida is unique. There's a lot of competition for fans here. Baseball parks are about as common as 7-Eleven convenience stores here, and the major leagues' spring training season has a way of stealing all the thunder. On top of that, the Rookie leagues start playing in June, bringing even more competition. Most of the clubs in the Florida State League are owned outright by their major league affiliates, but the teams must still work hard to put on a good show—and they do, too. If a team draws in the neighborhood of 100,000 fans during the season, they've had a very good year.

The Florida State League is made up of fourteen teams, which are scheduled to play 140 games during the regular reason. First-half division winners play second-half division winners in a best-of-three series. If the same team wins both halves, it gets a bye for the first round. Division playoff winners then play each other in a best-of-five series for the league championship.

Brevard County Manatees

(Florida Marlins)

Space Coast Stadium
5800 Stadium Parkway
Melbourne, FL 32940

When the Florida Marlins bought the very successful Sarasota White Sox franchise in 1993 and moved it to their new spring training complex way outside of town in the middle of farmland, they gambled that baseball fans in Brevard County would find their way on a regular basis to see their new Class A team play. Not much of a gamble. First off, the franchise itself was blessed with luck, having made it to the playoffs four times since 1987. By the end of the 1994 season, the new "Brevard County Manatees" had drawn over 140,000 Marlins loyalists, as well as local fans who had been starved for baseball ever since the nearby Cocoa Astros left town in 1977.

Space Coast Stadium, located south of Cape Canaveral, sits on an eighty-acre tract and is sur-rounded by grazing land, alligator ponds, horse pastures, lakes, and farmland. Sadly, this bucolic setting will gradually disappear over the next twenty-five years or so to give way to the already-planned future city of Viera. New county buildings, schools, malls, and hospitals will emerge around the ballpark. For now, though, Melbourne is the closest city.

The new (1994) stadium is aptly named in honor of NASA's achievements over the past decades, and the space theme plays out every-where. On the large landscaped entry plaza sits a permanent exhibit of the Space Ship X30, a proto-type of the NASA miracle machine of the future that will be able to blast off from New York City, rocket into space, and descend in Hong Kong in two hours. Over the ramp into the stadium hangs a huge digital count-down clock that ticks off the hours and seconds to game time. To your right on the breezy concourse is the Orbit Grill (try the chicken sandwich), and to your left is the Galaxy Grill (on Friday nights, try the special, the fried baloney and cheese sand-wich). In dead center field is the Black Hole, a twenty-four-by-eighty-foot stretch of outfield wall painted, that's right, *black*. The huge score-

In their debut season at spectacular Space Coast Stadium, the 1994 Manatees challenged but lost to Tampa in the championship playoffs.

board left of center has an old-fashioned look to it, but it comes with high-tech thrills. In the event of a Manatee home run a gigantic neon-bright baseball, spewing smoke, bursts from the center of the board as if it were a rocket taking off. The fans go nuts, music plays, and the announcer cries out, "We have liftoff, we have liftoff—it's outta here."

The grandstand and bleachers extend down both baselines, seating 7,381 fans close-to-the-grass and on-top-of-the-action. An eleven-foot grassy berm extends from left field to center beyond the outfield fence. For $1 a ticket you can sit out there and bring your own food and beverage, lawn chairs, and blankets. On Fridays, the hill turns into a Berm Bash. From 5:00 to 7:00 P.M. it's a come-as-you-are carnival where you can pitch horseshoes, eat barbecue, listen to live bands, shoot baskets, get free haircuts, and sing karaoke. Players show up for autographs and photos, too.

Manatees fans don't seem to need a mascot for morale. At least two trumpet-playing fans in the crowd sound the call to charge at every game and the universal goodbye to the yanked pitcher: "na na na na—na na na na—hey, hey—goodbye." The club does host some terrific promotions and memorable events. Early in the season, try to get in on the Bonfire of the Manatees, a big rally and cookout to welcome the players to town. Later on, when the 100,000th fan comes through the gate, he or she stands to win $100,000 if a Manatee hits a grand slam during a selected inning. Berm Bingo (that's right—that outfield berm transforms into a bingo board) is a weekly draw. And speaking of memorable events, fans are still talking about "rocket man's" entrance on opening day 1994! He jetted high over the outfield fence, turned flips in the air, and made a pinpoint landing on the mound to deliver the ball for the first pitch. F-14s flew overhead, and there were fireworks, too.

Gates open one hour before game time. You can also get autographs if you come out early and wait down by the dugout.

GETTING THERE

The Melbourne area has thirty-three miles of beaches, which are separated from the mainland by the beautiful Indian River. The Kennedy Space Center is a must-see. There are fine hotels, beachside resorts, riverside motels, cottages, and RV parking right in Melbourne Beach.

To get to Space Coast Stadium from the south, take I-95 north to Wickham Road (exit 73). Go left and stay on Wickham as it turns and becomes Lake Andrew Drive, which leads into Stadium Parkway, which takes you right into the stadium. From the north, take I-95 south to Fiske Road (exit 74). Go left and stay on Fiske right to the stadium. There is plenty of parking, which costs $1.

Box seats are $4, while reserved seats go for $3. General admission tickets cost $2.

For schedule of events and ticket information, call (407) 633-9200.

For tourist information, contact the Melbourne-Palm Bay and the Beaches Convention and Visitors Bureau, 1005 E. Strawbridge Avenue, Melbourne, FL 32901, (407) 724-5400 or (800) 771-9922.

HOMETOWN STATS—BREVARD COUNTY
*The Last Ten Years**

Affil.	Year	League	Wins	Losses	Attendance
FLO	1994	Florida State	78	61	144,688

*Statistics are given only for the year in which the team played in Brevard County.

Charlotte Rangers

(Texas Rangers)

Charlotte County Stadium
2300 El Jobean Road
Port Charlotte, FL 33948

The Texas Rangers bought the old Daytona Beach Admirals, a coop franchise, in 1986 and moved it to Port Charlotte in 1987. It didn't take long for the "Charlotte Rangers" to feel at home. In 1989 they took the league championship, and they placed first in the western division in 1990 and again in 1993. About half the players on the 1994 Texas Rangers roster played their first professional innings here—Ivan Rodriguez, Dean Palmer, Jeff Frye, David Hulse, Kevin Brown, Kenny Rogers, and Rusty Greer were all from Charlotte. Other players in the majors—Sammy Sosa, Rey Sanchez, and Wilson Alvarez—started here as well.

Charlotte County Stadium sits in a beautiful wooded area outside of town. The entry plaza is warm and welcoming—decked with flowers, palm trees, flags, and a stone bed that spells out RANGERS. Inside the gate, the concourse is bustling with activity before the game. A fast-pitch machine and a three-putts-for-$1 putting contest attract lots of players. The aromas of fresh-grilled hot dogs and burgers mingle with the just-baked smells of Vinnie's Gourmet Pretzels (be sure to have one). Around 5:30 P.M., music starts up in the party pavilion in the picnic area down off right field. Until 7:00 P.M. every night, live bands play, and everybody dances (country is big here). The 5,000-seat main grandstand tucks up to first base and third, and bleachers continue down the lines. It's all roofless and wide open. About three dozen foul balls zing out nightly and go home with the dozen kids who are waiting outside for them. Thirty-foot

Mr. Fireball is about to astound fans by blowing himself up and walking away unharmed. Really!

palm trees line the outfield fence, and beyond that are thick and verdant pine woods. The view is peaceful and serene; many fans here feel that the view is unrivaled by any park in the minor leagues.

Promotions are legendary here. People are still talking about the Boot Scootin' Boogie Bash—named after the popular line dance. Fans signed up at local country bars to learn the "boot scootin' boogie." Then they got a free pass to the game. After the last out, 1,000 fans swarmed onto the field to do the biggest boot scootin' boogie ever. Fans come out in big numbers for Stupid Pet Tricks Night, too. One time the trick was actually pretty smart. Luke the bloodhound tracked the scent of a fan all the way through a maze of fans to his seat off third base. On Turn Back the Clock Night there's a live ragtime band, hot dogs go for twenty-five cents, and the teams wear 1930 uniforms.

Every game features the Fun Cruise Fourth Inning, when some fan tries to win a vacation cruise by rolling jumbo dice on the field. If he does well he can even win a cruise for everybody in his section. Lucky number prizes like car washes and free pizzas go to fans each game, too.

On Mondays, bring your Sunday church bulletin and get in for half-price. On Tuesday, any kid who is a member of the team-sponsored Knothole Gang gets in for five cents. On Wednesdays, families or groups of five people get in for $5. On Thursdays, beer costs fifty cents until a visiting player gets a hit. (The poor guy gets booed mercilessly.)

The team mascot, Pop-Up, is a huge yellow bear who is best known for his Zorro disguise (Uncle Sam, too).

Gates open one and a half hours before game time. Come early to get autographs down by the dugout, or wait outside the clubhouse in right field after the game.

GETTING THERE

Charlotte County, on Florida's Gulf Coast, has a total population of 119,000; 107,000 of those people live in Port Charlotte, which is only thirty-five years old and has 165 miles of man-made waterways. There are accommodations of all kinds, including fancy resorts.

Charlotte County Stadium is four miles west of I-75 between Port Charlotte and Englewood. Take I-75 to Toledo Blade Blvd. West (exit 32). Go about five miles past a traffic light and one more mile to a stop sign. That's State Road 776. Turn right and go one mile. The stadium is on your left. There is plenty of parking, which costs $1.

Box seats are $4. General admission tickets cost $3.50, $2.50 for kids and seniors.

For schedule of events and ticket information, call (813) 625-9500.

For tourist information, contact the Charlotte County Chamber of Commerce, Inc., 2702 Tamiami Trail, Port Charlotte, FL 33952, (813) 627-2222.

HOMETOWN STATS—CHARLOTTE
*The Last Ten Years**

Affil.	Year	League	Wins	Losses	Attendance
TEX	1987	Florida State	69	74	100,238
	1988		72	65	117,275
	1989		75	64	122,060
	1990		85	53	122,478
	1991		62	70	97,399
	1992		73	62	92,996
	1993		84	49	90,792
	1994		60	76	75,821

*Statistics are given only for the years in which the team played in Port Charlotte.

Clearwater Phillies

(Philadephia Phillies)

Jack Russell Memorial Stadium
800 Phillies Drive
Clearwater, FL 34615

Back in 1985 when the Phillies brought their new Class A minor league franchise to Clearwater, the locals were not particularly excited; a measly 44,000 fans came out that year. But the club persisted, playing decent ball over the next years and sending up notables like Bruce Ruffin, Pat Combs, and Pete Smith to the major leagues. Gradually, more and more fans pushed the annual attendance up until in 1990, when the team coincidentally suffered its worst season with only fifty wins, the fans topped out at 91,834. From then on, things got better. The club made it to the playoffs the next two years running, and in 1993 won the league championship. So far, more than two dozen players have gone from Clearwater to the majors—Mickey Morandini, Kevin Stocker, Ricky Jordan, Kim Batiste, Bob Wells, and Donnie Elliott are some of them.

Now there are fans who show up no matter what. They stream in just after the gates open to get a chance to greet the Phillies before the game.

The players lean over the fence next to the dugout and talk to the fans as they would to family. Women send boxes of cookies into the dugout, and kids hand the players bags of licorice and bubble gum. By the third inning, the Clearwater dugout is strewn with candy wrappers.

Jack Russell Memorial Stadium dates back to 1955 and is named for the city commissioner who fought so hard for it. Russell himself was a major league pitcher whose notorious misfortune was giving Babe Ruth his forty-seventh home run in 1926. Be that as it may, he'll be well remembered for this park. From the old-fashioned metal roof over the grandstand to the underbelly of steel column supports visible from the street entrance, this park has charm and character. On a snug concourse, tucked under the grandstand, the smell of grilled sausage and onions (or bratwurst, if your prefer) arouses the feel of yesteryear, too.

Inside the stadium, grandstand seating starts way down by the left field foul pole, sweeps in close to home plate, and extends just past the first base bag. The 7,300 individual seats (no bleachers at all) make this a relaxing, user-friendly park. The ryegrass field is the most verdant we've seen, and the double-tiered outfield wall is wildly colorful with forty billboards. The view beyond is filled with those stately Florida palms and the front yards and roofs of the old homes that make up the surrounding neighborhood.

Clearwater players conduct baseball clinics for kids several times a season.

The game atmosphere is full of character, too. Organist Wilbur Snapp, who's been with the Phillies since the beginning, sits in the stands behind home plate with a tip jar on his console. Wilbur was actually ejected from a game back in 1985 after the umpire called a Phillie out at the plate and he played "Three Blind Mice." Then there's Ruben Washington, a 6'3" basso-voiced peanut vendor, who makes his sales by singing out "PEAAAANUTS, ANYBODY WANT SOME PEAAANUTS." Between-innings action features the team mascot, Phrazzle, a red bird-thing, kind of a fat road runner—we give up. In Phrazzle's Home Run Inning, he pitches whiffle balls to kids in shallow left. If a kid hits one into the stands he gets a prize. In Blackjack a guy with a cordless mike plays blackjack with a lucky fan, who wins a cruise just for playing. Everybody in his section goes on a cruise, too, if he actually wins. About twenty giveaway nights each season send fans home with bats, helmets, caps, and beach towels. There's a huge turnout when the Phillie Phanatic comes to town. The big league mascot gets away with antics most folks would be ejected for—like the night he handed the umpire a baby, then ran off. Mom, who was in on the prank from the start, finally showed up to save the flustered ump. If you come around the 4th of July, you might try to get in on the fireworks—another big night.

Gates open one hour before game time. Come early if you want to get autographs down by the dugout.

GETTING THERE

The Clearwater area (Clearwater Beach), due west of Tampa on the coast, is renowned for its fine beaches, deep-sea fishing, and water sports like sailing, windsurfing, water skiing, and so on. There are beachside resorts, hotels, motels and camping in town proper.

Jack Russell Memorial Stadium is right in downtown Clearwater. From the east, take Route 60 West into Clearwater. Go downtown to Greenwood Avenue and turn north. The stadium is 7 blocks up on your right. There is plenty of free parking.

Box seats are $4. General admission tickets cost $2.

For schedule of events and ticket information, call (813) 441-8638.

For tourist information, contact the St. Petersburg, Clearwater, and Dunedin Convention & Visitors Bureau, Thunderdome, 1 Stadium Drive, Suite A, St. Petersburg, FL 33705, (813) 582-7892 or (800) 345-6710.

HOMETOWN STATS—CLEARWATER *The Last Ten Years*					
Affil.	Year	League	Wins	Losses	Attendance
PHI	1985	Florida State	69	72	44,081
	1986		63	74	53,824
	1987		66	70	55,570
	1988		52	86	50,456
	1989		57	79	68,591
	1990		50	87	91,040
	1991		81	49	82,631
	1992		75	59	91,834
	1993		75	60	86,508
	1994		72	62	82,494

Daytona Cubs

(Chicago Cubs)

Jackie Robinson Ballpark
105 East Orange Avenue
Daytona Beach, FL 32115

Daytona Beach has been home to a minor league team on and off since 1920. The most recent off period began in 1987 after the Daytona Beach Admirals left town. Six years later, in 1993, fate smiled down on Daytona Beach. Jordan Kobritz, a rather bored and unfulfilled lawyer from Maine who had taken the plunge into minor league ball business back in the 1980s, arrived. Kobritz actually went down to Florida to develop a minor league hockey circuit. But when he heard that Anheuser-Busch wanted to sell its Class A Kansas City Royals franchise, which was based at the Boardwalk and Baseball theme park in Baseball City, Florida, he was intrigued. Then he found out that Daytona Beach was aching to have a team move into Jackie Robinson Ballpark. Fate? Or "just one of those things?" In any case, Kobritz put a deal together and in the spring of 1993, the Daytona Cubs were born.

The D-Cubs had little time to get ready for their inaugural season, and they ended up just a little short in the overall standings—tenth in a league of thirteen teams. But the fans didn't mind at all. They were so happy to have baseball back in town that they set the second-best attendance record in the league that year; over 95,000 came through the gate. Of course, it did help when Chicago sent future Hall of Famer Ryne Sandberg to Daytona for a two-day rehab.

Jackie Robinson Ballpark is a fifty-six-year-old park that is the site of one of the greatest moments in baseball history. On March 17, 1946, Jackie Robinson took the field here in a spring training game that pitted the Triple-A Montreal Royals against their parent Brooklyn Dodgers. For the first time in this century, an African-American player played on an integrated professional baseball team. On September 15, 1990, Rachel Robinson paid tribute to Daytona Beach when she helped dedicate the statue of the "All-American Hero" that now stands at the entrance to the Ballpark.

The ballpark is in an idyllic setting on City Island, virtually surrounded by palm trees, water, and pleasure-craft marinas. The place may be old, but it is full of character and the kind of quirks that make it fun to watch a game there. A traditional wooden grandstand that extends from home plate to the first base bag is covered. Another grandstand, with no roof, stretches bleacher-style from home plate down past third base; the last rows are actually up higher than the roof of the first base grandstand. The view is great from up there. Down the right field line is the popular Pavilion, which offers cafe eating with a view of the game. All in all, the old park accommodates 4,200 nicely.

Every Sunday afternoon the Cubs offer reduced ticket prices and special promotions for kids. Billy Bird and Company come to town once or twice a season, and the park sells out. Seasonal giveaways at the gate are good ones—bats, balls, helmets, and so forth. One night a year the club gives away a USAir package to Chicago, which includes tickets to see the big league club play.

Cubby the mascot is a cool bear in a uniform, sunglasses, and backward cap who can't keep from dancing, especially when the Village People blast through the speakers.

Gates open one hour before game time. You can get autographs before the game after infield practice along the third base grandstand, or after the game outside the clubhouse.

GETTING THERE

The Daytona Beach area is divided by the Halifax River. On the "beachside" there are twenty-three miles of sandy beaches. On the "mainland" there's the International Speedway. There are over

Historic Jackie Robinson Ballpark sits on an island—the perfect setting for a late-afternoon game.

16,000 guest rooms (of all kinds) and even RV parks beachside in Ormond.

Jackie Robinson Ballpark is on City Island on the mainland side of the Halifax River. From the north, south, and west, take I-95 to the International Speedway Boulevard exit and go east approximately six miles to Beach Street, then south to Orange Avenue and left to the ballpark. From the east, take the Silver Street Bridge to the ballpark (or take International Speedway Boulevard to Beach, etc.). Parking is free in the lots beyond the outfield.

Box seats cost $4, and general admission tickets go for $3.50, $2.50 for kids and seniors.

For schedule of events and ticket information, call (904) 257-3172.

For tourist information, contact the Daytona Beach Area Convention & Visitors Bureau, 126 East Orange Avenue, Daytona Beach, FL 32114, (904) 255-0415 or (800) 854-1234.

HOMETOWN STATS—DAYTONA BEACH *The Last Ten Years*†*					
Affil.	**Year**	**League**	**Wins**	**Losses**	**Attendance**
COOP	1985	Florida State	53	87	30,736
TEX	1986		40	97	42,774
CWS	1987		69	70	54,132
CUB	1993		57	76	95,089
	1994		61	73	96,756

*Statistics are given only for the years in which the team played in Daytona Beach.

†Daytona Beach did not have a baseball team from 1988 to 1993.

Dunedin Blue Jays

(Toronto Blue Jays)

Dunedin Stadium at Grant Field
373 Douglas Avenue
Dunedin, FL 34698

In 1980, after a brief tenure of two seasons, the original independently owned Dunedin Blue Jays were sold and moved out of town. But in the short time they were here, they produced major league talents like Jesse Barfield and Dave Stieb. When the Jays came back in 1987 it was with Toronto as their owner/operator, and they've been thriving ever since. The team made the playoffs in 1990 as well as setting the all-time league record for the most wins in the first half-season. The team went to the playoffs again in 1992, and catcher Carlos Delgado was selected league MVP and Minor League Player of the Year. There have been more than fifty major league players who say they took their first strides in Dunedin—Mike Timlin, Jeff Kent, Ryan Thompson, Domingo Cedeno, David Weathers, Denis Boucher, and Vince Horsman are a few.

Dunedin Stadium at Grant Field is an easy-access ballpark in a residential part of town, just a ten-minute walk from Main Street and three (cool breeze) blocks from the Gulf. It was built in 1938 and dedicated in honor of then Mayor Grant. In 1990 the city of Dunedin rebuilt the entire stadium, increasing seating capacity to 6,200 while being careful to preserve the cozy, old-fashioned feeling of the park. Consequently, every seat is so close to the field that you can smell the pine tar on the bat. Well, almost.

Dunedin fans are an exuberant mix of hard-core baseball nuts and low-key fans out for a good time. And they do come out—about 1,200 each game. They're here early for dinner at the Bull Pen Cafe, an open grill just inside the main gate. Or you can find them milling about the airy concourse before the game, testing themselves at the speed pitch and checking the "where are they now" board to keep up on past Dunedin players. These people get attached to the players and form long-lasting relationships with those who come back for spring training every year. One young couple claims that their baby's first words were "el-mingo eh deno"—close enough to "Domingo Cedeno."

GM Gary Rigley and staff do a good job of keeping the fans coming back. Fridays and Saturdays are Premium Giveaway Nights, when you might get a Louisville Slugger, beach towel, cap, and so forth. Tuesday is a big day for kids; any kid who's a member of the Knothole Gang gets in free and gets a chance to win a trip to Toronto.

Every game offers all kinds of chances to win something between innings: Get a strike while bowling on the infield and win a dinner for two. Sink three putts on a swatch of AstroTurf and win a prize. And every night is Bingo Night at Dunedin; your card is in the program right next to the scorecard. During the Home Run Inning, when the player who's batting for your lucky number comes up to the plate, you could win something like a year's worth of fresh-baked pies from the Village Inn. All he has to do is hit a grand slam.

Blueper the mascot, the biggest blue jay you'll ever want to contend with, tosses peanuts and boxes of Cracker Jacks into the crowd when "Take Me Out to the Ball Game" is played during the seventh-inning stretch. He will race your kid around the bases, too. And lose.

Here's something unusual: the organist who plays all the classic ballpark music, as well as crowd-rousers like that famous call to "charge!" sits right in the grandstand behind home plate and takes requests.

Gates open one hour before game time. Players spend a lot of time with the fans, talking and signing autographs along the third base line fence.

Dunedin Stadium at Grant field is exposed to cool refreshing breezes that blow in from the nearby Gulf.

GETTING THERE

Dunedin, directly north of Clearwater, is a small, quiet community on the beach. The town has two lovely state parks, Caladesi Island State Park and Honeymoon Island State Park. Accommodations include small hotels, motels, and campgrounds.

To get to Dunedin Stadium at Grant Field from US Alternate 19, turn left at Main Street. Go to Douglas Avenue and turn right to the stadium.

Box seats go for $4. General admission tickets cost $3, $2 for kids and seniors.

For schedule of events and ticket information, call (813) 733-9302.

For tourist information, contact the St. Petersburg, Clearwater, and Dunedin Convention & Visitors Bureau, Thunderdome, 1 Stadium Drive, Suite A, St. Petersburg, FL 33705, (813) 582-7892 or (800) 345-6710.

| | | HOMETOWN STATS—DUNEDIN | | | |
| | | *The Last Ten Years** | | | |
Affil.	Year	League	Wins	Losses	Attendance
TOR	1987	Florida State	76	64	29,905
	1988		65	75	33,540
	1989		69	71	41,231
	1990		84	52	65,348
	1991		59	72	67,040
	1992		78	59	74,983
	1993		68	64	77,382
	1994		65	68	80,126

*Statistics are given only for the years in which the team played in Dunedin.

Fort Myers Miracle

(Minnesota Twins)

William H. Hammond Stadium
Lee County Sports Complex
14400 Six Mile Cypress Parkway
Fort Myers, FL 33912

If you find yourself at a baseball game where kids are running the entire operation (Kids for Kids Night), where a ghoulish character appears from a cloud of smoke from one of the dugouts (Phantom of the Ballpark), where horror movies are shown afterward projected onto sheets (Field of Screams), where Madame Zelda tries to conjure up the spirit of a great inventor (the Thomas Edison Seance), and where the mascot has four legs (Toucan the Diamond Dog), you are, no doubt, in Florida. Fort Myers, Florida, to be more exact—and in the hands of Mike Veeck, son of the late great promoter (and major league club owner) Bill Veeck. Mike has been called "crazy," "whacko," "absolutely nuts," and "bananas," and this is by people who *love* him!

The Miracle franchise was born in 1927 as the Miami Base Ball Club. Through the years the club would be known as the Wahoos, the Flamingos, the Sun Sox, the Marlins, the Amigos, and, finally, the Miracle. Throughout much of the 1980's right on through 1992, the team was independent and really struggled. In fact, the team was downright awful, it was the joke of minor league baseball. In 1989 there was some hope when the team got new owners, including Bill Murray and Jimmy Buffett, but the team kept losing and losing.

Then Mike Veeck (as in wreck) entered the picture. Veeck moved the team to Fort Myers and a brand-new stadium in 1992. The last year that the Miracle played in Miami the team attracted only 14,972 fans all season. Their first game in Ft. Myers in 1992 attracted almost half that number—

7,269 fans. In 1993 Veeck established Class A affiliation with the Minnesota Twins, and in 1994 the Miracle had its first winning season since 1985. Overall, through bad times and good, some major names have come out of the Miracle's organization, among them Jim Palmer, Mike Flanagan, Jose Canseco, Eddie Murray, Cal Ripken, and Benito Santiago.

William H. Hammond Stadium is part of the Lee County Sports Complex, which also has softball and soccer fields, lake fishing, and picnicking. The stadium is quite beautiful, the facade more reminiscent of a grand old Florida-style racetrack than a ballpark. The $15 million ballpark seats 7,500 and has separate facilities (practice fields, indoor hitting tunnels, etc.) that are state-of-the-art and second to none. Besides being home to the Miracle, the complex serves as the Twins' spring training site. The Bill Murray picnic area down the left field line can be reserved for parties of thirty or more; you can watch the game relaxing on the grass or at one of the original picnic tables moved from Chicago's historic Comiskey Park.

Veeck's goal is to attract 100,000 fans a year. We bet he'll do it, too. Be it giant fireworks displays, giveaways, or appearances by The Famous Chicken, Max Patkin, Elvis Presley, the Addams Family's Morticia, or the Beach Boys, something is always going on. You never quite know what to expect either. One evening you might encounter "The Miracle Players Present the Murder Most Foul"—an audience participation event. As "dead bodies" (actors) keep piling up between innings, the fans are furnished with clues. Whoever solves the mystery first wins free tickets to a future game. Best of all, you can get a $6 haircut over near third base while all this is going on!

When Jericho the Miracle Dog, an eleven-year-old golden retriever, retired as team mascot in 1993 the fans gave him a big send-off. He came to the game in a limo, and children brought him baskets of candy. His son Toucan, "the Diamond Dog," has succeeded him, learning to bring out the extra balls—and to carry the Gatorade to the umpires between innings, as Jericho used to do. For the mascot race, dozens of kids line up at first and try to race around the bases before Toucan can fetch a ball from the outfield and beat them to home plate. Toucan will also, on occasion, retrieve foul balls. He spends much of the game in his dog-house, located next to the Miracle dugout.

Gates open one hour before game time. The best time to get autographs is between 6:00 P.M. and 6:30 P.M. down by the dugouts.

GETTING THERE

There are literally hundreds of islands to explore off Fort Myers on Florida's Gulf Coast. Do visit the Thomas Edison Museum. There are 20,000 hotel rooms in Lee County, ranging from budget to resort—and countywide, an unbelievable 3,500 campsites and 50 RV sites!

To get to William H. Hammond Stadium in the Lee County Sports Complex, take I-75 to Daniels Parkway (exit 21). Go west on Daniels to Six Mile Cypress Parkway. Take a left on the Parkway and continue to the stadium. There is plenty of parking, which costs $1.

Box seats go for $4, and general admission tickets cost $3. (There are no reserved seats.) Kids and seniors get $1 off.

Toucan the Diamond Dog is the Miracle's official mascot.

For schedule of events and ticket information, call (813) 768-4210.

For tourist information, contact the Lee County Visitors & Convention Bureau, 22180 West First Street, Fort Myers, FL 33902, (813) 335-2631 or (800) 533-4753.

HOMETOWN STATS—FORT MYERS *The Last Ten Years*†					
Affil.	**Year**	**League**	**Wins**	**Losses**	**Attendance**
KCR	1985	Florida State	82	57	46,163
	1986		50	85	42,083
	1987		54	87	27,369
COOP	1992		46	85	105,578
MIN	1993		55	79	95,054
	1994		71	63	95,688

*Statistics are given only for the years in which the team played in Fort Myers.

†Fort Myers did not have a baseball team from 1988 to 1992.

Kissimmee Cobras

(Houston Astros)

Osceola County Stadium
1000 Bill Beck Boulevard
Kissimmee, FL 34744

The Houston Astros had been affiliated with Daytona Beach from 1978 through 1984, when they bought the franchise outright and relocated to their brand-new spring training complex here in Kissimmee. The early years were successful ones on the field. The team went to the playoffs in 1985 and in 1987 to the league championship series. In 1992 they advanced to the playoffs again, but then in 1993 the team set a franchise record for the worst season ever. They finished at 56–74, 26½ games back of the Charlotte Rangers. In spite of this off-year, the Cobras (the Osceola Astros until 1995) have one of the best records in the league, and their all-time roster glistens with the names of big league players. Thirty-two players have come through Kissimmee on their way to the majors. Gold Glove outfielder Kenny Lofton had a great 1990 here, batting .331. Longtime Astro third baseman Ken Caminiti started here. So did catcher Scott Servais. Al Osuna and Brian Williams pitched here, too.

Osceola County Stadium opened in 1985 and sits alongside the four practice fields and official buildings of Houston's spring training camp. It's a sleek park with a white and coral grandstand that sweeps down past first and third bases. Behind the outfield fence is a line of fern palms that provides the lush tropical view we've come to expect in Florida. And beyond the trees is a huge pond that, they tell us, is stocked with bass (some ten-pounders).

Unfortunately, the Cobras are in a tough fan market to crack. It's not easy to compete with nearby Disney World, Epcot Center, Universal Studios, and MGM. The club feels fortunate to draw 1,000 fans into the park on any night. The die-hard fans who do come get the benefit of a number of promotional events during the season, like fireworks shows and guest appearances by the Blues Brothers and Max Patkin and a Rainbow Kids concert. There are premium giveaways throughout the season, too.

Quazzie, the team mascot, is about as famous as any major league Astro, and it's worth a trip just to catch his act. We'd describe him as a huge (6-foot), orange (midnight blue in 1995 is a possibility) foam-rubber marshmallow wearing a happy face, oversized sunglasses, and an Astros hat. A local sportswriter once described him as a sweet potato on steroids or perhaps a mutant navel orange. Poor Quazzie. One day Quazzie got the hoist for allegedly taunting the umpires—something that seems (to us anyway) to be part of any mascot's job description. Well, the umpires must have been having a collective bad day because when Quazzie came out on the field to select a kid for the Mascot Race, they told him to get lost. Unofficial word had it that the umpires were furious with Quazzie for mimicking them, holding his nose at calls he didn't like. They tossed him for inciting the crowd, as well. Quazzie was stunned. The little kids were, too—they cried as he slumped out of the stadium. The story appeared in *USA Today* and *Baseball Weekly*—even ESPN ran it. Quazzie got over his humiliation, naturally, and hasn't missed a game since.

Gates open one hour before the game. You can get autographs before the game from 6:15 P.M. to 6:45 P.M. down both foul lines, or after the game outside the clubhouse.

GETTING THERE

Kissimmee is virtually right next door to Walt Disney World, Sea World, and the brand-new "Splendid China" theme park, so there is no shortage of things to do. There are literally hundreds of hotels and motels and plenty of camping in and around Kissimmee.

To get to Osceola County Stadium, take the Florida Turnpike to Exit 244. Take a right onto Highway 192; then turn right again onto Bill Beck Boulevard and to the stadium. There is plenty of free parking.

Admission is $3.50 for adults, $2.50 for kids and seniors.

For schedule of events and ticket information, call (407) 933-5500.

For tourist information, contact the Kissimmee-St. Cloud Convention & Visitors Bureau, P.O. Box 422007, Kissimmee, FL 34742, (407) 847-5000 or (800) 327-9159.

Mascot Quazzie warms up in the on-deck circle.

HOMETOWN STATS—KISSIMMEE *The Last Ten Years*					
Affil.	**Year**	**League**	**Wins**	**Losses**	**Attendance**
HOU	1985	Florida State	77	58	38,082
	1986		59	78	36,135
	1987		80	59	38,068
	1988		83	54	44,023
	1989		72	65	53,566
	1990		72	66	46,421
	1991		64	63	48,341
	1992		72	62	49,870
	1993		56	74	51,527
	1994		46	89	38,496

Lakeland Tigers

(Detroit Tigers)

Joker Marchant Stadium
2301 Lakeland Hills Boulevard
Lakeland, FL 33805

Lakeland Tiger fans start out young.

The Lakeland Tigers have been headquartered here—in Tigertown, Detroit's facilities for spring training—since 1967, and they're owned (since 1992) by Mike and Marion Ilitch, the founders of Little Caesar's (Pizza, Pizza!) Pizza. In twenty-five-plus years, the Tigers have won five Florida State League championships, and from 1987 through 1993 they put together an impressive golden streak, making it to the playoffs seven times. Major league veterans like Kirk Gibson, Howard Johnson, and John Smoltz made their starts here. Newer major league stars include Sean Bergman and Shawn Hare.

Joker Marchant Stadium is named after the official from the Parks and Recreation Department who labored for its cause back in the 1950s. Located in downtown Lakeland, the stadium has a facade that actually abuts Lakeland Boulevard. Recent renovations (about $600,000 worth) have given this place a nostalgic feel. There's a large sign reading TICKETS in big carnival-like green and orange letters that hangs above the ticket window. Two traditional wrought-iron entry gates open onto a lively concourse full of colorful vendors. There's a courtyard with tables and umbrellas next to a rustic, barn-wood burger shack. Concessions stands are lit up with 1950s-vintage neon signs and trimmed with bright awnings. On weekends, live musicians and clowns perform on the concourse. Inside, the roomy grandstand and bleachers seat 7,000. Over the (billboardless) outfield wall, there's a great view of Lake Parker and what is really a power plant, but what we swear looks like a launching pad when it's lit up at night.

Until recently, the Tigers shared fans with the nearby Florida State League Winter Haven Red Sox team and the Baseball City Royals. When those two franchises moved out in 1993, the Tigers were left as the only team in Polk County. However, the lack of local rivalry (and a lousy two-year record) has hurt attendance.

The Tigers' premium giveaways are plentiful each season and include the best of the usual—bats, gloves, T-shirts, helmets, and so on. Promotional events include a big 4th of July celebration of fireworks that packs the park to near capacity, and other special events. It's like a party from the first pitch to the last out. In Spin to Win fans are chosen to come down out of the stands to spin a casino wheel set up behind home plate. If the spinning arrow stops on the number the player has called he or she wins a weekend getaway, a color TV, or a dinner for two. In Couch Potato of the Night in the second inning a fan is chosen to watch the game with three friends on a big comfy couch behind third base. Free snacks are provided, too. A fan chosen to guest-sing "Take Me Out to the Ball Game" during the seventh-inning stretch wins something, too, like tickets to a game, a large pizza, or a car wash.

Southpaw the Tiger and Little Tiger are agile team mascots who dance on top of the dugout, and instigate a wave or two.

Gates open one hour before game time. The best time to get autographs is after the game along the first base side.

GETTING THERE

Lakeland, midway between Tampa and Orlando on I-4, is most famous for Frank Lloyd Wright's The Child of the Sun Collection, which is a grouping of twelve Wright buildings on the Florida State University campus. There are a few hotels and numerous motels, with camping just to the east.

To get to Joker Marchant Stadium from Orlando take I-4 west (from Tampa, take I-4 east) to Exit 19 onto Lakeland Hills Boulevard heading south. Go about two miles and you'll see the stadium on your left. Parking is free.

Box seats are $4. General admission tickets cost $3.

For schedule of events and ticket information, call (813) 499-8229.

In 1993, the Lakeland Tigers battled the St. Lucie Mets in the division playoffs but lost 2–1 in a best-of-three series.

For tourist information, contact the Central Florida Convention & Visitors Bureau, P.O. Box 1839, Bartow, FL 33831, (813) 534-4372.

| | | HOMETOWN STATS—LAKELAND | | | |
| | | *The Last Ten Years* | | | |
Affil.	Year	League	Wins	Losses	Attendance
DET	1985	Florida State	56	84	50,229
	1986		54	79	53,147
	1987		74	61	61,255
	1988		77	61	53,818
	1989		77	59	54,409
	1990		83	49	57,967
	1991		72	56	51,464
	1992		70	62	56,951
	1993		65	63	25,248
	1994		63	68	21,996

St. Lucie Mets

(New York Mets)

Thomas J. White Stadium
525 NW Peacock Blvd.
Port St. Lucie, FL 34986

In 1988, when the New York Mets bought the Class A Daytona Beach Admirals (with the White Sox at the time) and moved the franchise to Port St. Lucie, no one could have predicted the quick return they would get for their buck. The St. Lucie Mets literally took the Florida State League by storm that year, and took the 1988 league championship to boot! They haven't let up, either, having qualified for the playoffs every year since that championship season. Major league stars like the versatile infielder Chris Donnels played here. Donnels, in fact, was league MVP in 1989. And St. Lucie's Randy Curtis was MVP in 1993. Pete Schourek, Butch Huskey, Eric Hillman, and Tim Bogar are others who made their first strides with these Class A Mets.

Actually located in St. Lucie West, a few miles from the center of Port St. Lucie, Thomas J. White Stadium is the crown jewel in a seven-field complex that is the spring training/minor league headquarters of the New York Mets. The white facade literally gleams amid the thick green woods and swamps and the acres of fruit orchards that surround it. Named for the president of the St. Lucie West Corporation, the ballpark sits in the heart of a planned town that has just begun to pop up. In time, we imagine, there will be a thriving community here. Right now what you see, as you gaze over the outfield wall, is the green of the Mets' training fields and woods.

This is a beautiful park for watching baseball, and about 70,000 fans show up every year. The stadium is roomy, with comfortable seating for 7,500. So sit back and enjoy the ocean breeze that wafts in from the nearest beach about seven miles away and marvel at a sunset that's worth writing home about. It's so friendly and relaxed here that fans often come back just for the ambience. With an average attendance of 1,100, GM Ross Vecchio and his staff can practically greet every fan at the gate. And they do—or at least try to.

Pay one price ($4) and you can sit almost anywhere in the park unless it's Sunday Five for $5 Night, when five people get in for five bucks. Monday is Two for the Price of One Night with a coupon from the sponsor. On Tuesday any kid who is a member of the Knothole Gang gets in for twenty-five cents. Wednesday is a kind of flea market giveaway night, when you might get a player's broken bat or a grab bag of leftovers from past giveaways. On Thursdays ladies' admission is only $1, and soda and beer cost only fifty cents. On weekends, count on big giveaways and promotions.

Every game has a few between-inning contests like Strike O and Dash for Cash. At least once each game a kid gets to try to sail a Frisbee through a window to win a free hamburger.

Thomas J. White Stadium is a shining, sleek structure surrounded by palms and verdant woods.

What St. Lucie players won't do for the fans! Here they rehearse the National Anthem, which they went on to sing at game time, May 7, 1993.

Sometimes Lou, the seven-foot pink (they tell us he's sunburned) bull mascot, will help the little contestant win that burger.

PA announcer Phil Scott is one of the treasures of the Mets organization. With one of the deepest bass voices we've heard in any park, he leads a particularly powerful rendition of "Take Me Out to the Ball Game" during the seventh-inning stretch. Scott also emcees a contest the fans look forward to each night: Scott's Stupid Trivia. How he even knows Lucy Ricardo's middle name, we can't guess. But that might be the stupid trivia question, and if any fan knows it they win a prize.

Gates open one hour before game time. Autographs are easy to get if you arrive early and head down by the dugout.

GETTING THERE

Port St. Lucie, an agricultural and fishing community, is located on Florida's "Treasure Coast" (East Coast)—so named because of a Spanish treasure fleet (now excavated) that was wrecked in 1715, leaving over $14 million on the barrier reef. Accommodations range from moderately priced motels to luxury resorts.

Thomas J. White Stadium is located in St. Lucie West. From I-95 take Exit 63C onto St. Lucie West Blvd. Turn left on NW Peacock. From the Turnpike, take the Port St. Lucie exit and follow the signs. From US Route 1, take Prime Vista Boulevard right to the stadium. There's plenty of free parking.

All adults pay $4 for open seating, it's $2.50 for kids and seniors.

For schedule of events and ticket information, call (407) 871-2100.

For tourist information, contact the St. Lucie County Chamber of Commerce, 1626 SE Port St. Lucie Boulevard, Port St. Lucie, FL 34985, (407) 335-4446.

		HOMETOWN STATS—ST. LUCIE *The Last Ten Years**			
Affil.	Year	League	Wins	Losses	Attendance
NYM	1988	Florida State	74	65	68,150
	1989		79	55	66,041
	1990		76	58	65,597
	1991		72	59	79,961
	1992		74	62	66,899
	1993		78	52	69,078
	1994		71	65	67,999

*Statistics are given only for the years in which the team played in Port St. Lucie.

St. Petersburg Cardinals

(St. Louis Cardinals)

Al Lang Stadium
180 2nd Avenue SE
St. Petersburg, FL 33701

Minor league ball began in St. Petersburg in 1920 and ended abruptly when the old Florida State League disbanded in 1928. In 1955 the city came back into the reactivated league, and baseball has been thriving ever since. Some say that the affiliation between St. Pete and St. Louis was a match made in heaven. It has endured since 1966, and major league stars like World Series veteran Terry Pendleton, four-time Gold Glover Andy Van Slyke, and All-Star catcher Terry Kennedy made their starts here in Al Lang Stadium. Sparky Anderson even managed here, in 1966.

In spite of the strong alliance with St. Louis, these local Cards have been struggling since their last championship in 1987. When the present owner, Joel Schur, bought the club in 1989, things began to look up. Briefly, anyway. The fans came out in league-leading numbers of 2,600 each game to watch the likes of young Brian Jordan help the team qualify for the playoffs. Unfortunately, over the next three years the team slumped, finishing eleventh in the overall standings in 1992. The fans kept coming, however, and finally in 1993 the team managed to finish third best in the league. Okay, so it's not a real golden moment. Let's call it a tribute to endurance.

Al Lang Stadium is an old (almost fifty years old) but comfortable park that sits right on the Tampa Bay waterfront about a five-minute walk from the beach. It's a very friendly 7,500-seat place. The grandstand is close to the diamond, and bleachers extend behind the bullpens down left and right field. There are cookout smells from the BBQ area off first base. The outfield fence is covered with traditional billboards, and the view from the stands? Well, it's common to see twenty or thirty sailboats serenely cruise by during the game. Foul balls and home runs regularly head for the bay too, along with dozens of kids hoping to catch them. It gets very hot here, but once the sun sets and the breeze blows in off the water there's no better place to be (win or lose) for baseball. At least, that's how they feel in St. Petersburg.

Owner Joel Shur is an ardent fan. By day he's a real estate magnate in New York City, but by night he's the loud one cheering in the front row. A good time for all, no matter what, is his prescription for the St. Petersburg fans. There are fifty-five promotions scheduled for seventy home games. Premium giveaways like bats, jackets, T-shirts, and so forth, and guest appearances by Billy Bird are big draws on the weekends. Kids Night is an exciting kind of a combination treasure hunt/career night for kids six to fourteen. The first 500 kids to enter the stadium get a number. Scattered over the field before them is a sea of great prizes—gloves, hats, balls, bats, and jackets, each with a number on it. At the "go" signal, music pumps through the speakers, the kids scramble to find *the* prize with *their* number, the announcer calls the action, parents help the little ones, and the kids help each other until everybody is matched up. Then during the game some kids get to work in the ticket booth or alongside ushers or even with radio broadcasters in the press box. At another special event, Turn Back the Clock Night, the seniors get a 1940s big band, and Cokes and hot dogs cost ten cents.

Gates open one hour before game time. Players will sign autographs if you get there early and approach them by the dugout.

Fifty-year-old Al Lang Stadium is blessed with sea breezes and hefty attendance records.

GETTING THERE

St. Petersburg, on the tip of the peninsula that separates Tampa Bay from the Gulf of Mexico, is a cultural center with many museums, including the famous Salvador Dali Museum. There are first-class hotels, lots of motels, and waterside camping at Fort De Soto.

Al Lang Stadium is located in the heart of St. Petersburg, right on the Tampa Bay waterfront. From Orlando, take I-275 south to First Street (exit 9). Take First Street south for two blocks to the stadium. There's limited free parking in the stadium lot, but plenty of street parking within walking distance.

Box seats are $4. General admission tickets cost $3, $2 for kids and seniors.

For schedule of events and ticket information, call (813) 822-3384.

For tourist information, contact the St. Petersburg, Clearwater, and Dunedin Convention & Visitors Bureau, Thunderdome, 1 Stadium Drive, Suite A, St. Petersburg, FL 33705, (813) 582-7892 or (800) 345-6710.

| | | HOMETOWN STATS—ST. PETERSBURG | | | |
| | | *The Last Ten Years* | | | |
Affil.	Year	League	Wins	Losses	Attendance
STL	1985	Florida State	78	62	136,689
	1986		88	48	126,242
	1987		85	57	121,732
	1988		68	68	170,534
	1989		75	64	202,383
	1990		60	74	190,146
	1991		47	84	155,946
	1992		57	76	121,763
	1993		75	58	123,275
	1994		74	65	108,283

Sarasota Red Sox

(Boston Red Sox)

Ed Smith Stadium
2700 12th Street
Sarasota, FL 34237

After twenty-three years in Winter Haven and one year in Fort Lauderdale, these Class A Red Sox moved in 1994 to Sarasota, where they play in the White Sox spring training facilities. This is the team that graduated future Red Sox power hitter Jim Rice, Cy Young Award winner Roger Clemens, the flamboyant Oil Can Boyd, and 1992 All-Star Brady Anderson to the big leagues.

So although Sarasota is beautiful and the fans are great, the Sox really want to be in Fort Myers at the Red Sox spring training facility there. They might get their way, too, if they can convince the Fort Myers Miracle, the Twins' Class A affiliate, that having another team in town would be so good for business that it would be worth it to them to waive their territorial rights. Until such a day, however, the Red Sox are here in Sarasota. The local fans actually don't care who's playing whom, or where. They come out, about 1,100 per game, no matter what. Attendance is actually much better here in Sarasota than in Winter Haven or Fort Lauderdale, where some nights saw as few as 300 in the stands.

Ed Smith Stadium is named for the local community activist who has done so much to improve baseball in Sarasota. A grandstand of 25 rows seats 6,500, and bleachers down both baselines take care of an additional 1,000. Built in 1988, the stadium sits in a quiet residential area just north of downtown and is one of those modern parks with an old-fashioned feel to it. It could be because of the traditional ten-foot-high billboarded outfield fence or the quirky placement of the bullpens—the players go through gates in the outfield wall into the bullpens, which sit on the other side of the fence in either corner. Or perhaps it's the tent down left field that serves as a picnic area, the foul balls that fly over the grandstand and into the yards of houses nearby, or the kids who wait outside with mitts ready. But more than anything, this park is just plain fun. There's a welcome mat at each turnstile (just try to keep from smiling). And a waitress is there to serve you in the box seats section.

There are lots of between-inning contests, too. A live organ plays for a game of Musical Chairs (kids only). There's the Dizzy Bat Race and the Long Drive Golf contest—whoever's whiffle ball flies the farthest into the outfield wins a weekend getaway, or dinner for two. On Friday and Saturday nights, at the end of the fifth or sixth inning the Frisbee Toss grabs everybody's attention. Somebody tries to sail the disc so that it will land in the bed of a pickup truck. What's so tough about that? The truck happens to be rolling along the warning track. Splash for Cash has an interesting twist here: the contestant who goes splashing for coins in a kiddie pool is blindfolded! Big promotions like 4th of July fireworks and premium giveaways at the gate take place on the weekends. On Thursdays, all general admission seats cost only a buck.

Gates open one hour before game time. The players are more than happy to sign autographs before the game if you come down to the edge of the dugout.

GETTING THERE

Sarasota, with the new Asolo Center for the Performing Arts, the astonishing Van Wezel Performing Arts Hall, the Ringling Museum of Art, and much, much more, is often called the cultural center of Florida. The city, on the Gulf Coast, has all kinds of accommodations from inexpensive to luxurious.

To get to Ed Smith Stadium, take I-75 to University Parkway (exit 40) and go west for three miles to Tuttle Avenue; take a left on Tuttle and proceed to 12th Street and the Stadium. Parking costs $1.

Box seats cost $4, while general admission tickets go for $3, $2 for kids and seniors.

For schedule of events and ticket information, call (813) 365-4460.

For tourist information, contact the Sarasota Convention & Visitors Bureau, 655 N. Tamiami Trail, Sarasota, FL 34236, (813) 957-1877 or (800) 522-9799.

The Red Sox (catcher Walt McKeel shown here) lost the third and deciding game of the 1994 division playoffs to Tampa 1–0 in an exciting 14-inning battle.

| | | HOMETOWN STATS—SARASOTA | | | |
| | | *The Last Ten Years** | | | |
Affil.	Year	League	Wins	Losses	Attendance
CWS	1989	Florida State	79	57	52,061
	1990		63	75	51,775
	1991		75	56	84,951
	1992		85	48	91,574
	1993		77	57	91,883
BOS	1994		69	64	68,781

*Statistics are given only for the years in which the team played in Sarasota.

Tampa Yankees

(New York Yankees)

Red McEwen Field
University of South Florida
4202 Fowler Avenue
Tampa, FL 33620

Owned by the Yankees' George Steinbrenner et al., this team recently moved to Tampa after a thirty-year stay (1962–1992) in Fort Lauderdale. While there, they played in twelve playoffs, winning the league championship seven times. Now they've set up temporary quarters at Red McEwen Field on the University of South Florida campus, but the plan is to move in 1996 to a brand-new Yankees minor league/major league spring training and athletic complex twelve miles away. The 10,000-seat stadium that is being designed and built is an exact miniature of Yankee Stadium.

In the meantime, the team is getting by at Red McEwen Field, a tiny old-fashioned place named after the father of veteran sports writer Tom McEwen. Good things come in small packages, however, and Steinbrenner and club management staff make sure that local fans see baseball here that is worthy of the Yankee tradition. After all, this very same franchise has sent up the likes of Don Mattingly, Scott Kamieniecki, and Jim Leyritz. Steve Balboni whacked twenty-six homers for these A-Yankees in 1979, and a young Jose Rijo set a league record with fifteen wins and a 1.68 ERA when he was league MVP in 1983.

On opening day of the 1994 season, 3,200 fans jammed into the 2,500-seat park. Many saw nine innings on their feet, but if it hadn't been for Steinbrenner himself, who showed up in time to see the long line of about-to-be-turned away fans, they wouldn't have seen anything. Steinbrenner stayed outside with them for a good hour, signing autographs and posing for photos until the GM and staff found seating or standing room for everyone. The only thing some of them missed that day was the first pitch by Reggie Jackson.

From that day on this Yankee team has aimed to please. Walk through the one main gate, and you immediately notice the sawdust and circuslike feeling of the small concourse, where concessions and souvenir stands are housed under colorful tents and canopies. The smell of fresh grilled chicken, Italian sausage, burgers, and hot dogs fills the air. An entire Little League team dressed in their uniforms might file in behind you. A different team gets in free each night to take part in a pregame tradition called Field of Dreams: a little player stands on the field next to a big player during the singing of the National Anthem. Inside, the Yankees have added new bleachers down right field, and down the left field line behind home dugout is another tent with

Reggie Jackson and the Yankees' Gene Michael appeared at 1994 opening day ceremonies. Tampa finished as league champs.

picnic tables for pregame parties (reservations required).

The atmosphere on game night is very laid-back. One reason might be the heat and humidity that settles in over Tampa. Another reason might be that Steinbrenner and partners chose to make this a no-alcohol park. That's right—no beer here! But for the 1,100 or so fans who show up on a regular basis, that seems to be just fine. Between-inning contests like the Dizzy Bat Race, Water Balloon Pitch, and Baseball Trivia are popular. During the seventh-inning stretch some lucky fan gets to take the mike and lead the crowd in "Take Me Out to the Ball Game." For that he or she wins two tickets to some upcoming event at the Tampa Bay Performing Arts Center—maybe even voice lessons.

Foul balls fly everywhere, including up over the grandstand, across the road, and into the Sun Dome parking lot. Kids beware: If you want to hang around outside with your mitt ready for a foul, your parents have to be with you.

Gates open one hour before game time. Autographs are easy to get down by the dugout before the game or after, when the players exit through the main gate and walk across the road to their locker room in the Sun Dome Arena.

GETTING THERE

Tampa Bay, discovered by Ponce de Leon in 1513, is "a city built on, in and beside water." Visit the historic Latin Quarter, Ybor City, where you can still get handmade cigars. There are luxury hotels, resorts, myriad motels, campgrounds, and RV parks.

Red McEwen Field is situated on the University of South Florida campus. From 275 South take the Fowler Avenue exit. Go left for about five miles and you'll see a sign for the Sun Dome. Turn left. Look for the Sun Dome and you'll see Red McEwen Field right across the street. There's plenty of free parking in the Sun Dome lot or on the street.

All seats are bleacher-type. Reserved seats are $3, and general admission tickets are $2. Kids under twelve and seniors get in for $1 (that's really $1).

For schedule of events and ticket information, call (813) 632-9855.

For tourist information, contact the Tampa/Hillsborough Convention & Visitors Association, 111 Madison Street, Tampa, FL 33602, (813) 223-2752 or (800) 44-TAMPA.

Affil.	Year	League	Wins	Losses	Attendance
CIN	1985	Florida State	73	62	60,764
	1986		79	57	57,930
	1987		64	76	62,394
CWS	1988		71	59	55,900
NYY	1994		80	52	60,855

*Statistics are given only for the years in which the team played in Tampa.

†Tampa did not have a baseball team from 1989 to 1994.

Vero Beach Dodgers

(Los Angeles Dodgers)

Holman Stadium
4001 26th Street
Vero Beach, FL 32960

A Vero Beach fan wins plenty in the Cash Scramble.

Dodgertown might not be the granddaddy of the spring training/minor league enterprises, but it has been around for a long time. The Brooklyn Dodgers first came south in 1948 and settled into the barracks of the old navy base that was here. Today, there's little trace of those barracks. Instead, spread out over 450 acres of woods and citrus orchards are several buildings that are used as a conference center after spring training, five full-sized playing fields, two half-fields, and two golf courses (a 9-hole and an 18-hole). The streets here, named after the likes of Vin Scully, Sandy Koufax, and Don Drysdale, come complete with streetlamps that are shaped like baseballs.

The Class A Vero Beach Dodgers have taken two league championships since their first season in 1980, one in 1983 and the latest in 1990. They've gone to the playoffs several times, and they've sent some stellar players on to the major leagues. Henry Rodriguez, Alejandro Peña, Sid Bream, and Ramon Martinez were all Vero Beach Dodgers. Peña had one of his best years ever here, throwing ten wins in 1980.

Located smack in the middle of Dodgertown is Holman Stadium, which is named after the city official who brought the Brooklyn Dodgers here in the first place. The park opened and was dedicated in his honor in March 1953. Due to several renovations since then, this is a very comfortable park with a lively, traditional feel about it. There are 6,500 seats in the stadium, and each one is so close to the action that fans can hear the base coaches and players talking. The foul area is no more than ten feet wide, and the grandstand, just seventeen rows deep, sweeps from foul pole to foul pole.

This is a lush setting for a game. Unlike in other minor league parks, the outfield fence is simple chain-link, beyond which is a landscaped berm and then more than a dozen palm trees. From the top row in the stadium, you can see the golf course beyond the palm trees. A kind of lovable oddity of this stadium is the absence of dugouts; the players sit on a bench separated from the fans by only a three-foot fence.

The atmosphere is very relaxed and casual. Down the left line is a picnic area, where for $9 you can have a complete burger cookout supper and watch the game. $15 will get you a New York steak. Seating is open, so unless a season ticket holder owns a seat you have your eye on, sit anywhere.

General manager Tom Simmons and his staff put on nights of entertainment that keep lots of fans coming out. Weekend promotions like the three big fireworks shows every season really draw the crowds. Contests like Steal a Deal are very popular, too. In this contest the host offers a fan the choice of a Dodger cap, for instance, or whatever is in the box. Sound familiar? Could it be a great jacket or a can of sardines in the box? The same guy shows up in the stands between the next innings challenging fans to produce anything with a Dodger logo on it in order to collect $10. The Cash Scramble lets four fans run on the infield for one minute to collect as many one-dollar bills as they can. There are 4,900 singles (real money!) and one hundred-dollar bill out there. A Brinks truck and guard stand by—a great touch.

The concourse is full of good smells. Be sure to try a grilled Dodger Dog. The fresh-squeezed lemonade is some of the best-tasting in the country.

Gates open one hour before game time. Ask for autographs before the game over the fence by the dugout uh, bench.

Vero Beach players successfully turn a double play.

GETTING THERE

Vero Beach, just north of Port St. Lucie on the Indian River, has twenty-seven miles of ocean beaches and fabulous offshore reefs to explore. The famous Indian River grapefruit is grown here on the mainland side. There are plenty of resorts and motels—and camping at Sebastian Inlet State Park.

Dodgertown and Holman Stadium are located near the heart of Vero Beach. From U.S. 1 take State Route 60 west through Vero Beach to 43rd Avenue. Go north and almost immediately you'll see the WELCOME TO DODGERTOWN sign. From I-95 take State Route 60 east to 43rd Avenue. Turn north. There is plenty of free parking.

All seats are $3.50.

For schedule of events and ticket information, call (407) 569-4900.

For tourist information, contact the Tourist Council, Vero Beach–Indian River County Chamber of Commerce, 1216 21st Street, Vero Beach, FL 32960, (407) 567-3491.

		HOMETOWN STATS—VERO BEACH			
		The Last Ten Years			
Affil.	**Year**	**League**	**Wins**	**Losses**	**Attendance**
LAD	1985	Florida State	67	73	81,800
	1986		68	70	81,919
	1987		62	76	82,676
	1988		75	62	81,831
	1989		69	66	87,178
	1990		79	56	94,832
	1991		79	52	95,900
	1992		53	82	79,447
	1993		56	77	72,861
	1994		60	75	68,903

West Palm Beach Expos

(Montreal Expos)

West Palm Beach Municipal Stadium
715 Hank Aaron Drive
West Palm Beach, FL 33401

Rattlesnakes in the outfield, alligators in the dugouts, and bunnies (the Playboy kind) running the bases are all part of this team's colorful early history. Welcome to West Palm Beach, where since 1928, with several teams playing off and on in three different leagues, anything has—and still does—happened.

This current franchise joined the Florida State League in 1965 as affiliates of the then–Milwaukee Braves. In 1969, the Montreal Expos bought it outright and set up their Class A farm club here. The following year Fred Whitacre became GM, and Montreal sold him the team for $1. Six years later, Whitacre sold it to Bob Sowers for $50,000. When Sowers died in 1985, his wife Ann ran the team for three and a half years before she sold it back to Montreal for $500,000! We love stories like this one.

The first player the WPB-Expos sent to the majors was southpaw Balor Moore, who pitched a no-hitter against Key West back in 1969, the Expos' very first year. The team won its first league championship in 1974 and since then has had some incredible years. In 1990 they finished with a 92–40 record, the best in *all* of organized baseball; and in 1994 they went to the division playoffs. More than 130 players have gone from WPB to the majors, among them Razor Shines (whose nickname came the day he handed out safetyrazors and a handshake to 1,000 men who came through the gate), Bobby Ramos, Gary Carter, Larry Walker, Bill Gullickson, and seven-time All Star outfielder Tim Raines.

The West Palm Beach Municipal Stadium is right in the middle of the action in West Palm Beach. Near the beach, the mall, and downtown, it's been a fixture here since the 1960s, when it was built. And although the park adds character to the town, it hasn't aged well and will be replaced by a brand-new park by opening day 1996. In the meantime, fans will come out all through the 1995 season to say goodbye to this well-loved park.

There are only 4,200 seats here, but each one is practically right on top of the players. The grandstand roof behind home plate gives this place quite a bit of character. Perhaps it's the way the roof ripples and waves, or the way it angles so sharply toward the sky. At any rate, it makes the park look a little like a spaceship out of *Close Encounters* or a *Star Trek* movie. Down the left field line is a casual picnic area that is popular with kids, who love to run around. The team mascot, gorilla Willie P. Bananas, is also a hit with the kids. Willie is so named because his initials are the same as West Palm Beach.

The usual giveaways go home with fans each season. And when The Famous Chicken comes to entertain, he sells out the park. But the team is really most famous for postgame entertainments. Besides some spectacular fireworks shows, there have been more than a few wacky events over the years. Puppies and ponies have been given away. Skydivers have descended into the park, and hot-air balloons have raced to the finish on the field. Several fans and players have said their wedding vows right at home plate. And one year the famous Captain Dynamite, who blows himself up and out of a box, somehow managed to burn up the pitcher's mound and the infield grass! (He hasn't been asked back.)

Gates open one hour before the game. Come early and you can get autographs before the game down by the dugouts, or after the game you can get them outside the clubhouse and in the parking lot.

GETTING THERE

In Palm Beach County there are more than 145 golf courses, 1,100 tennis courts, 16 croquet clubs, 47 miles of ocean beaches, and some of the most expensive shops and real estate around. Lodging ranges from absurdly expensive resorts to moderately priced lakeside campgrounds.

West Palm Beach Municipal Stadium is conveniently located near the downtown area. Take I-95 to Palm Beach Lakes Boulevard (exit 53). Head east for half a mile to the stadium. There is ample free parking.

All seats cost $5 for adults, $3 for kids and seniors.

For schedule of events and ticket information, call (407) 684-6801.

For tourist information, contact the Palm Beach County Convention and Visitors Bureau, 1555 Palm Beach Lakes Boulevard, West Palm Beach, FL 33401, (407) 471-3995.

The Expo marquee marks the entrance to West Palm Beach Municipal Stadium.

| | | HOMETOWN STATS—WEST PALM BEACH | | | |
| | | *The Last Ten Years* | | | |
Affil.	Year	League	Wins	Losses	Attendance
MON	1985	Florida State	74	66	114,659
	1986		80	55	97,481
	1987		75	63	110,633
	1988		71	63	85,733
	1989		74	64	84,316
	1990		92	40	83,673
	1991		72	59	105,787
	1992		76	61	121,574
	1993		69	67	69,289
	1994		71	60	72,097

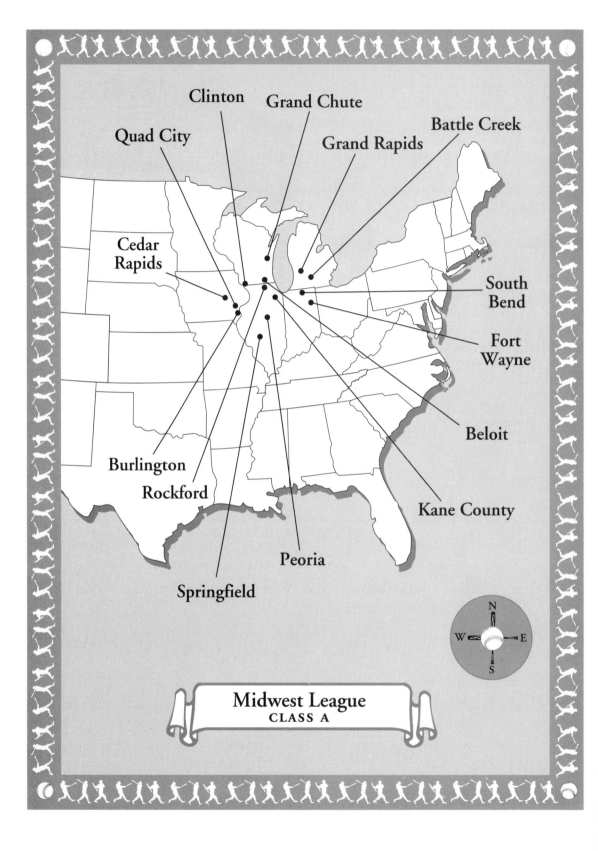

Clinton

Grand Chute

Battle Creek

Quad City

Grand Rapids

Cedar
Rapids

South
Bend

Fort
Wayne

Beloit

Burlington

Rockford

Kane County

Peoria

Springfield

Midwest League
CLASS A

N

W   E

S

Midwest League

Class D 1956–1962; Class A 1963–

The Midwest League actually began play in 1949 under the banner of the Mississippi-Ohio Valley League. Of the charter cities—Centralia (IL), West Frankfort (IL), Mattoon (IL), Paducah (KY), Mt. Vernon (IL), and Belleville (IL)—only Mattoon was around when the league was reorganized and renamed the Midwest League in 1956. None of those original six teams exist today.

The oldest member city today in the Midwest League is Clinton, Iowa, which first joined the Mississippi-Ohio Valley League in 1953 and is the only surviving member of the Midwest League's inaugural year. The newest city to come into the fold (1995) is Battle Creek, Michigan, which is now home to the St. Louis Cardinals' franchise that was previously the Madison Hatters. There hasn't been professional baseball in Battle Creek since 1921, and since the West Michigan Whitecaps in Grand Rapids shattered all attendance records in 1994, its inaugural season, expectations are great in Battle Creek. The franchise's move east, however, has resulted in the league's realignment into three divisions: Western, Central, and Eastern.

The Midwest League is made up of fourteen teams, which are scheduled to play 140 games during the regular season. Division winners, plus the team with the next best overall record, participate in a best-of-three playoff series. The first-round winners then play each other in a best-of-five series for the league championship. This is, however, subject to change.

Battle Creek
Golden Kazoos

(St. Louis Cardinals)

C.O. Brown Stadium
1392 Capital Avenue, NE
Battle Creek, MI 49017

The story of the St. Louis Cardinals' Class-A Midwest League affiliate is somewhat of a sad tale that began in Springfield, Illinois, back in 1982. That was the year the Cardinals established a Midwest League franchise there to replace its Triple-A affiliate that had relocated to Louisville. Springfield fans were so crazy about the Cardinals organization that they supported the new Class A franchise with just as much gusto as they had the Triple-A team. And why not? They were rewarded with consistently good baseball.

The Springfield Cardinals went to the Midwest League playoffs eight times in the twelve years they were in Springfield. There are at least seven players on the current St. Louis roster who played in Springfield, including Rod Brewer, Bernard Gilkey, Ray Lankford, Marc Ronan, and Todd Zeile, who had a league-leading 106 RBIs for the Cards in 1987. Curt Ford (1983) and Jim Lindeman (1984) went on to become part of the 1987 World Series-contending St. Louis team, and Danny Cox (1982) played not only in the 1987 Series, but in the 1985 Series (both of which St. Louis lost) and then once again in the 1993 Series, this time with the Toronto Blue Jays.

It came as a real shock to Springfield fans when it was announced after the winter meetings in 1993 that the team was leaving town because the city of Springfield wouldn't guarantee needed stadium improvements. The team left in anger, pulling up stakes with nowhere to go. They set up shop temporarily in Madison, Wisconsin, which had actually just lost its team to Grand Rapids, Michigan, because Madison would not commit to stadium improvements. They played the 1994 season as the Madison Hatters (pun definitely intended) and drew 69,000 fans—less than half what the franchise drew in Springfield. In the meantime, the West Michigan Whitecaps (the team that left Madison for Grand Rapids the year before) was well on its way to setting all kinds of attendance records, and western Michigan began looking awfully good as a home base for the wandering Cardinals affiliate. Battle Creek, in particular, with its new and underutilized C.O. Brown Stadium, seemed like the perfect spot. It came as no surprise when the team announced that it was moving to Battle Creek (about 65 miles south of Grand Rapids) in 1995. The new team name is inspired by the proximity of Battle Creek to Kalamazoo.

C.O. Brown Stadium was named after sporting goods entrepreneur Cooper Othneil Brown, who donated the land on which the original stadium was built. In 1935, he was a founder and Vice President of the Athletic Institute, the forerunner of the American Amateur Baseball Congress—an umbrella organization for various amateur and youth baseball leagues. The original 1,700 seat brick stadium was built in 1936. The stadium was demolished in 1989 and a new 6,500-seat ballpark was built on the same spot. The stadium is part of Bailey Park Complex, which also contains eight softball fields and two auxilliary baseball diamonds. Though the sideline exterior walls are aluminum, the exterior that wraps around the main entrance and ticket office, directly behind home plate, is brick-faced. The seats here are comfortable and the view over the outfield wall is bucolic: trees and the Battle Creek River.

For the 1995 season, Battle Creek management has lined up a number of fireworks displays and has scheduled appearances by all the minor league personalities; Max Patkin, Dynamite Lady, Phillie Phanatic, Blues Brothers and so forth. There will be lots of contests and giveaways. Hopes are high in Battle Creek.

Gates open one hour before game time. The best place to get autographs, before and after the game, is outside the clubhouse doors, which open right onto the concourse.

GETTING THERE

Battle Creek, home of Kelloggs (and the World's Longest Breakfast Table), calls itself the "Cereal Capital." While there, visit the Kellogg Bird Sanctuary Lake northwest of town and historic Marshall, ten miles to the east. There are first-class hotels, inexpensive motels, and campsites nearby.

Bailey Park Complex and C.O. Brown Stadium are about four and a half miles north of town on Capital Avenue, which is the main north/south artery in Battle Creek. There are two parking lots, each of which charge $1.50 for parking.

Box seats (if available) cost $5, while reserved seats go for $4. General admission tickets cost $3.

For schedule of events and ticket information, call (616) 660-2287.

For tourist information, contact the Greater Battle Creek/Calhoun County Visitor & Convention Bureau, 34 W. Jackson Street, Battle Creek, MI 49017, (616) 962-2240.

C. O. Brown Stadium, which was rebuilt and reopened in 1990, seats 6,500.

Beloit Snappers

(Milwaukee Brewers)

Harry C. Pohlman Field
2301 Skyline Drive
Beloit, WI 53511

Except for a mediocre team that had a brief stint with the Class D Wisconsin Association in 1905, the Snappers (formerly the Brewers) are the only professional baseball team ever to play in Beloit. There had been semipro ball here going way back to 1866, when a team of local college kids called the Olympians played in independent leagues. And in 1920, a local industry's team called the Fairies played here. That team included former Chicago White Sox third baseman Buck Weaver, who had been banned from the majors for his part in the 1919 Black Sox scandal. The Brewers brought Class A minor league ball to town in 1982, and even with an average fan attendance of only 1,000 per game this club is doing just fine, thank you.

Beloit is located about ninety miles southwest of Milwaukee on the Wisconsin–Illinois border. Fans call Beloit baseball the "State Line's Greatest Show on Dirt." The B-Brewers, as they were called until 1995, have put together some hard-hitting, if not championship, seasons. In 1984 they won 86 games, and in 1992 they wound up with a 77–58 overall standing. They went to the playoffs in 1992 but lost the championship to Cedar Rapids. A goodly number of players from Beloit have gone on to the big leagues. In recent years pitcher Bill Wegman and third baseman B. J. Surhoff moved up. And Milwaukee's Greg Vaughn finished 1987 in Beloit with a .305 average and thirty-three home runs.

Beloit's Snappers is one of the few teams in minor league baseball that is community-owned and not-for-profit—that is, all profits go back into the team, the ballpark, and this community of 32,000 citizens. More than 250 volunteers take care of general maintenance at the stadium, man the ticket booths, and work the concession stands.

Pohlman Field is a small place with a quaint and friendly atmosphere. Located in Telfer Park, it seats 2,800, but for some big events it has held as many as 3,500. The place is so small and the seats are so close that we aren't kidding when we say you can really hear word-for-word any arguments between players. The ballpark underwent a $1,000,000 renovation recently to comply with the new major league codes. Now the grandstand extends down both the right and left field lines. The view beyond the traditional billboarded outfield fence remains remarkably serene—thick trees, neighborhood homes. The three-tiered picnic area down the first base line is called "On Deck," and it's *the* place to get some of the best grilled Wisconsin bratwurst you'll ever taste.

Popular on-field contests include Basepath Bowling: if the player gets a strike or spare everyone in the stands gets one free game at the local bowling alley.

Giveaways take place throughout the season. Some of the good ones include helmets, caps, bats, and cowbells. Fireworks nights are big here—call ahead to make sure you can get a seat.

Gates open one hour before game time. The best time to get autographs is before the game down by the dugouts or after the game outside the clubhouse.

GETTING THERE

Beloit, on the Wisconsin–Illinois border, was settled by a French-Canadian fur trader in 1824. It's a land of rivers, lakes, and, amazingly enough, virgin forests. Lodging consists mostly of motels and inns, with some excellent campgrounds in Beloit and nearby.

Pohlman Field is located in Telfer Park on the eastern edge of Beloit. To get there, take I-90 to Exit 81 West, and take a right on Cranston Road

Harry C. Pohlman Field in Beloit, Wisconsin, has been home to Class A baseball since 1982.

to the stadium. There are two parking areas, both of which are free but very limited in capacity. There is no problem parking on the streets in the neighborhood.

Box seats cost $4, and general admission tickets go for $3.

For schedule of events and ticket information, call (608) 362-2272.

For tourist information, contact the Beloit Convention & Visitors Bureau, 1003 Pleasant Street, Beloit, WI 53511, (608) 365-4838.

	HOMETOWN STATS—BELOIT				
	The Last Ten Years				
Affil.	**Year**	**League**	**Wins**	**Losses**	**Attendance**
MIL	1985	Midwest	79	57	93,638
	1986		70	69	101,127
	1987		76	64	87,419
	1988		66	74	96,616
	1989		62	72	93,166
	1990		72	63	95,876
	1991		70	67	77,487
	1992		77	58	60,999
	1993		60	74	65,728
	1994		76	64	60,650

Burlington Bees

(San Francisco Giants)

Community Field
2712 Mt. Pleasant Street
Burlington, IA 52601

Burlington has had professional baseball off and on and in one league or another since the late 1800s, and has been a member of the Midwest League since 1962. The team became the Bees for the first time in 1963 when they affiliated with the then–Kansas City A's; "B's" or "Bees" seemed like a good idea. Then came the Rangers in 1982, followed by the Expos, Braves, and Astros. When Montreal came back to Burlington in 1993, the team became the Bees again, and remain so under their new affiliation with the San Francisco Giants.

Burlington teams may have produced more major league players than any other team in the Midwest League; future Cubs slugger and Hall of Famer "Sweet-Swinging" Billy Williams played here in 1958; Vida Blue was pitching here not long before his call up to the A's in 1970; future All Stars Chet Lemon and Paul Molitor played in Burlington in the 1970s. Recent graduates include Cubs pitcher Jose Guzman, the A's Ruben Sierra, and Braves catcher Javier Lopez.

Community Field was built in 1970 to replace the original Community Field, which had burned down. It's a pleasant, no-frills ballpark that sits in a lovely park setting surrounded by trees. Even though the park is right in the middle of the town's main strip area, surrounded by hotels and retail stores, there's a sense of quiet as you drive up to the stadium and park in the grass lot.

The playing field is the smallest in the league, with only 338 feet to left, 370 to center, and 315 to right. The seats in this 4,000-seat stadium are so close to the action that the players and fans often recognize and greet each other by name.

If you are seriously into baseball, you will have lots of good company here. Some "bleacher bums" come to the game every single night and sit on the third base side. This is a family-oriented crowd, too, and once school's out kids are everywhere. Kids' favorite place for watching the game is the open area off right field near the speed-pitching

About 84,000 fans show up to watch Bees baseball each season.

machine. This is also a good place to catch foul balls; there is a mad dash every time the crack of a bat sends one sailing that way.

There is a fairly new two-tiered Brat Garden Picnic Area that has a fine view of the field. If it hasn't been booked up already, it's open to everybody for grilled brats, chicken, and pork chops.

The management puts on fireworks shows three times a season, and appearances by such minor league celebrities as The Famous Chicken, Billy Bird, the Phillie Phanatic, and the Blues Brothers pack the park. And when it comes to on-field contests, the Bees claim to have the best-officiated Dizzy Bat Race. The contestants must place their foreheads fully down on the bat and spin a complete ten turns around the bat before they make the run of twenty yards and back. Coaches and players spot the runners to make sure no one gets hurt. In the Flipper Race two fans in scuba-diving fins race each other to second base. In the Sumo Wrestlers contest fans take each other on around the sixth inning. The Velcro Wall Leap might be on the night when you are there, too. A contestant wearing a Velcro vest runs, bounces off a small trampoline, and hurls himself forward toward a Velcro wall. If he sticks to it, he wins. Prizes vary.

Gates open one hour before game time. Although you can sometimes get autographs before the game by the gates near the dugouts, the best time is after the game outside the main gate as players leave the ballpark.

GETTING THERE

Burlington, atop the bluffs overlooking the Mississippi, was founded in 1805. The city has several remarkably large areas (with some 200 buildings) named in the National Register of Historic Places. Heritage Hill has nearly 160 structures reflecting Victorian, Greek and Gothic Revival, Italian Villa, Queen Anne, and Georgian architecture. Lodging consists mostly of motels, inns, and bed-and-breakfasts.

To get to Community Field, take Highway 61 North (Roosevelt Avenue) to Mt. Pleasant Street. Take a right on Mt. Pleasant and go one block to the stadium. There is ample free parking.

Box seats go for $4, and general admission tickets cost $3, $2 for kids and seniors.

For schedule of events and ticket information, call (319) 754-5882.

For tourist information, contact the Burlington Area Convention & Visitors Bureau, 807 Jefferson Street, Burlington, IA 52601, (319) 752-6365 or (800) 82-RIVER.

HOMETOWN STATS—BURLINGTON *The Last Ten Years*					
Affil.	Year	League	Wins	Losses	Attendance
TEX	1985	Midwest	50	88	64,763
MON	1986		69	71	68,457
	1987		62	75	71,098
ATL	1988		60	80	78,308
	1989		60	77	82,936
	1990		78	59	81,230
HOU	1991		67	70	81,811
	1992		47	89	69,679
MON	1993		64	71	77,492
	1994		55	82	83,927

Cedar Rapids Kernels

(California Angels)

Veterans Memorial Stadium
950 Rockford Road, SW
Cedar Rapids, IA 52404

In 1891 they were the Cedar Rapids Canaries. In 1896 they became the Rabbits, but then by 1904 they had somehow regressed to the Bunnies. The Bunnies, in turn, became the Raiders in 1934, then the Rockets, the Raiders again, and from 1962 through 1992 the team took on affiliation names: they were the Braves, Reds, Cardinals, Astros, Giants, and Reds again until Cincinnati abruptly ended their thirteen-year association the very day after Cedar Rapids won the 1992 Midwest League championship!

In 1993, when Cedar Rapids signed up with the California Angels, the team decided to create their own identity. The name "Kernels" was one of six possibilities from more than 800 entries in a name-the-team contest. When the owners saw the logo for the Kernels—a baseball, instead of corn, bursting from a husk—they knew they had a winner. (The logo has won so many awards that Kernels merchandise flies off the shelves.)

The Kernels, owned by a group of more than fifty local stockholders, has been red-hot over recent years, although attendance suffered dramatically (as it did in most of the Midwest League) in 1993 when the area had sixty inches of rain. Even so, they drew 114,000 fans that year; under normal conditions average attendance would have been about 140,000.

Cedar Rapids fans have cheered on a lot of great players to the majors. All-Stars Paul O'Neill, Eric Davis, Chris Sabo, and Chili Davis are graduates. Veteran pitcher Tony Cloninger played here in 1959, and so did two-time All-Star Ron Hunt in 1960. Going way back, the legendary John J. McGraw played here in 1891. Known as "Little Napoleon," McGraw was the feisty third baseman for Baltimore who helped the team win titles in 1894, 1895, and 1896. He also went on to manage the world champion New York Giants.

Veterans Memorial Stadium was built in 1949. It sits on a hill above the parking lot, so getting to the main entrance is a bit of a climb. Also known as "the Vet," the 6,000-seat stadium has recently undergone renovations; the clubhouses, press boxes, and umps' room have all been remodeled. When you enter, the main concession areas present you with an array of good eating choices: steak sandwiches, grilled chicken sandwiches, bratburgers, brats, chili dogs, and foot-long hot dogs. There's an ice cream stand and a nothing-but-candy stand, too.

One of the most enjoyable features about this ballpark is the large (250 seating capacity) picnic area near the home team bullpen in left field. It's a great place to watch the game. Kids roam everywhere, including outside the ballpark, in hopes of catching foul balls. There's not much of a view over the left or right field walls because of billboards, but you can see the city skyline over center—very pretty at night.

The Kernels host lots of special events, like pregame clinics for Little Leaguers, performing marching bands, and school choirs. On Kids' Carnival Night the park is packed with people who come out for the rides and games; the proceeds benefit critically ill, disabled, and disadvantaged children. On regular game nights some of the popular on-field contests are the Dash for Cash, the Strike 0 (dugout bowling), and Miniature Car Racing (by remote control between home and first base).

Gates open one hour before game time. The best time to get autographs is between 6:15 and 7:00 P.M. down by the left field bleachers. The players usually hang around briefly down by the dugouts after the game.

A Kernels fan gets in on the act as the Blues Brothers entertain between innings at Veterans Memorial Stadium.

GETTING THERE

Cedar Rapids, on the banks of the Cedar River, is surrounded by some of America's richest farmland. Iowa's number-one attraction, the Amana Colonies—communal villages settled in the 1800s by religious Germans—is nineteen miles to the southwest. Lodging includes hotels, motels, inns, and bed-and-breakfasts. There are extensive campgrounds south of town near Coralville Lake.

To get to Veterans Memorial Stadium, take I-380 north to Wilson Avenue and then go west on Wilson to Rockford Road. Take a right on Rockford and go about one mile to the stadium. There is plenty of free parking.

Box seats are $4, and general admission tickets cost $3, $2 for kids and seniors.

For schedule of events and ticket information, call (319) 363-3887 or (800) 860-3609.

For tourist information, contact the Cedar Rapids Area Convention & Visitors Bureau, 119 First Avenue SE, Cedar Rapids, IA 52406, (319) 398-5009.

Affil.	Year	League	Wins	Losses	Attendance
HOMETOWN STATS—CEDAR RAPIDS *The Last Ten Years*					
CIN	1985	Midwest	78	61	155,034
	1986		70	70	131,534
	1987		70	70	144,279
	1988		87	53	166,121
	1989		80	57	181,189
	1990		88	46	121,340
	1991		66	74	132,820
	1992		82	56	133,899
CAL	1993		54	80	114,105
	1994		77	62	137,795

Clinton LumberKings

(San Diego Padres)

Riverview Stadium
6th Avenue N. and 1st Street
Clinton, IA 52732

Baseball in Clinton dates back to 1906 and the Class D Iowa State League. In 1937 the Clinton Owls joined the Three I League as affiliates of the Brooklyn Dodgers. After a couple of years, the club signed on with the Giants (New York, of course). Through the years they've been the Cubs, Steers, Pirates, White Sox, Pirates again, Pilots, Dodgers, and from 1980 through 1994 Giants once again (now San Francisco). 1995 marks their first year with the Padres. They have been members of the Midwest League since 1954, when it was called the Mississippi-Ohio Valley League,

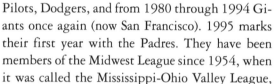

and have had a remarkable record, generally finishing in the top four every year.

Even more impressive, Clinton teams have produced over 300 players for the majors, including Detroit's wunderkind pitcher of the 1960s, Denny McLain, and All-Stars Ron LeFlore and Orel Hershiser. Young Matt Nokes may have hit only three homers when he played for Clinton in 1982, but he went on to hit thirty-two for Detroit in 1987 to help win the division title.

The club only recently changed its name to the LumberKings, trying, like other teams, to have more of a local identity. Chosen from 354 name-the-team entries, "LumberKings" has historical significance. Clinton was once the lumber center of the country and had more millionaires per capita than anywhere else. Today the team is owned not by a millionaire, however, but by over 600 stockholders, who paid $10 per share for the honor. The market is small compared to other minor league areas, but the community is

Clinton finished first in the league's overall standings in 1993, but then struggled to wind up thirteenth in 1994. That's baseball!

willing to support the team in attendance and through taxes. The mayor is even on the board of directors.

Riverview Stadium is, as the name suggests, on the banks of the Mississippi, about fifty yards from the river. Like Davenport, the old park suffered during the floods of 1993. At one point the field level was nine feet below the river level. The 3,000-seat stadium, which was built in 1937 as a WPA project, not only survived the floods but continues to provide the old-fashioned warmth and rustic charm that the fans here count on. You eat well here, too—pork chop sandwiches, meat nachos, grilled bratwurst, and barbecued beef.

There is usually some kind of pregame activity, perhaps a softball game, Little League clinic, or our favorite, the Famous Cow Chip Toss. Giveaways for early arrivals at the gates include the usual posters, T-shirts, and baseballs. During the game a Sweetheart of the Night receives a corsage. There is also the Attendance Guess, Trivia Contest, and Catch a Thief (guess the number of stolen bases the team will have, and win $100).

One of the all-time favorite events is Elvis Night. The King himself shows up, and anybody who dresses up like him gets in free. During a karaoke contest, prizes are given to the best—and worst—Elvis impersonation.

Gates open one hour before game time. Autographs are easiest to get after the game by the front gate, since the players have to walk right by it to leave the park.

GETTING THERE

Clinton, located on the bluffs of the Mississippi River, calls itself the River City. Clinton has its own showboat complete with the Lillian Russell Theater, which produces professional summer theater. Accommodations are mostly motels, with some camping nearby.

Riverview Stadium is located one and a half miles north of US 30 at the Mississippi River Bridge. There is ample free parking.

Box seats go for $3.50, and general admission tickets cost $2.50, $1.50 for kids and seniors.

For schedule of events and ticket information, call (319) 242-0727.

For tourist information, contact the River City Chamber of Commerce, 333 4th Avenue S., Clinton, IA 52733, (319) 242-5702.

HOMETOWN STATS—CLINTON The Last Ten Years					
Affil.	Year	League	Wins	Losses	Attendance
SFG	1985	Midwest	71	69	101,499
	1986		63	76	100,326
	1987		72	67	112,826
	1988		78	62	127,251
	1989		55	84	68,487
	1990		76	58	75,325
	1991		81	58	83,943
	1992		59	79	79,374
	1993		80	54	62,873
	1994		57	82	62,317

Fort Wayne Wizards

(Minnesota Twins)

Memorial Stadium
4000 Parnell Avenue
Fort Wayne, IN 46805

In March 1993, just fifteen minutes after tickets for the opening game of the Fort Wayne Wizards went on sale, the place was sold out. It was the first sign that the return of professional baseball to Fort Wayne, after an absence of over fifty years, would be a major success. And a major success it is. Over 318,000 fans flocked to Memorial Stadium that first year, giving Fort Wayne the third-highest attendance in the thirty-nine-year history of the Midwest League, just falling short of the successful Kane County Cougars, who set league records in both 1992 and 1993.

Baseball and Fort Wayne go way back to 1871, when the Kekiongas played in what many consider to be the first major league, the National Association (1871–1875). From 1903 through 1948, however, hometown teams played mostly in the Class B Central League and produced some very colorful players. The great Pirates' center fielder Max Carey played here in 1907 when he had no money to go to Lutheran Divinity School (we're glad he gave up his calling). Hall of Famer Jesse Haines and another Hall of Famer, Detroit's Charlie (the mechanical man) Gehringer, played here in 1914 and 1920. Although their 1993 season finished at 68–67 the current Wizards have plenty to look forward to with exciting young players like catcher Rene Lopez and pitcher LaTroy Hawkins, who was chosen the Twins Minor League Player of the Year.

Memorial Stadium officially opened on April 19, 1993. It is a beautiful, 6,000-seat, state-of-the-art facility that is, interestingly enough, mostly concrete and precast. With the two elevator towers near the main gate, it looks very modern. The stadium is in a complex that also houses an 8,000-seat arena and exposition center. Beyond the left field wall you can see the University of Indiana. Over center and right fields are views of the St. Joseph River and Johnny Appleseed Park (he is actually buried there). What you can't readily see over the left field wall is Coliseum Boulevard, one of the busiest thoroughfares in Fort Wayne. To protect the cars, management has hung a forty-foot net called the Tater Sack (Tater is slang for home run) from the center field pole to beyond the left field pole.

Wizards fans are wildly enthusiastic about their ball club and their parks—they turn out at an average of 4,000 per game. On game nights the place is buzzing. Team mascot Wayne the Wizard doesn't have to do much to get these fans cheering. Between innings, the on-field contests get the cheers. A big favorite is Human Bowling, which we've seen in a few other parks. The contestant climbs into a four-foot steel-ribbed ball and is then rolled into 6'5" bowling pins. He wins a shirt and a hat if he gets a strike. We think he should win something just for climbing into the ball in the first place.

The Wizards host special events like postgame fireworks shows and guest appearances of the Phillie Phanatic and others. There are many giveaway nights, featuring premiums like duffle bags, lapel pins, key chains, and backpacks in addition to the regular sports fan freebies.

Gates open one hour before game time. Autographs are very easy to get down by the dugouts; the players have to walk through the crowd to get to and from the clubhouse.

GETTING THERE

Fort Wayne is touted as Indiana's "second largest city"! The city sits on the banks of three rivers—the St. Mary's, St. Joseph's, and Maumee.

The Wizards' mascot, Wayne, greets fans, does dance routines atop the dugout, leads cheers, and races fans around the bases between innings.

There are more than eighty parks in Fort Wayne, including the Rivergreenway, which follows the three rivers. Modern Fort Wayne has the familiar hotel and motel chains, bed-and-breakfasts, and camping facilities nearby.

To get to Memorial Stadium, take I-69 to Coldwater Road (exit 112) and go south to Coliseum Boulevard. Turn left (or east) onto Coliseum (Highway 30) and continue one mile to the stadium on the right. There is plenty of parking, which costs $2.

Box seats are $6, while reserved seats go for $5. General admission tickets cost $4, $3 for kids and seniors.

For schedule of events and ticket information, call (219) 482-6400.

For tourist information, contact the Fort Wayne Convention and Visitors Bureau, 1021 South Calhoun Street, Fort Wayne, IN 46802, (219) 424-3700 or (800) 767-7752.

HOMETOWN STATS—FORT WAYNE *The Last Ten Years**					
Affil.	Year	League	Wins	Losses	Attendance
MIN	1993	Midwest	68	67	318,506
	1994		66	73	266,670
Statistics are given only for the years in which the team played in Fort Wayne.					

Kane County Cougars

(Florida Marlins)

Philip S. Elfstrom Stadium
34W Cherry Lane
Geneva, IL 60134

When the struggling Orioles affiliate the Wausau Timbers moved to Geneva, Illinois, in 1991, some thought it seemed like risky business. Their new home was just forty miles west of Cubs and White Sox territory. As it turned out, the club had relocated to the middle of one of the fastest-growing regions in the United States, home to legions of commuters who work in Chicago but choose not to live there. Consequently, the Cougars have set a modern-day attendance record for all of Class A baseball, with an average attendance of 6,000. And that's in a stadium with a capacity of 4,800! Thousands of fans have had a chance to root for the likes of Charles Johnson, the catcher from the University of Miami who was the Marlins' number-one draft pick in 1992. As of May 1994, Johnson was already hitting home runs for the Marlins. Brad Pennington, now with the Orioles, was the first Cougar to ever make it to the majors. Others to watch are Todd Pridy, Chris Sheff, Rey Mendoza, and Vic Darensbourg.

Philip S. Elfstrom Stadium, named after the man who helped make it happen, sits in a beautifully scenic and wooded area of town. A plan for additional seating is in the works, but for now this place is a tight fit. The grandstand hugs the field, and a deck over the right field wall and grassy hills down both lines provide extra space for the large crowds. Blankets and lawn chairs are welcome in the grassy areas.

The Cougar organization puts on quite a show here between innings. Every night there's a Horse Race—cardboard horses beyond the outfield wall.

Dizzy Bat Race is a favorite too. It seems that some lucky fan is always being pulled out of the stands for a chance to win something, but if you can steal away from the action to get to the concession stand, try one of Kane County's pork chop sandwiches.

Mascot Ozzie T. Cougar loses the Race-the-Mascot Race every night. He once lost his head, too. On July 4, 1993, in a widely reported incident, teenagers stole the cougar's head from the laundry room. The original was never recovered, but after a brief recuperation period a reconstructed cougar returned.

Among the special events during the season are fireworks shows, the Old-Timers' Game, and appearances by The Famous Chicken and Max Patkin. Cougars' giveaways are about the most unusual we've seen. Besides bats, caps, helmets, and baseballs, you might get a bike bottle, megaphone, checkbook cover, ice cream watch, frisbee, golf towel, flashlight, Mickey Mouse hat, floppy hat, growth chart, memo board, or cassette sampler just by coming out to the game.

The ballpark is open during the day and closes two hours before game time. Gates reopen one and a half hours before the game. Players will sign autographs down by the dugout. On Sundays whole families can gather with players on the field for autographs and photos for a half hour before the game.

GETTING THERE

Geneva, one hour straight west of the Chicago Loop on the Fox River, was settled in 1833 and is renowned for its Victorian houses and gaslit streets. Geneva is also noted for its distinctive retail and antique shops. This is the suburbs, however; accommodations are limited to a few inns and motels and The Herrington, a slightly expensive, charming riverfront inn that was once a late 1800s butter and cheese manufacturing center.

To get to Elfstrom Stadium, take I-88 to the Farnsworth North exit in Aurora. Go six and a half

The very popular Cougars mascot, Ozzie, takes time out to rest on his laurels.

miles to Cherry Lane and then go west on Cherry Lane to the stadium. Or take Route 59 to Route 64. Go west on 64 to Kirk Road, south on Kirk to Cherry Lane, and then west on Cherry Lane. Parking, which costs $1, is a little tight, so it's best to get there early.

Box seats are $6, while reserved seats go for $5. General admission tickets (lawn) cost $3.

For schedule of events and ticket information, call (708) 232-8811.

For tourist information, contact the Geneva Chamber of Commerce, 8 South Third Street, Geneva, IL 60134, (708) 232-6060.

			HOMETOWN STATS—KANE COUNTY *The Last Ten Years**			
Affil.	Year	League	Wins	Losses	Attendance
BAL	1991	Midwest	68	67	240,290
	1992		61	76	323,769
FLO	1993		75	62	354,327
	1994		71	68	417,744

*Statistics are given only for the years in which the team played in Kane County.

Peoria Chiefs

(Boston Red Sox)

Pete Vonachen Stadium
1524 W. Nebraska Avenue
Peoria, IL 61604

Baseball returned to Peoria in 1983 after a twenty-six-year absence when the Danville Suns, an Angels affiliate, moved to town. Local businessman Pete Vonachen bought the club in 1984 and renamed it the Chiefs in honor of a team that had played here in the mid-1950s. Vonachen even resurrected the 1950s logo. In 1985 he signed the club up with the Chicago Cubs, and the union continued until 1995, when the Cubs took over the Rockford franchise and the Red Sox came in.

Pete Vonachen is one of the most familiar faces in Peoria (he made most of his money through Peoria Blacktop, but also owns interests in several restaurants and motels, lots of real estate, and an auto dealership). Vonachen sold the team in 1989 to a limited partnership in Chicago. Interestingly enough, when he ran the club, it was wildly successful at the gate. It led the Midwest League in attendance and was the first to draw over 200,000 in one season. Future notables like All-Stars Devon White and Greg Maddux are still remembered by fans here. Wally Joyner started in Peoria, as did catcher Joe Girardi and the Cubs' Mark Grace, who finished the 1986 season here with a .342 average.

Support for the team, however, dwindled under the new owners. So in 1993 Pete and other local investors bought the team back. The good news is that since Pete is back, so is community interest, and attendance figures are up, too.

Pete Vonachen Stadium is a royal blue concrete structure that was renovated prior to the 1992 season. The 6,200-seat stadium is open-air (no roof), and every fan is as close to the field as rules will allow. There are two picnic decks—the Cubby Hole and the Friendly Confines—in addition to the Hardball Cafe gazebo. The butterflied pork chop sandwich is all the rage here; don't miss it. Then there are the ribeye steak sandwiches, mesquite-grilled chicken, quarter-pounder hot dogs, nachos, and Spotted Cow ice cream.

Pregame activities are tied to the promotion of the night. Dixieland bands and school marching bands perform on occasion, and on Firefighters Night a fire engine roars onto the field, siren blaring, while Shriners' clowns entertain. Count on something always going on here—skydivers, acrobats, gymnasts. Special guests like the Blues Brothers or the Pirate Parrot and other mascots are booked, too.

The Chiefs' mascot is a woolly buffalo named Chip, whose favorite pastimes are hugging people and losing the Mascot Race. On-field contests like the Dizzy Bat Race are big here in Peoria. And one of our all-time favorite contests takes place here, too—Kiss the Pig. All that we'll say is that it definitely involves the players!

Gates open one hour before game time. Before every home game, two players man the autograph booth on the concourse. You can also get autographs down along the left field line. The clubhouse is beyond the left field wall, so the guys have to walk down the line to and from the field.

GETTING THERE

Dating back to the late 1600s, Peoria, on the Illinois River, was the first permanent settlement in what is now the state of Illinois. The town was named after the Peoria Indians. There are many landmark buildings and historic sites to visit. Hotels, motels, and bed-and-breakfasts provide lodging. Camping is available to the east.

To get to Pete Vonachen Stadium, take I-74 to University Street North (exit 91B) and go to Nebraska Avenue. Take a left on Nebraska to the stadium. There is plenty of free parking.

Box seats go for $5, while reserved seats go for $4, $3 for kids and seniors. General admission tickets cost $3, $2 for kids and seniors.

For schedule of events and ticket information, call (309) 688-1622.

For tourist information, contact the Peoria Area Convention & Visitors Bureau, 403 NE Jefferson Street, Peoria, IL 61603, (309) 676-0303 or (800) 747-0302.

In 1994, Peoria fans made an attendance comeback (after a two-year slump) to well over 175,000.

HOMETOWN STATS—PEORIA
The Last Ten Years

Affil.	Year	League	Wins	Losses	Attendance
CUB	1985	Midwest	75	65	165,053
	1986		77	63	179,183
	1987		71	69	195,832
	1988		70	70	207,294
	1989		80	59	225,757
	1990		55	82	195,671
	1991		62	76	212,159
	1992		62	74	172,560
	1993		59	79	100,811
	1994		68	70	176,603

Quad City River Bandits

(Houston Astros)

John O'Donnell Stadium
209 S. Gaines Street
Davenport, IA 52802

Most of us won't ever forget the pictures coming out of the Midwest during the great floods of 1993—and the one we remember best is the stunning photograph of a mostly submerged John O'Donnell Stadium. The overflowing Mississippi had flooded downtown Davenport, and when the waters (12 feet deep) finally receded they left behind several inches of mud, destroying the field. It's been a tough comeback for the Quad City River Bandits.

Going back some, the Davenport Blue Sox played here in the 1920s with the Class D Mississippi Valley League and into the 1940s with the Class B Three-I League. Since then, there has always been a Quad City team named after one major league affiliate or another. It was the Quad City Angels who won the league championship in 1990. And it was the following year, in 1991, that the Angels decided to break with tradition and become the River Bandits, thereby connecting themselves a little more deeply to the big river. Future major league players who developed their stuff here in Davenport were Carney Lansford, who would go on to have a great hitting career with the Oakland A's; also Brian Harper, Chad Curtis, and pitchers Mike Cook, Hilly Hathaway, Chuck Finley, and Roberto Hernandez.

One of the reasons that the image of flooded John O'Donnell Stadium was so vivid is that the ballpark, built in 1932, is a colorful piece of Americana. With its brick facade and arches throughout, the stadium for many is even more nostalgic than Wrigley Field. And the setting—in a park complete with bandshell on the banks of the Mississippi River, with gambling riverboats paddling by—is nothing less than perfect, or so it seemed until the floods came.

The grandstand is totally covered, which just adds to the classic atmosphere here. For private parties there is the Brat Garden down off left field. The stadium, which was named in honor of the *Quad City Times* sports editor of the 1940s and 1950s, seats 5,500, but when the grass areas around the park are opened up, 12,000 to 14,000 can squeeze in.

The team mascot, Rookie, is a giant raccoon who, we are told, lives under the stadium and shows up at every game just to lose the Mascot Race. Other on-field contests include the Chip Shot (whiffle balls chipped off the dugout and into a bucket win a $100 spree at a local restaurant) and the Dice Game (3-foot dice are rolled off the *top* of the stadium down the protective screen behind home plate onto the field—a 12 or 2 wins dinner on a riverboat).

The Bandits host postgame concerts and five or six fireworks displays a season. Count on fireworks at each game, too—they burst from the scoreboard unpredictably. Promotional giveaways include some of the best baseball fan paraphernalia—gloves, bats, caps, jerseys, and so forth. Food not to miss: grilled cheddar wurst, and the Bandit's Pie—corn chips smothered with chili and cheese.

Gates open about one hour before game time. To get autographs before the game, get there early. There is an eight-foot fence along the third base side that is open between 6:30 P.M. and 6:45 P.M. The players are very willing, but time is short.

GETTING THERE

They call the Quad Cities—Moline and Rock Island (Illinois side) and Bettendorf and Davenport (Iowa side)—the Mississippi River Playground. Riverboat gambling is popular and river mansions and other historic sites abound. Lodging is varied; there are lovely bed-and-breakfasts and campgrounds.

To get to John O'Donnell Stadium from I-74, get off at State Street (exit 67) and take State to River Drive; turn right on River Drive and go about three miles to the stadium. From I-80, get off at Harriston Street (exit 61) and take Harriston to River Drive; turn right on River Drive and go about three blocks to South Gaines and the stadium. There is ample free parking.

Box seats are $6, while reserved seats go for $5. General admission tickets cost $4, $3 for kids and seniors.

For schedule of events and ticket information, call (319) 324-2032.

For tourist information, contect the Quad Cities Convention & Visitors Bureau, 1900 Third Avenue, Rock Island, IL 61204, (309) 788-7800 or (800) 747-7800.

One of the great ballparks in the country, John O'Donnell Stadium was built in 1932 on the banks of the Mississippi.

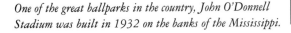

	HOMETOWN STATS—QUAD CITY				
	The Last Ten Years				
Affil.	**Year**	**League**	**Wins**	**Losses**	**Attendance**
CAL	1985	Midwest	66	74	153,414
	1986		62	78	116,062
	1987		47	91	60,999
	1988		60	79	115,459
	1989		72	63	191,825
	1990		81	59	204,889
	1991		74	63	242,322
	1992		91	46	250,745
HOU	1993		56	74	103,797
	1994		57	81	260,471

Rockford Cubbies

(Chicago Cubs)

Marinelli Field
101 15th Avenue
Rockford, IL 61104

They tell us that Albert Spalding, of Spalding Sporting Goods, played for Rockford in 1867. Cap Anson played in 1871. That's the same Cap Anson who is traditionally credited with originating the notion of spring training. (As coach of the Chicago White Stockings he took the team to Hot Springs, Arkansas, to "boil out the booze of winter.") And yes, there really was an all-women's team called the Rockford Peaches, as featured in the movie *A League of Their Own.*

The current team is an expansion club from 1988. They began as the Expos, but the team was sold to the Chicago Cubs in 1992. The Cubs, however, were not quite ready for a new farm team, so they allowed Rockford to sign up with Kansas City (temporarily). Rockford finally will start up with the Cubs in 1995. Lots of players have gone to the majors in the meantime, including Delino DeShields, Mel Rojas, Chris Nabholz, and Greg Colbrunn. All in all, twenty-three players moved up in the team's first six years.

Marinelli Field was built (or actually rebuilt) in 1988 around the existing diamond. The 4,500-seat stadium was named in honor of Louis F. Marinelli, a legend among gifted amateur baseball coaches, who died at the young age of thirty-six. Located right on the banks of the Rock River in Blackhawk Park, the ballpark has a simple look, with a plain blue awning over the main gate and ordinary chain-link fence stretching around.

The picnic area off left field has tables set out on grass. Usually reserved for private parties before the game, it opens up to everybody once the game begins. Head on down there for the concessions: flame-broiled hamburgers, brats, and barbecued pork chop or chicken sandwiches are all first-rate.

Pregame activities tend to be community-oriented, like exhibitions by the YMCA girls pompom team, tumbling groups, and the high school bands. Once the game is on, there is never a dull moment. PA announcer Lisa Fielding is one of the few women in the business. A news reporter for local radio by day, Lisa brings her quick wit and collection of sound effects out to the ballpark on game nights. The fans love her.

Meanwhile, team mascot Rocky the Duck turns cartwheels on the dugout roof, signs autographs in the crowd, and delivers

On grassy berms, Cubbies fans can have their picnics and baseball, too.

232

the pizza during the Pizza Scream contest. There are Auto Races along the outfield wall, and Trivia and Frisbee Toss contests, too. On Saturn Sundays, if a home player hits a grand slam, someone wins a new car. If the grand slam happens during a Denny's Special Inning, the local Denny's serves a Grand Slam Breakfast to everybody in the stands as well. On one Friday the 13th, Denny's offered everybody free breakfast if the team got thirteen hits. Lucky for Denny's that there were only 800 people left in the stands when it happened.

Gates open one hour before game time. You can get autographs down on the third base side before the game, and outside the clubhouse after the game.

GETTING THERE

Rockford, ninety minutes west of Chicago on the banks of the Rock River, has some fine examples of nineteenth-century architecture. There's a variety of hotels, motels, and bed-and-breakfasts, including several resorts. Camping is nearby.

To get to Marinelli Field from the east, take I-90 west to US 20 west (toward Freeport). Go eight miles and get off at the Main Street exit (Route 2 North). Go north to 15th Avenue (second stop light). Take a right onto 15th and continue to the stadium just across the Rock River. From south I-39, head north to US 20 west and follow the same directions. There is plenty of free parking.

Box seats go for $5, while reserved seats are $4.

In 1993, the league's top prospect, Johnny Damon (LEFT), and All-Star MVP Steve Sisco helped bring Rockford to the division playoffs.

General admission tickets cost $3. Kids, seniors, and the military get $1 off.

For schedule of events and ticket information, call (815) 964-5400.

For tourist information, contact the Rockford Area Convention & Visitors Bureau, 211 North Main Street, Rockford, IL 61101, (815) 963-8111 or (800) 521-0849.

	HOMETOWN STATS—ROCKFORD				
	*The Last Ten Years**				
Affil.	Year	League	Wins	Losses	Attendance
MON	1988	Midwest	84	56	158,674
	1989		74	59	139,338
	1990		56	80	140,864
	1991		76	61	66,524
	1992		66	70	50,900
KCR	1993		78	54	68,206
	1994		89	50	70,527
*Statistics are given only for the years in which the team played in Rockford.					

South Bend
Silver Hawks

(Chicago White Sox)

Stanley Coveleski Regional Stadium
501 West South Street
South Bend, IN 46601

The Silver Hawks began life as the expansion South Bend White Sox when the Midwest League grew from twelve to fourteen teams in 1988. The club changed its name in 1994 to Silver Hawks, a name the owners thought might add local color. It does. Studebaker, the maker of Silverhawk cars, was once the city's largest employer. The plant closed in 1963, but the building still stands today just beyond the outfield fence, and we're told there are still unfinished car frames left sitting on the assembly line.

The Silver Hawks baseball team, however, is hardly standing still. This franchise took the Midwest League championship in 1989, took it again in 1993, and has been sending up a load of talented players to the majors year after year. Jason Bere, Roberto Hernandez, Rodney Bolton, Bob Wickman, Mike Maksudian, and Scott Radinsky are just a few of them. Radinsky, who went from Coveleski to Chicago's Comiskey in 1990, was the first pitcher to jump from Class A straight to the Show since Dwight Gooden did it in 1984. And Silver Hawks fans haven't been sitting, either. They've been streaming into the ballpark at an average of nearly 4,000 each game.

Stanley Coveleski Regional Stadium was built in 1986 and named in honor of South Bend's most famous big league player and Hall of Fame pitcher. "The Cove," as fans have nicknamed it, seats 5,000. The concourse, which offers a bird's-eye view of the field, is covered from end to end. So are the last couple of rows of the grandstand, which stretches almost to the foul poles. Grassy berms complete the sidelines and then wrap around both the left and right outfield fences. The berms are "preferred seating" as far as the kids are concerned. Dead center in the billboarded outfield fence is a unique feature for a minor league park— a forty-foot blank wall, not a billboard in sight. Hmmmm. Another unique feature in the park is something called the Upper Deck, an enclosed room above the press box that is available for groups of twenty-five or more. Not only is there a great view of the game from up there, but virtually any sporting event in the world can be broadcast over any one of eleven television monitors serviced by satellite and cable. The Batters Box is a luxurious suite right behind home plate that's pretty well rented out for the season, but the Outdoor Cafe, located at the end of the first base concourse, is available on short notice and serves groups of fifty or more before the game.

The Silver Hawks provide lots of ballpark entertainment for the fan dollar. There are back-to-back nights of fireworks extavaganzas around July 4th, and special appearances by all the popular big league mascots, Hall of Famer Bob Feller, the Clown Prince Max Patkin, and the Blues Brothers. At-the-gate giveaways are plentiful throughout the summer.

The team mascot, Covey (named after Coveleski), is a uniform with a big humanlike head with an equally big moustache. Covey signs autographs for the kids before every game by the front gate.

Gates open one hour before game time. The best time to get autographs is down by the dugouts after the game.

GETTING THERE

South Bend, on the banks of St. Joseph's River in northern Indiana, is best known as the home of Notre Dame University. The Studebaker Museum (with Studebaker innovations ranging from Conestoga wagons to the Avanti) is a must-see. There's

Over 3,500 fans per game show up to watch the Silver Hawks play at Stanley Coveleski Regional Stadium.

a variety of lodgings, including a campground in Granger.

Stanley Coveleski Regional Stadium is located right downtown. Go west on Western Avenue to Taylor, then south on Taylor to the stadium. There is ample parking, which costs $2.

Box seats are $6, while reserved seats go for $4.

General admission tickets cost $3.

For schedule of events and ticket information, call (219) 235-9988.

For tourist information, contact The Convention & Visitors Bureau of South Bend/Mishawaka, 401 East Colfax Avenue, South Bend, IN 46634, (219) 234-0051 or (800) 828-7881.

		HOMETOWN STATS—SOUTH BEND *The Last Ten Years**			
Affil.	Year	League	Wins	Losses	Attendance
CWS	1988	Midwest	59	81	171,444
	1989		85	47	203,197
	1990		77	57	212,485
	1991		69	70	221,071
	1992		71	62	213,951
	1993		77	59	229,883
	1994		72	67	258,424

*Statistics are given only for the years in which the team played in South Bend.

Sultans of Springfield

(Kansas City Royals)

Lanphier Park
1351 N. Grand Avenue
Springfield, IL 62702

Springfield almost lost professional baseball in 1994. Trouble had been brewing for most of 1993, so it wasn't a big surprise around the inner circles of the minor leagues when, after the winter meetings in 1993–1994, the news became official. The Springfield Cardinals (with St. Louis) were leaving town after twelve successful years. But the news did come as a huge shock to Springfield fans, who had no clue of the political intrigue and budgetary stubbornness that had led to the flight of the team.

It seems that the city had been too slow in guaranteeing the improvements (mostly at the stadium) that the team desperately needed. So while the Cardinals were off setting themselves up as the new Madison (WI) Hatters in the spring of 1994, Springfield's baseball fans, corporate sponsors, and community organizations were in a rage so hot that it could be felt by city and county officials. After all, the team had been here since 1982—long enough to just about fill any major league roster. Todd Zeile was Midwest Player of the Year when he played in Springfield in 1987. Rod Brewer was here in 1988. So were Ray Lankford and Mike Perez. And it wasn't as if the club hadn't drawn a healthy number (about 153,000) of fans a season—placing about fourth in attendance in the league of fourteen.

Fortunately, the politicos who were feeling the heat got somewhat of a break. The same kind of scenario had been unfolding in Waterloo, Iowa, where the Padres affiliate, the Diamonds, had been playing since 1989. They were looking for a new home, too. Enter the Midwest League officials, who in late winter of 1994 quickly arbitrated an agreeable lease between the Diamonds owners and Springfield, now willing to make promises and guarantees. There was no time for a name contest when the Diamonds arrived, so the owners picked up the dictionary and went through every word beginning with "S" until they hit "Sultan." They loved it and all the drama it conjured up—a saber, a snake charmer, a snake.

The Sultans' new logo (complete with saber) was up near the main gate, but the management was still lining up concessionaires when the team had their grand opening game at Lanphier Park on April 19. Things pulled together quickly, though, as the team jumped into first place in their division. The club, even in Waterloo, had always been strong in pitching. The Padres currently have three pitchers who were important to this franchise—Mike Ettles, Scott Sanders, and Tim Worrell. But even so, the fans, still bitter over the loss of the Cardinals, didn't come. A mere

Lanphier Park has been a neighborhood landmark in Springfield since 1923.

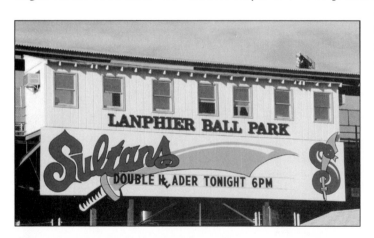

54,000 showed up. The Kansas City Royals, who have replaced the Padres, hope to turn things around in 1995.

Lanphier Park is in a residential neighborhood next to the high school. It was built in 1923, rebuilt in 1952, refurbished in 1960, and now seats 5,000 in the grandstand and bleachers. A snug concourse runs down either baseline, and the main concession stand is right behind home plate. Traditional billboards cover the right and left outfield walls, but the fence in center field is plain chain-link. A grove of pine trees fills the view there, providing the deep green background, or what's called "the batters' eye," for the hitter at the plate.

Two announcers, Len and Amy, who are also local radio stars, host the stadium action. He sits in the booth, announcing players; she roams the crowd with a wireless mike, playing Let's Make a Deal with fans, or instigating the "Sultan Wave." All the while Sinbad the mascot, a big purple genie who carries a magic lantern, grants wishes and gives out prizes. The Sultan Swat is a contest here that's a bit of a twist on Water Pitch. Two fans in swim fins, scuba masks, and snorkels use a Little League bat to try to hit the most pitched water balloons in thirty seconds.

Gates open one hour before game time. It's easy to get autographs here before or after the game because the players have to go down a walkway in order to get to and from the clubhouse. You'll see lots of kids hanging out here.

GETTING THERE

When in Springfield, Illinois's state capital, must-visits include Abe Lincoln's home (from 1844 to 1861), the original law office where he practiced, the Old State Capitol, Lincoln's Tomb, and more. There are lots of motels, some fine hotels, and numerous campgrounds.

To get to Lanphier Stadium from I-55 North, take the Clear Lake exit and turn right onto 11th Street. Take another right on N. Grand Avenue and proceed about a half mile to the ballpark.

Box seats go for $5, while general admission tickets cost $4.

For schedule of events and ticket information, call (217) 544-7300.

For tourist information, contact the Springfield, Illinois Convention & Visitors Bureau, 109 N. Seventh Street, Springfield, IL 62701, (217) 789-2360 or (800) 545-7300.

		HOMETOWN STATS—SPRINGFIELD			
		The Last Ten Years			
Affil.	Year	League	Wins	Losses	Attendance
STL	1985	Midwest	66	74	149,069
	1986		87	53	151,815
	1987		94	46	154,148
	1988		81	58	155,416
	1989		73	62	164,012
	1990		63	76	161,271
	1991		58	79	175,017
	1992		84	56	152,942
	1993		78	58	110,189
SDP	1994		69	71	54,218

West Michigan Whitecaps

(Oakland Athletics)

Old Kent Park
4500 West River Drive
Comstock Park, MI 49321

The West Michigan Whitecaps are fairly new to Comstock Park and Grand Rapids, having played their first season here in 1994. The franchise moved from Madison, Wisconsin, after the 1993 season, where they had been the Madison Muskies for eleven years. For five of those years the club had made it to the playoffs. Some recent major league players who came out of that era are Walt Weiss and the Canseco twins—Jose played in 1983, Ozzie in 1986 through 1988.

The Whitecaps are named after the fierce and persistent white-caps on the great Lake Michigan. The team is owned by a group of twenty-seven local investors headed by Lew Chamberlin. Corporate support for this team has been tremendous; an awful lot of people worked for a long time to bring minor league baseball to the West Michigan area after a forty-three-year absence (professional baseball began as early as 1902 but ended in 1951). They can't really miss. There's a huge fan base, practically the entire western region of the state. Almost from the day the season opened, the Whitecaps were number one in attendance in Class A baseball and ended the season with an all-time Class A record of 475,212.

The Whitecaps play in Old Kent Park, located five miles north of the city in a beautiful setting on the Grand River. Old Kent Park is actually not at all old. It was completed on April 11, 1994, and opened the very next day. The name refers to the Old Kent Bank, which paid for naming rights and, by so doing, gave the team instant credibility. The whole venture has been funded privately. And as other minor league teams have discovered, a brand-new ballpark seems to ensure success.

Because the stadium is located on a flood plain, it was built up high; it's a thirty-step climb to the main gate. The official capacity is 5,701, but the Whitecaps have been averaging over 6,000 fans per game. Grassy berms at either end of the grandstand handle the overflow. On the way to the berms there are picnic areas with tents and grills where brats, chicken, and pork chop sandwiches are sold.

On the concourse—which, by the way, is made of solid pine flooring (kind of rare)—a clown, juggler, or barbershop quartet might be entertaining before the game. There is some kind of giveaway every night—seat cushions, gloves, balls, bats, and so forth—and every night offers a special admission discount or special event. On Monday, for example, anyone with a Sunday church bulletin gets in for half-price; on Wednesday, fans fifty and up get free bingo cards; on Ball Blast Saturday players from both teams toss about 300 baseballs into the stands; Sundays are Family Days—anybody can go down on the field before the game and talk to the players.

The team mascot, Crash the River Rascal, looks like a woodchuck, and is all over the place. Every night there is a Sweetheart of the Game who gets a dozen roses, chocolates, and a free lunch! On-field events like the Slingshot Contest are real popular on hot days. Water-soaked spongy Nerf balls are shot with a slingshot into the stands. Whoever catches one—well, gets wet. Fans also like to toss a beach ball around in the stands, and they seem to take great pride in their wave.

Gates open one hour and fifteen minutes before game time. Autographs are fairly easy to obtain, or should we say the players are readily available, but there's always a crush, sometimes fifteen deep! There's a designated area down the first base line and near the bullpens, but the lines are long. After

Old Kent Park in Comstock, Michigan, is actually brand new, having just opened in 1994.

the game, an unbelievable 500 to 600 fans wait by the locker room door for as long as an hour and a half trying to get autographs. Yikes!

GETTING THERE

Grand Rapids, Michigan's second-largest city, is the "gateway to West Michigan" and a short distance from the sandy beaches of Lake Michigan. Grand Rapids is known for its ethnic and art festivals and its numerous museums, including the Gerald R. Ford Museum. There are first-class hotels, a variety of motels, and several campgrounds outside town.

Old Kent Park is just north of Grand Rapids in Comstock Park. To get there, take US 131 north to West River Drive. Exit through the intersection and into the stadium parking lot. There is plenty of parking, which costs $1.

Box seats go for $6 and reserved seats are $4.50. General admission tickets cost $3.

For schedule of events and ticket information, call (616) 784-4131.

For tourist information, contact the Grand Rapids/Kent County Convention and Visitors Bureau, 245 Monroe NW, Grand Rapids, MI 49503, (616) 459-8287 or (800) 678-9859.

HOMETOWN STATS—GRAND RAPIDS *The Last Ten Years**					
Affil.	Year	League	Wins	Losses	Attendance
OAK	1994	Midwest	74	65	475,212
*Statistics are given only for the year in which the team played in Grand Rapids.					

Wisconsin Timber Rattlers

(Seattle Mariners)

Wisconsin Timber Rattlers Stadium
Casaloma Drive at Wisconsin Avenue
Grand Chute, WI 54911

1994 fan attendance was up about 35 percent over Wisconsin's 1993 counts.

If you have $5 and live in Appleton, Grand Chute, or any of the nearby cities on the Fox River, where they've had professional baseball since 1890, you can own a piece of the Timber Rattlers. That's right, $5. The team, formerly the Appleton Foxes, is community-owned, and since it was formed in 1940 it has brought home ten championships.

From 1891, when they belonged to the Independent Western State League, until 1953, you could count on the team from Appleton to be called the Papermakers (the state's major industry at the time). In 1953, the club broke the tradition when they affiliated with Milwaukee and became the Braves. By 1962, when they joined the Midwest League, they were the Fox Cities Foxes, soon followed by the Appleton Foxes. The team changed its name once again in 1994 to the Wisconsin Timber Rattlers.

Through several affiliations with the Phillies, Browns (St. Louis), Braves, Orioles, White Sox, Indians, Royals, and now Mariners, the franchise has sent some true greats to the big leagues. In the 1960s Earl Weaver managed here before going on to the Orioles and becoming one of the winningest managers of all time. Cal Ripken Sr. managed here, too. Slugger Boog Powell hit his way from here right to the Orioles. In the 1970s, Bucky Dent, Mike Squires, and Pete Vuckovich were among those who moved up, while the 1980s and 1990s have given us the likes of Daryl Boston, Doug Drabek, Bobby Thigpen, and Steve Shifflett.

Fox Valley residents have recently made a big commitment to keeping baseball in northeast Wisconsin—a new stadium. The fifty-three-year-old Goodland Field had all the traditional charm of a neighborhood park—surrounded by an ivy-covered fence, it was set amid homes, within walking distance of people's front yards. But the old park also adjoined an electronics plant with power generators that more or less nixed any fireworks shows. And although the feeling there was always upbeat, the team was drawing only 500 to 600 fans a game. The deteriorating facilities, inadequate parking and rest rooms, uncomfortable seating, and congested traffic were keeping people away. And besides, the park didn't meet the new

The Packer Pass game board makes a fine maze when it's not in use for the popular on-field contest.

major league baseball requirements needed by 1995. So, instead of a Band-Aid approach, the club and the residents of the ever-growing Fox Cities area decided to do what other thriving baseball towns have done—build. The new stadium, already dubbed "the Snake Pit," is located in Grand Chute just west of Highway 41 and opened for the 1995 season.

It hasn't been easy the last couple of years. The then–Appleton Foxes' management had to scale back on special promotions because of the cost of a new stadium. Then-GM Frank Gahl tried to fill in by getting out front before the game and making balloon animals for the kids instead of hosting elaborate pregame events. The kids adored the animals—and Frank, too!

The new ballpark is worth it. Located outside Appleton, on forty-five acres of open space, it's built amphitheater-style, with a traditional brick facade. The stadium seats 4,000. Grass berms envelop the place from down the sidelines to around the outfield fence. For $3 a ticket anyone can bring a blanket or chair and sit on the grass. Premium giveaways sponsored by local companies are some unusual ones, like *real* thirty-two-inch bats, hats, seat cushions, and beer steins (this is Wis-consin!). On-field activities include the Dizzy Bat Race and the Packer Pass (this is Green Bay territory)—throw a football through a hole and win.

Gates open one hour before game time. You can get autographs before the game down the third base line.

GETTING THERE

The Fox Cities are a series of towns, Kaukauna to Neena—Appleton being the largest—on the Fox River and Lake Winnebago in east central Wisconsin. Appleton is also the childhood home of Houdini. Accomodations are varied, but are mostly motels. Camping is nearby.

To get to Wisconsin Timber Rattlers Stadium take the Wisconsin Avenue exit off Highway 41 to Casaloma Drive and turn right. The stadium is right there. There's plenty of parking, which costs $1.

Box seats go for $5, reserved seats cost $4, and berm spots are $3.

For schedule of events and ticket information, call (414) 733-4152.

For tourist information, contact the Fox Cities Convention & Visitors Bureau, 110 Fox River Drive, Appleton, WI 54915, (414) 734-3358.

HOMETOWN STATS—APPLETON/GRAND CHUTE *The Last Ten Years*					
Affil.	**Year**	**League**	**Wins**	**Losses**	**Attendance**
CWS	1985	Midwest	85	54	76,860
	1986		56	83	60,001
KCR	1987		71	69	81,208
	1988		58	82	85,310
	1989		67	68	76,223
	1990		62	71	84,396
	1991		58	81	72,601
	1992		70	62	46,576
SEA	1993		62	73	56,036
	1994		75	64	76,281

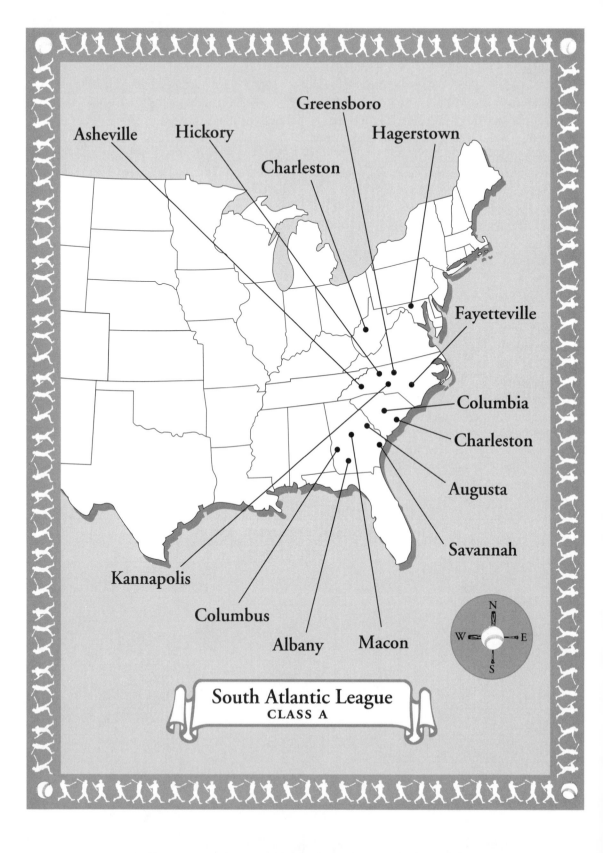

Asheville   Hickory   Greensboro   Hagerstown

Charleston

Fayetteville

Columbia

Charleston

Augusta

Savannah

Kannapolis

Columbus

Albany   Macon

N
W   E
S

South Atlantic League
CLASS A

South Atlantic League

Class A 1980–

The South Atlantic League, often called the Sally League, has had two incarnations, the first as the predecessor to the Southern League. That original league was established in 1904 as a Class C league. It worked its way up the ranking ladder, ending up at the Double-A level when it regrouped and formed the current Double-A Southern League in 1964.

Today's Class A South Atlantic League actually grew out of the old Class A Western Carolinas League, which was in existence from 1963 through 1979. (The Class D Western Carolina League existed from 1948 through 1952 and 1960 through 1962). That league was made up of teams playing in North and South Carolina. When it expanded into Macon, Georgia, in 1980, it was decided to rename the league. The original members of the resulting new South Atlantic League were Anderson, Charleston, and Spartanburg in South Carolina; Asheville, Gastonia, Greensboro, and Shelby in North Carolina; and Macon. The league ventured into West Virginia (Charleston) in 1987.

The South Atlantic League is made up of fourteen teams, which are scheduled to play 142 games during the regular reason. First-half division winners play second-half division winners in a best-of-three series. If the same team wins both halves, it gets a bye in the first round. Division playoff winners then play each other in a best-of-five series for the league championship.

Albany Polecats

(Montreal Expos)

Polecat Park
1130 Ballpark Lane
Albany, GA 31705

The Polecats have been here since 1992, and frankly, some people still haven't gotten used to them. Although baseball in the Albany area goes back to 1906, there hadn't been a team in town since 1958, when this new team, the Flyers, moved in from Sumter, North Carolina, where it began playing in 1991 as a new expansion team affiliated with Montreal. When the owners asked for suggestions for a new name, many area residents wanted something that hooked into the heritage of the Seminoles, whose territory this once was. Ninety percent of the names suggested were, in fact, Native American. There were some other ideas too—like Peaches, Pine Cones, and Nuts—that had an agricultural flavor. Then the team's announcer came up with "Polecats." When owner Rick Holtzman (who also owns the Tucson Toros, Chattanooga Lookouts, and Quad City River Bandits) heard about it, he had to call the front office to find out just what a polecat actually was. "Skunk," they told him. But Holtzman's partner, ex–big leaguer Barry Foote, not only knew what a polecat was but flipped for the idea. People would sit up and take notice, he thought. Did they ever!

The town's people just hated it, but the team went ahead with the polecat idea anyway. A local vet finally stood up for the name *and* the honorable reputation of the skunk, which helped some. But what really helped was team mascot Pepper the Polecat, who was introduced early in the first season. Even though he's a skunk, Pepper's big fluffy head, bushy tail, and mischievous ways made him an instant hit, not only with the kids, but with a lot of grown-ups, too!

The Polecats went on to have a good inaugural season. Their first alumnus, first baseman Cliff Floyd, made it to Montreal (through West Palm Beach, Harrisburg, and Ottawa) in 1993. Pitcher Brian Looney, also with Albany in 1992, followed the same route (skipping Ottawa) on his way to the Expos in 1993. But playing in a temporary stadium that year didn't do much for attendance; the games drew about 98,000. The next year with the Baltimore Orioles, ensconced in brand-new Polecat Park in the Paul Eames Sports Complex, attendance shot up to 140,000! Montreal re-signed with Albany for the 1995 season.

Named Polecat Park, the 4,200-seat stadium is part of a sports complex, with other fields and a stadium nearby. It's a very friendly place. The picnic area down the left field foul line holds up to 1,000 for reserved parties before the game, but opens up to everybody during the game. You can count on clusters of kids down there waiting for foul balls. The twenty-foot outfield wall is wildly colorful with billboards. We think the fence painter is a bit of an illusionist. On the IHOP board, the pat of butter on the stack of pancakes turns out to be a net on closer inspection. If a player hits a ball into the net, some lucky fan wins $10,000. The ball came within five feet on opening night!

This ballpark is an extra-safe place for kids. The play area is supervised; the security is tight and child-oriented. And Pepper is always around to help out. When Pepper doesn't get his way, however, he's been known to use his squirt gun. Once he raised his tail at an ump—and was tossed! Pizza Scream, Dizzy Bat Race, Frisbee Throw, and the Water Balloon Pitch and Batting are some of the on-field contests. Concessions include the usual, but also good chicken fingers and great jalapeño dogs. It's very hot and humid here on game nights, so anything cold is popular. The

Little League teams are often honored guests at Polecat games.

Pepsi Freeze (like a slush puppy) has become a craze—and the snow cone and ice cream stands are always jammed.

Gates open one hour before game time. Before the game the players are easily accessible for autographs adjacent to the dugouts and along the retaining wall of the ramp that leads from the clubhouse to the field.

GETTING THERE

Albany, situated in the southwest corner of the state, has beautiful lakes, rivers, and mineral springs. (Take a side trip to FDR's Little White House in Warm Springs.) Accommodations are mostly motels, but there are two riverfront campgrounds right in town.

To get to Polecat Park, take the Baylock Street exit off U.S. 19 and U.S. 82. Take Ballpark Lane into the Paul Eames Sports Complex and follow the signs to Polecat Park. There is plenty of parking, which costs $1.

Box seats go for $6, and reserved seats are $5. General admission tickets cost $3.50; kids, seniors, and the military get $1 off.

For schedule of events and ticket information, call (912) 435-6444.

For tourist information, contact the Albany–Dougherty Chamber of Commerce, 225 West Broad Avenue, Albany, GA 31701, (912) 434-8700.

		HOMETOWN STATS—ALBANY *The Last Ten Years**			
Affil.	**Year**	**League**	**Wins**	**Losses**	**Attendance**
MON	1992	South Atlantic	72	70	97,810
BAL	1993		71	71	140,140
	1994		63	74	124,520
*Statistics are given only for the years in which the team played in Albany.					

Asheville Tourists

(Colorado Rockies)

McCormick Field
30 Buchanan Place
Asheville, NC 28801

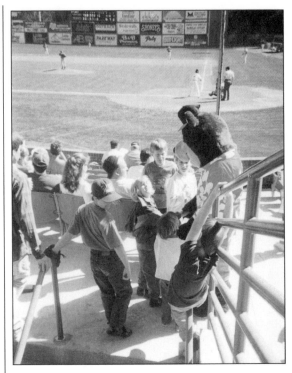

The Tourists' lovable mascot, Teddy, is continually hunted down by kids seeking hugs and autographs.

The first professional game played on Asheville's McCormick Field on April 3, 1924, pitted the Asheville Skylanders of the Class B Sally League against the Detroit Tigers in an exhibition game. Ty Cobb was on that Detroit team. So were Harry Heilmann and Heinie Manush, who, as a matter of fact, blasted the first home run out of the park that day. Other greats—Babe Ruth, Lou Gehrig, and Jackie Robinson—played in exhibition games here, too.

Asheville teams have belonged to nine different leagues since 1910, the first year baseball was played here. Although the home team has had a few different names over the years, Tourists is the one that has stuck and become traditional. Asheville, you see, has always been a major tourist mecca, sitting as it does at the junction of the Blue Ridge and Great Smoky Mountains. The Tourists have had some great players over the years. Willie Stargell, who played here in 1961, is probably the most famous. Eddie Murray, Sparky Anderson, Dave Concepcion, and, more recently, Craig Biggio, Eric Anthony, Luis Gonzalez, Tom Henke, and Mike Simms, who holds the league record for the thirty-nine home runs he hit in 1987, all spent time on McCormick grass.

The original stadium, built in the early 1920s, was named for Dr. Louis McCormick, who, after moving to Asheville in 1904, launched a campaign called Swat the Fly, which helped rid the city of houseflies. (Sad to say, people are still swatting.) It was the oldest ballpark in the minor leagues (fourth oldest in all of baseball) until 1992, when the place was torn down and totally reconstructed. The new 3,500-seat McCormick Field is a charming brick structure that has a landmark look to it. Lots of real-life tourists drop by just to see it and recall the scenes from the movie *Bull Durham* that were filmed here (albeit in the old park). By the way, if you call ahead, you can check out Kevin Costner's uniform, which is on display in the Tourists' management office.

The entrance walkway through the main gate is paved with personalized bricks, each one donated by a company or individual who wanted to help build the new park. The grandstand starts and stops just beyond the dugouts. If you sit in a box seat, you get waitress service (be sure to try the Polish Sausage Dog). Sit in general admission off first, and you'll have a good shot at catching a foul ball. There's a terrific view beyond the outfield fence—hills that look close enough to touch are lush with thick trees and wild honeysuckle.

Tourists fans are exceptionally loyal. Even though the team placed dead last recently, the fans set attendance records. This doesn't mean they are easy on the players. At the opening ceremonies of one game in the 1993 season, when the Tourists were in another bad slump, Little Leaguers in uniform took the field with the Tourists players and stood at attention for the National Anthem. (This is a popular ceremony that's done at lots of games in many parks. After the National Anthem, the kids run off and the game begins.) This night, the crowd cheered the kids instead of the players!

Regular theme nights include Magic Mondays and fifty-cent Hot Dog (plus free haircuts) Tuesdays. There are special appearances by big league mascots and Ronald McDonald, too. Giveaways include the best of the usual: T-shirts, baseballs, even stadium blankets. Best of all are the Delta Airlines Trip Giveaways. One lucky fan wins a free trip anywhere Delta flies within the continental USA. On another night a fan wins a trip anywhere Delta flies in the world.

Gates open one hour before game time. You can easily get autographs before the game down by the bullpen and dugouts, or after the game outside the clubhouse.

GETTING THERE

Asheville, a Blue Ridge Mountain resort city, is famous for its historic Art Deco downtown district, its art galleries, the incredible Biltmore Estate (the Vanderbilt mansion), and more. There are grand resorts, hotels, bed-and-breakfasts, motels, and camping within 5 miles.

To get to McCormick Field, take I-240 (Beltway) to the Charlotte Street exit and go south on Charlotte to Buchanan Place. Turn left onto Buchanan just before Biltmore. The parking is free, but the lot is small and cars spill over into the lot at the top of the hill. Many fans park on Biltmore as well.

Box seats cost $6, for kids and seniors, $4. General admission tickets are $4, students, $3.50, seniors, $3, and kids, $2.50.

For schedule of events and ticket information, call (704) 258-0428.

For tourist information, contact the Asheville Convention & Visitors Bureau, P.O. Box 1010, Asheville, NC 28802, (704) 258-6111 or (800) 257-1300.

HOMETOWN STATS—ASHEVILLE
The Last Ten Years

Affil.	Year	League	Wins	Losses	Attendance
HOU	1985	South Atlantic	76	62	73,888
	1986		90	50	101,962
	1987		91	48	104,060
	1988		65	75	95,252
	1989		68	70	96,178
	1990		66	77	101,193
	1991		55	83	117,625
	1992		74	66	119,115
	1993		51	88	121,573
COL	1994		60	73	118,146

Augusta Greenjackets

(Pittsburgh Pirates)

Augusta/Richmond County Stadium
78 Milledge Road
Augusta, GA 30904

Augusta was always a fine town for minor league ball, with one team or another playing in the Sally League from 1904 almost straight through into the early 1960s. So it was a grim day for everybody when in 1963 the South Atlantic League regrouped, and the Yankees affiliate moved out to Columbus (GA) and joined the Southern League. Augusta was left high and dry, without a team, without even the promise of a team. For twenty-five years, fans pined. One man in particular, Richard Heaton, finally raised $25,000 and almost single-handedly built a ballpark so that they (any team) would come. When Heaton finished in 1988, the new 3,800-seat stadium looked fifty years old. Everything was secondhand—from the concession stands to the bleachers, which had come from an old 1940s drag-strip stadium. But it worked! They came! After four years down in Macon, Georgia, the Class A Pirates affiliate moved into Heaton Stadium in time for opening day 1988. The Augusta Pirates made themselves right at home, winning the South Atlantic League championship in 1989. They drew better than 100,000 fans in their first seasons here, and in the process sent up some great talent to the major leagues, too. Moises Alou, Orlando Merced, Carlos Garcia, Wes Chamberlain, and Tim Wakefield all played for the Augusta Pirates.

In 1993, club owner Bill Scripps (of the Scripps-Howard newspaper and media group) determined that a new look and name could send roots deeper into the community and give the team some local character. First came the logo—a cool-looking little yellowjacket, wearing a green blazer exactly like the prestigious one that the winners of the Masters golf tournament, held in Augusta, wear. Taking it all one step further, the Augusta Greenjackets were born. By June of that year, the Greenjackets were drawing almost 40 percent more fans than the years prior, and their fitted baseball cap (with new logo) was the biggest seller in all of the minor leagues. With an average of nearly 1,800 fans coming in every night, the strain on the bare-bones park and upon the fans and players who put up with it led to a new deal with the city and county. $3,000,000 was committed to bulldoze the old park and build anew for 1995 on the same ground.

The new ballpark is still located just north of town in the picturesque recreational area right next to Lake Olmstead. Before the game you can play softball, enjoy a picnic, and even go boating on the lake, which is only about twenty feet from the stadium. The brand-new individual seats still give the fans that close-to-the-field feeling of the old park. The fierce wind that blows in from center is still present, too, making any home run a wild moment to remember. There's a picnic area that serves hot dogs, pizza, and fried chicken and biscuits, as well as Beer Island, a popular hangout from the old park (complete with sand and a Tiki hut), down the right field line.

The Greenjacket fans are zealots. There's a rally they get going that has literally shaken the dugout bench on occasion. The third base stands yell "Green" and the first base stands answer "jackets" again and again, building in volume and rhythm until everyone is on their feet and wild.

Sting, the mascot, is a yellow jacket wearing shades who first met the fans when his limo, escorted by motorcycle cops, drove onto the field. Nowadays he delivers surprise birthday cakes to kids in the stands and executes extraordinary dance moves on top of the dugout. On-field contests give fans plenty of chances to win money and dinners for two.

The stadium is open during the day until two hours before the game starts. Gates reopen one houre before game time. Get autographs down by the dugouts before the game, or outside the club-house after the game.

GETTING THERE

Augusta, on the banks of the Savannah River, is Georgia's second-oldest city and former capital, known for its magnolia-lined streets and beautiful old homes in Olde Town and Summerville. There are lovely hotels and inns, plenty of motels, and camping, too.

To get to Augusta/Richmond County Stadium, take I-20 to Washington Road South (exit 65) and follow Washington past the Augusta National Golf Course for one mile to Broad Street. Take the exit ramp down to the right and then turn left, which takes you under Washington to the top of a hill and a stoplight. Take a left onto Milledge Road and continue half a mile to the stadium, which is on the right. There is ample free parking.

Box seats go for $5.50, while reserved seats are $4.50. General admission tickets cost $3, $2.50 for kids, seniors, and the military.

For schedule of events and ticket information, call (706) 736-7889.

For tourist information, contact the Augusta–

Catcher Sergio Mendez was one of the first to be photographed in the new 1994 Greenjackets uniform.

Richmond County Convention & Visitors Bureau, 32 Eighth Street, Augusta, GA 30903, (706) 823-6600 or (800) 726-0243.

HOMETOWN STATS—AUGUSTA *The Last Ten Years**					
Affil.	Year	League	Wins	Losses	Attendance
PIT	1988	South Atlantic	78	60	123,626
	1989		77	67	119,153
	1990		73	70	125,105
	1991		68	74	100,141
	1992		67	74	83,247
	1993		59	82	115,051
	1994		50	86	115,909

*Statistics are given only for the years in which the team played in Augusta.

Capital City Bombers

(New York Mets)

Capital City Stadium
301 S. Assembly Street
Columbia, SC 29201

Columbia was a founding member of the South Atlantic League, and except for a twenty-one year hiatus between 1962 and 1983 and a few other years here and there, there's been a professional team in this capital city since 1904. They've been called the Comets, Palmettos, Teddy Bears, Reds, and Gems. In 1983 the Mets moved their franchise to town from Shelby (NC), and until 1992 the team went by the name the Columbia Mets. The team became the Capital City Bombers in 1993 to honor the famous Doolittle Raiders, who trained here in Columbia for their historic World War II mission, the first bombing raid over Japan.

Owned by Eric Margenau and a group of investors, who also own the Class A Fort Wayne Wizards, the team has done very well. They've taken two league championships—one in 1986, the other in 1991—and they've fallen below .500 only twice since 1983. Frank Robinson, who played for the

Reds long ago, might be the most famous player from Columbia. Strangely enough, he didn't have such a great season here in 1955, batting only .263 and hitting twelve home runs. But the Reds moved him up to Cincinnati the next year anyway, where he had a record 122 runs and was named Rookie of the Year. More recently Todd Hundley, Pete Schourek, Butch Huskey, Tito Navarro, Tim Howard, Jose Martinez, Pat Howell, Randy Myers, Dave Magadan, and Bobby Jones have moved up to the major leagues through Columbia.

Before Bill Shanahan came to town as GM attendance was pretty sad. Even in their championship season of 1991, and in a newly renovated stadium, the team drew a paltry 79,000. Since Shanahan has taken over, the team has shattered Columbia's all-time baseball attendance records, most recently topping 145,000 in 1994.

Capital City Stadium, built in 1927 and renovated in 1991, is located right downtown. It has a modern feel, but some old-fashioned touches remain here and there, like the huge wrought-iron main gate that actually squeaks as it opens onto the concourse. On your way into the grandstand, a Bomber Girl Usherette will help you find your seat. The grandstand, which extends just beyond the first and third bases, seats 6,000 and everybody claims there's not a bad seat in the house.

The Hard Ball Cafe is a relaxed place down the left field foul line, where there's a playland for kids, too. The outfield wall is double-stacked with colorful billboards. If a Bomber batter hits the bull on the Longhorn Steak billboard, the player and a lucky fan win a steak dinner (shades of Durham). Get there early enough to catch the col-

Here's a rare photo: Capital City's usually busy Bomber Girl usherettes are all in the same place at the same time!

orful pregame announcer Jim Seay down on the field as he entertains during first pitch ceremonies. And you definitely want to be there when the Bombers take the field. Air-raid sirens wail, bombs burst, and fireworks explode in the sky above the park.

Bomber fans are loud and loyal. There are a lot of characters, too. One big man (240 pounds maybe) has been coming out to the park ever since the club moved here. At every game he dresses in a Bombers uniform (XX-Large, we would think) and rallies fans by dancing on the dugout roof. There are plenty of on-field contests between innings. Besides the ubiquitous Mascot Race with Bomber the Mouse and the ever-popular Dizzy Bat Race and Dash for Cash, there's a Cow Race (contestants dress up in cow costumes—front and back—and race each other for a steak dinner at Longhorn's) and Human Bowling—a fan gets strapped inside a giant bowling ball and then rolled off a truck, down a ramp, and toward the pins! Ouch! Come on a Wednesday if you like sumo wrestling between innings. Promotional giveaways include some of the best—baseballs, gloves, bats, caps, and so forth.

Gates open about one hour before game time. The best place to get autographs is in the picnic area on the third base side before the game.

GETTING THERE

Columbia, South Carolina's capital city, has an abundance of nineteenth-century charm. Historic buildings, ancient trees, and fine museums await the visitor. There are luxury hotels, lovely inns, and bed-and-breakfasts, and camping fifteen miles northwest at Lake Murray.

To get to Capital City Stadium from the south, take I-277 into downtown Columbia and exit at Elmwood Street. Go right on Elmwood and then left on Assembly Street. The stadium is about two miles down on Assembly on the righthand side. From the west, take I-26 to I-126 to downtown and straight onto Elmwood Street. Take a right on Assembly and go two miles to the stadium. There is ample parking, which costs $1.

Super boxes, the first four rows with waitress service, are $5, and regular box seats go for $4.50. Reserved seats and general admission tickets cost $4. Kids, seniors, and the military get $1 off.

For schedule of events and ticket information, call (803) 256-4110.

For tourist information, contact the Columbia Metropolitan Convention and Visitors Bureau, P.O. Box 15, Columbia, SC 29202, (803) 254-0479 or (800) 264-4884.

| | HOMETOWN STATS—COLUMBIA | | | | |
| | The Last Ten Years | | | | |
Affil.	Year	League	Wins	Losses	Attendance
NYM	1985	South Atlantic	79	57	101,277
	1986		90	42	106,403
	1987		64	75	92,855
	1988		74	63	114,172
	1989		73	67	85,862
	1990		83	60	99,385
	1991		86	54	79,564
	1992		79	59	124,508
	1993		64	77	144,054
	1994		59	76	146,676

Charleston Alley Cats

(Cincinnati Reds)

Watt Powell Park
3403 MacCorkle Avenue
Charleston, WV 25304

There has been professional baseball in Charleston since 1910, when the city was a charter member of the Class D Virginia Valley League, which folded after just one season. Over the years, Charleston teams have belonged to nine different leagues. The current team arrived as a coop team in 1987 when the SAL expanded from ten teams to twelve. The original owners had family ties to the Charleston Stern Wheelers, which plied the Kanawha River, and until 1995 they were the Wheelers.

The Alley Cats (formerly The Whalers) have been affiliated with the Cincinnati Reds since 1990. Obviously it was a good move, because the team promptly went out and won the league championship! Over the past few years they have consistently made the playoffs—thanks mostly to the quality of the Reds' farm system. Some major league players who trained in Charleston are Dan Wilson, Bobby Ayala, Chris Hammond, Kevin Roberson, and Cincinnati pitcher Tim Pugh, who as of 1994 had the best year of his career while playing in Charleston in 1992, with 15 wins and a 1.93 ERA.

Fan support for the team has been incredible since the team signed up with Cincinnati, but then this city identifies with the Reds. Cincinnati games are broadcast over the radio here, so the fans really relate to the players, following them all the way to the top.

Watt Powell Park is a cinderblock stadium built in 1949 and named after the man who put up the money for it after the old wooden one burned

Charleston's 4th of July extravaganza is always a sure sellout.

down. It sits right on one of the busiest streets in Charleston, where restaurants, museums, shops, and office buildings are all within a short walk. One of the quirky features of the 6,800-seat park is the right field cinderblock (not padded) wall. When a ball hits the wall directly, it gets a true bounce right back to the outfielder. If it hits a support column, however, forget it. It's like a pinball effect—anything can, and does, happen.

The die-hard fans sit in the third base bleachers and really dish it out to the visiting team and umps. They are hard to ignore, too, since all the seats here are right on top of the field. If the picnic area has not been booked, it's open to everybody. Rib sandwiches, grilled hamburgers and hot dogs, barbecued chicken, and imported beer are served up. If you are a foul ball hunter, the picnic area is a great spot. So is the parking lot behind the first base bleachers, where most of the kids wait. Over the right field wall is a view up a deep green hollow, down from which spills a nice breeze. A mountain rises at the end of the hollow, and the old train trestles near the park serve as bleachers for opportunistic fans who want to sneak a look at the game.

The team has a ton, *a ton*, of between-inning contests and prizes. Win a new car by picking the one right envelope out of 102. During the Grand Slam Inning you could win $10,000. Play Let's Make A Deal and win gift certificates or (sorry) two rubber bands. And there's more. If the pitcher strikes out the side, you could win a new truck. Or cast a whiffle ball that's hooked on your fishing line into a wading pool off first base, and your whole section wins free fries. How about winning a lunch date with your favorite player! Come early for pregame pizza-eating contests, and stay late for fireworks on July 4th.

Gates open one hour before game time. There is an autograph booth in the lobby area that is open before the game. Kids also go down by the picnic area that borders the bullpen.

GETTING THERE

Charleston, the capital of West Virginia, is noted for its classic capitol building and its restored turn-of-the-century downtown district. Nearby whitewater rafting is extremely popular here. There are good motels, hotels, and some nice campgrounds close by.

To get to Watt Powell Park, take I-64 east to the 35th Street Bridge exit. The stadium is at the bottom of the hill. Or take I-64 west and get off at the first Charleston MacCorkle exit. Take a right on MacCorkle and proceed four miles to the stadium. There is plenty of parking, which costs $1.

Box seats go for $4.50, while general admission tickets cost $3.50. Kids and seniors get $1 off.

For schedule of events and ticket information, call (304) 925-8222.

For tourist information, contact the Charleston Convention & Visitors Bureau, 200 Civic Center Drive, Charleston, WV 25301, (304) 344-5075 or (800) 733-5469.

HOMETOWN STATS—CHARLESTON
*The Last Ten Years**

Affil.	Year	League	Wins	Losses	Attendance
COOP	1987	South Atlantic	66	73	97,563
CUB	1988		51	86	125,998
	1989		58	76	130,293
CIN	1990		77	66	152,350
	1991		92	50	185,389
	1992		77	64	135,010
	1993		76	64	110,118
	1994		65	75	103,985

*Statistics are given only for the years in which the team played in Charleston.

Charleston RiverDogs

(Texas Rangers)

College Park
701 Rutledge Avenue
Charleston, SC 29403

Professional baseball in Charleston goes all the way back to 1886. After the city became a charter member of the old South Atlantic League in 1904, Charleston saw a string of teams—the Sea Gulls (through 1917) and then the Gulls, Palmettos, Pals, Rebels and a few others—before the Rainbows, affiliated with the San Diego Padres, took the field in 1985. Unfortunately, in their seasons with the Padres the Rainbows were always the worst team in minor league baseball, usually finishing up twenty to thirty games below .500. Then the Texas Rangers came to town in 1993, and the new Rainbows team had a great year, even though they still only finished in the middle of the pack.

There were many fine major leaguers who stopped off in Charleston on their way up. Willie Randolph, Tony Pena, John Candelaria, Roberto Alomar, Sandy Alomar Jr., Carlos Baerga, David Cone, who went 9–2 in 1982, and Danny Jackson, who went 10–1 the same year, all played here.

In 1993 Marvin Goldklang, who bought the club in 1990 and who also owns the Fort Myers Miracle (Florida State), the Hudson Valley Renegades (New York-Penn), and the St. Paul Saints (the independent Northern), wanted a team name with a bit more bite than "Rainbows." A contest sponsored by a local grocery chain produced more than 10,000 entries, and "RiverDogs" came up the winner, "River" because the team was to move into a brand-new stadium in 1995 on the banks of the Ashley River (which didn't happen), and "Dogs," well, because there are no other "canines" in the minors. Whatever the reason, everybody has taken to the fierce but friendly name.

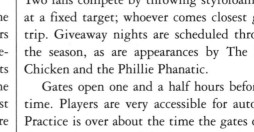

The new stadium, now scheduled to open in 1996, will have a spectacular view of the Ashley River and will have 7,100 seats. Old College Park, where the team plays now, was built in 1938, and its wooden grandstand seats 4,000. You enter the stands from either end (first base or third). A huge mechanical bull looms above the home bullpen. The bull will make the move to the new park. The fans still go wild when a RiverDog hits one over, and the bull bellows and snorts, blows smoke from its nostrils, flashes its eyes, and whips its tail. There's an outdoor picnic area off right field that can be reserved for private parties. Reserve now— it's sold out every game. There are about forty concessions located behind the grandstand. All kinds of foods are available in addition to great grilled dogs, burgers, and barbecue: seafood salads, fried shrimp, pizza, nachos, burritos, deli sandwiches, funnel cakes, lemonade, frozen yogurt, and on and on.

The team mascot, Charlie the RiverDog, is a mischievous mutt who makes unpredictable entrances on a speeding four-wheeler. He steals the spotlight during the first five innings, and then during the sixth he takes it easy in his fishing shack down the left field line, where he signs autographs. Come out to the park on Continental-sponsored Fly-Away Fridays and try for a chance to win a free trip anywhere in the USA or Mexico. Two fans compete by throwing styrofoam gliders at a fixed target; whoever comes closest gets the trip. Giveaway nights are scheduled throughout the season, as are appearances by The Famous Chicken and the Phillie Phanatic.

Gates open one and a half hours before game time. Players are very accessible for autographs. Practice is over about the time the gates open, so the guys hang around signing autographs near the dugouts.

GETTING THERE
Charleston, South Carolina, is truly one of America's most beautiful cities—it's almost like a living museum. There are grand hotels and inns,

Young RiverDogs fans can always find the team's mascot, Charlie, lounging outside his fishing shack in left field during the late innings.

historic bed-and-breakfasts, a variety of motels, beach resorts, and camping right on nearby James Island.

To get to College Park, take I-26 into Charleston to Exit 217A (Rutledge Avenue). Follow Rutledge for one mile to the stadium on the right. There is limited free parking at the stadium. Most fans find parking on nearby streets.

Box seats are $6. General admission tickets cost $4, $3 for kids, seniors, and the military.

For schedule of events and ticket information, call (803) 723-7241.

For tourist information, contact the Charleston Trident Convention & Visitors Bureau, P.O. Box 975, Charleston, SC 29402, (803) 853-8000.

		HOMETOWN STATS—CHARLESTON			
		The Last Ten Years			
Affil.	**Year**	**League**	**Wins**	**Losses**	**Attendance**
SDP	1985	South Atlantic	78	61	105,647
	1986		63	69	131,696
	1987		68	71	87,185
	1988		85	53	55,909
	1989		72	68	78,438
	1990		46	96	76,133
	1991		69	72	119,080
	1992		55	85	103,824
TEX	1993		65	77	98,670
	1994		56	81	105,701

Columbus RedStixx

(Cleveland Indians)

Golden Park
100 4th Street
Columbus, GA 31901

A ceremony at home plate in 1993 celebrated the nuptials of RedStixx manager Mike Brown and his wife, Claudette.

Things will never be the same in Columbus, Georgia. When it was announced in July 1993 that this city had been chosen to host the women's fast-pitch softball competition for the 1996 summer Olympics, a chain reaction of enthusiasm resulted in a brand-new athletic and entertainment complex overlooking the Chattahoochee River. This complex includes eight state-of-the-art softball fields and a brand-new Golden Park.

The historic forty-five-year-old stadium was one of the most charming parks in the South Atlantic League. However, due to insufficient parking, failing wiring and plumbing, and cramped conditions, the old park was torn down, except for the original concrete grandstand and the roof. The old facade, clubhouses, concession space, restrooms, offices, and press areas are gone! One thing that most players (well, outfielders, in any case) do not miss is the famous, or rather infamous, brick outfield wall. Besides outfielders' constant terror of crashing into it, the wall had an unpredictable effect on balls coming off it. A lot of would-be doubles suddenly turned into triples. Hitters, of course, loved it.

Although Columbus has had a remarkably steady diet of baseball since 1906, the RedStixx were an expansion team when they started playing here in 1991. Named after the local Native American tribe that once lived on the banks of the Chattahoochee, they have been affiliated with the Cleveland Indians since the start. They've done pretty well for a new club, too. For the 1994 season they had the league's best overall record, and two of their young players have already reached the majors. Pitcher John Carter (17–7 in 1993)

wound up in Cleveland, and outfielder Willie Canate (110 runs in 1992) eventually went to Toronto. But they just can't seem to get out of the gate at the playoffs. Nonetheless, the fans have remained interested, increasing in numbers every year to better than 133,000 in 1994. We predict that even more will come through the gates of the newly renovated Golden Park.

The stadium sits practically on the banks of the Chattahoochee River, which separates Georgia from Alabama. The grandstand seating stops at the base bags, while grassy areas for picnics and a kids' playground continue down right and left field lines. The view over the outfield wall is of stately Georgia pines, from one end of the field to the other.

Summers are awfully hot and humid in the South, and the crowds have a tendency to be a little laid-back despite the efforts of the team mascot, FreddStixx, an oversized red fox. But he does his job well, as does another character in the park, Willie Bowman, "The Good-Goody Peanut Man." He's the only vendor we've heard of whose entrance into the park is announced over the PA. "It's time for Willieeeee the Peanut Man" comes the intro in the second inning, and in runs the vendor, selling and tossing his bags of peanuts. If you're not in the mood for peanuts, try one of the eight food vendors located in the RedStixx mini–food court. The menu varies from pizza and chicken to yogurt and funnel cakes.

On-field contests between innings include one of our favorites, the Pizza Scream, where a large pizza goes to whoever makes the most noise. Water Balloon Smash is popular here, too. There are fireworks during the season and special appearances by The Famous Chicken and the Flying Elvises (those skydiving impersonators). Giveaways are good and plentiful.

Gates open one hour before game time. The best place to get autographs is down by the dugouts before the game, or outside the clubhouses after the game.

A RedStixx fan plans his own strategy.

GETTING THERE

Columbus, home of Fort Benning, is called Georgia's "West Coast," located as it is on the Chattahoochee River. The Riverwalk, the promonade along the banks of the Chattahoochee, in uptown Columbus is really charming. There are a few hotels, lots of motels, and a couple of state parks with camping close by.

To get to Golden Park, take I-185 to Victory Drive North (Exit 1 North) and continue for five and a half miles to Olympic Boulevard. The stadium is right there on the left. There is ample parking, which costs $1.

Box seats cost $5, and general admission tickets go for $4. Kids and seniors get $1 off.

For schedule of events and ticket information, call (706) 571-8866.

For tourist information, contact the Columbus Convention & Visitors Bureau, 802 Front Avenue, Columbus, GA 31902, (706) 322-1613 or (800) 999-1613.

		HOMETOWN STATS—COLUMBUS			
		*The Last Ten Years**			
Affil.	**Year**	**League**	**Wins**	**Losses**	**Attendance**
HOU	1985	Southern	79	65	109,603
	1986		70	70	134,964
	1987		67	76	128,845
	1988		69	74	110,621
	1989		71	72	95,689
	1990		67	77	94,265
CLE	1991	South Atlantic	73	69	96,736
	1992		77	62	118,243
	1993		86	56	122,137
	1994		87	51	133,351

Fayetteville Generals

(Detroit Tigers)

J. P. Riddle Stadium
2823 Legion Road
Fayetteville, NC 28306

Fayetteville fans have been cheering their home teams on since 1909. In the 1950s they rooted for the Highlanders of the old Class B Carolina League and the likes of pitcher Leonard Matarazzo, who had twenty-two wins and nine shutouts in 1952. And then, after the 1956 season, Fayetteville fans had to wait thirty years before they could once again get behind a home team. When baseball came back in 1987, thanks to an expansion of the South Atlantic League, the new team signed on with the Detroit Tigers. And since Fayetteville is home to Fort Bragg, one of the largest military bases in the country, "Generals" seemed like the perfect name.

The Generals have been to the playoffs twice, and eighteen players have made it to the big leagues. The most successful is Travis Fryman, third baseman for the Tigers, who was an American League All-Star two years in a row. And then there's Danny Bautista, a recent graduate, and Scott Aldred, Phil Clark, Milt Cuyler, John DeSilva, Kurt Knudsen, Torey Lovullo, Rusty Meacham, and Randy Nosek, among others.

J. P. Riddle, for whom the stadium is named, gave the land on which the ballpark sits, in a residential area just south of downtown. As you walk through the gate you find yourself right in the middle of an open-air concourse, where on game night something is always going on. There might be a karate demo, or a radio DJ doing a live broadcast, or a local band doing its thing. There's a video arcade and batting cage, speed-pitch, and one-hole miniature golf, too. A kids-only concession stand has steps up to the counter so that even the littlest fans can order their own cotton candy. Inside the small 3,800-seat stadium, the grandstand wraps from just beyond first base to just beyond third. There are picnic areas at each end of the grandstand, just before the left and right field bleachers. They are closed for an hour before the game for private parties, but are then opened to everybody. Thick pine trees hug the outfield wall, giving the ballpark a cozy feeling. Over 100,000 fans came through the gates in 1994, many of them from Fort Bragg and from Pope Air Force Base, which is next to Fort Bragg.

The team mascot, the Bleacher Creature, is a cockeyed fuzzy orange thing who delivers a half-dozen roses to the woman who is the Sweetheart of the Night. In one on-field event, a fan hits a plastic ball off a batting tee with a plastic bat (not so tough) and tries to get it through a hole sixty feet away (that's tough!). The prize is a $15,000 new car. A few have come close, but so far, no cigar! Here's one of our favorites— the annual Broken Bat Scramble. The Generals save all broken bats throughout the season, then line them up in the outfield and turn a pack of kids loose to scramble for their own major (minor) league broken bats. The ratio is usually something like 500 kids to 300 bats. It's a madhouse.

The club puts on three fireworks shows during the season, which tend to pack the park, as do the appearances by such noted minor league legends as Billy Bird and Homer the Dragon. Some popular premium giveaways include bats, steins, coffee mugs, fanny packs, and baseballs. A very popular event is the Used Car Giveaway.

Gates open one hour before game time. You can get autographs before or after the game as the players make their way back and forth to the clubhouse down the first base line.

Getting There

Fayetteville, on the Cape Fear River, has a rich history dating back to the early 1700s and wonderful examples of eighteenth- and nineteenth-century

In 1993, Fayetteville finished strong, with the Generals challenging in the division playoffs. At right, a skydiver achieves a pinpoint landing on the pitcher's mound for the Generals' opening day ceremonies.

architecture. Accommodations are mostly motels. There are two camping facilities just outside of town.

To get to J. P. Riddle Stadium take I-95 to Business 95 (U.S. 301) and exit at Owen Drive. Go west on Owen to Legion Road. Take a left on Legion and go one and a half miles to the stadium. From Fort Bragg, take the All American Freeway to Legion and take a right to the stadium. There is plenty of free parking.

Box seats are $6, while reserved seats go for $5. General admission tickets cost $3.

For schedule of events and ticket information, call (910) 424-6500.

For tourist information, contact the Fayetteville Area Convention and Visitors Bureau, 515 Ramsey Street, Fayetteville, NC 28301, (910) 483-5311 or (800) 255-8217.

Affil.	Year	League	Wins	Losses	Attendance
DET	1987	South Atlantic	65	74	95,008
	1988		62	73	57,543
	1989		70	69	65,931
	1990		82	61	95,040
	1991		58	79	88,380
	1992		74	67	100,226
	1993		75	66	100,321
	1994		62	75	104,379

HOMETOWN STATS—FAYETTEVILLE
*The Last Ten Years**

*Statistics are given only for the years in which the team played in Fayetteville.

Greensboro Bats

(New York Yankees)

War Memorial Stadium
510 Yanceyville Street
Greensboro, NC 27405

Greensboro teams have been affiliated with various major league clubs and have played in several different leagues since 1902, when the city was a charter member of the short-lived (one year) Class D North Carolina League. This current franchise came to town in 1979 as a member of the Western Carolina League. The team was affiliated with Cincinnati, and previously had ties to Shelby (NC). For years the team was called the Hornets, and they had a reputation for being a tough, competitive club, consistently placing second or better in the overall standings (ten times since 1980). Since signing on with the New York Yankees in 1990, they've made it to the championship series once, in 1993. Some major leaguers who were once on the Greensboro roster are Don Mattingly, Otis Nixon, Mike Pagliarulo, Reggie Sanders, Roberto Kelly, and Phillies pitcher Curt Schilling, who had a record fifteen *losses* here in 1987.

The old Hornets became the new Bats in 1994, when the team owners went for a new identity and color scheme for the club. John Horshok, one of the owners, designed the new logo himself. And the fans seem to love it. These fans, in fact, have always been terrifically supportive. Greensboro led the league in attendance for fourteen years straight until the upstart Hickory Crawdads (NC) broke their record in 1993. Although they are not a particularly volatile bunch, Bats fans aren't overly polite, either. They are very knowledgeable and aren't afraid to boo the umpire when he makes a call against the Bats.

War Memorial Stadium was built in 1926 and dedicated in honor of all the Greensboro residents who served and died in World War I. Right outside the stadium is a large bronze plaque listing their names. When you enter, you pass through the original stone and conrete archways and into the main lobby of the concourse. The 7,500-seat stadium has a unique shape. It's built like a backward J—the grandstand and bleachers start at first base, curve around home and then stretch from home down into left field. By the left field foul pole is a multilevel bar and party area called the Grandstand. This is the center of all kinds of pregame group fun and postgame band concerts.

There is a picnic area behind the stands that's

The team's strong performance in 1993 and 1994 boosted Greensboro fan attendance at War Memorial Stadium up more than 40 percent over 1992 stats.

great for large groups. At the concession stands the nightly specials are always good, the favorite being Italian sausage with peppers and onions. A variety of beer is served here; Red Oak Amber, a local beer, is the most popular. And for some reason, even though the average temperatures are only in the seventies, snow cones are very big.

Some of the on-field promotions here include the Dizzy Bat Race, the Pizza Scream, and the Merchandise Scream (works the same as the pizza scream but shirts, hats, and other stuff are given away). The best event, though, is Sumo Wrestling—fans get dressed up in inflatable suits (that look like sumos) and have a wrestling match in the sixth inning. Some lucky fan can also win a cellular phone during the home run inning if a player hits a homer over the Cellular One sign. The fan not only wins a phone, but free service, too.

Gates open one hour and fifteen minutes before game time. The players have to go through a tunnel area near the stands to get from the dugouts to the field and back, so it's fairly easy to get autographs here. Also, there is a walkway in front of the bleachers, so it's very easy for fans to come down by the dugouts and bullpens for autographs.

GETTING THERE

Greensboro was named after Revolutionary War hero General Nathanael Greene, whose victory at the Guilford Battleground (now a historical site) was a pivotal turning point. There's a variety of motels, and camping just south of town in Pleasant Garden.

War Memorial Stadium is just east of downtown in a residential area. To get there, take I-40 or I-80 to the Elm-Eugene Street exit. Go north to Market Street, then east to Dudley, and then north again on Dudley to the corner of Lindsay and Yanceyville streets. Parking is very limited (only 325 spaces) and costs $1.50. Most fans end up parking on the streets.

Box seats go for $7, while reserved seats are $5. General admission tickets cost $4, $3 for kids and seniors.

For schedule of events and ticket information, call (910) 333-2287.

For tourist information, contact the Greensboro Area Convention & Visitors Bureau, 317 South Greene Street, Greensboro, NC 27401, (910) 274-2282 or (800) 344-2282.

		HOMETOWN STATS—GREENSBORO *The Last Ten Years*			
Affil.	Year	League	Wins	Losses	Attendance
BOS	1985	South Atlantic	74	63	172,626
	1986		75	63	180,715
	1987		55	85	166,208
CIN	1988		79	60	168,675
	1989		78	60	157,927
NYY	1990		59	85	153,232
	1991		73	68	191,048
	1992		74	67	156,387
	1993		85	56	201,222
	1994		71	69	218,410

Hagerstown Suns

(Toronto Blue Jays)

Municipal Stadium
274 E. Memorial Boulevard
Hagerstown, MD 21740

Although the current Hagerstown Suns have been here only since 1993, baseball has thrived in the area since 1915. The Hubs played in the Old Blue Ridge League from 1915 until 1930, when it became the Mid Atlantic League. Teams that followed were: the Owls, who played from 1941 to 1949; the Braves, 1950 to 1952; the Packets, 1953 to 1955; and the Suns, a Class A Carolina League team, from 1981 to 1988. In 1989 the Suns joined the Eastern League as a Double-A franchise and played through the 1992 season, when new ownership moved the team to Bowie, Maryland. Suddenly the future of baseball in Hagerstown looked bleak. Enter Winston Blenckstone. Blenckstone had sold his Baltimore gas operation and moved to Myrtle Beach, South Carolina, to take life easy. He ended up buying the rights to the Class A Florence (SC) Blue Jays, which had been defunct for six years. After failing to get the city to build a new stadium, he brought the franchise to Hagerstown. The club kept the name Suns, and as members of the South Atlantic League brought baseball back to Municipal Stadium.

As soon as you drive into the parking lot, you're hit with nostalgia. There are giant shade maple trees, the smell of new-mown grass, and the original limestone ballpark facade in the distance. Municipal Stadium was built in 1931. This is where Willie Mays made his professional debut with the Trenton Giants on June 24, 1950. Babe Phelps played here, and so did first baseman Jesse Levan, who was eventually barred from baseball for gambling. Hagerstown teams have always been pretty good—more than sixty players have gone on to the majors after playing here. The new team is no exception. Keep an eye on D. J. Boston and Jose Silva, top prospects in the Blue Jays organization. In 1994, the Suns drew over 110,000 fans, which is not bad for a town of 36,000—one and half hours from Washington, D.C.—especially with the Frederick Keys of the Carolina League only twenty-three miles away.

Municipal Stadium is a comfortable 5,140-seat place, with some old quirks but lots of modern conveniences. The grass field is lush, even if not exactly level. The rise in left center field is due to a large deposit of limestone, which just can't be moved, so it stays. The three-tiered picnic area is reserved for groups, and if it's not booked up it's open to the general public. There is also a nice playground for kids, which is supervised throughout the game by an adult (to keep out older kids). The outfield walls are covered three-deep with billboards (that's 26 feet). Out over left field is the Washington County Hospital; the view from everywhere else is of nothing but maple trees.

There's a carnival atmosphere before the game and wonderful smoky aromas from open-flame grills: hamburgers, apple-smoked hot dogs, Italian sausages, and chicken filets. And do try the Coney Island hot dogs, BBQ pork sandwiches, giant soft pretzels, and marvelous boardwalk-style fries cooked in peanut oil and served with salt, vinegar, and/or catsup. Wash it all down with old-fashioned lemonade; this is the real stuff—with half a lemon in each cup. Average summer-night temperatures average between 81° and 85°F, and Suns fans think this park is the perfect place to be.

Special events take place before the game —fireworks, the Blues Brothers, The Famous Chicken, the Dynamite Lady, and the like. Some of the premiums given away at the gate are caps, baseball cards, jerseys, magnetic schedules, team photos, and bats.

Gates open one hour before game time. The best place to get autographs is along the first base line, in front of the box seats, before the game.

Municipal Stadium was built and dedicated in 1931, the brand-new home for the then–Hagerstown Hubs. In 1994, the fans watched the Suns contend for but lose the championship to Savannah 3–0 in the best-of-five series.

GETTING THERE

Hagerstown sits in a valley surrounded by the Blue Ridge Mountains. Its historic sites from the German frontier days, the French and Indian War, the Revolutionary War, and the Civil War are remarkable. The area has plenty of motels, inns, bed-and-breakfasts, and campsites.

To get to Municipal Stadium from the east, take I-70 west to Exit 32B and proceed two and a half miles to Cleveland Avenue. Turn left and continue straight on into the stadium. From I-81 south, take Exit 6A and proceed through town to Cleveland Avenue. Turn right and continue straight on into the stadium. There is plenty of free parking.

Box seats are $6. General admission tickets cost $4, $2 for kids and seniors.

For schedule of events and ticket information, call (301) 791-6266.

For tourist information, contact the Washington County Convention & Visitors Bureau, 1826-C Dual Highway, Hagerstown, MD 21740, (301) 791-3130 or (800) 228-STAY.

HOMETOWN STATS—HAGERSTOWN *The Last Ten Years*					
Affil.	Year	League	Wins	Losses	Attendance
BAL	1985	Carolina	65	72	112,978
	1986		91	48	144,161
	1987		72	68	135,059
	1988		79	61	135,380
	1989	Eastern	67	72	161,630
	1990		67	71	167,725
	1991		81	59	193,753
	1992		59	80	130,331
TOR	1993	South Atlantic	74	68	95,702
	1994		80	56	111,660

Hickory Crawdads

(Chicago White Sox)

L. P. Frans Stadium
2500 Clement Boulevard
Hickory, NC 28601

1993 was the Crawdads' first year in Hickory (they were previously the Gastonia Rangers)—and what a year it was. They came in thirteenth out of fourteen teams (they were equally awful in Gastonia), but they broke attendance records left and right. Not only did they set the all-time high of 283,727 for the South Atlantic League, they outdrew the whole White Sox farm system, not including the Triple-A Nashville Sounds.

Hickory hosted baseball sporadically from 1939 through 1960. The teams were usually called the Rebels and belonged to various leagues, beginning with the Tar Heel League and ending with the Western Carolina League. In their last year, 1960, the attendance was a meager 14,503. This might explain why Hickory was without baseball for the next thirty-two years. Times sure have changed. Why, the Crawdads draw more than that in three games! And why not, when you have youngsters like Harold Wilson with twenty-two homers, Jeff Abbott batting .371, and Dave Lundquist winning twelve games in 1994.

L. P. Frans Stadium opened in 1993. The facade, offices, and utility buildings are brick, giving the park a warm, old-fashioned quality. The right field wall, in a takeoff of Fenway's "Green Monster," is called the "ad" monster because the fence is *four* billboards high! Looking out over the outfield walls (center and left, that is) you see mostly trees, and through one clearing a glimpse of the Blue Ridge Mountains. The 5,100 seats are full on weekends. Even during the week, the team draws at least 4,000. These numbers are virtually unheard of in Class A ball. This team must be doing something right.

The Crawdad Cafe (air-conditioned, take note) is located in the right field area adjoining the administration building. Appetizers and sandwiches are served, and there is a full bar. The Cafe is also hooked up to cable and satellite TV, so you can keep up with other games. There is one catch, however: before and during the game the Cafe is open only to box and reserved seat ticketholders.

Conrad the Crawdad is the team mascot. One year he made his entrance by parachuting into the ballpark. The next he arrived by hot-air balloon. A couple of the contests here are unusual. For instance, at one point between innings, a pickup truck pulls out on the warning track. A selected Crawdad player gets one try at hitting a fly ball that will land in the bed of the pickup. No bouncing *and* the ball has to stay put in the bed of the truck. If he does it, some lucky fan wins a $500 savings bond. It's never been done. There is also the Ford Explorer billboard on the left field wall with the front passenger window missing (cut out). A homer through the window could win somebody a cruise for two. That's never been done, either.

The fireworks shows each season pack the park to overflowing, as does Turn-Back-the-Clock Night and special appearances by the Phillie Phanatic, Billy Bird, and the Dynamite Lady. You can see some of the goings-on from outside the stadium along the field lines, where kids often wait to catch foul balls. Giveaways include the usual seat cushions, pennants, umbrellas, and caps, but you can only get giant foam-rubber claws here in Hickory.

Gates open one and a half hours before game time. You can get autographs before the game down by the railings near the dugouts.

GETTING THERE

Hickory, "Gateway to Northwestern North Carolina," boasts that 60 percent of *all* U.S.—made furniture is manufactured right in this area.

In 1994, fans packed the picturesque L. P. Frans Stadium to cheer the Crawdads on to their first division playoff.

The furniture malls and antique malls here are incredible. There's a variety of motels and quite a few campgrounds in the region.

To get to L. P. Frans Stadium, take I-40 to Exit 123 (Lenoir North), then turn left on Clement Boulevard. The stadium is half a mile down on the right. There is parking for 800 cars, which costs $1. Most fans park on nearby streets.

Box seats cost $6.25, while reserved seats go for $5.25. (Kids and seniors get $1 off.) General admission tickets are $4.25, $3 for kids and seniors.

For schedule of events and ticket information, call (704) 322-3000.

For tourist information, contact the Hickory Convention & Visitors Bureau, P.O. Box 1828, Hickory, NC 28603, (704) 328-6111 or (800) 849-5093.

HOMETOWN STATS—HICKORY					
The Last Ten Years*					
Affil.	Year	League	Wins	Losses	Attendance
CWS	1993	South Atlantic	52	88	283,727
	1994		86	54	270,880
*Statistics are given only for the years in which the team played in Hickory.					

Macon Braves

(Atlanta Braves)

Luther Williams Field
Central City Park/7th Street
Macon, GA 31201

Macon was a founding member of the original South Atlantic League in 1904 and had fairly constant baseball right up through 1987, when the Pittsburgh Pirates moved their franchise from Macon to Augusta. This current team moved to Macon in 1991 after a five-year stint (1985 through 1990) as the Sumter Braves in Sumter, North Carolina. The Atlanta Braves organization has always given its Class A franchise a lot of credit. Almost all its World Series–caliber players have come up through its farm system—Mark Lemke, Jeff Blauser, Dale Murphy, and David Justice are just a few of them. The first *Macon* Brave to make it to the majors is shortstop Larry "Chipper" Jones, who moved up in 1994.

Luther Williams Field is one of the landmark ballparks in the National League system. Built in 1929 and named after a former mayor, it's a truly old-fashioned park that is located at the State Fairgrounds in Macon. The old brick-and-iron gates and the brick archways leading into the stadium really do take you back to another era. Preserving all this nostalgia while bringing the park up to major league standards has required extensive capital. It's been well worth it, however, and the Braves' groundskeepers have the reputation for being the best in the league.

The grandstand starts at first base and stops at third and is completely covered. There is a picnic area down the left field line that has wooden bleachers, and although it is reserved for groups before the game, anyone can go in during the game. The casual and open grassy area off right field is popular with those who want to go home with a foul ball. When you're sitting in the stands, you can see a softball complex off to the left—and trains in a freight yard off to the right. Homers hit over the right field wall often go sailing into the open freight cars. It has been said that the longest home run in the world was hit in Macon and ended up in Seattle! The coaches consider the trains part of the Braves' home field advantage. When they bump into each other or a whistle blows a warning at the crossings, visiting players can be somewhat startled, breaking their concentration just enough to make a few mistakes.

One of the nice touches here, as in so many minor league

Players as well as fans enjoy the relaxed atmosphere of Braves baseball at Luther Williams Field.

parks, is that every night a different Little League team is honored. The kids get to go down in the dugout before the game and accompany the Braves players out on the field for the National Anthem. If a little one trips or falls, he's likely to get picked up and carried by a Brave. After the anthem, as the team takes the field, the announcer plays the sound of tom-toms over the PA system; the "tomahawk chop" is very big in Macon.

Prizes include a free car wash for the parking lot's filthiest car, duly announced over the loudspeakers. If three players are struck out in one inning by a Macon pitcher, everybody in the stadium gets a certificate for a free hamburger at Krystal's. (During the first half of 1993, over 25,000 burgers were given away!) One of the most popular events is Used Car Night. Only one car is given away, but nine keys are passed out. Whoever has the key that starts the car wins it. There are special appearances by skydivers, the Dynamite Lady, Billy Bird, and others. Giveaways are scheduled throughout the season.

Gates open one hour before game time. There is an autograph booth by the souvenir stand that is usually manned by two players before the game. The players will also stop and sign autographs by the dugouts before and after the game.

GETTING THERE

Macon is a city of parks and elaborate mansions that was originally designed with the ancient Gardens of Babylon in mind. It's also an important archaeological site—some artifacts date back 10,000 years. There are plenty of hotels and motels, with camping nearby.

Luther Williams Field is located in Central City Park on 7th Street. To get there, take I-75 to I-16. Take the second exit off I-16 to Riverside Drive, which takes you right to the park. There is plenty of free parking.

Box seats go for $5, while general admission tickets cost $4 for adults, $3 for seniors and the military, and $2 for kids. (Kids 6 and under are free.)

For schedule of events and ticket information, call (912) 745-8943.

For tourist information, contact the Macon-Bibb County Convention & Visitors Bureau, 200 Cherry Street, Macon, GA 31201, (912) 743-3401.

Affil.	Year	League	Wins	Losses	Attendance
PIT	1985	South Atlantic	56	82	39,679
	1986		54	84	37,816
	1987		73	64	41,728
ATL	1991		83	58	107,059
	1992		58	81	88,833
	1993		74	67	96,450
	1994		73	64	83,597

HOMETOWN STATS—MACON
The Last Ten Years*†

*Statistics are given only for the years in which the team played in Macon.

†Macon did not have a baseball team from 1988 to 1991.

Piedmont Phillies

(Philadelphia Phillies)

Fieldcrest Cannon Stadium
Moose Road
Kannapolis, NC 28082

Hi Ho Phillie gives his last mascot performances in 1995!

This Philadelphia Phillies franchise moved north from Spartanburg, South Carolina, after the 1994 season and will be in a brand-new stadium in Kannapolis, North Carolina, for the 1995 season. The Phillies, that is to say the Spartanburg Phillies, had played in Spartanburg since 1963—first in the Western Carolinas League and then in the Sally League. Two of Spartanburg's legends were Rocky Colavito and Ron Allen, who in 1966, as legend has it, hit a ball so hard out of Spartanburg's Duncan Park that it cleared the trees over the right field fence and landed 600 feet away! Others who have gone on to The Show from Spartanburg are Luis Aguayo, Dave Baker, Kim Batiste, Rocky Childress, Ryne Sandberg, and George Bell, who back in 1979 hit twenty-two homers and thirteen triples.

Although the team has won six championships since 1963, including back-to-backs in 1966–1967 and 1972–1973, they have not done all that well lately, and fan support in Spartanburg was extremely erratic. The Phillies drew only 16,833 in 1986, a year in which they finished 47½ games back of first place. Then attendance jumped dramatically to 94,120 in 1989 (they finished 30½ games back), only to drop again. When the club finally made it to the playoffs once again in 1992, just 47,274 fans turned out. The team's new owner, Larry Hedrick, made a concerted effort in 1994 to get the fans into the ballpark, but nothing seemed to have much of an impact—a discouraging 58,138 showed up that year. Giving up, Hedrick and company headed north to Kannapolis.

Kannapolis is only twenty miles northeast of Charlotte and the Triple-A Charlotte Knights, but because the Knights actually play in Fort Mill, South Carolina, the Phillies will be just outside the Knights' twenty-two mile protected territory limit. The club, however, is not counting on drawing fans from Charlotte. Instead, it will draw from an area that includes Concord just to the south of Kannapolis and Salisbury to the north—an area that has a population of 200,000. Kannapolis, by the way, is home to corporate Philip Morris and Fieldcrest Cannon.

The team will temporarily be called the Piedmont Phillies in 1995—the Piedmont being the plateau between the Atlantic seaboard and the Appalachian Mountains. The move to North Carolina was so sudden that the club didn't have a chance to hold a name-the-team contest. So they are open to suggestions up until the 1995 All-Star break. The winning entry will be announced late

Female fans, during the annual Diamond Dig, use spoons to hunt for a real diamond hidden somewhere in the infield dirt. (Shown here in Spartanburg.)

in the season and the team will take its new name in 1996.

The new $5 million stadium, which overlooks Lake Fisher, is brick and will have a total of 4,500 seats. It was designed by the same architects that built L.P. Frans Stadium in Hickory and is named after the Fieldcrest Cannon company, which paid $300,000 for the naming rights. Although the stadium will not have a picnic area open for the 1995 season, there are plans in the works to have one ready for 1996.

The team mascot, Hi Ho Phillie, may or may not make his final appearance during the 1995 season. Phillie, a big fuzzy horse, was extremely popular with the fans in Spartanburg, though not with the person wearing what was dubbed the "costume from hell." The heavy costume required the wearer to don an ice vest to survive the humid ninety-degree weather. There will, of course, be a new mascot for the 1996 season.

The Dizzy Bat Race will likely be revived in Kannapolis, along with the Water Balloon Smash and Airplane Toss (in which a fan attempts to sail a styrofoam airplane into a pool fifty feet away). There will also be plenty of promotional giveaways.

Gates open about one hour before game time. You will be able to get autographs down by the dugouts before the game.

GETTING THERE

Cabarrus County, in which Kannapolis lies, is home to three of North Carolina's most popular attractions: Cannon Mills and Cannon Village in Kannapolis and the Reed Gold Mine and Charlotte Motor Speedway in nearby Concord. There are plenty of familiar hotels, chain motels and campgrounds in the area.

To get to Fieldcrest Cannon Stadium, take I-85 to Lane Street (exit 63). Go west on Lane Street for about half a mile to China Grove Road. Take a right and continue to the next intersection, which is Moose Road. Turn right on Moose Road. The stadium is on the right. (The stadium is within view of I-85 and may get its own exit ramp.) There's plenty of parking, which costs $1.

Premium box seats (right behind home plate) cost $7.50, while the regular box seats go for $6.50. Reserved seats are $5.50 and general admission tickets cost $4.50. Kids and seniors get $1 off reserved and general admission.

For schedule of events and ticket information, call (704) 932-3267.

For tourist information, contact the Cabarrus County Visitors Center, 200 West Avenue, Concord, NC 28025, (704) 938-4550 or (800) 848-3740.

Savannah Cardinals

(St. Louis Cardinals)

Grayson Stadium
1401 E. Victory Drive
Savannah, GA 31404

Savannah's first team took the field in 1904, and over the years baseball fans have seen some great players play the game here. Babe Ruth, Ty Cobb, Mickey Mantle, and Hank Aaron all played here in exhibition games. Savannah teams have also produced some of their own impressive players. Alumni include such greats as Curt Flood, Milt Thompson, Donn Clendenon, Brook Jacoby, and Steve Bedrosian and more recently, Geronimo Pena, Donavan Osborne, Allen Watson, Bernard Gilkey, and pitcher Mark Clark, who had a league-leading fourteen wins in 1989.

The Savannah Cardinals, affiliated with the St. Louis Cardinals since 1984, are owned by a group of New Yorkers, among them Gerry Cooney, the heavyweight prizefighter. The team has been playing great ball these last couple of years, winning the league championship in 1993 and 1994. Quite a turnaround from 1992, when they went 62–78. The team's performance brought in the fans, too. As the club improved, old attendance records fell by the wayside. Better than 110,000 fans showed up each year, and the numbers will keep going up. The best news is that St. Louis is stocking the team with quality young players, so the future looks very bright for the Savannah Cardinals.

Grayson Stadium is located in Daffin Park, a beautiful setting with recreational facilities such as tennis courts, baseball fields, softball fields, and basketball courts. The stadium was built in 1941 and named after General William Grayson, a war hero in the Spanish-American War. This is a very informal place. You enter the park through a simple gate set in a brick facade. A small concession area leads to ramps that take you right into the stands behind home plate. The covered grandstand and bleachers seat 8,500, making this the largest ballpark in Class A baseball. But because every fan is close to the field and everybody can hear just about every word the players say, there is a real feeling of intimacy here.

The outfield wall is worth mentioning. The center and right field walls are double-stacked with billboards. The left field wall has a single row of billboards, bleachers above, and then another single row of billboards over the bleachers. On that top row a grocery cart has been nailed to the Kroger's Grocery Store billboard. If any player hits the ball into the cart during the game, some lucky fan wins $1,000.

There's a new grill and barbecue area in the park, and no matter where you sit irresistible aromas surround you. The picnic area on the third base side is rented out to groups of twenty-five or more. If all the tables aren't full, they are opened up to the general public around 8:00 P.M. The Cardinals do not have a mascot, but they still provide a lot of fun. There's the Pizza Run between innings, in which two participants start at second and run in opposite directions to home plate for a pizza prize. They also have the Dizzy Bat Race, Water Balloon Toss, and Best Seat in the House contest.

Gates open one hour before game time. Getting autographs before the game isn't too easy—you have to go stand by the first base side gate. Visitors' autographs are much easier to get, since the fence along third base is only waist-high. However, Cardinal players are happy to sign autographs after the game as they leave the locker rooms.

GETTING THERE

Savannah was designed by General James Oglethorpe in the 1730s on a grid of broad avenues, braided at regular intervals with spacious public squares. It's a remarkable city with world-class

Loyal Savannah fans were rewarded in 1994 as the Cardinals won their second consecutive league championship title.

hotels and inns. There are campgrounds right in town and on nearby islands.

Grayson Stadium is on the west side of town. To get there, take I-16 west to the 37th Street exit. Go left at the end of the ramp and take a right on Abercorn Street and then a left on Victory Drive to the stadium. There is ample free parking.

Box seats (always sold out) are $5.25, while re- served go for $4.25. General admission tickets cost $3.50, $3 for kids, seniors, and the military.

For schedule of events and ticket information, call (912) 351-9150.

For tourist information, contact the Savannah Area Convention & Visitors Bureau, P.O. Box 1628, Savannah, GA 31402, (912) 944-0456 or (800) 444-2427.

HOMETOWN STATS—SAVANNAH
The Last Ten Years

Affil.	Year	League	Wins	Losses	Attendance
STL	1985	South Atlantic	57	78	34,287
	1986		75	60	44,787
	1987		69	69	33,363
	1988		68	67	58,311
	1989		69	70	76,287
	1990		73	68	94,686
	1991		61	77	99,399
	1992		62	78	79,589
	1993		94	48	106,287
	1994		82	55	111,143

The Other Minor Leagues

The Independent Leagues

It's remarkable how many different leagues exist today. With the exception of the Japanese Leagues, which are highly regarded, the National Association of Professional Baseball Leagues (NAPBL) tends to overlook any league that is not a member of the Association, calling them "semi-pro," "shams," and worse. But it shouldn't dismiss them so easily, as the independent minor leagues are providing fierce competition in some markets. The Northern League, putting down roots in the Upper Midwest, is giving everybody fits. It's wildly successful; there is already a long list of cities wanting franchises. Founded by Baseball America president Miles Wolff, the new league has been a boon for players looking for a second chance, or often, as it's turning out, that first chance. On any given night you'll find a few major league scouts in the stands. And the fans are flocking to independent team games in places like Sioux City, Iowa, where the Explorers play in a brand-new stadium, and St. Paul, where Mike Veeck (you remember Mike from the Fort Myers Miracle, with Toucan, the Diamond Dog) is working his magic with the Saints in the Twin Cities' outdoor ballpark—only now it's Saint the Pig who's getting all the attention. In 1994, the Colorado Silver Bullets, an all-female fellow Northern League team, made its debut, but found the competition too overpowering. Phil Niekro, the Bullets' coach, said that many of the players in the Northern League were major league material and just too strong for the rookie Silver Bullets. There is talk of forming an all-female league, but in the meantime, the Silver Bullets will play exhibition games. They won their first game, by the way, on May 27, 1994, against the Richfield (MN) Rockets, a thirty-five-and-over men's semipro team.

The Frontier League, playing in Ohio, Pennsylvania, West Virginia, and Kentucky, got a lot of bad press in 1994 over bad playing (and living) conditions: no money, no equipment, bad lighting, low salaries ($12 a game), and so on. One team, the Kentucky Rifles, still managed to make positive headlines by signing twenty-three-year-old Oklahoma State University female softball star Kendra Hanes for their outfield. The big question remains, however: Will the league live to see '95?

The Northeast League was to have begun its inaugural season in 1994, but it didn't quite make it off the ground. They will try again, adding Glen Falls and Albany (NY), which both recently lost NAPBL teams, to their schedule. Northeast League commissioner Lee Mazzilli has plans for scheduling 160 games per season, giving the league a big edge over their competition, the New York-Penn League, which is a short season (starting in June) league playing only 76 games total.

The Texas-Louisiana League, which began operating in 1994, is made up of eight teams—Mobile (AL), Alexandria (LA), and, in Texas, Amarillo, Beaumont, Corpus Christi, Rio Grande (Edinburg/McAllen), Tyler, and San Antonio (where they plan to go head to head with the San Antonio Missions of the Double-A Texas League). While it might be a bit of an overstatement to say that all eyes are on the T-L League, there is definitely interest in whether the league will succeed, since the league itself owns and runs all the franchises, trying to maintain stability.

Not far away, the Mid-South Baseball League

hopes to get going in 1995 with Biloxi (MS), Greenville (MS), Gretna (LA), Meridan (MS), Quad Cities (AL), Slidell (LA), and Tupelo (MS). It will also be worth watching California, where the Golden State Baseball League may get under way with member teams from the Antelope Valley, Henderson (NV), Northern San Diego County, Oxnard, Palm Springs, Santa Barbara, and San Luis Obispo. The GSBL was originally named the Western League, which briefly made matters somewhat confusing since another league calling itself the Western League hopes to install itself in the Northwest with member teams ranging from Portland to Reno, reaching into southern Canada as well.

Now for the matter of winter baseball! There is a Dominican League, Puerto Rican League, Australian League, and Venezuelan and Hawaii Winter Leagues. And last, but certainly not least, is the Arizona Fall League. The Arizona Fall League is jokingly referred to as "A League of Their Own." Disgruntled by what the majors see as deteriorating conditions in the traditional winter leagues, the AFL is a coop of sorts, established by major league clubs to provide a safe and controlled atmosphere for players who need extra work. Each major league team is furnishing the league with at least six prospects. It started up in 1992. Everyone seems more than happy with the situation even though attendance has been sparse. Things looked better for the 1994 season—Michael Jordan was on the roster.

THE BUSH LEAGUE

There was a time when the term "bush league" might have referred to many of the abovementioned leagues, but nowadays it has taken on a new meaning. The Boston-based Bush League cashes in on the popular (and lucrative) minor league franchising phenomenon by selling merchandise with fictional logos—made-up teams. In the 1994 season the Bush League ran ads in *Baseball America* and *Baseball Weekly* promoting merchandise for the Titusville Flamingos. Only problem was, as *Baseball America* found out, no such team existed. It was strictly a money-making gimmick. *Baseball America* stopped running the ads, even though there's nothing illegal. Buyer beware, if you want a cap, shirt, or jacket from a real team.

Wrapping Up the NAPBL

The other members of the National Association of Professional Baseball Leagues are listed below. The Mexican League, which is classified Triple-A, is made up of 16 teams and plays a schedule of 132 games. Though basically an entity in its own right, the Mexican League has provided a good training ground for many a future major league ballplayer; Fernando Valenzuela is perhaps the best known. The remaining leagues are the short season leagues, which do not start playing until the middle of June and then play a maximum of seventy-six games. Not listed here is the Dominican Summer League, which seems to change so fast that it is hopeless trying to keep track. At the moment, the league is made up of twenty-one teams that play seventy to seventy-two games. They all have major league affiliates; some are coops, shared by as many as three major league teams.

Triple-A / Mexican League

Northern Zone
Aguascalientes Railroadmen
Jalisco Cowboys
Monclova Steelers
Monterrey Industrials
Monterrey Sultans
Owls of the Two Laredos
Saltillo Sarape Makers Owls
Union Laguna Cotton Pickers

Southern Zone
Campeche Pirates
Mexico City Red Devils
Mexico City Tigers
Minatitlan Oilers
Puebla Parrots
Tabasco Olmecas
Veracruz Eagles
Yucatan Lions

Class A Short Season Teams

New York-Penn League

McNamara Division
New Jersey Cardinals (Cardinals)
Oneonta Yankees (Yankees)
Pittsfield Mets (Mets)
Utica Blue Sox (Red Sox)

Stedler Division
Batavia Clippers (Phillies)
Hudson Valley Renegades (Rangers)
Jamestown Jammers (Tigers)
St. Catharines Blue Jays (Blue Jays)
Vermont Expos (Expos)
Welland Pirates (Pirates)

Pinckney Division
Auburn Astros (Astros)
Elmira Pioneers (Marlins)
Williamsport Cubs (Cubs)
Watertown Indians (Indians)

Northwest League

Northern Division
Bellingham Giants (Giants)
Everett Mariners (Mariners)
Spokane Indians (Royals)
Yakima Bears (Dodgers)

Southern Division
Bend Rockies (Rockies)
Boise Hawks (Angels)
Eugene Emeralds (Braves)
S. Oregon Athletics (Athletics)

Rookie Teams

Appalachian League

Northern Division
Bluefield Orioles (Orioles)
Burlington Indians (Indians)
Danville Braves (Braves)
Martinsville Phillies (Phillies)
Princeton Reds (Reds)

Southern Divsion
Bristol White Sox (White Sox)
Elizabethton Twins (Twins)
Huntington Cubs (Cubs)
Johnson City Cardinals (Cardinals)
Kingsport Mets (Mets)

Pioneer League

Northern Division
Billings Mustangs (Reds)
Great Falls Dodgers (Dodgers)
Lethbridge Mounties (Coop)
Medicine Hat Blue Jays (Blue Jays)

Southern Division
Butte Copper Kings (Coop)
Helena Brewers (Brewers)
Idaho Falls Padres (Padres)
Ogden Raptors (Independent)

Gulf Coast League

Northern Division
Melbourne Marlins (Marlins)
St. Lucie Mets (Mets)
West Palm Beach Braves (Braves)
West Palm Beach Expos (Expos)

Western Division
Bradenton Pirates (Pirates)
Fort Myers Red Sox (Red Sox)
Fort Myers Royals (Royals)
Fort Myers Twins (Twins)
Port Charlotte Rangers (Rangers)
Sarasota Orioles (Orioles)
Sarasota White Sox (White Sox)

Eastern Division
Dunedin Blue Jays (Blue Jays)
Osceola Astros (Astros)
Osceola Cubs (Cubs)
Tampa Yankees (Yankees)

Arizona League

Chandler Brewers (Brewers)
Chandler Cardinals (Cardinals)
Chandler Rockies (Rockies)
Mesa Angels (Angels)

Peoria Padres (Padres)
Peoria Mariners (Mariners)
Scottsdale Athletics (Athletics)
Scottsdale Giants (Giants)

Weekend Jaunts and Vacation Itineraries

If you're thinking about heading to the beach this season, try sunny Florida, where the summer rates are cheap and baseball and beaches are part of everyday life. Or if you have a yen for hills, mountains, and lakes, North Carolina and Tennessee have the best of both. History? New York's got it in spades. Or follow California's Highway 99 from Stockton to Bakersfield and pick a few strawberries along the way. If your time is more limited, try one of the suggested day trips—or even a weekend outing.

NORTHEAST

New York State of Mind

Perhaps we are prejudiced—we do live here. New York State is a wonderful place to spend a vacation, and what's more, there's more baseball here than you can shake a bat at. There are twelve Triple-A, Double-A and Class A Short Season teams in New York alone.

The New York "BIG DEAL" Baseball Tour

If you have two weeks, this is a *great* tour. You can see the best of baseball and the best of New York State. We are not suggesting that you hit every town on the tour, though if you plan ahead carefully, just maybe you'll manage to watch every team play and visit Cooperstown and Niagara Falls, too.

First stop, a day game with **Hudson Valley Renegades** of the Short Season New York-Penn League in Fishkill. New team, new stadium, very pretty setting, and only seventy miles from New York City. Head straight up the Hudson River via the Taconic State Parkway (or go up the Palisades Parkway in New Jersey) to I-84. Head west to Fishkill.

Next stop, the **Oneonta Yankees**, another New York-Penn team, about 120 miles from Fishkill. The road takes you through the Woodstock area and the heart of the Catskills, so there are plenty of places to stop and explore. Take I-84 west to I-87 north and then go northwest on Route 28 to Oneonta.

From Oneonta, continue on designated scenic Route 28 for about forty-five minutes and stop in Cooperstown for lunch and a visit to the Baseball Hall of Fame. If you've never been to Cooperstown, spend the night. It's charming. In the morning continue on 28 to I-90 and head west to Utica, where you can catch another New York-Penn team, the **Utica Blue Sox**, in action, or continue west into Syracuse and the Triple-A **Syracuse Chiefs** of the International League (page 50).

Continuing straight west on I-90 toward Buffalo, we suggest a detour through Rochester, about ninety miles away on Lake Ontario, and a visit to Silver Stadium, home of the Triple-A **Rochester Red Wings** (page 46). The stadium, built in 1929, is one of the oldest in the country, but do see it in 1995. As of 1996, the Red Wings will be playing in a brand-new ballpark.

On your way to Buffalo from Rochester, drop in on the **Batavia Clippers** just off I-90 if they're playing a day game. Back on I-90 and heading west, it's another forty-five miles to Buffalo, nearby Niagara Falls, and, of course, the Triple-A

Buffalo Bisons (page 16). When you're ready to head back, get on I-90 east to Route 60 and go down to Jamesport on Lake Chautauqua, about an hour and a half away. (Or mosey down the longer scenic Route 5 along Lake Erie.) Take in a short season **Jamestown Jammers** game and buy a CD or two for the three-and-a-half-hour trip to Elmira and the **Pioneers**—or four and a half hours, if you continue on to Binghamton. Relax in Binghamton and take in a couple of **Mets** games (page 80) before driving the final 200 miles back to New York City.

For Further Information on the Short Season Teams

Hudson Valley Renegades: (914) 838-0094
Oneonta Yankees: (607) 432-6326
*National Baseball Hall of Fame and Museum
 (Cooperstown):* (607) 547-9988
Utica Blue Sox: (315) 738-0999
Batavia Clippers: (716) 343-7531
Jamestown Jammers: (716) 664-0915
Elmira Pioneers: (607) 734-1811

Some Day Trips from New York City

Before 1994, the closest minor league team to New York City was in New Britain, Connecticut. It was a Double-A **New Britain Red Sox** (now the Hardware City Rock Cats) (page 86) game that inspired this book. The game, which the Sox won, was great; the strange mascot, a very tired and rumpled bee, was hilarious; and Beehive Field, well, it seemed more like a college field than a pro ballpark. All in all, we had a great time. Sadly for us, though not for anyone else, Beehive Field will be replaced by 1996, so if you want to see what inspired two baseball fans to go out and write a tome on the minor leagues, get there in 1995. To get to New Britain, simply take the Hutchinson River Parkway to I-684 north to I-84 east to New Britain. It's about 115 miles, or a two-hour-and-fifteen-minute drive.

Another easy trip for a night or day game is to the brand-new Mercer County Waterfront Park in Trenton, New Jersey, to see the Double-A **Trenton Thunder** (page 98) play. Trenton is about seventy-five miles from New York City. You can either take the Jersey Turnpike and head west to Trenton on I-95 or take U.S. 1 and drive through the Princeton area.

A little farther away, about 120 miles, are the Triple-A **Scranton/Wilkes-Barre Red Barons** (page 48). We've done it at night and just whizzed back to New York on I-80 (and I-280). Lackawanna County Stadium is a big modern ballpark set in the woods at the bottom of a mountain, so day games are great, too. You can cool off at the Delaware Water Gap on your way. Or take a detour in New Jersey up Route 94 to Highway 206 into Augusta and catch a night game with the short season New Jersey Cardinals at brand-new Skylands Park, (201) 579-7500.

A Connecticut Weekend

New Yorkers (us included) have a real need to get out of town on summer weekends. One perfect getaway is Norwich, Connecticut, about 137 miles away. Leave early Saturday morning and head straight out I-95 to I-395 and up to Norwich, which takes about two hours and forty minutes. Spend part of the day in Norwich and then take scenic Route 12 to charming old Mystic on Long Island Sound. Head back to Norwich for the Double-A **Norwich Navigators** (page 92) game. The next morning, drive the sixty miles down to West Haven in time to see the Double-A **New Haven Ravens** (page 90) take on the "Visitors" at Yale Stadium. If time allows, be sure to walk around the Yale University campus.

Philadelphia Freedom Loop

Philadelphia is on everybody's list of cities to visit. It's a great place to start a one-week trip through the Pennsylvania Dutch country and the Early American and Civil War towns of both Pennsylvania and Maryland. Reading, Pennsylvania, in the heart of Berks County, is home to the Double-A **Reading Phillies** (page 96) and the first destination. The most direct route from Philadelphia is via the Pennsylvania Turnpike (I-76) to I-176 north to Reading. It's about a one-hour-and-fifteen-minute drive.

From Reading, it's on to Harrisburg either by way of the Turnpike for an hour-and-fifteen-minute drive, or via a picturesque detour down Highway 222 and a stop in Lancaster. It will add about twenty-five minutes to your driving time, but will be worth every minute. Once in Harrisburg, give yourself some time to wander around City Island and Waterfront Park before catching a Double-A **Senators** (page 88) game.

Hagerstown, Maryland, home of the Class A **Hagerstown Suns** (page 262), is your next stop. You can either take I-81 straight there, which is about seventy miles, or take the scenic route, Highway 15, through Gettysburg, which really doesn't add that many miles, but does take a lot longer, of course. And remember as you are driving through Civil War country that it was during that period of our history that baseball took root.

Frederick is another example of Americana at its most charming. It's only twenty-six miles from Hagerstown, so if you catch the Class A **Frederick Keys** (page 168) for a day game, you can easily drive the seventy miles to Washington, D.C. after the game. From Washington, take a day trip over to Bowie (on the way to Annapolis) and see the Double-A **Bowie Baysox** (page 82) play in their new Prince George Stadium. It's only a seventeen-mile jaunt. On your way back to Philadelphia, drop in on the Class A **Wilmington (DE) Blue Rocks** (page 178), about two and a half hours north of DC on I-95. From there it's about thirty miles back to Philadelphia.

MID-SOUTH

Goin' to Carolina on Our Minds

You could spend weeks trying to visit all the baseball teams in the Carolinas. We counted fourteen—and now that Spartanburg has decamped from South to North, the North has eleven of

them. If you're flying in, the Raleigh-Durham airport is about halfway between the two cities.

Raleigh is the capital of North Carolina, so we'll start there. And while you are there, either on business or vacation, take the time to head east for twenty miles on Highway 264 and catch a Double-A **Carolina Mudcats** (page 104) game out in Zebulon. And not to be missed are the Class A **Durham Bulls** (page 166). Durham is only twenty-five miles from Raleigh, so you can zip over while in Raleigh, or stop on your way west. The Bulls, one of the most famous minor league teams ever, open their new park in 1995—and yes, they took the bull with them!

I-40 west takes you all the way from the Raleigh-Durham area to Asheville, the tip end of this tour, about 223 miles. On that interstate system, there are six teams, including Durham. Burlington, about thirty-one miles to the west, is home to the Appalachian League's **Burlington Indians**, (910) 222-0223. And twenty-five miles west of Burlington is Greensboro, where you can catch the **Bats** (page 260) in action in the vintage 1926 War Memorial Stadium. Stay on I-40 and you'll come to Winston-Salem, about thirty miles west of Greensboro, and hopefully you'll catch the **Warthogs** (page 180) in town.

The next stop on I-40 is Hickory, home of the famous Class A **Crawdads** (page 264). Love those Crawdads. Then it's on to Asheville, eighty-one miles away, and the Class A **Asheville Tourists** (page 246). Newly-renovated McCormick Field sits at the foot of the Appalachians and is a hot tourist spot.

From Asheville, start your return trip by heading down south to Greenville, South Carolina, where the Double-A **Greenville Braves** (page 108) make their home. Greenville's about an hour and twenty minutes from Asheville via I-240, I-26, and Highway 25, or take the scenic Blue Ridge Parkway southwest for about twenty miles to Route 215 and go south on 215 past Sassafrass Mountain and on into Greenville via Highways 178 and 123.

From Greenville, it's more or less a straight ninety-mile shot up I-85 to the Triple-A **Char-**

lotte Knights (page 34). Charlotte is the largest metropolitan area in the state and a good place to spend the night and enjoy a game at the new stadium in nearby Fort Mill (SC).

The last stop on the tour, or last baseball stop, we should say, is in Kannapolis, the new home of the Class A **Piedmont Phillies,** just twenty-one miles up I-85 from Charlotte. From Kannapolis, back to the Raleigh-Durham area is 135 miles on I-85 and I-40.

You are going to need sustenance, so about thirty-five or so miles out of Kannapolis take a detour onto Highway 29-70 and go north four or five miles to Lexington, the home of some of the best barbecue in the Carolinas. There are *sixteen* barbecue joints in town. Lexington Barbecue No. 1 right on the highway is the one you want. It's smooth sailing after that.

Waltzing Through Tennessee

No rushing this trip. Go in the spring when the dogwoods and azaleas are in bloom. Spend some time in Nashville taking in the country and western flavor and then catch a few games with the Triple-A **Nashville Sounds** (page 24), one of the South's oldest baseball teams. Not to be missed—the 115-foot-high, guitar-shaped scoreboard. We cheat a little here and wander into Alabama to Huntsville, which is about 110 miles almost due south of Nashville. You can take I-85 most of the way, but remember that this a "waltz." Instead, take I-24 to Murfreesboro, about thirty-one miles, and then take designated scenic Highway 231 straight south into Huntsville.

The **Huntsville Stars** (page 110) put on a good show. There are lots of promos and fireworks displays and lots of tourists, too, who have come to Huntsville for the U.S. Space & Rocket Center.

Then it's off to Chattanooga, a great vacation spot on the Tennessee River. It's 102 miles from Huntsville, and there are two ways to get there. You can take Highway 72 east and then north along the Tennessee River, which is a designated scenic route. Or go back up Highway 231 to Fayetteville, Tennessee, and then follow scenic Highway 64 and then 41 into Chattanooga.

There's so much to see and do in Chattanooga, you should spend a few days there. Yes, be sure to see the Double-A **Chattanooga Lookouts** (page 106) in historic Engel Stadium, a registered historical landmark complete with brick walls, awnings, wrought-iron gates, and antique lamp lights. The park is open to the public during the day.

From Chattanooga it's about 117 miles to Knoxville up I-75, but no interstates just yet. Instead, take I-75 northeast for just twenty-one miles to Highway 64. Go east to Ducktown and pick up Route 68 going north. The next thirty-three miles take you through the Appalachians and Cherokee National Forest. When you hit Highway 411, take it northeast to Maryville. Pick up Route 33 and go north to Knoxville.

Knoxville is your destination not only because it is in the heart of the scenic East Tennessee Valley and surrounded by TVA lakes, but also because it's the home of great baseball. The Double-A **Knoxville Smokies** (page 114), the Blue Jays affiliate, have played top-notch ball over the years. You can either end your trip here and head back to Nashville, west on I-40 for 178 miles, or you can keep going east on I-40 113 miles to Asheville and beyond, or head into northeastern Tennessee and into the Virginias, where there are a slew of Appalachian League teams.

Appalachian League

For information on team locations, call the league office in Bristol, West Virginia, at (703) 669-3644.

SOUTH

We're Going to Disney World!

And so is everybody else over five. But let us quickly add that all the Orlando tourist attractions are really worth the trip. A little kitschy here and there, but for the most part, Orlando is a nice destination. It also happens to be within easy reach of lots of baseball action. Right in Orlando, you have the Southern League Double-A **Orlando Cubs** (page 118). The Cubs play in historic Tinker Field, which, though rebuilt in 1963, was originally constructed in 1914.

Some Day Trips from Orlando

Kissimmee, home of the Class A **Kissimmee Cobras** (page 196), is only fifteen miles down Highway 17. Aside from the Cobras, Osceola County Stadium also hosts semipro and state college baseball playoffs. If it's the beach you want, head to Daytona Beach. If you're lucky, no one will have bought the Class A **Daytona Cubs** (page 190) before you get there. (Daytona, for some reason, has a history of losing baseball teams.) Daytona Beach is about an hour's drive up I-4 from Orlando. Baseball fans of all stripes drop by during the day to visit the bronze statue honoring Jackie Robinson located at the park entrance.

Melbourne, where the Class A **Brevard County Manatees** (page 184) await you, is about sixty miles away, depending on where you are staying in the Orlando area. If you're near Kissimmee, take the Space Coast Parkway (Highway 192) straight to Melbourne. If you're farther north—and especially if you want to spend some time at Cape Canaveral—head due east from Orlando on the Bee Line Expressway (Route 528). Continue on to the Kennedy Space Center or take I-95 and head south to the brand-new Space Coast Stadium.

A Gulf Coast Weekend

Leave Friday afternoon from Orlando and head west on I-4 for thirty miles to Lakeland. Spend some time walking around the Florida State University Campus before catching the Class A **Lakeland Tigers** (page 198). (You might keep Lakeland in mind for a day trip as well.) From Lakeland, continue west on I-4 for forty-eight miles to Tampa. There's a lot to see and do in the Tampa Bay area, which is home to not one but *four*

baseball teams—all within a thirty-minute drive of Tampa.

For starters, there's George's Class A **Tampa Yankees** (page 206), which are temporarily playing on the campus of the University of South Florida. Then cross Tampa Bay to St. Pete and catch the Class A **St. Petersburg Cardinals** (page 202) at Al Lang Stadium right on the Tampa Bay waterfront. From St. Pete, head north on Ft. Harrison Avenue (Alt. 19) to Clearwater and take in a **Phillies** (page 188) game at Jack Russell Memorial Stadium. Or continue on to Dunedin and take in a Blue Jays game. The Class A **Dunedin Blue Jays** (page 192) play in reconstructed Dunedin Stadium, which sits just three blocks from the Gulf. From Dunedin, it's about one hundred miles back to Orlando.

MIDWEST

Chicago, Chicago . . .

When a strike hits the majors, as in 1994, it's bad enough if you have one major league team to mourn. When you have two, it can all be a bit much. Fortunately for Chicagoans, there are three minor league teams within a hundred miles of downtown.

Some Day Trips from Chicago

Most of Chicago's western suburbanites already know about the Class A **Kane County Cougars** (page 226), just thirty-eight miles west out I-280 and I-88. This team has a huge following, so it's a good idea to check in advance to make sure you can get tickets before heading out that way. Geneva is a pretty town, so plan to spend some time there.

1995 marks the first year that the Class A **Rockford Cubbies** (page 232) take the field. They will be a big hit—count on it. You can get to Rockford in under two hours by taking I-90 northwest out of Chicago and then connecting with Highway 20, which takes you into Rockford. If you feel up to it, make this a weekend trip and bop on up I-90 another seventeen miles and catch a Class A **Beloit Snappers** (page 216) game.

South Bend, in the other direction, is about seventy-five miles east of Chicago straight out I-90. South Bend is home to Notre Dame and to the Class A **South Bend Silver Hawks** (page 234), who play in Stanley Coveleski Regional Stadium, otherwise known as "The Cove."

A West Michigan Weekend

Holland, with its Dutch heritage, and Grand Haven, with its penchant for festivals, are two of Michigan's most popular lakeside (Lake Michigan, that is) resorts—and just a short hop from Grand Rapids and nearby Comstock Park, where the Class A **West Michigan Whitecaps** (page 238) play in Old Kent Park. Grand Rapids is about a three-and-a-half-hour trip from Chicago. Old Comstock Park is ten minutes north on the Grand River.

The "Field of Dreams" Tour

The Mississippi River attracts a lot of visitors yearly. Most tourists travel up the river from St. Louis or drive over from Chicago. We suggest starting out in Des Moines, Iowa's state capital and home to the ever-popular Triple-A **Iowa Cubs** (page 20), who play in the brand-new (1992) 10,500-seat Sec Taylor Stadium.

From Des Moines, it's 122 miles northeast to Cedar Rapids via I-80 and I-380. Cedar Rapids is where the red-hot Class A **Kernels** (page 220) play in Veterans Memorial Stadium, built in 1949. From Cedar Rapids you can head east on Highway 30, eighty-three miles directly into Clinton. Or you can make the pilgrimage to Dyersville, where the movie *Field of Dreams* was shot. Take Highway 151 north out of Cedar Rapids to Route 136 to Dyersville. The excursion will add about seventy miles to your itinerary.

The site is on Lansing Road in Dyersville. Just ask anybody where it is. The movie set was act-

ually built on two farms: Don Lansing's (see **Carolina Mudcats**, page 104), where the field, bleachers, and house were, and a neighbor's, where the corn grew. The neighbor plowed his part under after filming, but so many people were making the trek to pay homage that he quickly restored it. These gentlemen have even set up a souvenir and concession stand.

From Dyersville take Highway 20 west to Dubuque and then follow Highways 52 and 67 for sixty-two miles into Clinton. The Class A **Clinton LumberKings** (page 222) play in Riverview Stadium right on the banks of the Mississippi, which was not an asset during the rains of 1993. Although the stadium, which was built in 1937, was flooded, it's none the worse for wear. Downriver from Clinton about forty miles on Highway 67 is Davenport, home to the Class A **Quad City River Bandits** (page 230). Another flood victim, John O'Donnell Stadium, with its red-brick facade and archways, became the photographic symbol of the disaster that took place that year along the Mississippi River. But it, too, has nicely recovered.

Continuing down the Mississippi from Rock Island, follow the local roads along the riverbanks until you reach Route 99, which takes you into Burlington. The trip should take about an hour and forty-five minutes. Community Field, where the Class A **Burlington Bees** (page 218) play, was built in 1970 in a park right in the middle of town.

On the way back to Des Moines, which is 162 miles from Burlington, you can take the quick way by way of Highways 34 and 218 back to I-80 and then west to Des Moines. But we like the Woodlands Scenic Byway. From Burlington, swing down Highway 61 to Fort Madison and go west on Route 2. Take a detour into Bentonsport and Vernon on the Des Moines River to catch a glimpse of the steamboat era. Then, back on 2, continue west through beautiful forests and into Amish country. When you get to Highway 63 go north through Bloomfield to Ottumwa and then back to Des Moines on Route 163.

WEST

California, Here I Come

This great western state has more to offer than panoramic views of wild ocean, giant redwoods, towering mountain ranges, desert valleys, sandy beaches, freeways, movie sets, theme parks, and earthquakes! There's a rich minor league heritage here. Remember that California (and the West) has only had major league baseball since 1958, when the Giants and Dodgers moved west. 'Till then it was minor leagues all the way.

A Day Trip from San Francisco

You say the Giants aren't at Candlestick this weekend? Check your minor league schedule— they might be in San Jose, just under an hour's drive south of San Francisco on Highway 101. We're talking, of course, about the Class A **San Jose Giants** (page 158). On the way there, be sure to stop off in beautiful Palo Alto, home of Stanford University and thousands of trees. Really, the city is known for its trees, and on a hot summer day Palo Alto is the place to be. The name actually means "tall tree," and you can see the city's namesake on Palo Alto Avenue near Alma Street. This is a great place to stop for lunch, by the way, if you're making a day of it.

Old California Route 99

Old Route 99, which begins inland from San Francisco, is a stretch of road that offers vintage California League Class A baseball—and more. This is John Steinbeck country, and the land of the great white waters of the California Delta. From north to south spans the agricultural gold mine of the great Central San Joaquin Valley. If you time your trip right in spring and early summer, you'll not only see highly competitive baseball—the teams on old 99 are fierce rivals—you'll also hit food festivals, wineries, and roadside berry and vegetable stands all the way down.

Starting in San Francisco, it's about eighty miles (an hour-and-thirty-minute drive) east toward Stockton. Halfway there on I-580, you'll no-

tice the big difference in air quality from the congested Bay Area. The **Stockton Ports** (page 160) are very popular in town, and almost everybody knows where Billy Hebert Field is. (*Day Option:* After baseball, you might want to explore the fantastically gorgeous Gold Rush country up in the mountains no more than two hours east of Stockton. You can still pan for gold there.)

Picking up Route 99 off I-205 from Stockton, it's about two hours south to Modesto and the home of the **Modesto A's** (page 150). The A's are Stockton's archrival, and the small stadium is packed when these teams play each other. (*Day Option:* The entrance to Yosemite National Park is about two hours east of Modesto.)

On to Visalia, straight down 99 passing through towns that will remind you of the movie *American Graffiti*—Turlock, Merced, Fresno—and finally into the heart of the San Joaquin Valley and the home of the **Visalia Oaks** (page 162). (*Day Option:* the entrance to Sequoia National [redwoods] Park is about 50 miles east of Visalia.)

The last city on Route 99 is Bakersfield, known for **The Blaze,** of course (page 144), and also for its cotton, crops, Basque food, cowboy boots, and country music. After the game, eat hearty and dance. The next day, L.A. will still be two hours away.

Some Day Trips from Los Angeles

Most Angelenos don't realize how near they are to five important minor league baseball teams. Here are some suggested baseball outings that take you to the foothills, coast, and desert.

From the heart of downtown L.A. to the beautiful new Epicenter, home of the Class A **Rancho Cucamonga Quakes** (page 152), is only about a forty-five-minute trip. To get there, head east on the San Bernardino Freeway for about thirty-five miles. Continuing on another thirty minutes will bring you into San Bernardino, where the Class A **Spirit** (page 156) have been playing for ten years. Both teams are located in the foothills of the great San Bernardino National Forest and are right on the way to the mountain play areas of Lake Arrowhead and Big Bear Lake.

About halfway down the coast between Los Angeles and San Diego (1 hour 30 minutes from either city), off I-5 and just inland from the great surfing beaches of San Clemente and San Onofre, is the historic town of San Juan Capistrano, the site of the famous mission founded by Padre Juan Junipero Serra in 1776. Yes, the swallows do come back there every year on March 19. Another twenty minutes inland through beautiful foothill terrain on Route 74 is the tiny town of Lake Elsinore, where the Class A **Lake Elsinore Storm** (page 148) opened a new stadium in 1994 practically right on the famous lake.

One of the best places to see turn-of-the-century California architecture—those large, elegant, and rambling Spanish-style buildings and homes bedecked with palms, cyprus, and oaks—is Riverside, which just fifty years ago was surrounded by thousands of acres of orange trees.

Even the Class A **Riverside Pilots** (page 154) play in such a lush setting. And although from downtown L.A. the distance looks great, Californians assure everyone that on a good day (no traffic) Riverside is a mere forty-five minutes away. We'd give it an hour or so. Head southeast on the Santa Ana Freeway, pick up the Pomona Freeway, and continue east to Riverside.

About two hours from L.A., or one hour from San Bernardino via I-15 through the 4,000-foot Cajon Pass in the San Bernardino Mountain range, are the high desert communities of Victorville and Apple Valley. To the west, plopped between the Mojave River and Mirage (dry) Lake, is Adelanto, the home of **High Desert Mavericks** (page 146). Yes, it's hot and dry here in summer, but the nights! The nights are beautifully cool and crisp, with dark, dark skies full of stars.

Ballpark Talk

You can play baseball anywhere—that's part of the attraction of the game. Some places, however, are more exciting than others for watching the game and can actually add to (or detract from) your enjoyment. Here are a few minor league ballparks known for either their historical importance and/or charm, picturesque settings, size, modern style, or quirky characteristics. When you're traveling, be sure to look them up. Some historic parks are open all day long.

NORTHEAST

Historic

McCoy Stadium in Pawtucket, Rhode Island, was built in 1942 and has been maintained as an authentic park of the era. The **Pawtucket Red Sox** (page 42) play there.

Silver Stadium, where the **Rochester Red Wings** play in upstate New York (page 46), was built in 1929. 1995 will mark its last season and your last chance to see it. The city will be building the team a new park in 1996.

Landmark **Yale Field,** in West Haven, Connecticut, was built in 1927 as an exact model in miniature of old Yankee Stadium. Newly renovated, it is home to the **New Haven Ravens** (page 90).

Others to Note

See the **Harrisburg (PA) Senators** (page 88) play at **RiverSide Stadium.** The ballpark sits on City Island in the middle of the Susquehanna River as part of a sixty-two-acre waterfront park.

Binghamton Municipal Field, home to the **Binghamton (NY) Mets** (page 80), is a new, classic-looking park right downtown.

Pilot Field in Buffalo, New York, is the biggest minor league park in the region. 19,500 fans watch the **Buffalo Bisons** (page 16) play there.

MID-ATLANTIC AND MID-SOUTH

Historic

Engel Stadium in Chattanooga, Tennessee, is a restored 1920s registered historical landmark. Don't miss it. The **Chattanooga Lookouts** (page 106) play there.

Grainger Stadium, where the **Kinston (NC) Indians** play (page 170), is a charming 1940s-style park in a residential area.

McCormick Field is home to the **Asheville (NC) Tourists** (page 246) and was rebuilt carefully in 1992 on the site where the old McCormick had stood since 1924. It's worth the trip just for the nostalgic look of the place.

Municipal Stadium in Hagerstown, Maryland, was built in 1931. The **Hagerstown Suns** (page 262) play on the same field where Willie Mays made his pro debut. Nostalgia is everywhere.

War Memorial Stadium in Greensboro, North Carolina, home of the **Greensboro Bats** (page 260), was built in 1926 and is very well preserved. The original stonework remains.

Others to Note

Built right in town, the **Durham Bulls'** (page 166) new ballpark in Durham, North Carolina, is a must-see for its architectural homage to the past and to downtown Durham.

Visit **Charlotte Knights Stadium** near Charlotte, North Carolina, where the **Charlotte Knights** (page 34) play. The view of bucolic pastureland complete with cows and clear blue skies is charming. The seating is even in a rainbow of different colors. Get there early and see it.

SOUTH

Historic

Jackie Robinson Ballpark, home to the **Daytona Cubs** in Daytona Beach, Florida (page 190), opened in 1939. It is the historic park where Jackie Robinson broke the color barrier in baseball in 1946.

Luther Williams Field, home of the **Macon (GA) Braves** (page 266), is a brick-and-wrought-iron landmark built in 1929. Part of its charm is its location—the State Fairgrounds.

Tinker Field is where the **Orlando (FL) Cubs** (page 118) play. Originally constructed in 1914 and rebuilt in 1963, it's wonderfully nostalgic.

Others to Note

One of the nicest settings is at **Al Lang Stadium** in St. Petersburg, Florida, where the **St. Petersburg Cardinals** (page 202) play. The park, practically on Tampa Bay, offers a serene view of sailing boats and cruisers.

Grayson Stadium, the simple 1940s-style home of the **Savannah (GA) Cardinals** (page 270), has much old-fashioned simplicity, beginning with the brick facade and ending with the fully covered grandstand.

William H. Hammond Stadium in Fort Myers, Florida, is home to the **Fort Myers Miracle** (page 194) and is a must-see for its architectural reminiscence of late-nineteenth-century Florida.

For simple squeaky-new state-of-the-art comfort and convenience, visit **Space Coast Stadium,** home to the **Brevard County Manatees** (page 184), in Melbourne, Florida.

In the quirky charm department, at **Privateer Park,** where the **New Orleans (LA) Zephyrs** (page 26) play, there are big holes in the outfield fence, which allows fans in trucks and vans to pull up and watch the game.

MIDWEST

Historic

John O'Donnell Stadium in Davenport, Iowa, is the beautiful home of the **Quad City River Bandits** (page 230). It was built in 1932 and still stands right on the banks of the Mississippi.

The new (1992) **Sec Taylor Stadium** in Des Moines, Iowa, where the **Iowa Cubs** (page 20) play, has replaced the old park and has twice as much warmth and charm.

Others to Note

The biggest minor league park anywhere is **Cardinal Stadium,** in Louisville, Kentucky, where the **Redbirds** (page 22) play. It holds 33,000. The second largest is **Rosenblatt Stadium,** where the **Omaha (NE) Royals** play (page 30); the "Blatt" fills up with 22,000.

Among the newer stadiums, **Philip S. Elfstrom Stadium** in Geneva, Illinois, is home to the **Kane County Cougars** (page 226) and offers a fantastic setting in scenic woods.

In the smallest park department, **Pohlman Field,** where the **Beloit (WI) Snappers** (page 216) play, might take the prize. Capable of seating 3,500, it really only seats 2,500 comfortably. Not to be outdone, **Community Field,** home to the **Burlington (IA) Bees** (page 218), claims to be so small that the players often recognize the fans in the stands and wave.

In the charming quirks department is **Cooper Stadium,** home of the **Columbus (OH) Clippers** (page 36), which has the same asymmetrical (unpredictable ball-bouncing) outfield as Yankee Stadium.

WEST

Historic

Among the ballparks that were built in California during the 1940s and set in lovely town park groves, these have maintained their warmth and simplicity and are worth a visit: **Recreation Park** in Visalia, which is home to the **Vasalia Oaks** (page 162); **Riverside Sports Center** in Riverside, where the **Riverside Pilots** (page 154) play; and **Billy Hebert Field** in Stockton, where the **Stockton Ports** (page 160) play.

Hi Corbett Field, home to the **Tucson (AZ) Toros** (page 72), is a warm, old-fashioned place that was built in 1937 and is quite often used as a movie set, most recently for *Major League II*.

Others to Note

An interesting quirk of **Albuquerque Sports Stadium**, the home of the **Albuquerque (NM) Dukes** (page 56), is the lava rock drive-in view from the outfield.

In the sleek, modern, and user-friendly category is the **Epicenter**, home to the **Rancho Cucamonga (CA) Quakes** (page 152).

Lake Elsinore Diamond, where the **Lake Elsinore (CA) Storm** (page 148) play, is an architectural eye-catcher with brick entries, green steel girders, and a long entry walk lined with colorful flags. The lake is right there, too.

As for spectacular settings, **Nat Baily Stadium**, home of the **Vancouver Canadians** (page 74) in Vancouver, British Columbia, is a small place at the foot of the Queen Elizabeth Park. It was built in 1951 and patterned after the famous Sicks Seattle Stadium, considered a showcase of minor league baseball.

In the neighborly department, Sky Sox Stadium, a big, comfortable home to the **Colorado Springs Sky Sox** (page 60) in Colorado Springs, offers fans hot tub seating in right field.

The Glossary of Fun & Games

(What Goes On Between Innings)

There are celebrity softball games, dances, and exhibitions before the game, fireworks and concerts afterward, and in between innings there are always six to ten contests that keep the fans involved, and sometimes hilariously entertained.

More than any other element, these contests separate the majors from the minors and make the game experience something of a family picnic, church bazaar, small-town carnival, TV game show, or relaxing walk in the park. We mention some specific contests when we talk about the teams in this book, but we don't always explain or describe them. While minor league management is uproariously creative and new contests come and go every season, we thought it worthwhile to include a list of what are both classic and current.

Bash for Cash: Two or more baseball players are matched up with two or more fans and each player has maybe three chances (the number varies) to hit the ball into the outfield and break the headlight of a truck that's been parked out there. If he does, the fan wins big money.

Bat Scramble: A kids' race in most places. The team saves broken bats until there are enough to give away and kids race to the outfield for them.

Beer Strikeout: Beer and soda are only half-price until the opposing pitcher strikes out one of our guys. Lots of variations on this one.

Bingo: Really big in Florida. Cards are in the programs and the PA announcer calls numbers between innings.

Dash for Cash: Basically there is a lot of money (real or fake) scattered around and the contestants have 15 or 30 seconds to grab as much as they can. There are tons of variations on this—the money could be blowing around inside a phone booth or scattered around the infield (see also Splash for Cash).

Diamond Dig: A big Mother's Day favorite. The first 50, 100, or 200 women through the gate win the right to look for a diamond that has been buried in the infield. There's a "go" signal and a time limit. Each contestant has a tablespoon to do the job. This usually happens after the last out of the game.

Dirtiest Car of the Game: Somebody's license number is called out. They usually win a car wash.

Dizzy Bat Race: This race has become as popular as the hot dog. Two or more (usually adult) contestants stand near home plate, place their foreheads on the end of a bat that is standing upright on the ground, and spin around ten times. Then they try to race somewhere—like up the first base line. They are so dizzy they can barely stand up. In some places, there are spotters along the route to make sure no one gets hurt. Lots of variations on this one—sometimes runners, err, stumblers have to carry an open box of pizza, a bucket of water . . .

Dugout Bowling, aka Baseline Bowling: Anywhere from three to ten pins are set up on the dugout roof. The contestant tries to bowl a strike for a prize, which is quite often free passes to the sponsoring bowling alley.

Dugout Golf: The contestant must try to sink putts on an AstroTurf green laid out on the dugout roof.

Eating Contest: Usually a pregame event. Tacos in California/ice cream in Virginia/ribs in North Carolina, and so on.

Egg Toss: Teams of two each try to keep the egg unbroken as they play catch with it and move farther apart.

Fan of the Night: All kinds of variations on this one, but basically, fans are chosen by lot or lucky number to sit in a special seat and get free food and service all through the game.

Flipper Race: Race to first base wearing swim fins.

Frisbee Toss: Sail a Frisbee through some kind of hole in some kind of target. There are a dozen variations of this.

Grand Slam Inning: A player and a fan are matched up. If in a designated inning, the player hits a grand slam, the fan wins tons of money, or a year's worth of pies, or a getaway vacation, or . . .

Home Run Inning: The same rules as Grand Slam, except player hits a homer only.

Horse Race, aka Pig Race or Bug Race or Dog Race: Large wooden or cardboard cutouts on long poles, handled by humans, race (or seem to) over the outfield wall. Sometimes the color of the animal corresponds to a section of the stands and the cheers from the section make the animal run.

Human Bowling: The contestant, strapped inside a biosphere, rolls head over heels down a ramp and hopes that the ball he or she is in knocks down giant pins.

Lucky Number: In every fan's program is a stamped number. If the PA announcer calls it, they can win anything from free tickets to a color TV.

Make a Deal, aka Steal a Deal: An MC in the stands or on the field with a wireless mike offers a deal to a fan—let's say, a T-shirt with the team logo OR whatever's in the box.

Mascot Race: Also as popular as hot dogs. A fan (usually a kid, but not always) races the mascot around the bases, and the mascot always loses. The fun is in how he loses—it's different everywhere, every time.

Pizza Scream: The mascot or an usher walks around with a large pizza in a box. Whoever is screaming the loudest wins the pizza.

Pop-Up: Three fans in the outfield try to catch flies from the pop-up machine. Whoever catches the most wins something.

Roll to Win: A contestant rolls a pair of jumbo (usually made of foam or cardboard) dice off the dugout or the grandstand roof. Rules vary, but usually preset winning combinations win something like an all-expenses-paid trip for two to go see the parent major league club play. Some combos can win something for everybody in the park!

Splash for Cash, aka Big Splash: A kiddie pool is filled with water and hundreds of dollars in coins. The contestant(s) get into the pool and fill their pockets with as much money as they can in 15 or 30 seconds. In some places they do it blindfolded.

Spin to Win: A fan's lucky number in the program gives him or her a chance to spin the casino wheel and win—weekend cruises in Florida, grocery shopping sprees, airline tickets, a set of tires, and so forth.

Strike-O, aka Board Toss, aka Barrel Toss, aka Ball Toss: A fan (usually a kid) gets three tries to get a ball through a hole in some kind of target, like a board or a barrel top, from three different distances. The first ball in from up close wins a little prize. The second ball in from a bit farther back wins a bigger one. And a third ball in from far away wins the best prize. Sometimes the prizes affect the whole stadium, for example, one ball in and everyone wins a free soda, three balls in and everyone wins free pan pizza from Pizza Hut.

Sumo Wrestling: Two fans in inflatable costumes that make them look like huge Sumo wrestlers try to be the one left standing.

Sweetheart of the Night: A female fan is awarded flowers and prizes, at her seat.

Trivia: Usually related to baseball, often to minor league baseball. Fan with the answer wins tickets, free meals . . .

Used Car Giveaway: Big in Triple-A and Double-A. Sponsored by a local dealership; sometimes one is given away each inning to fans drawn by lot. All kinds of variations.

Water Balloon Pitch, aka Water Toss, aka Water Pitch: Contestants have a bat (sometimes a Little League bat), and someone pitches water balloons. Whoever hits and breaks the most out of ten wins. This is a wet one.

You Make the Call: Usually sponsored by a cellular phone company. A fan wins a two- to five-minute phone call from the stands to anywhere in the USA.

Photography Credits

Page 17: Buffalo Bisons; page 19: Mark Wick; page 20: Iowa Cubs; page 23: Louisville Redbirds; page 25: Nashville Sounds; page 26: New Orleans Zephyrs; page 29: Oklahoma 89ers; page 30: Omaha Royals; page 35: Charlotte Knights; page 36: Columbus Clippers; page 38: H. E. Skip Banner; page 39: Norfolk Tides; page 41: *Ottawa Sun*; Moe Doiron; page 42: Pawtucket Red Sox; page 43: Pawtucket Red Sox; page 45: Richmond Braves; page 47: *Left and right:* Barbara Jean Germano; page 48: David M. Schofield; page 49: Lewis Geyer; page 51: Syracuse Chiefs; page 52: Toledo Mud Hens; page 56: Pat Barrett; page 58: Calgary Cannons; page 61: Ernie Ferguson; page 62: Edmonton Trappers; page 64: Richard Torrento; page 65: Edd Lockwood; page 67: Phoenix Firebirds; page 69: Norm Perdue; page 70: Michael R. Sage; page 72: Tucson Toros; page 73: Tucson Toros; page 75: Vancouver Canadians; page 81: Michael Seaman; page 82: Benjamin F. Koerber, Jr.; page 83: Bowie Baysox; page 85: Canton-Akron Indians; page 86: Robert Muirhead; page 89: Stephen G. Eddy; page 91: Art Rich Photography; page 93: Michael Seaman; page 94: Portland Sea Dogs; page 95: Portland Sea Dogs; page 96: David M. Schofield; page 97: David M. Schofield; page 99: David M. Schofield; page 102: Beth Bracknell; page 105: Marty Coward; page 107: Chattanooga Lookouts; page 109: Greenville Braves; page 110: Huntsville Stars; page 111: Huntsville Stars; page 113: Jacksonville Suns; page 115: Wade Payne; page 116: Kevin Lewter; page 117: Kevin Lewter; page 118: Janet Jordan; page 121: Generic; page 125: Arkansas Travelers; page 126: El Paso Diablos; page 129: Lee R. Schmid; page 131: Midland Angels; page 132: Kemp Davis; page 135: Shreveport Captains; page 136: Tulsa Drillers; page 137: Tulsa Drillers; page 139: Dan Moore; page 144: Todd Stanger; page 147: High Desert Mavericks; page 148: John George; page 151: Modesto A's; page 152: Rancho Cucamonga Quakes; page 153: Rancho Cucamonga Quakes; page 155: Riverside Pilots; page 156: San Bernardino Spirit; page 158: Ted Orssten; page 161: Stockton Ports; page 162: Todd Stanger; page 166: Durham Bulls; page 169: Benjamin F. Koerber, Jr.; page 170: Kinston Indians; page 172: Dr. Donald Garlock; page 174: Prince William Cannons; page 177: David M. Schofield; page 179: Bradford Glazier; page 181: Winston-Salem Warthogs; page 184: Smith Aerial Photography; page 186: Charlotte Rangers; page 188: Clearwater Phillies; page 191: Daytona Cubs; page 193: Ed Strohmayer; page 195: Fort Myers Miracle; page 197: Kissimmee Cobras; page 198: Lakeland Tigers; page 199: Lakeland Tigers; page 200: St. Lucie Mets; page 201: St. Lucie Mets; page 203: St. Petersburg Cardinals; page 204: Sarasota Red Sox; page 206: Cliff Welch; page 208: Vero Beach Dodgers; page 209: Vero Beach Dodgers; page 211: West Palm Beach Expos; Page 215: Battle Creek Golden Kazoos; page 217: Beloit Snappers; page 218: Burlington Bees; page 221: Cedar Rapids Kernels; page 222: Clinton LumberKings; page 225: Fort Wayne Wizards; page 227: Kane County Cougars; page 228: Peoria Chiefs; page 231: Boyd Fitzgerald;

Directory of Teams